The Ultimate Guide to filing for Bankruptcy

The
Personal
Bankruptcy
Toolkit

The Ultimate Guide to Filing For Bankruptcy

The Personal Bankruptcy Toolkit

DANIEL SITARZ, ATTORNEY-AT-LAW

Nova Publishing Company
Small Business and Consumer Legal Books
Carbondale Illinois

ISBN13 978- 1-892949-42-4   Book/CD   ($29.95)
ISBN 10 1-89294942-3
Cataloging-in-Publication Data
    Sitarz, Dan, 1948-
        the personal bankruptcy toolkit/by Daniel Sitarz -- 1st ed. --
        Carbondale, Ill. : Nova Pub. Co., c2009
        256 p. cm. -- CD-ROM (4 3/4 in.)
        (Legal Toolkit series).
        At head of title: The ultimate guide to filing for bankruptcy
        CD contains forms and includes Adobe® Acrobat® reader software. Includes index.
        ISBN13: 978-1-892949-42-4   Book/CD   ($29.95)
        1. Bankruptcy—United States—Popular works. 2. Bankruptcy—United States—
        States—Popular works. 3. Bankruptcy—United States—Forms. I. Title. II: Ultimate guide
        to filing for bankruptcy. III. Series.
        KF 1524.85 .S48 2009   346.7307/8--dc22   0901

Nova Publishing Company is dedicated to providing up-to-date and accurate legal information to the public. All Nova publications are periodically revised to contain the latest available legal information.

1st Edition; 1st Printing   January, 2009

This publication is designed to provide accurate and authoritative information in regard to the subject matter covered. It is sold with the understanding that the publisher and author are not engaged in rendering legal, accounting, or other professional services. If legal advice or other expert assistance is required, the services of a competent professional person should be sought.
    —From a Declaration of Principles jointly adopted by a Committee of
    the American Bar Association and a Committee of Publishers

DISCLAIMER

Because of possible unanticipated changes in governing statutes and case law relating to the application of any information contained in this book, the author, publisher, and any and all persons or entities involved in any way in the preparation, publication, sale, or distribution of this book disclaim all responsibility for the legal effects or consequences of any document prepared or action taken in reliance upon information contained in this book. No representations, either express or implied, are made or given regarding the legal consequences of the use of any information contained in this book. Purchasers and persons intending to use this book for the preparation of any legal documents are advised to check specifically on the current applicable laws in any jurisdiction in which they intend the documents to be effective.

Nova Publishing Green Business Policies

Nova Publishing Company takes seriously the impact of book publishing on the Earth and its resources. Nova Publishing Company is committed to protecting the environment and to the responsible use of natural resources. As a book publisher, with paper as a core part of our business, we are very concerned about the future of the world's remaining endangered forests and the environmental impacts of paper production. We are committed to implementing policies that will support the preservation of endangered forests globally and to advancing 'best practices' within the book and paper industries. Nova Publishing Company is committed to preserving ancient forests and natural resources. Our company's policy is to print all of our books on 100% recycled paper, with 100% post-consumer waste content, de-inked in a chlorine-free process. In addition, all Nova Publishing Company books are printed using soy-based inks. As a result of these environmental policies, Nova Publishing Company has saved hundreds of thousands of gallons of water, hundreds of thousands of kilowatts of electricity, thousand of pounds of pollution and carbon dioxide, and thousands of trees that would otherwise have been used in the traditional manner of publishing its books. Nova Publishing Company is very proud to be one of the first members of the Green Press Initiative, a nonprofit program dedicated to supporting publishers in their efforts to reduce their use of fiber obtained from endangered forests. (see:www.greenpressinitiative.org). Nova Publishing Company is also proud to be an initial signatory on the Book Industry Treatise on Responsible Paper Use. In addition, Nova Publishing Company uses all compact fluorescent lighting; recycles all office paper products, aluminum and plastic beverage containers, and printer cartridges; uses 100% post-consumer fiber, process-chlorine-free, acid-free paper for 95% of in-house paper use; and, when possible, uses electronic equipment that is EPA Energy Star-certified. Nova's freight shipments are coordinated to minimize energy use whenever possible. Finally, all carbon emissions from Nova Publishing Company office energy use are offset by the purchase of wind-energy credits that are used to subsidize the building of wind turbines on the Rosebud Sioux Reservation in South Dakota (see www.nativeenergy.com). We strongly encourage other publishers and all partners in publishing supply chains to adopt similar policies.

Nova Publishing Company
Small Business and Consumer Legal Books and Software
1103 West College St.
Carbondale, IL 62901
Editorial: (800) 748-1175
www.novapublishing.com

Distributed by:
National Book Network
4501 Forbes Blvd., Suite 200
Lanham, MD 20706
Orders: (800) 462-6420
free shipping on internet orders

Table of Contents

CHAPTER 5: Filling out the Bankruptcy Forms

How to Install Personal Bankruptcy Forms-on-CD

This book is part of Nova Publishing Company's continuing Legal Toolkit series. The various legal guides in this series are prepared by experienced attorneys who feel that public access to the American legal system is long overdue. The books in this series are designed to provide concrete information to consumers in order to assist them in understanding and using the law with a minimum of outside assistance.

However, in an area as complex as bankruptcy, it is not always prudent to attempt to handle every situation that arises without the aid of a competent professional. Although the information presented in this book will give readers a basic understanding of bankruptcy, it is not intended that this text entirely substitute for experienced professional assistance in all situations. Throughout this book there are references to those particular situations in which the aid of a professional is strongly recommended.

Regardless of whether or not an attorney or other professional is ultimately retained in certain situations, the information in this handbook will enable the reader to understand the framework of bankruptcy and effectively use this knowledge. To try and make that task as easy as possible, technical legal jargon has been eliminated whenever possible and plain English used instead. When it is necessary in this book to use a legal term that may be unfamiliar to most people, the word will be shown in *italics* and defined when first used. A glossary of bankruptcy legal terms most often encountered is included at the end of this book.

Quick Start Installation:
1. Insert the enclosed CD in your computer's CD drive.
2. The installation program will start automatically. Follow the on-screen dialog and make the appropriate choices.
3. If the CD installation does not start automatically, click on START, then RUN, then BROWSE and select your CD drive and then the file "Install.exe". Finally, click OK to run the installation program.

Installation Instructions for MAC:
1. Insert the enclosed CD in your CD drive and click on it.
2. Copy the folder "Bankruptcy\Forms for MACs" to your hard drive.

Chapter 1

Understanding Bankruptcy

The ability to file for bankruptcy and obtain a fresh start is an important and long-standing part of American law. Your right to file for bankruptcy is guaranteed under federal law and the U.S. Constitution. There are various chapters in the Federal Bankruptcy Code under which you may file for bankruptcy. Each chapter has certain requirements and each offers certain relief from creditors and debt. This book describes the process for filing for bankruptcy under Chapter 7 of the Federal Bankruptcy Code, which is commonly known as a personal bankruptcy. (Information regarding the other types of bankruptcy is included at the end of this chapter.) The culmination of a successful Chapter 7 bankruptcy is the elimination of most of your debts and the prevention of any efforts by creditors to collect on those debts.

In April of 2005, the U.S. Congress passed and President Bush signed the "Bankruptcy Abuse Prevention and Consumer Protection Act of 2005." The new law took effect on October 17, 2005. This new law provided for the most extensive changes in bankruptcy law in over a generation. This chapter provides an explanation of Chapter 7 personal bankruptcy under the new bankruptcy law. The extensive changes to bankruptcy law that were enacted will be explained later in this chapter.

An Overview of Chapter 7 Bankruptcy

Chapter 7 bankruptcy is designed for debtors in financial difficulty who do not have the ability to pay their existing debts. The new 2005 Bankruptcy Act has limited Chapter 7 bankruptcy, in most cases, to those debtors whose income is less than the median income in the state in which they live. This is determined by a *means test*, that will be explained later in this chapter. Another new aspect of the new bankruptcy laws is that you must take a *credit counseling course* within 180 days before filing for bankruptcy and you must also, generally, complete a *financial management course* before your bankruptcy will be granted. These new aspects of bankruptcy will be explained in more detail later in this chapter.

> **⛯Toolkit Tip!**
>
> Even though you file for bankruptcy, you will be allowed to keep much of your personal property and even certain real estate (such as your home) in certain instances.

By obtaining a personal bankruptcy, individuals are able to re-start their economic lives without the burden of their prior debts. There are several effects of filing for a Chapter 7 bankruptcy. Immediately upon filing for bankruptcy, an *automatic stay* goes into effect. This is a court order that prohibits creditors from harassing you or taking any further action to collect your debts while your bankruptcy is in court (Note: the new bankruptcy laws contain limitations on the scope of an automatic stay; these will be explained later in this chapter.) A bankruptcy court trustee then takes possession of all of your property, except the property that you may claim as exempt under state or federal law. *Exempt property* is property that the law allows you to keep, even after you are granted a bankruptcy. Much personal property and real estate is exempt from being seized in a bankruptcy. You may also be allowed to keep property that you have purchased which is subject to a *security interest* (secured property). The trustee then *liquidates* (sells) your non-exempt property and uses the proceeds to pay your creditors according to the priorities of the Bankruptcy Code. The final result of filing Chapter 7 bankruptcy is to obtain a *discharge* of your existing debts, that is, their total elimination. If, however, you are found to have committed certain kinds of improper conduct described in the Bankruptcy Code, your discharge may be denied by the court, and the purpose for which you filed the bankruptcy petition defeated. If your bankruptcy is granted, however, most of your debts will be wiped clean forever. If you receive a discharge of your debts through bankruptcy, you will not be allowed to file for bankruptcy again for a period of eight years (this time limit was increased to eight years–from six years–by the 2005 Bankruptcy Act).

Non-Dischargeable Debts

Even if you receive a discharge in bankruptcy, there are some debts that are not discharged under the law. These are referred to as *non-dischargeable debts*. Therefore, even after a successful bankruptcy, you may still be responsible for the following non-dischargeable debts:

> **Toolkit Tip!**
>
> There are a number of types of debts that are NOT cancelled through a bankruptcy. These are referred to as "non-dischargeable" debts.

- Federal, state, and local income taxes that came due within the last three years. The 2005 Bankruptcy Act added student loans to private Financial Institutions to this category
- Student loans that became due within the last seven years
- Court-ordered alimony and child support payments. Also, property settlements or other divorce-related debts if your spouse objects to their discharge
- Criminal restitution and court-ordered fines
- Debts for death or personal injury caused while driving while intoxicated from alcohol or drugs
- Debts you incurred to pay off non-dischargeable taxes, fines or penalties
- Debts that you failed to list on your bankruptcy filing papers (Note: because debts that you fail to list are not eliminated by bankruptcy, it is very important to make certain that you include every one of your debts on bankruptcy paperwork)
- Debts based on fraud, theft, or dishonesty. The new 2005 Bankruptcy Act increases the scope of this area of non-dischargeable debt, which now Includes debts of over $500.00 that you incurred for loans or credit purchases of *luxuries* within 90 days of filing for bankruptcy, cash advances of $750 or more within 70 days of filing, and any debts incurred when you knew you couldn't pay them. Luxuries are generally considered to be anything (goods or services) other than absolute necessities for a basic "no-frills" lifestyle.
- Certain condominium association fees and charges
- and, finally, any debts that arise *after* you have filed your petition for bankruptcy. Any debts incurred *after* you file for bankruptcy will NOT be discharged in the course of a successful bankruptcy.

Understanding Chapter 7 Bankruptcy

> **⚡ Warning!**
>
> You must be entirely honest in completing your bankruptcy forms. The Bankruptcy Court will not tolerate any attempts to hide your property or money.

Chapter 7 bankruptcy is also referred to as a *liquidation bankruptcy*. Chapter 7 requires you, the debtor, to pay the bankruptcy court a $299.00 filing fee (which includes a $39.00 administrative fee and a $15.00 trustee surcharge) upon filing. The filing fee may be paid in installments if you are unable to pay it all at one time upon filing. The new 2005 Bankruptcy Act also allows for these fees to be waived entirely if you are truly unable to pay them. In order to file for a bankruptcy of this type, you fill out various official forms that detail your entire recent economic life. These forms will require you to inform the court of the following:

- **The location and value of all of your real estate**. All of your real estate will have to be surrendered to the court unless you claim it as exempt from bankruptcy under a federal or state exemption, or you agree in some manner to keep current on the payments.
- **The location and value of all of your personal property**. All of your personal property will have to be surrendered to the court unless you claim it as exempt from bankruptcy under a federal or state exemption, you agree to pay the creditor what it is worth (if it was pledged as collateral for a debt), or you agree in some manner to keep current on the payments.
- **The type of real estate and/or personal property you claim is exempt from being surrendered to the bankruptcy court**. You will be allowed to keep all of the property that is exempt. In most states, you will generally be allowed to keep much of your property. Every state allows you to use their own state exemptions. In addition, some states also allow you to choose to use federal bankruptcy exemptions instead of the state exemptions.
- **The details of any debts for which you have pledged any type of property as collateral or on which a lien has been created**. These are referred to as *secured debts*. Your liability for these debts may be eliminated by a bankruptcy (unless it is a type of debt that is non-dischargeable). However, you may have to surrender the collateral to the creditor.
- **The details of any debts that are specified by bankruptcy law as having priority in their repayment**. These debts will be repaid first from any money or property that you will surrender

to the bankruptcy court. These are referred to as *unsecured priority debts*. If there is insufficient money to pay off these debts, they will also be wiped out by bankruptcy, unless the debts are non-dischargeable.

- **The details of any debts for which you have not pledged any collateral and which are not priority debts**. These are referred to as *unsecured non-priority debts*. If there is any money left after paying all other creditors, these debts will be paid off proportionately. Then they too will be eliminated forever, unless they are considered non-dischargeable.
- **The details of any outstanding contracts or leases**. These may also be voided unless the court feels that they can earn you income that can be used to pay off your creditors.
- **The identity of any cosigners for any of your debts**. If you are successful in obtaining a bankruptcy, your liability on a dischargeable debt will be eliminated. However, anyone who has cosigned or guaranteed a debt will still be held liable for payment on your debt.
- **The amount and sources of your current income**. Your ability to pay off your debts will be scrutinized by the court.
- **The amount and type of expenses that you currently pay**. Your spending on monthly expenses will also be carefully examined by the court.
- **Any financial transactions within the last two years that may have an effect on your ability to pay your current creditors**. The bankruptcy court has the power to void transactions if you have transferred property to a family member to shelter it from surrender, or if you have paid off one debt to the detriment of other creditors. If you made any transactions with the intention of hiding assets or otherwise tricking creditors, your entire bankruptcy may be denied.

Upon filing the forms containing this information, an *automatic stay* or court order is put into effect that prevents most creditors from trying to collect on their debts. Then a bankruptcy trustee, and perhaps your creditors, will meet with you to go over your documents. The trustee will then take possession of your non-exempt property. If necessary, the trustee will sell your non-exempt property and use the proceeds to pay off your creditors as much as possible. Finally, the bankruptcy judge *discharges* or wipes out all of your current dischargeable debts that have not been paid off.

Other Types of Bankruptcy

There are four chapters of the Federal Bankruptcy Code under which you may file a bankruptcy petition. This book describes the Chapter 7 bankruptcy in detail. Each of the other types of bankruptcy is described, in general, as follows:

> ### ☼ Toolkit Tip!
>
> If you feel that you can pay off your loans if a reasonable payment plan can be setup, you might consider filing for a Chapter 13 bankruptcy.

Chapter 13: This type of bankruptcy is referred to as "Repayment of All or Part of the Debts of an Individual with Regular Income." Chapter 13 is designed for individuals with regular income who are temporarily unable to pay their debts, but would like to pay them in installments over a period of time. A provision of the new 2005 bankruptcy law is that you may be forced into a Chapter 13 repayment-type bankruptcy even if you file under Chapter 7 for a discharge-type bankruptcy, but are found to have an income high enough to actually pay back your debts over a period of five years. This is determined by a "means test" that will be explained later in this and the following chapter. Under Chapter 13, you must file a plan with the court stating how you will repay your creditors all or part of the money that you owe them, using your future earnings. Usually, the period allowed by the court to repay your debts is three years, but no more than five years. Your plan must be approved by the court before it can take effect. Under Chapter 13, unlike Chapter 7, you may keep all of your property, both exempt and non-exempt, as long as you continue to make payments under the plan. After completion of payments under your repayment plan, your debts are discharged, except for certain taxes, student loans, alimony and child support payments, criminal restitution, debts for death or personal injury caused while driving while intoxicated from alcohol or drugs, and long-term secured obligations. Chapter 13 bankruptcies are also available to small sole-proprietorship businesses and will allow the business to remain open while paying off burdensome debts over a period of up to five years.

A Chapter 13 bankruptcy has advantages over other types of bankruptcies in certain instances. If you are behind in payments on your house, you may file a Chapter 13 plan to keep your house and take three to five years to make up your delinquent payments. A Chapter 13 bankruptcy may be the best alternative if you have a large amount of secured debts (debts for which you have pledged some type of collateral). If you have a mortgage on your home, the mortgage debt is a secured debt. Under a Chapter 7 bankruptcy, you may lose your home. Under a Chapter 13 bankruptcy, however, you will be allowed to keep it. If this is your situation and you would like to keep your house, you should consult a competent attorney.

Chapter 11: This type of bankruptcy is referred to as a "Reorganization." Chapter 11 is designed primarily for the reorganization of a business, but is also available to consumer debtors. Its' provisions are quite complicated and any decision by an individual to file a Chapter 11 petition should be reviewed with an attorney.

Chapter 12: This bankruptcy is a specialized type of bankruptcy only available to a family farmer. Chapter 12 is designed to permit family farmers to repay their debts over a period of time and is, in many ways, similar to Chapter 13. The eligibility requirements are restrictive, however, limiting its use to those whose income arises primarily from a family-owned farm.

> **Toolkit Tip!**
> If you are a farmer whose income is primarily from your own farm, you should investigate a Chapter 12 bankruptcy. Please see a qualified attorney for advice.

Changes in the 2005 Bankruptcy Act

The 2005 Bankruptcy Act brought extensive changes to bankruptcy law, many designed expressly to discourage the use of bankruptcy to eliminate debts. Many of the new provisions make filing for bankruptcy far more complex and confusing. The new law requires mandatory credit counseling before filing for bankruptcy that may take as long as three months to complete (during which time your late bills and charges may continue to pile up). It is likely that the coming years will bring additional changes to bankruptcy law as Congress and the Federal Bankruptcy Courts struggle with balancing creditors' rights with the constitutional right of debtors to obtain bankruptcy relief. The major changes to bankruptcy that were introduced by the 2005 law are as follows:

Means Test: Perhaps the most dramatic change in bankruptcy law was the introduction of a "means test," essentially a complex mathematical calculation to determine if a particular debtor's income, expenses, and debts falls above or below the median in the state where the debtor lives. If the Bankruptcy Court finds that a debtor's income level appears to be enough to pay off their debts, the Court may order that the debtor be involuntarily shifted into a Chapter 13 repayment-type bankruptcy and that they not be allowed to completely discharge their debts using a Chapter 7 bankruptcy. This is a major change from prior law which allowed a debtor to voluntarily choose between Chapter 7 (discharge-type bankruptcy) or Chapter 13 (repayment-type bankruptcy).

The calculations for this determination are now the most complicated portion of a Chapter 7 bankruptcy and are performed on Official Bankruptcy Form B22A. In brief, the calculations on this form entail determining your gross monthly income from all sources (from wages, salary, business, rental income, interest dividends, pension, child or spousal support, unemployment and any other source).

If your gross monthly income from all sources is less than or equal to the median family income for your state (based on the number of people in your household), then you are allowed to file for a discharge-type bankruptcy under Chapter 7 and your dischargeable debts may be entirely eliminated. Currently, for example, this income cut-off level ranges from $31,152.00 for a single earner in Mississippi up to $99,504.00 for a family of four in Connecticut. However, if your gross monthly income is greater than your state's median family income, there are many additional calculations that must be performed for this "means test."

To determine how much of your income may be available to pay off your debts, the calculations provide that from your gross monthly income, you may deduct monthly expense amounts as follows:

- Expenses for food, clothing, household supplies, and personal care items, as determined on a national basis by the Internal Revenue Service (IRS)
- Housing and utility expenses (other than rent or mortgage costs) based on the average for the county that you live in, as determined by the IRS
- Rent or mortgage expenses based on the average for the county that you live in, as determined by the IRS

💡 Toolkit Tip!

The current bankruptcy laws include calculations (referred to as a "means test") to determine if you are even eligible to obtain a Chapter 7 personal bankruptcy, or if you will be required to pay back your debts over time through a Chapter 13 bankruptcy.

- Transportation expenses (either for your own vehicle or public transportation) based on the average for the county you live in, as determined by the IRS
- Tax expenses (other than real estate or sales taxes)
- Any mandatory payroll deductions (such as retirement plans, union dues, or uniform expenses)
- Life insurance premiums
- Alimony or child support payments (if ordered by a court)
- Expenses for education that are a condition of your employment
- Expenses for a physically or mentally challenged child
- Child care expenses
- Health care expenses that are not covered by health insurance
- Phone expenses, including cellphones and possibly internet services
- Health and disability insurance, including Health Savings Account expenses
- Expenses for the care of any family member who is elderly, chronically ill or disabled
- Expenses to maintain your family's safety under the federal Family Violence Prevention and Services Act
- Any home energy costs in excess of the amount allowed by the IRS
- Educational expenses for children under the age of 18
- Any additional food or clothing expenses
- Any charitable contributions

 Warning!

The form that you will use for the 'means test' is extremely complicated, but this book provides step-by-step instructions for its completion. Take your time and you will be able to complete this form successfully.

After making all of the above deductions, you then must determine the average monthly payments that will be due in the next 5 years for your secured and priority debts (such as mortgage payments, alimony and child support payments, any debts secured by collateral, etc.). This amount is also deducted from your gross monthly income. The final amount determined by these calculations provides the figure that is used to determine whether or not you are presumed to have enough income to repay your debts and, thus, should be required to proceed under a Chapter 13 repayment-type bankruptcy. If the amount of money left over after deducting all allowed expenses from your total monthly income is more than $100.00 per month (as spread over a 60-month period), you may be forced into a Chapter 13 bankruptcy. Note that these calculations have very little to do with your actual expenses, but are based on IRS calculations of a bare-bones budget that are used by IRS auditors when determining tax re-payment plans to be set up by delinquent taxpayers.

Mandatory Credit Counseling: Within 180 days prior to filing for bankruptcy, debtors are now required to receive credit counsel-ing from an "approved non-profit budget and credit counseling agency." If a plan to manage your debts is developed during your credit counseling sessions, this plan must be filed with the Bankruptcy Court. A list of approved credit counseling agencies is contained in Appendix C.

Non-dischargeable Debts: Any debts that are owed to a single creditor which total more than $500.00 for luxury goods and were incurred within 90 days of filing for bankruptcy are presumed to be non-dischargeable. In addition, any cash advances taken on a credit card for $750.00 or more and which were made within 70 days of filing for bankruptcy are also presumed to be non-dischargeable.

Time between Discharges: If you receive a Chapter 7 discharge of your debts, you will not be allowed to file for another bankruptcy within eight (8) years. This is an increase in the time limit from the previous limit of six (6) years.

Use of State Exemptions: You may only elect to use state exemptions in the state in which you live if you have lived in that state for 2 or more years (730 or more days). If you have lived in the state less than 2 years (730 days), you must use the state exemptions for the state in which you lived for the majority of time in the 6 months (180 days) preceding the 2-year period (730 days). This provision was enacted to prevent "exemption shopping" or moving to a new state specifically for the purpose of being able to use a state's more lenient bankruptcy exemptions. A list of state exemptions is contained in Appendix A.

Homestead Exemptions: Additionally, a debtor may only ex-empt up to $136,875.00 of his or her interest in a homestead property, if that property was acquired within 1,215 days (3 and 1/3 years) prior to filing for bankruptcy. (Note that this restric-tion on a homestead exemption does not include, however, any amount of equity which was rolled over from one house

Toolkit Tip!

Before you can even file for your bank-ruptcy, you *must* obtain 'credit coun-seling' that is designed to help you seek alternatives to bankruptcy.

Toolkit Tip!

Appendix A of this book provides a complete guide to each state's listing of exempt property.

to another during this 3 and 1/3 year period). This provision of the new bankruptcy law was also enacted to stop "exemption shopping" relating to homestead exemptions. A few states (currently Florida, Iowa, Kansas, South Dakota, and Texas) allow for unlimited amounts of real estate to be exempted from bankruptcy proceedings and a number of other states have homestead real estate exemptions of higher than $136,875.00. In recent years, these states' exemptions were being abused by wealthy persons filing for bankruptcy (by moving to such states and then investing large amounts of their money in a personal home that is then exempt from bankruptcy).

The new law essentially caps homestead real estate exemptions at $136,875.00 unless you have lived in your state for more than 3 and 1/3 years. In addition, there are other caps on homestead exemptions that are part of the new law, relating to violations of securities law, fraud, and other criminal conduct. If you have a possible homestead exemption of over $136,875.00 and have lived in your home state for less than 3 and 1/3 years, you are strongly advised to seek the assistance of a qualified bankruptcy lawyer.

Reaffirmation of Debts: Under the new law, there are now extensive disclosure requirements informing debtors of their rights when confronting a *reaffirmation* of a debt. Reaffirmation of a debt is an agreement between a debtor and a creditor that the debtor will repay the debt, rather than include it in any discharge in bankruptcy. Thus, a reaffirmed debt becomes non-dischargeable. A debtor may choose to do this in order to hold onto the property for which the debt was incurred, if a bankruptcy discharge would force the debtor to relinquish the property to the Bankruptcy Court. The new disclosure requirements are designed to protect the debtor from any abuse by a creditor.

Changes in Automatic Stay: An automatic stay takes place upon a debtor filing a petition for bankruptcy. This is, essentially, an injunction against any collection actions being taken against the debtor or the debtor's property. The new 2005 Bankruptcy Act provides for some changes in how this automatic stay is used. If a debtor files for bankruptcy within one (1) year after a prior bankruptcy case was dismissed, the automatic stay only lasts for 30 days, unless the debtor is able to show that the bankruptcy

> **♀ Toolkit Tip!**
>
> If you are asked by a creditor to 're-affirm' a debt, and you are at all unsure of your rights, you should seek legal help prior to signing any documents.

filing is in good faith. In addition, in certain cases, an automatic stay will no longer prevent or halt an eviction proceeding (detainer action) if the debtor fails to pay any rent that is due after filing for bankruptcy. Finally, any domestic relations cases (such as paternity, support, custody, visitation, or domestic violence cases) are not stayed by a bankruptcy filing. An action for divorce is only stayed to the extent that it is seeks to divide a couple's property which is subject to the bankruptcy proceeding.

Required Documents and Schedules: Under the new bankruptcy laws, debtors are required to provide certain documents and information (in addition to the required schedules and forms). If the following documents are not provided to the court within 45 days after filing for bankruptcy (with a possibility of an additional 45 day extension for a good reason), the debtor's case for bankruptcy may be dismissed.

- Certificate of Credit Counseling
- Evidence of payments from employers (pay stubs) received within the 60 days prior to filing
- Statement by debtor that he or she has read the official Consumer Debtor Notice explaining bankruptcy
- Itemized statements of monthly income
- Statement of any changes in expenses anticipated after filing
- Tax returns for the most recent tax year
- Tax returns filed during the time the bankruptcy case is pending
- Disclosure of any interests in education IRAs or state tuition programs
- A photo ID

Mandatory Personal Financial Management Education: The new bankruptcy laws also require that debtors successfully complete a personal financial management course before being granted a discharge in bankruptcy. This course is to be taken after the debtor files the initial petition for bankruptcy and before the granting of a discharge. The Bankruptcy Court has prepared a list of approved non-profit agencies that will offer these instructional courses in personal financial management. This list is contained in Appendix D.

Toolkit Tip!

Prior to obtaining the final cancellation of your debts, you *must* also take a short course in 'personal financial management'.

Additional Changes: There are many other changes that the new 2005 Bankruptcy Act provided, many relating to technical details of how bankruptcy laws apply in cases of abuse or fraud. Any attempts at fraud or abuse of the bankruptcy process are now dealt by the Bankruptcy Court in a much harsher manner.

As you begin to determine your need for bankruptcy, you should be aware that there are various other alternatives to bankruptcy. You can often personally negotiate with your creditors to obtain relief from your debts, either in terms of making smaller payments, lengthening the time for paying the debt back, or actually lowering the amount of the debt. Most creditors will consider these options. You can also just sit tight and forego payments on your debts until your situation improves. You should also review your entire financial situation and determine how you got in over your head into debt in the first place. This may reveal strategies that you can use to lower your overall debt, for example, by giving up a second car or spending less on entertainment. Many of these strategies will be revealed during your mandatory credit counseling that you will undertake prior to filing for your bankruptcy. There are also specific circumstances when a Chapter 7 bankruptcy is not advisable, as listed below.

> **⚡ Warning!**
>
> The new bankruptcy laws deal harshly with any attempts at fraud. DO NOT attempt to hide any information or assets from the Bankruptcy Court.

When Chapter 7 Bankruptcy Isn't the Answer

There are certain situations when a Chapter 7 bankruptcy may not be the best alternative. In those situations, you may need to contact an attorney or other financial professional for advice. A Chapter 7 bankruptcy may not be the answer if:

- You own your own house or have a lot of equity built up on a major investment (such as an expensive car). Under Chapter 7, you may lose your house or car. Negotiation with your creditor or a Chapter 13 bankruptcy may be a better alternative. You should seek the assistance of an attorney.
- You have obtained a Chapter 7 bankruptcy within the past eight years. You will not be allowed to file for bankruptcy again until the eight-year period has elapsed.
- You filed a prior Chapter 7 bankruptcy petition within the previous 180 days and it was dismissed because you either

> **⚡ Warning!**
>
> If you fit any of the situations when 'bankruptcy is not the answer', you should seek the assistance of a qualified bankruptcy lawyer.

violated a court order or a creditor asked for relief from the automatic stay and you requested that your case be dismissed. Generally, you will not be allowed to file again until after 180 days. In addition, if you have previously filed for bankruptcy within the past year and had your case dismissed for any reason, the automatic stay will only remain in effect for 30 days, unless you can show the court that you had a good reason to file the second case.

- You have a cosigner on a debt. A Chapter 7 bankruptcy for you will leave your cosigner or guarantor liable for the entire debt.

- You're involved in a business partnership or business corporation. You should definitely consult with a lawyer before you file a Chapter 7 bankruptcy.

- You have been dishonest with your creditors in any manner, including lying on loan applications, concealing assets, or attempting to transfer property to relatives to avoid losing the property in bankruptcy.

- You have run up large debts in the last few months with no obvious way to repay them. The bankruptcy court will not discharge these types of debts.

- You have the ability to repay your debts over a five (5) year period. In this case, you will be required to file for a Chapter 13 bankruptcy. See the discussion earlier of the "means test" aspect of the new bankruptcy law.

- You have recently paid back loans, make gifts to, or transferred money to business colleagues or family members. In many cases, creditors can ask that a Bankruptcy Court undo such transactions and place any money back into your (and the court's) hands so that it is available to your creditors.

- You really don't have any assets or income that your creditors can take to pay off your debts. If you fit this category and also do not have any expectations of improving your situation, there is really no need to file for bankruptcy. This may be the situation if your only income is from Social Security or public disability income.

- Most of your debts are of the non-dischargeable type (for example, student loans or income taxes). Chapter 7 will offer little relief.

- You wish to *reaffirm* (pay off a debt, regardless of bankruptcy) a current debt. You may do so under Chapter 7. However, you should seek the assistance of an attorney.

> **⚡ Warning!**
>
> You will NOT be able to avoid debts that you have incurred in the last few months if it is clear that you had no obvious way to repay them when they were incurred.

- You wish to redeem property from the bankruptcy trustee. You may do so under Chapter 7. However, you should seek the assistance of an attorney.
- You wish to avoid a lien on your property. You may be able to do so under Chapter 7. However, you should seek the assistance of an attorney.
- You have had any complex financial transactions in your recent past. If so, you should consult an attorney qualified in bankruptcy.

If your situation fits any of the descriptions above, you should consult an attorney. If you have decided that Chapter 7 bankruptcy may be the correct decision for you, additional documents and instructions are necessary to complete the process of filing for bankruptcy.

If you decide to file for bankruptcy under Chapter 7, you also need to be aware that the court may disallow a final discharge of all debts, of whatever nature, if you (or your spouse), among other things:

- destroy or conceal property within one year before filing or after the date of filing, with the intent to hinder, delay or defraud a creditor
- conceal, destroy, falsify or fail to preserve records of his or her financial condition
- knowingly make a false account, oath, statement, or claim
- give, offer, receive, or attempt to obtain money, property or an advantage for acting or failing to act
- withhold from the court or the bankruptcy trustee any records related to his or her property or financial affairs
- fail to satisfactorily explain any loss of assets, or
- refuse to obey court orders or refuse to respond to questions posed by the court

Finally, the court may dismiss a Chapter 7 case if you (or your spouse, if you are filing jointly):

- unreasonably delay the proceedings to the creditors' harm
- fail to pay necessary fees or payments (unless waived by the court), or
- fail to file schedules

> **⚡ Warning!**
>
> Your bankruptcy case can be dismissed if you fail to pay your fees on time or fail to file the necessary paperwork on time. You must be ready to follow through with your bankruptcy before you begin the process.

Dismissal may also be justified if the debtor is an individual who has primarily consumer debt and the court finds that the granting of relief would be a substantial abuse of the bankruptcy process. Substantial abuse has been found by courts if the debtor is actually able to pay his debts when due. (Note: This is now generally determined by the mathematical calculations on Official Form B22A: *Statement of Current Monthly Income and Means Test Calculation.*)

As you can see, failure to be absolutely honest when you complete your bankruptcy papers will result in the dismissal of your case, and, perhaps subject you to criminal prosecution for fraud. The Bankruptcy Courts take dishonesty in bankruptcy filings very seriously.

⚡ Warning!

If you do not understand the instructions in this book or are unsure about how to properly complete the documents, you should seek professional assistance, either from a 'paid bankruptcy forms preparer' or a bankruptcy attorney

Finally, and this is **very important**: if you have trouble understanding the instructions in this book or other instructional documents or are in any way unsure about how to complete the forms or file the required documents, you should immediately seek professional help—either from a professional paid bankruptcy forms preparer or from a qualified bankruptcy attorney. Under the new 2005 Bankruptcy Act, the penalty for filing incorrect or incomplete forms with the Bankruptcy Court may be the dismissal of your bankruptcy case. Such dismissal could affect your efforts to refile your case with the correct forms, even if you eventually obtain a lawyer's help in preparing the correct forms. The dismissal of your case for errors in your forms will cause there to be a presumption that any subsequent refiling for bankruptcy will be in 'bad faith' and will have certain effects on the scope of the automatic stay in your second case. Thus, you must be very certain that you are filing forms that are complete, reveal all of your financial information correctly, and have been carefully proof-read to catch any errors. If you can not be certain that the forms are absolutely correct, you should seek the assistance of professional help.

Remember, however, that you have a legal constitutional right to file for bankruptcy. In fact, in the official bankruptcy court instructions, this statement is made:

An individual, of course, has the right to file a bankruptcy case without employing an attorney. Before doing so, the debtor should read a "self-help" book on filing bankruptcy.

By using this book and its accompanying CD, you are doing exactly what the bankruptcy court has advised. In addition, the court advises you to:

Read all instructions thoroughly before beginning to fill out any forms. A worksheet, from an extra copy of the form, should be completed for each form. After you have completed and reviewed each worksheet, and are satisfied that the forms have been completed correctly, you should transfer the information from each worksheet to a clean blank form. The completed forms should be set aside for signing and filing.

☀️ Toolkit Tip!

You should carefully read through the first four chapters of this book before you attempt to complete the official forms for your bankruptcy.

Chapter 2

The Chapter 7 Bankruptcy Process

Once you have considered the alternatives and have decided that a Chapter 7 bankruptcy may be the answer to your financial problems, you will need an understanding of the entire bankruptcy process. A Chapter 7 bankruptcy can generally be obtained, from start to final discharge, in about four to six months. The process consists, generally, of attending a credit counseling course, calculating whether you may proceed with a Chapter 7 bankruptcy, completing numerous forms to file with the court that detail your financial situation, meeting with the bankruptcy trustee (and perhaps creditors), turning over your non-exempt property to the trustee, taking another financial course, and finally eliminating your debts. Within this basic framework, there are various details that must be understood in order for you to emerge from your bankruptcy as financially intact as possible. Throughout the entire process of filing for bankruptcy, you must be entirely honest. All of your documents, statements, and dealings with the bankruptcy court will be under close scrutiny. The bankruptcy judges and trustees are extremely adept at detecting fraud or dishonesty. Your efforts to obtain a bankruptcy will be greatly diminished if you feel that you can trick the court or your creditors. Bankruptcy can provide a welcome relief from the burden of excessive debts. However, a bankruptcy court will not grant this relief to a person whom it feels has attempted to trick or defraud the court or creditors in any manner.

> **⌁Toolkit Tip!**
>
> Your bankruptcy will take approximately 4 to 6 months from the date you file your initial paperwork to the date of your final discharge (the cancellation of your debts).

There are nine basic steps in obtaining your bankruptcy:

- Attending a credit counseling course at an approved credit counseling agency
- Filling out draft copies of the bankruptcy forms
- Filling out the official bankruptcy forms and assembling all of the other required documents for filing
- Determining which property is exempt from being lost in the bankruptcy
- Completing a "means test" to determine if you are eligible to file for bankruptcy under Chapter 7 or will be required to use Chapter 13 and repay your debts
- Filing the completed forms and required documents with the bankruptcy court and paying the required fees ($299.00) or filing a request to pay the fees in installments or a request to have the fees waived
- Attending a short meeting with the court-appointed bankruptcy trustee
- Attending an additional personal financial management course
- Obtaining the final discharge of all your debts from the bankruptcy court

Attending a Credit Counseling Course

Under the new 2005 Bankruptcy Act, all debtors filing for a Chapter 7 bankruptcy (and Chapter 13 bankruptcies also) must attend a credit counseling course at an approved non-profit credit counseling agency in the 180-day period immediately preceding filing their petition for bankruptcy. The purpose of this requirement is to make certain that all persons who file for bankruptcy for relief from consumer debts understand that there are numerous alternatives to bankruptcy and that there are methods available to restructure one's debt to avoid bankruptcy. The credit counseling must be done for no charge if the debtor (you) is unable to pay for the service. This briefing can be done over the phone; it may be done over the internet; and it may be done as a group. It is, of course, also possible to have such a briefing in person on an individual basis. The credit counseling briefing must outline various credit counseling opportunities and it must assist

> **🔆 Toolkit Tip!**
>
> All debtors that file for a Chapter 7 personal bankruptcy are now required to attend a 'credit counseling course' during the 6-month period prior to filing for bankruptcy.

the debtor in performing an analysis of their budget. There is a list available of non-profit credit counseling agencies that have been approved by the Bankruptcy Court. Many of the listings are available for a national audience, and there are other listings that are only available to residents of a specific state. Please refer to this list in Appendix C to select an approved credit counseling agency for your pre-bankruptcy credit counseling. Note that you should be very specific in informing the agency that you choose that you are applying for the required credit counseling session only. In the past, there have been many instances of scams by credit counseling agencies, so be certain that you only deal with an approved agency and that you make certain that they are aware that you only want the necessary pre-bankruptcy credit counseling briefing. Once you have completed your counseling session, you will certify that you obtained such counseling on your *Voluntary Petition*, as explained further in the specific instructions for filing.

Note: There is a very limited exception to the requirement that credit counseling be obtained prior to filing for bankruptcy in cases where a debtor has requested counseling services but has been unable to obtain them within five (5) days of requesting them. In such cases, the debtor must attach a certification of "exigent circumstances" to the Voluntary Petition, and obtain the credit counseling within 30 days after filing the petition. In such cases, the assistance of a qualified bankruptcy attorney is necessary.

Filling out Your Draft Bankruptcy Forms

♀ Toolkit Tip!

To fill our your various bankruptcy forms, you will list all of your property (whether personal or real estate) as well as all of your debts.

The next step in obtaining your Chapter 7 bankruptcy will be to carefully fill in draft versions of the bankruptcy forms. On these forms, you will list all of the property that you own, both real estate and personal property. Every single piece of property that you own or possess must be listed, regardless of how trivial or special it may be to you. You will also list all of the various debts that you currently owe. Again, every debt that you owe must be listed. If you neglect to list a debt, that particular debt may not be wiped out by your bankruptcy. You must be scrupulously honest when filling out the official bankruptcy forms. If you attempt to hide your assets in any way to prevent them from being lost to bankruptcy, or if you lie on any of the forms or to the court, the bankruptcy judge will most likely deny your bankruptcy. You may also be subject to penalties for fraud and/or perjury, which can be up to $500,000.00 and/or five years in prison. On these forms, you will be asked to fill in considerable detail about both your property and your debts. Information regarding ownership, creditors' addresses, account numbers, and various other details will need to be listed. The gathering and recording of this information, however, will constitute the bulk of your efforts in obtaining a bankruptcy. You will need before you all of the paperwork you have that regards your finances. It will be necessary to consult your bills, payment records, paycheck stubs, mortgages, loan applications, checkbooks, tax returns, and all other financial information in order to complete these forms. If you are filing jointly, you will need to include totals for both spouses.

> **⚡ Warning!**
>
> The penalties for any types of fraud or dishonesty on your paperwork can be up to $500,000 in fines and up to 5 years in prison.

The *Voluntary Petition* (Official Form 1) is your official request for bankruptcy. The bankruptcy schedules (A through J) for the *Summary of Schedules* (Official Form 6) contain all of the details regarding your current assets, debts, income, and expenses. Schedules A and B contain the details of your real estate and personal property. Schedule C contains a listing of the property that you claim as exempt from bankruptcy, by virtue of either state or federal bankruptcy exemption laws. See "Determining Your Exemptions" later in the following section for details. On Schedules D, E, and F, you will divide your debts into three general categories: 1. *secured debts* (those for which you have pledged some type of collateral or against which a lien exists); 2. *unsecured priority debts* (those that are, by law, to be paid off first if you have any money or assets to apply to pay your debts); or 3. *unsecured nonpriority debts* (essentially, all of your debts that are not secured or priority debts). For all of your debts, you must also determine if they fit into four other subcategories: 1. *contingent debt* (a known debt with an uncertain value, such as a claim against you stemming from an auto accident, but has yet to be resolved by a court); 2. *disputed debt* (a debt for which you dispute either the amount of the debt or the entire debt itself); 3. *liquidated debt* (a debt of yours for which a court judgment has been issued); or 4. *unliquidated debt* (a known undisputed debt that has not been the subject of a court action). Note that the majority of most people's debts will normally be unliquidated debts. On Schedule G, you will list any outstanding contracts or unexpired leases. Schedule H will list any codebtors: either cosigners on a debt or guarantors of a debt. All of your current income will be listed on Schedule I and your current expenditures on Schedule J. You will also complete a *Statement of Financial Affairs* (Official Form 7) on which you will answer various questions regarding your financial situation and most recent transactions.

Determining Your Exemptions

> **∅ Definition:**
>
> **Exempt property:** This is property (personal and real estate) that you will be allowed to keep despite your bankruptcy. You will find your state's allowances in Appendix A.

The preparation of Schedule C: *Property Claimed as Exempt* of your bankruptcy papers is the most important form in terms of the property that you will get to keep at the end of your bankruptcy case. It is on this form that you will list all of your property that you claim is totally exempt from bankruptcy. Every state allows certain property to be excluded from being surrendered in bankruptcy. Many states also allow you to choose to use their list of exempt property or choose from the list of federal exemptions. In general, most states' exemption lists allow you to keep household goods, clothing, tools (up to certain limits), health aids (wheelchairs, crutches, etc.), public aid, unemployment, worker's compensation, pensions, and many insurance benefits. In addition, most states also allow you to exempt a certain value for a car and real estate. Most states also allow you to retain 75 percent of your wages. Some states are very liberal in their exemptions, allowing your residence to be retained regardless of value. Other states are far more restrictive. In those states that allow a choice between federal or state exemptions, you will need to carefully determine which set of exemptions will be most beneficial to you in your particular circumstances.

Calculating Your Eligibility for Chapter 7 Using the Means Test

An entirely new aspect of the 2005 Bankruptcy Act is the use of a mathematical test to determine whether a particular debtor is eligible to file for bankruptcy using Chapter 7, which allows the debtor to entirely eliminate most of their debts. The calculations for this portion of obtaining a bankruptcy are, perhaps, the most difficult part of filing. The form that must be used is (Official Form B22A: *Statement of Current Income and Means Test Calculation*). This form is exceedingly complicated and, perhaps intentionally, is made very difficult to complete. It requires a debtor to obtain many, many figures relating to standardized allowable expenses for their home state and local county. The required figures are available on several government sites on the internet or are supposed to be available from the clerk of the bankruptcy court in the judicial district in which a debtor is required to file (the district in which they reside). The "means test" is actually a two-part determination: first, a debtor calculates his or her (or both spouses, if filing for bankruptcy jointly) total gross monthly income from all sources. If this figure is less than the median income for a household of the same size in the same state as the debtor, then that debtor may proceed with filing a Chapter 7 bankruptcy and need not complete the second portion of the "means test".

If, however, a debtor (or debtor and spouse, if filing jointly) has income over the median for their state and household size, then many additional calculations are necessary to determine eligibility to file under Chapter 7. Average expense amounts for many, many items are used in these calculations, most of which are derived from U.S. Census figures and are used by the Internal Revenue Service to calculate payments from delinquent taxpayers. The final outcome of all of the second set of calculations is a determination as to whether or not a debtor has sufficient income to make payments on their debts. If the calculations reveal that the debtor(s) has over $100.00 per month left after the allowable expenses, then the Court may require the debtor to file under Chapter 13 and set up a repayment plan. If the calculations reveal that the debtor(s) have over $167.00 per month, then the Court will require the use of Chapter 13. Technically, in typical government bureaucratic double-talk, the paperwork refers to this calculation as a determination of whether or not "a presumption arises"– the "presumption" being whether or not allowing a debtor to file under Chapter 7 would be an abuse of the bankruptcy process (in that Chapter 7 would allow the debtor to avoid his or her debts, while a Chapter 13 bankruptcy forces the debtor to repay the debts).

⚡ Warning!

The "means test" that is part of Official Form B-22A is a very complex form. To complete the form, you will need either internet access or specific information from the bankruptcy court clerk in your district.

💡 Toolkit Tip!

If your 'means test' calculations indicate that you will have over $100 per month left after paying for your 'allowable' expenses, you may forced to file for a Chapter 13 repayment-type bankruptcy rather than a Chapter 7 type.

Filling out the Official Bankruptcy Forms

The next step in the process will be to prepare the official court forms for filing for bankruptcy. These consist of a three-page *Voluntary Petition*, Schedules A through J, a few additional forms (a summary of all of your schedules [Official Form 6], an application to pay the filing fee in installments, if desired [Official Form 3], a statement of your intentions regarding your secured debts if you have any [Official Form 8]), and a mailing list of your creditors' names and addresses. You will use your completed draft copies to transfer all of the information regarding your assets and debts to the appropriate official bankruptcy schedules. When you have completed these official forms, your work in obtaining a bankruptcy will almost be over. You will need to also compile certain personal and tax documents to file with the court. This will be explained below under: Filing Your Bankruptcy Papers.

Filing Your Bankruptcy Papers

 Toolkit Tip!

Make sure that you have your paperwork ready to go when you file your Voluntary Petition. You must file all of your bankruptcy papers within 15 days from the date on which you file your initial Voluntary Petition.

The filing of the *Voluntary Petition* is the act that officially begins your bankruptcy. If there is no emergency, you should file all of your completed official bankruptcy forms at the same time. However, if there is an emergency (such as a creditor about to foreclose on your property or garnish your wages), you may file the *Voluntary Petition* and *Mailing List of Creditors' Names and Addresses* first and the remaining documents within 15 days. The filing of your *Voluntary Petition* is your official request to the court for bankruptcy relief. It also creates the *automatic stay*. The automatic stay is an official court order that automatically goes into effect upon the filing of your *Voluntary Petition*. Its' effect is to prohibit your creditors from taking any action against you while your bankruptcy is pending. The stay has several effects:

- Lawsuits against you are suspended (with a few exceptions, such as paternity or child support suits).
- Creditors cannot repossess any of your property.
- Banks cannot foreclose on your home while the stay is in effect.
- Landlords cannot evict you (unless , in some cases, you fail

to pay rent after filing the Voluntary Petition).

- Utility companies cannot disconnect your utilities. However, this relief only lasts 20 days, at which time a utility company can insist that you furnish a security deposit for future payment of your bills.
- Even the Internal Revenue Service cannot collect on your past-due taxes.
- Creditors are blocked by the automatic stay from taking any action to collect or recover any debt. They may not call you or contact your place of employment and they may not harass or annoy you in any way.

There are a few exceptions to the blanket power of the automatic stay against creditors. Criminal prosecutions are not halted. The IRS can still audit you. Alimony and child support will likely be required to be paid, regardless of the stay. Creditors can also ask that the stay be lifted for certain debts or property. They may do this in particular to protect their collateral on one of your debts. In addition, a Chapter 7 automatic stay does not prevent a creditor from continuing collection procedures against a co-debtor, unless the codebtor is your spouse and you have filed a joint bankruptcy petition. The automatic stay is a powerful tool to help you as you struggle to get back on your financial feet. If necessary, to prevent immediate creditor action, you may decide to file your *Voluntary Petition* first in order to take advantage of this weapon against creditors. You, yourself, may then send a copy of your filed *Voluntary Petition* to creditors in order to alert them of the issuance of the automatic stay. In an emergency situation, waiting for the bankruptcy court to send notice of the automatic stay may take precious weeks.

⊘ Definition:

Automatic Stay: This is an automatic court order that, in most cases, prevents creditors from taking any action against you during the pendency of your bankruptcy proceedings.

The Creditors' Meeting

About a month after you file your *Voluntary Petition*, you will be required to attend a short creditors' meeting. Generally, no creditors will actually be present at this meeting, but they may attend if they seek to challenge some part of your claim to exemptions or dischargeability. Someone who will definitely attend the meeting, however, is the *bankruptcy trustee*. This is a court-appointed person who will take charge of your property and pay off your creditors with your assets to the best of his or her ability. All of your property and your right to receive property is together referred to as your *bankruptcy estate*. Upon filing for a personal bankruptcy, the bankruptcy court obtains total control over all of your property—your bankruptcy estate. Until your case is concluded, the court has full authority over your bankruptcy estate. While your bankruptcy case is pending, you must not sell, give away, or dispose of any property without notifying the bankruptcy trustee and obtaining permission. Your creditors' meeting will generally last less than one hour. At the meeting, your bankruptcy trustee will carefully review your documents with you. The trustee will look for any discrepancies, such as undervaluing property or claiming too many expenses. At this time, he or she will decide if there is any non-exempt property or cash that he or she feels can be used to pay off your creditors. If the trustee decides that there is certain property that is not exempt and that could be sold to pay off your creditors, he or she will ask that you surrender it to him or her. The same goes for any cash or bank accounts. Generally, the trustee will not take any used property with little cash value, even if it isn't exempt. After the meeting, the trustee will then use either the cash or proceeds from a sale of your non-exempt property to pay off your creditors according to a priority list set up by the Federal Bankruptcy Code.

Attending a Personal Financial Management Course

In addition to attending the pre-filing Credit Counseling course, you will also be required to attend an additional educational course regarding the effective management of your personal finances. You must take this course after you have filed your Voluntary Petition and other bankruptcy papers and before the bankruptcy judge will grant the discharge of your debts. This course must be taken from an approved non-profit agency that offers such financial management courses. Appendix D of this book includes a listing of all approved agencies at the time of the publication of this book.

⚡ Warning!

Before your bankruptcy will be made final, you must also attend a 'personal financial management course'. This is in addition to the 'credit counseling' course that is required prior to filing.

Your Final Discharge

Once the bankruptcy trustee has reviewed your case, collected any non-exempt property, and used the proceeds to pay your creditors, you will be granted a final discharge by the bankruptcy court. This will be the official elimination of the rest of your dischargeable debts. From that moment on, you will cease to have those debts. Your creditors can take no legal action to collect on those discharged debts. All of the exempt property that you were allowed to keep is yours, free and clear from any claims by your previous creditors. You are ready to begin anew. Up until your final discharge, you may voluntarily ask the court to dismiss your bankruptcy. You may wish to do this if you feel that you have become able to pay off your debts or if you have reached an agreement with your creditors. If you wish to have your bankruptcy dismissed, you are advised to seek legal assistance.

Definition:

Final Discharge: This is the official cancellation of all of your 'dischargeable' debts (those that are allowed to be eliminated).

Instructions for Married Couples

If you are currently married, you must decide how you will file for your bankruptcy. You have several choices. One of you may file individually, both of you may file individually, or you can file jointly. There are several factors that may influence your decision on which way to file for your bankruptcy. In general, there are benefits to jointly filing for bankruptcy. By doing so, all of the dischargeable debts, both joint and individual, belonging to both you and your spouse, will be wiped out. If you both file individually, you both will incur double filing and administrative fees. In addition, you will each have to complete a separate set of official bankruptcy forms. If you and your spouse have separated and have little or no jointly owned property or debts, you may wish to file alone. If your spouse individually owns valuable property that could be taken by the court in a joint bankruptcy, you may also wish to file for bankruptcy as an individual. In most cases, however, in which there is little property to be surrendered to the court, you will be safe in filing your bankruptcy petition jointly. Note that the forms have numerous places to indicate if you are filing jointly. If you have any questions regarding the choice on how to file, please consult a competent attorney. For

Toolkit Tip!

In general, it is best for married couples to file jointly for bankruptcy. However, you should review your individual circumstances to make certain that this is the best choice.

those married couples who live in community property states (Arizona, California, Idaho, Louisiana, Nevada, New Mexico, Texas, Washington, and Wisconsin [*Note*: Alaska allows spouses to designate property as community property if done in writing.]), some separate rules apply. If you both file jointly, your situation is similar to married couples in all other states. However, if one of you chooses to file for bankruptcy individually, the community property of the non-filing spouse may be taken by the court to pay off the bills and debts of the spouse who filed for bankruptcy. In addition, however, the *community debts* of both spouses (generally, those debts incurred during the marriage) will be totally discharged (providing that they are of the dischargeable type).

☞ Toolkit Tip!

Review the following two checklists very carefully as you work to complete your official bankruptcy paperwork.

On the next pages, you will find two checklists that will help you organize your activities in obtaining a personal bankruptcy. The first checklist details the various steps that you will need to personally take to obtain a bankruptcy. Check each action off as you complete each step. The following checklist indicates exactly which forms and paperwork must be completed to complete your filing for bankruptcy. It also indicates the cost of a Chapter 7 personal bankruptcy (official filing fees).

Checklist of Actions for Obtaining a Chapter 7 Bankruptcy

❑ Carefully read through all necessary forms and instructions.

❑ Gather all of your financial records, bills, deeds, titles, checkbooks, checkstubs, and other paperwork together in one place.

❑ Using your own financial documents, complete the bankruptcy questionnaire and the draft bankruptcy forms.

❑ Attend a credit counseling session with an approved non-profit credit counseling agency within 180 days of filing for bankruptcy.

❑ Contact the local bankruptcy court clerk for information on local court rules and mailing lists.

❑ Using your completed draft bankruptcy forms, fill in the official bankruptcy form. You will need to either type the fill-ins or use good handwriting in ink. However, your mailing list must be typed.

❑ Sign all official forms where indicated. If you are filing jointly, your spouse must also sign.

❑ Make the required number of copies of the completed official bankruptcy forms.

❑ File the original and required number of copies of your complete set of official forms. Retain an additional copy for yourself. Upon filing, you must either pay the required fees in full or fill out an application to pay the filing fee in installments.

❑ Attend a creditors' meeting and meet with the bankruptcy trustee.

❑ Surrender any non-exempt property to the bankruptcy trustee, if required.

❑ Attend a personal financial management course from an approved non-profit agency and file Certification to that effect with Court.

❑ Obtain a final discharge of all dischargeable debts from the bankruptcy court.

Checklist of Schedules, Statements, and Fees for a Chapter 7 Bankruptcy

❑ Filing Fee: $299.00 ($245.00 filing fee + $39.00 administrative fee + $15.00 trustee surcharge), payable in cash, money order, or certified bank check. You may choose to pay this fee in installments. If the fee is to paid in installments, the debtor must be an individual and must submit a signed application for court approval on an Application to Pay Filing Fee in Installments (Official Form 3A). You may also file for a complete waiver of these fees if you are unable to afford these fees by filing Official Form 3B: Application for Waiver of the Chapter 7 Filing Fee. These forms and all of the forms noted below can be obtained from the clerk of your local bankruptcy court (and are all contained on the enclosed CD).

❑ Voluntary Petition (Official Form 1): Names and addresses of all creditors of the debtor MUST be submitted with the petition. This is not required, however, if debtor submits schedules of debts (Schedules D through F) for Official Form 6 with the petition. (You will also need to file an Exhibit D of this form which is the Individual Debtor's Statement of Compliance with Credit Counseling Requirement. Exhibit D must be filed either with the Voluntary Petition or within 15 of its filing.)

❑ Notice to Individual Consumer Debtor under 11 U.S.C. Section 342(b): MUST be submitted with the petition or within 15 days.

❑ Certification of Credit Counseling and Debt Repayment Plan: This certification is part of the Voluntary Petition. Every debtor must complete a required credit counseling course within 180 days prior to filing for bankruptcy.

❑ Statement of Current Monthly Income and Means Test Calculation (Official Form B22A): MUST be submitted with the petition or within 15 days.

❑ Schedules of Assets and Liabilities (Official Form 6)–Schedules A through F: MUST be submitted with the petition or within 15 days.

❑ Schedule G: Executory Contracts and Unexpired Leases and Schedule H: Codebtors: MUST be submitted with the petition or within 15 days.

☐ Schedule I: Current Income of Individual Debtor(s) and Schedule J: Current Expenditures of Individual Debtor(s): MUST be submitted with the petition or within 15 days.

☐ Summary and Declaration Pages (Official Form 6): MUST be submitted with the petition or within 15 days.

☐ Statement of Financial Affairs (Official Form 7): MUST be submitted with the petition or within 15 days.

☐ Chapter 7 Individual Debtor's Statement of Intention (Official Form 8): Required only if the debtor is an individual and Schedule D: Creditors Holding Secured Claims contains consumer debts that are secured by property of the debtor. If so, this form MUST be submitted within 30 days of filing of the petition or by the date set for the creditors' meeting, whichever is earlier.

☐ Statement of Social Security Number(s) [Official Form 21]: MUST be filed with the Voluntary Petition (Official Form 1).

☐ Copies of all payment records or other evidence of payments received by debtor from any employer within 60 before the filing of the Voluntary Petition: MUST be submitted with the petition or within 15 days. This requirement can be satisfied with paystubs or copies of paychecks or any other evidence of payments for employment.

☐ Mailing List of Creditors' Names and Addresses: MUST be filed with the Voluntary Petition. This form varies with local bankruptcy courts. Check with the court for local rules.

☐ Debtor's Certification of Completion of Instructional Course Concerning Personal Financial Statement (Official Form 23): MUST be filed with the Court prior to the final discharge in bankruptcy.

☐ Copies of any tax returns for the most recent tax year and any tax returns filed during the time your banruptcy is pending MUST be submitted with your petition or within 15 days.

Chapter 3

Gathering Information For Your Bankruptcy

Before you begin to actually prepare your bankruptcy papers, you must have a clear record of what your assets, debts, income, and expenses are. This information regarding your current financial situation will help you understand your overall position and will eventually be used on the various bankruptcy forms which you prepare for the court. It is helpful to gather all of the information regarding your personal financial situation together in one place. The following Bankruptcy Questionnaire will assist you in that task and should provide you with all of the necessary information to make the actual preparation of your bankruptcy papers a relatively easy task. In addition, the actual process of filling out these questions will force you to think about your current financial situation. You must complete this questionnaire and the related bankruptcy papers with absolute honesty. Any attempts, however minor, to hide your property or trick creditors in any manner may result in the denial of your bankruptcy by the court.

To prepare this questionnaire, you will need in front of you all of the paperwork that you have regarding your finances. It will be necessary to consult your bills, payment records, paycheck stubs, mortgages, loan applications, checkbooks, tax returns, and all other financial information in order to complete this

☼Toolkit Tip!

The Questionnaire in this chapter is provided to help you organize all of the information that you will need to complete the official forms for your bankruptcy.

questionnaire. If you are filing jointly, include totals for both spouses.

Do not attempt to hide any information from the Bankruptcy Court. You are required by law to report every single detail of your personal financial situation. If you are holding property for someone else (for example: your mother's wedding ring), you must disclose it. This does not mean you will lose it in your bankruptcy, but if you fail to disclose assets such as this, you may be prevented from having any of your debts erased. This is very, very serious. If you have things that you do not want to disclose, you should not file for bankruptcy. If you file for bankruptcy and fail to disclose important financial aspects of your life, you could wind up in jail. The filing of false bankruptcy papers is a federal felony and bankruptcy judges and trustees take these matters very seriously. Keep this rule in mind as you complete the following questionnaire and all of the required documents for your bankruptcy: ***Do not attempt to hide any assets or transactions from the Bankruptcy Court.***

> ## ⚡ Warning!
> You must disclose every detail of your personal financial situation to the Bankruptcy Court. Do not attempt to hide any assets or transactions.

When you have finished completing the questionnaire, have it in front of you as you fill in your official bankruptcy forms. By referring to this completed questionnaire, you should be able to quickly and easily fill in all of the necessary legal documents for your bankruptcy.

Bankruptcy Questionnaire

What Are Your Assets?

Real Estate

Personal Residence
Description _____
Location _____
Market Value: $ _____
How held and percent held? (Joint tenants, tenancy-in-common, etc?)
_____ / _____ %
Value of your share .... $ _____
Amount of mortgage or other debt .... $ _____

Vacation Home
Description _____
Location _____
Market Value: $ _____
How held and percent held? (Joint tenants, tenancy-in-common, etc?)
_____ / _____ %
Value of your share .... $ _____
Amount of mortgage or other debt .... $ _____

Vacant Land
Description _____
Location _____
Market Value: $ _____
How held and percent held? (Joint tenants, tenancy-in-common, etc?)
_____ / _____ %
Value of your share .... $ _____
Amount of mortgage or other debt .... $ _____

Other Property
Description _____
Location _____
Market Value: $ _____
How held and percent held? (Joint tenants, tenancy-in-common, etc?)
_____ / _____ %
Value of your share .... $ _____
Amount of mortgage or other debt .... $ _____

Other Property

Description _____

Location _____

Market Value: $ _____

How held and percent held? (Joint tenants, tenancy-in-common, etc?)

_____ / _____ %

Value of your share .... $ _____

Amount of mortgage or other debt .... $ _____

Total Real Estate .... $ _____

Personal Property

Cash and Bank Accounts

Cash .... $ _____

Checking account .... $ _____

Bank _____

Address _____

Account # _____

Name(s) on account _____

Savings account .... $ _____

Bank _____

Address _____

Account # _____

Name(s) on account _____

Certificate of deposit .... $ _____

Held by _____

Address _____

Expiration date _____

Name(s) on account _____

Other account .... $ _____

Bank _____

Address _____

Account # _____

Name(s) on account _____

Total Cash and Bank Accounts .... $ _____

Security Deposits (Held by Utilities, Landlords, etc.)

Security deposit .... $ _____
Held by _____
Address _____
Reason for deposit _____
Name(s) on account _____

Security deposit .... $ _____
Held by _____
Address _____
Reason for deposit _____
Name(s) on account _____

Total Security Deposits .... $ _____

Miscellaneous Household and Personal Property

Household furnishings .... $ _____
Description _____
Location _____

Audio or video equipment .... $ _____
Description _____
Location _____

Computer equipment .... $ _____
Description _____
Location _____

Books, pictures, or artwork .... $ _____
Description _____
Location _____

Stamp, coin, or other collections .... $ _____
Description _____
Location _____

Clothing .... $ _____
Description _____
Location _____

Jewelry and furs .... $ _____
Description _____
Location _____

Firearms and sporting equipment .... $ _____
Description _____
Location _____

Camera and hobby equipment .... $ _____
Description _____
Location _____

Any other miscellaneous household and personal property .... $ _____
Description _____
Location _____

Total Miscellaneous Household and Personal Property .... $ _____

Insurance and Annuity Contracts

Life insurance (face value) .... Policy Amount $ _____
Policy # _____
Company _____
Address _____
Cash surrender value .... $ _____

Annuity contract (face value) .... Policy Amount $ _____
Policy # _____
Company _____
Address _____
Cash surrender value .... $ _____

Total Insurance and Annuity Contracts .... $ _____

Ira, Keogh, and/or Pension/Profit-Sharing Plans

Company or administrator _____
Address _____
Plan type _____
Net value .... $ _____

Company or administrator _____
Address _____
Plan type _____
Net value .... $ _____

Total IRA, Keogh, and/or Pension/Profit-Sharing Plans .... $ _____

Stocks and Mutual Funds

Company _____
CUSIP or Certificate # _____
Number and type of shares _____
Value .... $ _____

Company _____
CUSIP or Certificate # _____
Number and type of shares _____
Value .... $ _____

Total Stocks and Mutual Funds .... $ _____

Business Interests

Sole Proprietorship
Name _____
Location _____
Type of business _____
Your net value .... $ _____

Interest in Partnership
Name _____
Location _____
Type of business _____
Gross value $ _____
Percentage share held _____
Your net value .... $ _____

Corporation Interest
Name _____
Location _____
Type of business _____
Gross value $ _____
Percentage shares held _____
Your net value .... $ _____

Joint Venture Interest
Name _____
Location _____
Type of business _____
Gross value $ _____
Percentage share held _____
Your net value .... $ _____

Total Business Interests .... $ _____

Bonds and Mutual Bond Funds

Company _____
CUSIP or Certificate # _____
Number and type of shares _____
Value .... $ _____

Company _____
CUSIP or Certificate # _____
Number and type of shares _____
Value .... $ _____

Total Bonds and Mutual Bond Funds .... $ _____

Accounts Receivable

Accounts owed to you .... $ _____
Due from _____
Address _____

Accounts owed to you .... $ _____
Due from _____
Address _____

Total Accounts Receivable .... $ _____

Alimony, Support, or Property Settlements Owed to You

Alimony .... $ _____
Due from
Address _____

Property settlement .... $ _____
Due from _____
Address _____

Total Alimony, Support, or Property Settlements Owed to You .... $ _____

Other Debts Owed to You

Other debt owed to you .... $ _____
Due from _____
Address _____

Other debt owed to you .... $ _____

Due from _____

Address _____

Total Other Debts Owed to You .... $ _____

Tax Refunds Due to You

Federal income tax .... $ _____

Address of IRS office _____

State income tax .... $ _____

Name of state _____

Address of tax authority _____

Other tax .... $ _____

Name of tax authority _____

Address of tax authority _____

Total Tax Refunds Due to You .... $ _____

Miscellaneous Property Interests

Future interest and/or life estates .... $ _____

Description _____

Location _____

Interests in estates of decedents, etc. .... $ _____

Description _____

Location _____

Interests in another person's life insurance policy .... $ _____

Description _____

Location _____

Other contingent or unliquidated claims .... $ _____

Description _____

Location _____

Royalties, patents, copyrights, etc. .... $ _____

Description _____

Location _____

Licenses, franchises, etc .... $ _____
Description _____
Location _____

Auto, truck, or other vehicles .... $ _____
Description _____
Location _____

Boat, marine motor, etc. .... $ _____
Description _____
Location _____

Airplane and accessories .... $ _____
Description _____
Location _____

Office equipment, supplies, and furnishings .... $ _____
Description _____
Location _____

Machinery, business equipment, etc. .... $ _____
Description _____
Location _____

Business inventory .... $ _____
Description _____
Location _____

Animals .... $ _____
Description _____
Location _____

Crops (growing or harvested) .... $ _____
Description _____
Location _____

Farm equipment .... $ _____
Description _____
Location _____

Farm supplies and seed .... $ _____
Description _____
Location _____

Tools .... $ _____
Description _____
Location _____

Season tickets .... $ _____
Description _____
Location _____

Any other personal property not listed .... $ _____
Description _____
Location _____

Any other personal property not listed .... $ _____
Description _____
Location _____

Any other personal property not listed .... $ _____
Description _____
Location _____

Any other personal property not listed .... $ _____
Description _____
Location _____

Total Miscellaneous Property Interests .... $ _____

Summary of Assets

(Insert totals from previous pages)

Real Estate Total .... $ _____
Cash and Bank Accounts Total .... $ _____
Security Deposits Total .... $ _____
Miscellaneous Household and Personal Property Total .... $ _____
Insurance and Annuity Contracts Total .... $ _____
Ira, Keogh, and/or Pension/Profit-Sharing Plans Total .... $ _____
Stocks and Mutual Funds Total .... $ _____
Business Interests Total .... $ _____
Bonds and Mutual Bond Funds Total .... $ _____
Accounts Receivable Total .... $ _____
Alimony, Support, or Property Settlements Owed to You Total .... $ _____
Other Debts Owed to You Total .... $ _____
Tax Refunds Due to You Total .... $ _____
Miscellaneous Property Interests Total .... $ _____

Total Assets .... $ _____

What Are Your Debts?

Mortgages You Owe (Home or Business)

Payable to _____ Mortgage # _____
Address _____
Property location _____
Reason for debt _____
Place debt originated _____ Date incurred _____
Do you dispute debt? _____ Did you sign contract? _____
Any legal action on this debt? _____ Name of co-signer (if any)? _____
Length of term _____ Interest rate _____
Total amount now due.. $ _____

Payable to _____ Mortgage # _____
Address _____
Property location _____
Reason for debt _____
Has there been any legal action regarding this debt? _____
Place debt originated _____ Date incurred _____
Do you dispute debt? _____ Did you sign contract? _____
Any legal action on this debt? _____ Name of co-signer (if any)? _____
Length of term _____ Interest rate _____
Total amount now due.. $ _____

Total Mortgages You Owe .... $ _____

Loans You Owe (Finance Company, Bank, Auto, or Personal)

Payable to _____ Loan # _____
Address _____
Collateral _____ Reason for debt _____
Place debt originated _____ Date incurred _____
Do you dispute debt? _____ Did you sign loan contract? _____
Any legal action on this debt? _____ Name of co-signer (if any)? _____
Length of term _____ Interest rate _____
Total amount now due.. $ _____

Payable to _____ Loan # _____
Address _____
Collateral _____ Reason for debt _____
Place debt originated _____ Date incurred _____
Do you dispute debt? _____ Did you sign loan contract? _____
Any legal action on this debt? _____ Name of co-signer (if any)? _____
Length of term _____ Interest rate _____
Total amount now due.. $ _____

Total Loans You Owe .... $ _____

Accounts Payable You Owe (Medical, Dental, Stores, etc.)

Payable to _____ Account # _____
Address _____
Reason for debt _____
Place debt originated _____ Date incurred _____
Do you dispute debt? _____ Did you sign contract? _____
Is account past due? _____ Interest rate _____
Total amount now due... $ _____

Payable to _____ Account # _____
Address _____
Reason for debt _____
Place debt originated _____ Date incurred _____
Do you dispute debt? _____ Did you sign contract? _____
Is account past due? _____ Interest rate _____
Total amount now due... $ _____

Payable to _____ Account # _____
Address _____
Reason for debt _____
Place debt originated _____ Date incurred _____
Do you dispute debt? _____ Did you sign contract? _____
Is account past due? _____ Interest rate _____
Total amount now due... $ _____

Total Accounts Payable You Owe .... $ _____

Rent You Owe

Payable to _____
Address _____
Address of rental property _____ Date incurred _____
Do you dispute debt? _____ Did you sign lease? _____
Is rent past due? _____ Late charge _____
Total amount now due... $ _____

Payable to _____
Address _____
Address of rental property _____ Date incurred _____
Do you dispute debt? _____ Did you sign lease? _____
Is rent past due? _____ Late charge _____
Total amount now due... $ _____

Total Rent You Owe .... $ _____

Taxes Due

Federal income (name of tax authority _____) ...... $ _____
State income (name of tax authority _____) .... $ _____
Personal property (name of tax authority _____) .... $ _____
Real estate (name of tax authority _____) .... $ _____
Other (name of tax authority _____) .... $ _____

Total Taxes Due .... $ _____

Credit Card Debts

Credit card company _____ Credit card account # _____
Address _____
Reason for debt _____
Place debt originated _____ Date incurred _____
Do you dispute debt? _____ Did you sign contract? _____
Amount due... $ _____

Credit card company _____ Credit card account # _____
Address _____
Reason for debt _____
Place debt originated _____ Date incurred _____
Do you dispute debt? _____ Did you sign contract? _____
Amount due... $ _____

Credit card company _____ Credit card account # _____
Address _____
Reason for debt _____
Place debt originated _____ Date incurred _____
Do you dispute debt? _____ Did you sign contract? _____
Amount due... $ _____

Total Credit Card Debts .... $ _____

Miscellaneous Debts

To whom due _____
Address _____
Collateral _____ Reason for debt _____
Place debt originated _____ Date incurred _____
Do you dispute debt? _____ Did you sign contract? _____
Any legal action on this debt? _____ Name of co-signer (if any)? _____
Term _____ Interest rate _____
Amount due... $ _____

To whom due _____

Address _____

Collateral _____ Reason for debt _____

Place debt originated _____ Date incurred _____

Do you dispute debt? _____ Did you sign contract? _____

Any legal action on this debt? _____ Name of co-signer (if any)? _____

Term _____ Interest rate _____

Amount due .... $ _____

Total Miscellaneous Debts .... $ _____

Summary of Debts

(Insert totals from previous pages)

Mortgages You Owe Total .... $ _____

Loans You Owe Total .... $ _____

Accounts Payable You Owe Total .... $ _____

Rent You Owe Total .... $ _____

Taxes Due Total .... $ _____

Credit Card Debts Total .... $ _____

Miscellaneous Debts Total .... $ _____

Total Debts .... $ _____

What Is Your Monthly Income?

Occupation _____

How long employed? _____

Name of employer _____

Address of employer _____

Monthly Wage Income	*You*	*Spouse*
Gross wages, salary, and commissions		
(*pro-rate if not paid monthly*): .... $_____	$_____	
Estimated monthly overtime: .... $_____	$_____	
Total Monthly Wages .... $_____	$_____	
Less payroll deductions:		
Taxes .... $_____	$_____	
Social Security .... $_____	$_____	
Insurance .... $_____	$_____	
Union dues .... $_____	$_____	

Other (Specify: _____) .... $_____ $ _____
Other (Specify: _____) .... $_____ $ _____
Subtotal Of Payroll Deductions .... $_____ $ _____

Total Net Monthly Wage Income (take-home pay:
total monthly wages minus payroll deductions) .... $_____ $ _____

Do you anticipate any change of more than 10% in any of the above categories within the
next year? Explain: _____

Monthly Non-Wage Income   *You*   *Spouse*
Income from business, profession, or farm: .... $_____ $ _____
Income from real property: .... $_____ $ _____
Interest and dividends: .... $_____ $ _____
Alimony or child support payments: .... $_____ $ _____
Social Security or other government assistance: .... $_____ $ _____
Pension or retirement income: .... $_____ $ _____
Other monthly income: .... $_____ $ _____

Total Monthly Non-Wage Income .... $_____ $ _____

Do you anticipate any change of more than 10% in any of the above categories within the
next year? Explain: _____

Summary of Monthly Income

(Insert totals from previous pages)
                                                          You   *Spouse*
Total Net Monthly Wage Income .... $_____ $ _____
Total Monthly Non-Wage Income .... $_____ $ _____

Total Monthly Income   .... $_____ $

What Are Your Monthly Expenses?

Rent or home mortgage payment (include lot rent for mobile home): .... $ _____
Real estate taxes .... $ _____
Property insurance .... $ _____
Utilities:
    Electricity and heating fuel .... $ _____
    Water and sewer .... $ _____
    Telephone .... $ _____
    Other .... $ _____
    Subtotal of Utilities .... $ _____

Home maintenance (repairs and upkeep):.................................... $ _____

Food: .... $ _____

Clothing: .... $ _____

Laundry and dry cleaning: .... $ _____

Medical and dental expenses: .... $ _____

Transportation (not including car payments): .... $ _____

Recreation, clubs and entertainment, newspapers, magazines, etc.: .... $ _____

Charitable contributions:.. $ _____

Insurance (not deducted from wages or included in mortgage payments):

    Homeowner's or renter's .... $ _____

    Life.. $ _____

    Health.. $ _____

    Auto... $ _____

    Other .... $ _____

    Subtotal of Insurance .... $ _____

Taxes (not deducted from wages or included in mortgage payments): .... $ _____

Installment payments:

    Auto... $ _____

    Other .... $ _____

    Other .... $ _____

    Subtotal of Installment Payments .... $ _____

Alimony, maintenance, and support paid to others: .... $ _____

Support of dependents not living at your home: .... $ _____

Regular expenses from operation of business, profession, or farm: .... $ _____

Other: .... $ _____

Other: .... $ _____

Other: .... $ _____

Total Monthly Expenses .... $ _____

Do you anticipate any change of more than 10% in any of the above categories within the next year? Explain: _____

Financial Summary

(Insert totals from previous pages)

Total Assets .... $ _____

Total Debts .... $ _____

	You	*Spouse*
Total Monthly Income .... $_____		$ _____
Total Monthly Expenses		$ _____

Chapter 4

Using the Bankruptcy Forms-on-CD

All of the forms which are included in this book have been provided on the Forms-on-CD for your use on your computer. If you have completed the Forms-on-CD installation program, all of the forms will have been copied to your computer's hard drive. By default, these files are installed in the following folder which is created by the installation program. [Note for MAC users: see instructions below.]

C:\Personal Bankruptcy Toolkit\Bankruptcy Forms

The forms are provided as PDF forms which may be filled in on your computer screen and printed out on any printer. This particular format provides the most widely-used cross-platform format for accessing computer files. Files in this format may be opened as images on your computer and printed out on any printer. The files in Adobe PDF format all have the file extension: .pdf. Although this format provides the easiest method for completing the forms, the forms in this format can not be altered (other than to fill in the information required on the blanks provided). To access the PDF forms, please see below.

This CD also automatically installs Adobe Acrobat Reader® (if you do not already have this software installed on your computer). This software program is what allows you to fill in and print the PDF forms on any computer or printer. You may fill in the PDF forms when they have been opened in the Adobe Acrobat Reader® program. The Acrobat Reader® icon should have been placed on your desktop by the installation program.

Note for MAC users: You will need to copy the following folder to your computer's hard drive from the Forms-on-CD:

Personal Bankruptcy Toolkit\Form for for MACs

Once this folder is copied to your hard drive, open the Acrobat Reader® Installer folder and double click on the Adobe Acrobat Reader® Install.exe file. Follow the prompts to install this program on your computer. All of your PDF forms are included in the Personal Bankruptcy for MACs folder.

Forms and Files Provided

The Forms-on-CD installation program installs the following forms on your computer's hard drive. The default location for the forms is

C:\Personal Bankruptcy Toolkit\Bankruptcy Forms

The official title of the form is noted below first, followed by the computer file title.

Voluntary Petition (Official Form 1) = **voluntary petition.pdf**

Voluntary Petition Exhibit D (Official Form 1-Exhibit D) = **debtor statement of compliance.pdf**

Statement of Current Monthly Income and Means Test Calculation (Official Form B22A) = **means test.pdf**

Notice to Individual Consumer Debtor (Official Form B201) = **debtor notice.pdf**

Debtor's Certification of Completion of Instructional Course Concerning Personal Finance Management (Official Form 23) = **debtor certification.pdf**

Application to Pay Filing Fee in Installments (Official Form 3A) = **installments.pdf**

Application for Waiver of the Chapter 7 Filing Fee (Official Form 3B) = **waiver.pdf**

Bankruptcy Questionnaire = **bankruptcy questionnaire.pdf**

Chapter 7 Individual Debtor's Statement of Intention (Official Form 8) = **debtor statement of intention.pdf**

Continuation Sheet = **continuation sheet.pdf**

Declaration Concerning Debtor's Schedules (Official Form 6 - decl.) = **debtor declaration.pdf**

Schedule A - Real Estate = **schedule a.pdf**

Schedule B - Personal Property = **schedule b.pdf**

Schedule C - Property Claimed as Exempt = **schedule c.pdf**

Schedule D - Creditors Holding Secured Claims = **schedule d.pdf**

Schedule E - Creditors Holding Unsecured Priority Claims = **schedule e.pdf**

Schedule F - Creditors Holding Unsecured Non-priority Claims = **schedule f. pdf**

Schedule G - Executory Contracts and Unexpired Leases = **schedule g.pdf**

Schedule H - Codebtors = **schedule h.pdf**

Schedule I - Current Income of Individual Debtor = **schedule i.pdf**

Schedule J - Current Expenditures of Individual Debtor = **schedule j.pdf**

Statement of Financial Affairs (Official Form 7) = **financial statement.pdf**

Statement of Social Security Number(s) (Official Form 21) = **social security number.pdf**

Summary of Schedules (Official Form 6-summary) = **summary.pdf**

To Access Adobe PDF Forms

1. You must have already installed the Adobe Acrobat Reader® program to your computer's hard drive. This program is installed automatically by the installation program if you do not already have this program installed on your computer.

2. On your computer's desktop, you will find a shortcut icon labeled "Acrobat Reader®" Using your mouse, left double click on this icon. This will open the Acrobat Reader® program. When the Acrobat Reader® program is opened for the first time, you will need to accept the Licensing Agreement from Adobe in order to use this program. Click "Accept" when given the option to accept or decline the Agreement.

3. Once the Acrobat Reader® program is open on your computer, click on FILE (in the upper left-hand corner of the upper taskbar). Then click on OPEN in the drop down menu. Depending on which version of Windows or other operating system you are using, a box will open which will allow you to access files on your computer's hard drive. The files for Personal Bankruptcy are located on your computer's "C" drive, under the folder "Personal Bankruptcy Toolkit." In this folder, you will find a subfolder "Bankruptcy Forms." (Note: if you installed the forms folder on a different drive, access the forms on that particular drive).

4. If you desire to work with one of the forms, you should then left double-click your mouse on the sub-folder: "Bankruptcy Forms." A list of forms will appear and you should then left double-click your mouse on the form of your choice. This will open the appropriate form within the Adobe Acrobat Reader® program

Fill in Forms in the Adobe Acrobat Reader® Program

1. Once you have opened the appropriate form in the Acrobat Reader® program, filling in the form is a simple process. A 'hand tool' icon will be your cursor in the Acrobat Reader® program. Move the 'hand tool' cursor to the first blank space that will need to be completed on the form. A vertical line or "I-beam" should appear at the beginning of the first space on a form that you will need to fill in. You may then begin to type the necessary information in the space provided. When you have filled in the first blank space, hit the TAB key on your keyboard. This will move the 'hand' cursor to the next space which must be filled in. Please note that some of the spaces in the forms must be completed by hand, specifically the signature blanks.

2. Move through the form, completing each required space, and hitting TAB to move to the next space to be filled in. For information on the information required for each blank on the forms, please read the instructions in the book. When you have completed all of the fill-ins, you may print out the form on your computer's printer. (Please note: hitting TAB after the last fill-in will return you to the first page of the form.)

3. IMPORTANT NOTE: If you wish to save the filled-in form to your computer's hard drive, you should rename the form so that you will always have the oringinal of the form available.

Technical Support

Nova Publishing will provide technical support for installing the provided software. Please also note that Nova Publishing Company cannot provide any legal advice regarding the effect or use of the forms on this software. For questions about installing the Forms-on-CD installation, you may call Nova Technical Support at 1-800-748-1175.

In addition, Nova cannot provide technical support for the use of the Adobe Acrobat Reader®. For any questions relating to Adobe Acrobat Reader®, please access Adobe Technical Support at www.adobe.com/support/main.html or you may search for assistance in the HELP area of Adobe Acrobat Reader® (located in approximately the center of the top line of the program's desktop).

Chapter 5

Filling out the Bankruptcy Forms

On the following pages you will find instructions for filling in each of the required forms for a Chapter 7 bankruptcy. The instructions for each form will explain who will need to use the form and, specifically, how to fill in the form. After each set of instructions, you will also find a sample filled-in form, showing information from a fictional bankruptcy proceeding. Before you begin, you should carefully read through this entire chapter to gain an understanding of the entire procedure of bankruptcy form completion and to determine which forms you will personally need to use.

Please note that there are also instructions for a *Continuation Sheet*. This particular form is to be used, if necessary, to add additional information to bankruptcy schedules or forms. Bankruptcy *Schedules D, E, F* and *Form 8* already have pre-printed continuation sheets that you should use for additional information for those forms. As you prepare each of the necessary forms, you should have before you all of your financial information that you filled in on your Bankruptcy Questionnaire. Referring to a client's financial information is, in fact, the same method that a bankruptcy attorney would use to fill in these forms. The difference is that the attorney would be charging you over $200.00 per hour to fill in these forms.

You should then print out copies of the necessary forms from the CD-Rom that is included with this book, using the instructions in the previous chapter to access the forms. The copies must be on single-sided white 8½" x 11" paper. These copies will be your worksheets for completing the forms and you may fill them in with pencil. When you have completed your worksheet versions of these forms, you will use them to complete the final copies of the official forms using your computer as explained in the previous chapter.

Be absolutely honest in filling out these forms. Do not, in any way, attempt to hide property from the court. You must list every single piece of property that you own and every source of income that you have. If the court discovers any evidence of deceit, your case will most likely be dismissed and you will not be allowed to attempt to refile for bankruptcy for at least six months. You may also be subject to fines or imprisonment. Be extremely thorough. The schedules are the forms on which you will enter the information regarding what you own (your *assets*); what you owe (your *debts*) and to whom you owe them; what you make (your *income*); and what you spend (your *expenditures*). As you list your debts, assets, income, and expenditures, be certain that you have listed every possible item. It is very easy to overlook many common items or debts. Read the instructions and forms very carefully for clues on what you should include. The only debts that the bankruptcy court will eliminate are those that you list. If a debt is not listed by you on the appropriate schedule, you may go through bankruptcy and still owe that debt. Equally important is the careful listing of the exact address of each person or company that you owe. Creditors must be given notice that you are filing for bankruptcy or your debt to them will not be discharged. Recall that you need to include all transactions for a full year prior to your filing for bankruptcy. Also note that you have the right to amend your *Voluntary Petition* at any time, if you find that you made a mistake.

On the completed final copy, you will sign and date each form if necessary before filing it with the bankruptcy court. *Note:* Certain bankruptcy courts may require specific localized forms in addition to the main bankruptcy forms supplied in this book. Additional copies of official bankruptcy forms can be obtained from the clerk of the U.S. Bankruptcy Court for your area. Please check

> ### ⚡ Warning!
> Although you have been warned previously, here it is again: You MUST be totally honest in completing your bankruptcy forms. Bankruptcy judges and trustees have seen every type of attempt to fool or defraud the court and you will not succeed in tricking them.

the listing in Appendix B for the address of your area court. In addition, official bankruptcy forms may be downloaded from the internet at:

www.uscourts.gov/bkforms/

Note however that the forms used in this book have had corrected various programming errors that are found on the official bankruptcy forms available on that website.

☼Toolkit Tip!

The instructions and sample forms on the following pages should be followed carefully as you complete your own bankruptcy forms.

In general, you will use every form provided. Please refer to the instructions for each individual form. When filling in your copy of these forms, please be careful that your information is listed in the proper columns and on the correct form. Some of these forms are complicated and several forms are very similar. Do not make any stray marks on the forms. You may use legible handwriting in black ink to complete the forms (except the mailing list which must be typed), but you will find it much easier to complete the forms using your computer and the Forms-on-CD that are provided with this book. One final note: if there is not room on any of the forms for your information, you may use a *Continuation Sheet*.

Instructions for the Voluntary Petition (Official Form 1)

(Page 1 of Official Form 1)

The form that you will complete to actually request bankruptcy relief from the Bankruptcy Court is the Voluntary Petition. This form is your official request for bankruptcy. By filing this form, you are voluntarily agreeing to give control over everything you own to the court. In turn, you will be allowed to keep all of your property that is exempt from bankruptcy. If your bankruptcy is successful, all of your debts that are dischargeable in bankruptcy will be wiped out. It is with this form that you "declare bankruptcy." Filing this form generally operates to stop any action by your creditors to collect their debts. This form also operates as a rough outline of your case, allowing the court to assign a judge and make a general estimate of how complex your case will be.

IMPORTANT NOTE: By submitting this petition (and your other official forms), you are certifying that the information contained in the form(s) is complete, accurate, and truthful, to the best of your knowledge. There are severe penalties for fraud or deceit in filing bankruptcy papers and if you attempt to deceive the court in any way, your bankruptcy will be denied and you may face criminal charges. Also note that all of the papers that you file for bankruptcy become public documents, available to anyone who wishes to see them (with the exception of your social security number and your tax returns).

Court Name: Fill in the full name of the judicial district in which you will be filing your papers (such as "Southern District of Illinois"). This should be where you reside and maintain your primary home. Check Appendix B for the correct court to file in.

Name of Debtor: Fill in your full name (last name first) that you regularly use.

Name of Joint Debtor: Fill in your spouse's name, if you are married and filing a joint petition with your spouse. Use the name he or she regularly uses (last name first).

All Other Names used by the Debtor in the last 8 years: Fill in any other names that you have used (nicknames, shortened, maiden, or initials-only names, etc.). If you have recently operated a business, fill in any business name that you used.

All Other Names used by the Joint Debtor in the last 8 years: Fill in any other names that your spouse has used (nicknames, shortened, maiden, or initials-only names, etc.). If he or she has recently operated a business, fill in any business name that was used.

Last four digits of Soc. Sec. No./Complete EIN or other Tax I.D. No.: Fill in your (debtor) and your spouse's (joint debtor) last four Social Security number digits and/or any full Federal Employer Tax ID numbers, if applicable.

Street Address of Debtor and Joint Debtor: Fill in the actual street address of your home or homes. This cannot be a post office box or other address where you merely receive mail.

County of Residence or of the Principal place of Business: List the county of your main place of residence. "Place of business" does not apply.

Mailing Address of Debtor and Joint Debtor: Here is where you list your actual mailing address if it is different from your street address (can be a post office box).

Location of Principal Assets of Business Debtor: This is only for those debtors who have operated a business. Normally, this address will be that of your business, but if not, specify where the majority of your business possessions are located. If you have not operated a business, enter N/A for "not applicable."

Type of Debtor: Place an X in front of "Individual(s)." Note: Individual debtors must also complete the "Exhibit D" section on page 2 of the Voluntary Petition, as well as an actual Exhibit D as explained later in these instructions.

Nature of Business: Leave this box blank, unless you have operated a business which accounts for part of your income. If so, you will generally check the box titled "Other".

Tax-Exempt Entity: Leave this box blank.

Chapter of Bankruptcy Code Under Which the Petition is Filed: Place an X before "Chapter 7."

Nature of Debts: Most will place an X in front of "Non-Business/Consumer." However, if you have operated a business in the last few years and many of your debts are business-related, place an X in front of "Business."

Filing Fee: Check the first box if you will attach the entire filing fee of $299.00. Check the second box if you will be requesting to pay the fee in installments. If so, you will need to fill out an Application to Pay Filing Fee in Installments (Official Form 3A), explained later. Low-income debtors may request a waiver of the entire filing fee. Check the third box if you wish to pursue this option. You must then complete and file with the court an Application for Waiver of Chapter 7 Filing Fee (Official Form 3B), also explained later.

Chapter 11 Debtors: Leave all items in this box blank.

Statistical/Administrative Information: Check the first box if you estimate that you will have some money to pay off some of your unsecured debts. You may need to wait until you have completed more of your bankruptcy paperwork to accurately assess your ability to pay off portions of your unsecured debts. Check the second box if you estimate that there will be no money available to pay any unsecured creditors. For the next three areas, when you have a clear idea of the necessary amounts, check the appropriate boxes. The answers here may be your best estimates.

B 1 (Official Form 1) (1/08)

United States Bankruptcy Court **Northern District of Illinois**	**Voluntary Petition**

Name of Debtor (if individual, enter Last, First, Middle): Smith, Mary Ellen	Name of Joint Debtor (Spouse) (Last, First, Middle): Smith, John Alan
All Other Names used by the Debtor in the last 8 years (include married, maiden, and trade names): Ellen Smith, Ellen Harris (maiden)	All Other Names used by the Joint Debtor in the last 8 years (include married, maiden, and trade names): J.A. Smith
Last four digits of Soc. Sec. or Individual-Taxpayer I.D. (ITIN) No./Complete EIN (if more than one, state all): 5555	Last four digits of Soc. Sec. or Indvidual-Taxpayer I.D. (ITIN) No./Complete EIN (if more than one, state all): 8888
Street Address of Debtor (No. and Street, City, and State): 16 Main Street Centerville, IL ZIP CODE 61111	Street Address of Joint Debtor (No. and Street, City, and State): 16 Main Street Centerville, IL ZIP CODE 61111
County of Residence or of the Principal Place of Business: Superior County	County of Residence or of the Principal Place of Business: Superior County
Mailing Address of Debtor (if different from street address): PO Box 120 Centerville, IL ZIP CODE 61111	Mailing Address of Joint Debtor (if different from street address): PO Box 120 Centerville, IL ZIP CODE 61111
Location of Principal Assets of Business Debtor (if different from street address above): n/a ZIP CODE	

Type of Debtor (Form of Organization) (Check **one** box.)
- ☑ Individual (includes Joint Debtors) *See Exhibit D on page 2 of this form.*
- ☐ Corporation (includes LLC and LLP)
- ☐ Partnership
- ☐ Other (If debtor is not one of the above entities, check this box and state type of entity below.)

Nature of Business (Check **one** box.)
- ☐ Health Care Business
- ☐ Single Asset Real Estate as defined in 11 U.S.C. § 101(51B)
- ☐ Railroad
- ☐ Stockbroker
- ☐ Commodity Broker
- ☐ Clearing Bank
- ☐ Other

Tax-Exempt Entity (Check box, if applicable.)
- ☐ Debtor is a tax-exempt organization under Title 26 of the United States Code (the Internal Revenue Code).

Chapter of Bankruptcy Code Under Which the Petition is Filed (Check **one** box.)
- ☑ Chapter 7
- ☐ Chapter 9
- ☐ Chapter 11
- ☐ Chapter 12
- ☐ Chapter 13
- ☐ Chapter 15 Petition for Recognition of a Foreign Main Proceeding
- ☐ Chapter 15 Petition for Recognition of a Foreign Nonmain Proceeding

Nature of Debts (Check one box.)
- ☑ Debts are primarily consumer debts, defined in 11 U.S.C. § 101(8) as "incurred by an individual primarily for a personal, family, or household purpose."
- ☐ Debts are primarily business debts.

Filing Fee (Check one box.)
- ☑ Full Filing Fee attached.
- ☐ Filing Fee to be paid in installments (applicable to individuals only). Must attach signed application for the court's consideration certifying that the debtor is unable to pay fee except in installments. Rule 1006(b). See Official Form 3A.
- ☐ Filing Fee waiver requested (applicable to chapter 7 individuals only). Must attach signed application for the court's consideration. See Official Form 3B.

Chapter 11 Debtors
Check one box:
- ☐ Debtor is a small business debtor as defined in 11 U.S.C. § 101(51D).
- ☐ Debtor is not a small business debtor as defined in 11 U.S.C. § 101(51D).

Check if:
- ☐ Debtor's aggregate noncontingent liquidated debts (excluding debts owed to insiders or affiliates) are less than $2,190,000.

Check all applicable boxes:
- ☐ A plan is being filed with this petition.
- ☐ Acceptances of the plan were solicited prepetition from one or more classes of creditors, in accordance with 11 U.S.C. § 1126(b).

Statistical/Administrative Information — THIS SPACE IS FOR COURT USE ONLY
- ☐ Debtor estimates that funds will be available for distribution to unsecured creditors.
- ☐ Debtor estimates that, after any exempt property is excluded and administrative expenses paid, there will be no funds available for distribution to unsecured creditors.

Estimated Number of Creditors

☑ 1-49	☐ 50-99	☐ 100-199	☐ 200-999	☐ 1,000-5,000	☐ 5,001-10,000	☐ 10,001-25,000	☐ 25,001-50,000	☐ 50,001-100,000	☐ Over 100,000

Estimated Assets

☐ $0 to $50,000	☑ $50,001 to $100,000	☐ $100,001 to $500,000	☐ $500,001 to $1 million	☐ $1,000,001 to $10 million	☐ $10,000,001 to $50 million	☐ $50,000,001 to $100 million	☐ $100,000,001 to $500 million	☐ $500,000,001 to $1 billion	☐ More than $1 billion

Estimated Liabilities

☐ $0 to $50,000	☑ $50,001 to $100,000	☐ $100,001 to $500,000	☐ $500,001 to $1 million	☐ $1,000,001 to $10 million	☐ $10,000,001 to $50 million	☐ $50,000,001 to $100 million	☐ $100,000,001 to $500 million	☐ $500,000,001 to $1 billion	☐ More than $1 billion

(Page 2 of Official Form 1)

Name of Debtor(s): Enter your full name. If you are filing jointly, also enter your spouse's full name.

Prior Bankruptcy Case Filed Within Last 8 Years: Enter N/A if you, or your spouse if you are both filing jointly, have not filed for bankruptcy in the last eight years. If you have filed for bankruptcy within the last eight years, you may not be allowed to refile. In that case, you should consult an attorney. If you have filed for bankruptcy more than two times in the last eight years, you will need to attach an additional sheet that contains the information required.

Pending Bankruptcy Case Filed by any Spouse, Partner or Affiliate of this Debtor: Enter N/A if there are no other bankruptcy cases currently pending which involve your spouse, a partnership, or other business of which you are an owner. If there is a bankruptcy pending, consult an attorney.

Exhibit A: Leave blank. Exhibit A is not included in this kit. If the description applies to you or your spouse, you should consult an attorney.

Exhibit B: Enter N/A on the signature line.

Exhibit C: Check "No," unless your property includes very dangerous property. If your answer is "Yes," you should consult an attorney. Exhibit C is not included in this kit.

Exhibit D: This exhibit must be completed by each individual debtor. If your spouse is filing as a joint debtor, he or she must attach a separate Exhibit D to the Voluntary Petition. All individual debtors, should put an X in the first box. If someone Is filing with you as a joint debtor, the second box should also have a X placed in it. Note: Exhibit D and instructions follow the instructions for the Voluntary Petition.

Information Regarding the Debtor-Venue: You will generally check the first box: this certifies that you have been a resident of the judicial district in which you are filing for 180 days. You must check the second box if there is a bankruptcy case concerning a business partner, partnership or affiliate pending in the judicial district in which you are filing. If you check the second box, you are advised to seek legal assistance. If you fall under the provisions of the third item, you should consult an attorney.

Statement by a Debtor Who Resides as a Tenant of a Residential Property: If you are renting your home, apartment, or mobile home, you may need to complete this section. If you are current on your rent payments, you do not need to complete this section. If you are behind on your rent, but your landlord has not obtained a court judgment against you for past-due rent, you do not need to complete this section .However, if your landlord has previously filed a suit against you for unpaid rent and has obtained a court judgment for possession of your residence (ie. an eviction order), you will need to complete this section. If this is the case, you should consult an attorney in order to complete the rest of this section and understand your rights regarding your residence.

B 1 (Official Form 1) (1/08)		Page 2
Voluntary Petition *(This page must be completed and filed in every case.)*	Name of Debtor(s): Mary Ellen and John Alan Smith	

All Prior Bankruptcy Cases Filed Within Last 8 Years (If more than two, attach additional sheet.)		
Location Where Filed:	Case Number:	Date Filed:
Location Where Filed:	Case Number:	Date Filed:

Pending Bankruptcy Case Filed by any Spouse, Partner, or Affiliate of this Debtor (If more than one, attach additional sheet.)		
Name of Debtor:	Case Number:	Date Filed:
District:	Relationship:	Judge:

Exhibit A	**Exhibit B**
(To be completed if debtor is required to file periodic reports (e.g., forms 10K and 10Q) with the Securities and Exchange Commission pursuant to Section 13 or 15(d) of the Securities Exchange Act of 1934 and is requesting relief under chapter 11.)	(To be completed if debtor is an individual whose debts are primarily consumer debts.) I, the attorney for the petitioner named in the foregoing petition, declare that I have informed the petitioner that [he or she] may proceed under chapter 7, 11, 12, or 13 of title 11, United States Code, and have explained the relief available under each such chapter. I further certify that I have delivered to the debtor the notice required by 11 U.S.C. § 342(b).
☐ Exhibit A is attached and made a part of this petition.	X n/a Signature of Attorney for Debtor(s) (Date)

Exhibit C

Does the debtor own or have possession of any property that poses or is alleged to pose a threat of imminent and identifiable harm to public health or safety?

☑   Yes, and Exhibit C is attached and made a part of this petition.

☐   No.

Exhibit D

(To be completed by every individual debtor. If a joint petition is filed, each spouse must complete and attach a separate Exhibit D)

☐   Exhibit D completed and signed by the debtor is attached and made a part of this petition.

If this is a joint petition:

☑   Exhibit D also completed and signed by the joint debtor is attached and made a part of this petition.

Information Regarding the Debtor - Venue
(Check any applicable box.)

☑   Debtor has been domiciled or has had a residence, principal place of business, or principal assets in this District for 180 days immediately preceding the date of this petition or for a longer part of such 180 days than in any other District.

☐   There is a bankruptcy case concerning debtor's affiliate, general partner, or partnership pending in this District.

☐   Debtor is a debtor in a foreign proceeding and has its principal place of business or principal assets in the United States in this District, or has no principal place of business or assets in the United States but is a defendant in an action or proceeding [in a federal or state court] in this District, or the interests of the parties will be served in regard to the relief sought in this District.

Certification by a Debtor Who Resides as a Tenant of Residential Property
(Check all applicable boxes.)

☐   Landlord has a judgment against the debtor for possession of debtor's residence. (If box checked, complete the following.)

_____
(Name of landlord that obtained judgment)

_____
(Address of landlord)

☐   Debtor claims that under applicable nonbankruptcy law, there are circumstances under which the debtor would be permitted to cure the entire monetary default that gave rise to the judgment for possession, after the judgment for possession was entered, and

☐   Debtor has included with this petition the deposit with the court of any rent that would become due during the 30-day period after the filing of the petition.

☐   Debtor certifies that he/she has served the Landlord with this certification. (11 U.S.C. § 362(l)).

(Page 3 of Official Form 1)

Name of Debtor(s): Enter your full name. If you are filing jointly, also enter your spouse's full name.

Signature(s) of Debtor(s) (Individual/Joint): Sign the top line in the box and enter the appropriate date. If you are filing jointly, your spouse should sign the "Signature of Joint Debtor "line. Enter your phone number. By signing and filing this form, you will be officially asking the court to discharge your debts and you are certifying that the information that you filled in on this form is correct and true. If you are a debtor whose debts are primarily consumer debts (as opposed to business debts), you are also certifying that you have read the Notice to Individual Consumer Debtor Under Section 342(b) of the Bankruptcy Code (Official Form B201). This form is included in this kit and should be read, signed, and also submitted to the bankruptcy court clerk at the time that you file your Voluntary Petition .

Signature of Foreign Representative: Enter N/A in the box for the signature.

Signature of Attorney: Enter N/A in the box for the attorney signature.

Signature of Debtor (Corporate or Partnership): Enter N/A on the signature line.

Signature of Non-Attorney Petition Preparer: Enter N/A on the signature line, unless you are using the services of a paid bankruptcy-form preparer, in which case the box should be completed by the preparer.

B 1 (Official Form) 1 (1/08)	Page 3

Voluntary Petition
(This page must be completed and filed in every case.)

Name of Debtor(s):
Mary Ellen and John Alan Smith

Signatures

Signature(s) of Debtor(s) (Individual/Joint)	**Signature of a Foreign Representative**

Signature(s) of Debtor(s) (Individual/Joint)

I declare under penalty of perjury that the information provided in this petition is true and correct.

[If petitioner is an individual whose debts are primarily consumer debts and has chosen to file under chapter 7] I am aware that I may proceed under chapter 7, 11, 12 or 13 of title 11, United States Code, understand the relief available under each such chapter, and choose to proceed under chapter 7.

[If no attorney represents me and no bankruptcy petition preparer signs the petition] I have obtained and read the notice required by 11 U.S.C. § 342(b).

I request relief in accordance with the chapter of title 11, United States Code, specified in this petition.

X   Mary Ellen Smith (handwritten signature)
      Signature of Debtor

X   John Alan Smith (handwritten signature)
      Signature of Joint Debtor
      (444) 555-6666
      Telephone Number (if not represented by attorney)
      3/13/08
      Date

Signature of a Foreign Representative

I declare under penalty of perjury that the information provided in this petition is true and correct, that I am the foreign representative of a debtor in a foreign proceeding, and that I am authorized to file this petition.

(Check only **one** box.)

☐   I request relief in accordance with chapter 15 of title 11, United States Code. Certified copies of the documents required by 11 U.S.C. § 1515 are attached.

☐   Pursuant to 11 U.S.C. § 1511, I request relief in accordance with the chapter of title 11 specified in this petition. A certified copy of the order granting recognition of the foreign main proceeding is attached.

X   n/a
      (Signature of Foreign Representative)

      (Printed Name of Foreign Representative)

      Date

Signature of Attorney*

X   n/a
      Signature of Attorney for Debtor(s)

      Printed Name of Attorney for Debtor(s)

      Firm Name

      Address

      Telephone Number

      Date

*In a case in which § 707(b)(4)(D) applies, this signature also constitutes a certification that the attorney has no knowledge after an inquiry that the information in the schedules is incorrect.

Signature of Non-Attorney Bankruptcy Petition Preparer

I declare under penalty of perjury that: (1) I am a bankruptcy petition preparer as defined in 11 U.S.C. § 110; (2) I prepared this document for compensation and have provided the debtor with a copy of this document and the notices and information required under 11 U.S.C. §§ 110(b), 110(h), and 342(b); and, (3) if rules or guidelines have been promulgated pursuant to 11 U.S.C. § 110(h) setting a maximum fee for services chargeable by bankruptcy petition preparers, I have given the debtor notice of the maximum amount before preparing any document for filing for a debtor or accepting any fee from the debtor, as required in that section. Official Form 19 is attached.

      Printed Name and title, if any, of Bankruptcy Petition Preparer

      Social-Security number (If the bankruptcy petition preparer is not an individual, state the Social-Security number of the officer, principal, responsible person or partner of the bankruptcy petition preparer.) (Required by 11 U.S.C. § 110.)

      Address

X   n/a

      Date

Signature of bankruptcy petition preparer or officer, principal, responsible person, or partner whose Social-Security number is provided above.

Names and Social-Security numbers of all other individuals who prepared or assisted in preparing this document unless the bankruptcy petition preparer is not an individual.

If more than one person prepared this document, attach additional sheets conforming to the appropriate official form for each person.

A bankruptcy petition preparer's failure to comply with the provisions of title 11 and the Federal Rules of Bankruptcy Procedure may result in fines or imprisonment or both. 11 U.S.C. § 110; 18 U.S.C. § 156.

Signature of Debtor (Corporation/Partnership)

I declare under penalty of perjury that the information provided in this petition is true and correct, and that I have been authorized to file this petition on behalf of the debtor.

The debtor requests the relief in accordance with the chapter of title 11, United States Code, specified in this petition.

X   n/a
      Signature of Authorized Individual

      Printed Name of Authorized Individual

      Title of Authorized Individual

      Date

Instructions for Exhibit D of Voluntary Petition–Individual Debtor's Statement of Compliance with Credit Counseling Requirement:

Every individual debtor must complete an Exhibit D of the Voluntary Petition. If you are filing jointly with another debtor, each of you must complete a separate Exhibit D and attach it to the Voluntary Petition that you file with the Bankruptcy Court. Note that you must be able to truthfully answer one of the five statements in this form regarding compliance with the mandatory credit counseling requirement for filing for bankruptcy. You must also either attach the certificate from the credit counseling agency to Exhibit D or file such certificate within 15 days of filing for bankruptcy. If you have not received credit counseling or feel that you are not required to receive credit counseling for any reason (other than that the Bankruptcy Court has determined that the counseling requirement does not apply in your district), you may need the assistance of either a professional bankruptcy petition preparer or an attorney knowledgeable in bankruptcy law to continue.

Court Name: Fill in the full name of the judicial district in which you will be filing your papers (such as "Southern District of Illinois"). This should be where you reside and maintain your primary home. Check Appendix B for the correct court to file in.

In Re: Enter your full name. If you're filing jointly, include your spouse's name.

Case No.: Leave this blank if filed with your petition. The court clerk will assign you a case number.

Boxes # 1 through 5: There is a box before each of the five statements listed on this form. You must check one of these boxes. You should read each of the statements very carefully. Here is a brief explanation of the statements:

1. You received a credit counseling briefing within 180 days before filing for bankruptcy and you have a certificate to that effect. You must attach a copy of the certificate to Exhibit D and, if you received one, you must attach a copy of any debt repayment plan that was developed by the credit counseling agency for you.

2. You received a credit counseling briefing within 180 days before filing for bankruptcy and but you do not have a certificate to that effect. You must file a copy of the certificate and, if you received one, a copy of any debt repayment plan that was developed by the credit counseling agency for you, within 15 days after you file for bankruptcy.

3. You have requested credit counseling services but was unable to obtain the services within five days after having requested them. If this is the case, you will need to explain in simple language any circumstances (*exigent* means urgent) that make it necessary for you to proceed immediately with you bankruptcy petition.

4. You are not required to receive credit counseling because of your incapacity, disability, or your active military duty in a combat zone. **Note:** If this is the case, you will need to check the appropriate box.

5. The Bankruptcy Court or Trustee in your district has determined that credit counseling requirement does not apply in your district. You should check with the clerk of the Bankruptcy Court in your district to determine is this is the case.

Signature of Debtor: Under penalty of perjury, you should sign your full name certifying that the box that you have checked is true and correct. If you are filing jointly, each debtor will need to fill out and sign a separate form.

Date: Fill in the date on which you signed Exhibit D.

B 1D (Official Form 1, Exhibit D) (12/08)

UNITED STATES BANKRUPTCY COURT

Northern District of Illinois

In re Mary Ellen & John Alan Smith   Case No. (supplied by clerk)
          Debtor   *(if known)*

EXHIBIT D - INDIVIDUAL DEBTOR'S STATEMENT OF COMPLIANCE WITH CREDIT COUNSELING REQUIREMENT

Warning: You must be able to check truthfully one of the five statements regarding credit counseling listed below. If you cannot do so, you are not eligible to file a bankruptcy case, and the court can dismiss any case you do file. If that happens, you will lose whatever filing fee you paid, and your creditors will be able to resume collection activities against you. If your case is dismissed and you file another bankruptcy case later, you may be required to pay a second filing fee and you may have to take extra steps to stop creditors' collection activities.

Every individual debtor must file this Exhibit D. If a joint petition is filed, each spouse must complete and file a separate Exhibit D. Check one of the five statements below and attach any documents as directed.

☑ 1. Within the 180 days **before the filing of my bankruptcy case**, I received a briefing from a credit counseling agency approved by the United States trustee or bankruptcy administrator that outlined the opportunities for available credit counseling and assisted me in performing a related budget analysis, and I have a certificate from the agency describing the services provided to me. *Attach a copy of the certificate and a copy of any debt repayment plan developed through the agency.*

☐ 2. Within the 180 days **before the filing of my bankruptcy case**, I received a briefing from a credit counseling agency approved by the United States trustee or bankruptcy administrator that outlined the opportunities for available credit counseling and assisted me in performing a related budget analysis, but I do not have a certificate from the agency describing the services provided to me. *You must file a copy of a certificate from the agency describing the services provided to you and a copy of any debt repayment plan developed through the agency no later than 15 days after your bankruptcy case is filed.*

❏ 3. I certify that I requested credit counseling services from an approved agency but was unable to obtain the services during the five days from the time I made my request, and the following exigent circumstances merit a temporary waiver of the credit counseling requirement so I can file my bankruptcy case now. *[Summarize exigent circumstances here.]*

If your certification is satisfactory to the court, you must still obtain the credit counseling briefing within the first 30 days after you file your bankruptcy petition and promptly file a certificate from the agency that provided the counseling, together with a copy of any debt management plan developed through the agency. Failure to fulfill these requirements may result in dismissal of your case. Any extension of the 30-day deadline can be granted only for cause and is limited to a maximum of 15 days. Your case may also be dismissed if the court is not satisfied with your reasons for filing your bankruptcy case without first receiving a credit counseling briefing.

❏ 4. I am not required to receive a credit counseling briefing because of: *[Check the applicable statement.]* *[Must be accompanied by a motion for determination by the court.]*

❏ Incapacity. (Defined in 11 U.S.C. § 109(h)(4) as impaired by reason of mental illness or mental deficiency so as to be incapable of realizing and making rational decisions with respect to financial responsibilities.);

❏ Disability. (Defined in 11 U.S.C. § 109(h)(4) as physically impaired to the extent of being unable, after reasonable effort, to participate in a credit counseling briefing in person, by telephone, or through the Internet.);

❏ Active military duty in a military combat zone.

❏ 5. The United States trustee or bankruptcy administrator has determined that the credit counseling requirement of 11 U.S.C. § 109(h) does not apply in this district.

I certify under penalty of perjury that the information provided above is true and correct.

Signature of Debtor: handwritten signature (each sign separate form if filing jointly)

Date: date signed

Instructions for the Schedules for Official Form 6

Schedule A: Real Property

All of the real estate that you own or have an interest in will be listed on Schedule A. All of your personal property will be listed on Schedule B. However, don't include leases; these will go on Schedule G. Note that if you own a home, you may lose it in a Chapter 7 bankruptcy. You may be better off using a Chapter 13 bankruptcy and should consult an attorney for advice in this situation. If more space is needed, use a Continuation Sheet, as explained later.

In Re: Enter your full name. If you're filing jointly, include your spouse's name.

Case No.: Leave this blank if filed with your petition. The court clerk will assign you a case number.

Description and Location of Property: Enter a brief description of the property and its street address. You should enter all homes, land, condos, business property, and buildings in which you have any ownership interest. Your description can simply be "home" or "lot" or some other simple description and the address or location. If you do not own any real estate, enter the "None" box and put $0 in the space for "Total" and enter $0 on your Summary of Schedules (explained later) and proceed to Schedule B.

Nature of Debtor's Interest in Property: Check the ownership language on your deed or mortgage, but in most cases property is held as "fee simple." Enter the term "fee simple" (which refers to a full ownership), unless you are certain that your property is held in some other form, such as a "tenant in common" or other form of joint ownership. If you are purchasing real estate under a contract, describe the contract by date and name.

Husband, Wife, Joint, or Community: If single, enter N/A. If married, enter H (for husband), W (wife), J (joint), or C (community property), depending if the property is owned individually by the husband or wife, is owned jointly by both (as joint tenants or tenants-by-the-entireties), or is owned as community property. Check the ownership language on the deed or other document of ownership. In community property states (Arizona, California, Idaho, Louisiana, Nevada, New Mexico, Texas, Washington, and Wisconsin), property that was acquired during a marriage is generally considered community property. In all other states, the ownership of property depends on the names on the title document or deed.

Note: Spouses in Alaska can designate in writing that certain property is to be considered "community property."

Current Market Value of Debtor's Interest in Property, without Deducting Any Secured Claim or Exemption: You should enter the full value at which the property could be sold today. Do not deduct any money that you may owe on the property, like a mortgage. You may need to obtain a market value estimate from a real estate broker. However, you may determine the value yourself by checking the value of other similar property for sale in your locale. If you own the property jointly with someone who is not filing for bankruptcy with you, you should indicate your percentage of ownership and only note the market value of your share of the property (for example, your 33.33 percent ownership of a home owned jointly with both of your parents with a full market value of $150,000.00 would constitute a market value of $50,000.00 for your interest in the property).

Amount of Secured Claim: A secured claim is any mortgage, deed of trust, loan, lien, or other claim against the property that is in writing and for which the property acts as collateral. Enter the amount that is left to be paid on the mortgage or other obligation. You can get the current amount from the financial institution to which the money is owed. If there are no secured claims, enter the "None" box.

Total: Total the amounts in the "Current Market Value…" column (and from any continuation sheets if used), and enter here and also on the Summary of Schedules form, as explained later.

B6A (Official Form 6A) (12/07)

In re **Mary Ellen and John Alan Smith**   ,   Case No. (supplied by clerk)
_____   _____
               Debtor   **(If known)**

SCHEDULE A - REAL PROPERTY

Except as directed below, list all real property in which the debtor has any legal, equitable, or future interest, including all property owned as a co-tenant, community property, or in which the debtor has a life estate. Include any property in which the debtor holds rights and powers exercisable for the debtor's own benefit. If the debtor is married, state whether the husband, wife, both, or the marital community own the property by placing an "H," "W," "J," or "C" in the column labeled "Husband, Wife, Joint, or Community." If the debtor holds no interest in real property, write "None" under "Description and Location of Property."

Do not include interests in executory contracts and unexpired leases on this schedule. List them in Schedule G - Executory Contracts and Unexpired Leases.

If an entity claims to have a lien or hold a secured interest in any property, state the amount of the secured claim. See Schedule D. If no entity claims to hold a secured interest in the property, write "None" in the column labeled "Amount of Secured Claim."

If the debtor is an individual or if a joint petition is filed, state the amount of any exemption claimed in the property only in Schedule C - Property Claimed as Exempt.

DESCRIPTION AND LOCATION OF PROPERTY	NATURE OF DEBTOR'S INTEREST IN PROPERTY	HUSBAND, WIFE, JOINT, OR COMMUNITY	CURRENT VALUE OF DEBTOR'S INTEREST IN PROPERTY, WITHOUT DEDUCTING ANY SECURED CLAIM OR EXEMPTION	AMOUNT OF SECURED CLAIM
Personal home located at 16 Main Street, Centerville IL 61111	Fee simple	J	148,000.00	137,000.00

                                          Total▶ | 148,000.00 |
                                          (Report also on Summary of Schedules.)

Schedule B: Personal Property

On this form, you will list every other property that you own or have any claim of ownership in. Personal property includes all other property except real estate. This form includes extensive lists for many specific types of property. If your specific property is not listed, line 33 should be used for "other" property.

In re: Enter your full name. If you're filing jointly, include your spouse's name.

Case No.: Leave this blank if filed with your petition. The court clerk will assign you a case number.

None: If you do not own any of the type of property for that number, enter an X.

Description and Location of Property: Enter a brief description of the property and the street address of its location. You should separately enter each piece of individual property worth more than $25.00 in which you have any ownership interest at all. List wages that are owed to you under line 17 (liquidated debts). Your property should be listed under the appropriate number for that specific type of property (for example, enter an auto under line 23). Include a clear description of the property. For cash and bank accounts, list the source of the money (for example, from wages). At the top of this box, you may note that all of your property is located at a single address unless noted otherwise. If the property that you list is being held for you by someone else, you should list that person's name and address. If the property is owned by a minor child, do not include the name or address of the child. Simply state "a minor child."

Husband, Wife, Joint, or Community: If you are single, enter *N/A*. If you are married, enter *H*, *W*, *J*, or *C*, depending if the property is owned individually by the husband or wife, is owned jointly by both (as joint tenants or tenants-by-the-entireties), or is owned as community property in a community property state. Check the ownership language on the title or other document of ownership. In community property states (Arizona, California, Idaho, Louisiana, Nevada, New Mexico, Texas, Washington, and Wisconsin), property that was acquired during a marriage is considered community property. In all other states, the ownership of property depends on the names on the title document and if there is no title, then it is generally jointly owned if it was acquired while you were married. In most states, property that was individually owned prior to a marriage is still considered individually owned during the marriage. *Note*: Spouses in Alaska can designate in writing that certain property is to be considered "community property."

Current Market Value of Debtor's Interest in Property, without Deducting Any Secured Claim or Exemption: You should enter the full value at which the property could be sold today. Do not deduct any money that you may owe on the property, like a loan. For life insurance, enter the cash surrender value only, not the amount of the policy. For other property, you may need to obtain market-value estimates from a used-car Blue Book at the library or by checking the value of other similar property for sale in your area. For very valuable property, you may need to consult an appraiser. If you own the property jointly with someone who is not filing for bankruptcy with you, you should indicate your percentage of ownership and only note the market value of your share of the property. If more space is needed, use a *Continuation Sheet*, as explained later.

Instructions for specific property:
1. Cash on hand should be the amount in your actual possession on the date of filing.
2. Includes all financial accounts you have.
3. Includes all credit accounts and security deposits for your housing.
4–8. Include a brief description of the type of property. Include a lump sum total dollar amount for each category number.
9–14. Describe each item in detail. For Line 11, you must enter any interest that you have in either an Education IRA or a state tuition payment plan. For line 12, if your retirement plan is ERISA-qualified, do not enter an amount for its dollar value.
15. Include any personal or cashier's checks, money orders, or promissory notes.
16–18. Include any money owed to you.
19–21. Include any property that will become yours in the future.
22–23 Include trademarks, trade secrets, and any royalties.
24. If you operate a business and have collected customer information (such as a customer list), you must list such lists as assets under this section.
25–34. List each item in detail and include a continuation sheet if necessary.
35. List any property that does not fit into specific categories.

Total: On the last page, total the amounts in the "Current Market Value…" column on each page (and any continuation sheets) and enter here. Also enter this amount on the *Summary of Schedules* form (explained later). Enter the total number (if any) of continuations sheets that are attached.

B 6B (Official Form 6B) (12/07)

In re Mary Ellen and John Alan Smith_____, Case No. (supplied by clerk)_____
        Debtor   **(If known)**

SCHEDULE B - PERSONAL PROPERTY

Except as directed below, list all personal property of the debtor of whatever kind. If the debtor has no property in one or more of the categories, place an "x" in the appropriate position in the column labeled "None." If additional space is needed in any category, attach a separate sheet properly identified with the case name, case number, and the number of the category. If the debtor is married, state whether the husband, wife, both, or the marital community own the property by placing an "H," "W," "J," or "C" in the column labeled "Husband, Wife, Joint, or Community." If the debtor is an individual or a joint petition is filed, state the amount of any exemptions claimed only in Schedule C - Property Claimed as Exempt.

Do not list interests in executory contracts and unexpired leases on this schedule. List them in Schedule G - Executory Contracts and Unexpired Leases.

If the property is being held for the debtor by someone else, state that person's name and address under "Description and Location of Property." If the property is being held for a minor child, simply state the child's initials and the name and address of the child's parent or guardian, such as "A.B., a minor child, by John Doe, guardian." Do not disclose the child's name. See, 11 U.S.C. §112 and Fed. R. Bankr. P. 1007(m).

TYPE OF PROPERTY	N O N E	DESCRIPTION AND LOCATION OF PROPERTY	HUSBAND, WIFE, JOINT, OR COMMUNITY	CURRENT VALUE OF DEBTOR'S INTEREST IN PROPERTY, WITH-OUT DEDUCTING ANY SECURED CLAIM OR EXEMPTION
1. Cash on hand.		cash with debtors	J	90.00
2. Checking, savings or other financial accounts, certificates of deposit or shares in banks, savings and loan, thrift, building and loan, and homestead associations, or credit unions, brokerage houses, or cooperatives.		checking account at First Bank of Centerville 120 Broadway Centerville, IL 61111	J	137.00
3. Security deposits with public utilities, telephone companies, landlords, and others.		Centerville Electric Company 14 Center Street, Centerville, IL 61111	J	100.00
4. Household goods and furnishings, including audio, video, and computer equipment.		washer, dryer, refrigerator, TV, stereo, various household furnishings: all at family home	J	2,500.00
5. Books; pictures and other art objects; antiques; stamp, coin, record, tape, compact disc, and other collections or collectibles.		personal books, family photos, and 3 paintings	J	150.00
6. Wearing apparel.		personal clothing of debtors	J	400.00
7. Furs and jewelry.		Wedding rings	J	1,000.00
8. Firearms and sports, photographic, and other hobby equipment.		Nikon camera	J	140.00
9. Interests in insurance policies. Name insurance company of each policy and itemize surrender or refund value of each.		Prudential Insurance Company Policy 12345 - cash surrender value	W	1,200.00
10. Annuities. Itemize and name each issuer.	x			
11. Interests in an education IRA as defined in 26 U.S.C. § 530(b)(1) or under a qualified State tuition plan as defined in 26 U.S.C. § 529(b)(1). Give particulars. (File separately the record(s) of any such interest(s). 11 U.S.C. § 521(c).)	x			

B 6B (Official Form 6B) (12/07) -- Cont.

In re Mary Ellen and John Alan Smith_____, Case No. __(supplied by clerk)__
        Debtor   **(If known)**

SCHEDULE B - PERSONAL PROPERTY
(Continuation Sheet)

TYPE OF PROPERTY	N O N E	DESCRIPTION AND LOCATION OF PROPERTY	HUSBAND, WIFE, JOINT, OR COMMUNITY	CURRENT VALUE OF DEBTOR'S INTEREST IN PROPERTY, WITHOUT DEDUCTING ANY SECURED CLAIM OR EXEMPTION
12. Interests in IRA, ERISA, Keogh, or other pension or profit sharing plans. Give particulars.		IRA accounts held at First Bank of Centerville 120 Broadway, Centerville, IL 61111	J	150.00
13. Stock and interests in incorporated and unincorporated businesses. Itemize.	X			
14. Interests in partnerships or joint ventures. Itemize.	X			
15. Government and corporate bonds and other negotiable and non-negotiable instruments.	X			
16. Accounts receivable.	X			
17. Alimony, maintenance, support, and property settlements to which the debtor is or may be entitled. Give particulars.	X			
18. Other liquidated debts owed to debtor including tax refunds. Give particulars.	X			
19. Equitable or future interests, life estates, and rights or powers exercisable for the benefit of the debtor other than those listed in Schedule A – Real Property.	X			
20. Contingent and noncontingent interests in estate of a decedent, death benefit plan, life insurance policy, or trust.	X			
21. Other contingent and unliquidated claims of every nature, including tax refunds, counterclaims of the debtor, and rights to setoff claims. Give estimated value of each.	X			

B 6B (Official Form 6B) (12/07) -- Cont.

In re Mary Ellen and John Alan Smith   ,   Case No. (supplied by clerk)
                    Debtor   **(If known)**

SCHEDULE B - PERSONAL PROPERTY
(Continuation Sheet)

TYPE OF PROPERTY	N O N E	DESCRIPTION AND LOCATION OF PROPERTY	HUSBAND, WIFE, JOINT, OR COMMUNITY	CURRENT VALUE OF DEBTOR'S INTEREST IN PROPERTY, WITH-OUT DEDUCTING ANY SECURED CLAIM OR EXEMPTION
22. Patents, copyrights, and other intellectual property. Give particulars.	X			
23. Licenses, franchises, and other general intangibles. Give particulars.	X			
24. Customer lists or other compilations containing personally identifiable information (as defined in 11 U.S.C. § 101(41A)) provided to the debtor by individuals in connection with obtaining a product or service from the debtor primarily for personal, family, or household purposes.	X			
25. Automobiles, trucks, trailers, and other vehicles and accessories.		2006 Handa Accord, 2001 Chevy pick-up	J	13,000.00
26. Boats, motors, and accessories.	X			
27. Aircraft and accessories.	X			
28. Office equipment, furnishings, and supplies.	X			
29. Machinery, fixtures, equipment, and supplies used in business.	X			
30. Inventory.	X			
31. Animals.		1 dog (pet)		300.00
32. Crops - growing or harvested. Give particulars.	X			
33. Farming equipment and implements.	X			
34. Farm supplies, chemicals, and feed.	X			
35. Other personal property of any kind not already listed. Itemize.		tools used in trade as mechanic, and a piano	J	1,800.00

_____ 3 _ continuation sheets attached   Total▶ | $ | 20,967.00

(Include amounts from any continuation
sheets attached. Report total also on
Summary of Schedules.)

Schedule C: Property Claimed as Exempt

Important Note: This is one of the most important forms that you will complete. Be very careful that you understand the instructions regarding the exemptions and that you claim every possible exemption that is allowable in your situation.

You will use this form to claim the property that is exempt from being taken in your bankruptcy. Please consult Appendix A for details on the specific exemptions available in your state. In some states [Arkansas, Connecticut, District of Columbia (Washington D.C.), Hawaii, Massachusetts, Michigan, Minnesota, New Jersey, New Mexico, Pennsylvania, Rhode Island, South Carolina, Texas, Vermont, Washington, and Wisconsin] you have a choice between federal bankruptcy exemptions or state bankruptcy exemptions. In those states, fill in a separate copy of Schedule C for each set of exemptions (federal and state), compare the results, and then decide which is the better choice. File only the version of Schedule C that provides the most exemptions in your case. In all other states, you will use the state bankruptcy exemptions and federal non-bankruptcy exemptions. See Appendix A for details.

Note: You must have resided in your state for at least 730 days (two years) to use a state's exemptions. If you have not lived in the state of your current residence for two years, you must use the state in which you lived for the majority of time (at least 91 days) during the 180-day period immediately preceding the two year period prior to filing your Voluntary Petition.

In re: Enter your full name. If you're filing jointly, include your spouse's name.

Case No.: Leave this blank if filed with your petition. The court clerk will assign you a case number.

Debtor elects the exemptions to which debtor is entitled under: Select the top box if you choose to use the federal bankruptcy exemptions and the second box if you choose state and federal non-bankruptcy exemptions.

If you are claiming a homestead exemption for your principal place of residence and the amount claimed is over $136,875.00, you should check the box in the right-hand section under the main title. Note that the new 2005 Bankruptcy Act has capped homestead exemptions at $136,875.00, regardless of what the law of your state allows, unless you have lived in your state for more than 40 months. Those states that have allowed homestead exemptions greater than $136,875.00 are as follows: Arkansas, California (Option #1 and if over 65 or disabled), Florida, Iowa, Kansas, Louisiana (if debt is because of illness or injury), Massachusetts, Minnesota,

Montana, Nevada, Oklahoma, South Dakota, Texas, and Washington D.C. If you have been a resident of one of these states for less than 40 months and have a potential homestead exemption of over $136,875.00, you should consult an attorney. A Chapter 13 bankruptcy may be more appropriate in those situations.

Description of Property: Carefully go through the exemption list that you have chosen and your Schedules A and B and decide which property can be claimed as exempt. For each item of property that you decide is exempt, use the same description of that property that you used on Schedules A or B. List each grouping of property under subheadings such as "Real Estate," "Household Goods," "Tools," etc. For pensions, all ERISA pensions are exempt under either federal or state bankruptcy exemptions. Check with your employer to see if yours is an ERISA pension. If not, your state may specifically exempt your particular pension. If in doubt, you will need to consult a lawyer to be certain that you do not lose your pension.

Specify Law Providing Each Exemption: Using your state's listing in Appendix A, list the exact name and chapter of your state's law that provides the exemption. You may state at the top of the form that "All references are to..." and then list the name of your state's statute (for example: Idaho Code). Then just list the chapter numbers for each exemption.

Value of Claimed Exemption: Based on the statute exemption limits, list the amount that you claim as exempt for each piece of property. If you are married and filing jointly, you may double the amount of most exemptions, unless noted in Appendix A that your state does not allow such doubling. Some states have separate exemptions that may apply to a single piece of property. If so, list both exemption amounts up to the market value of the property. If the exemption amount is more than the value of the property, you may use the rest of the exemption on another piece of similar property until the exemption limit is reached. If the exemption amount is less than the market value of the property, the property may be sold by the court, the exemption amount given to you as cash, and the rest of the proceeds used to pay off your creditors.

Current Market Value of Property without Deducting Exemption: Enter the full market value of each piece of property exactly as you have previously listed it on Schedule A or B. Don't make any deduction for your exemption amount. Use a Continuation Sheet if necessary.

B 6C (Official Form 6C) (12/07)

In re _Mary Ellen and John Alan Smith_____,   Case No. _(supplied by clerk)_____
       Debtor   **(If known)**

SCHEDULE C - PROPERTY CLAIMED AS EXEMPT

Debtor claims the exemptions to which debtor is entitled under: ☐ Check if debtor claims a homestead exemption that exceeds
(Check one box) $136,875.
☑ 11 U.S.C. § 522(b)(2)
☐ 11 U.S.C. § 522(b)(3)

DESCRIPTION OF PROPERTY	SPECIFY LAW PROVIDING EACH EXEMPTION	VALUE OF CLAIMED EXEMPTION	CURRENT VALUE OF PROPERTY WITHOUT DEDUCTING EXEMPTION
personal residence	735-5/12-901	15,000.00	148,000.00
cash with debtors	735-5/12-1001(b)	90.00	90.00
checking account at First Bank of Centerville	735-5/12-1001(b)	137.00	137.00
security deposit Centerville Electric Company	735-5/12-1001(b)	100.00	100.00
household good and furnishings	735-5/12-1001(b)	2,500.00	2,500.00
pet - dog	735-5/12-1001(b)	300.00	300.00

Schedule D: Creditors Holding Secured Claims

The next three forms (Schedules D, E, and F) are used to list all of your debts. You should only list each debt once, even if the debt is partially secured or partially a priority claim.

Schedule D is used for listing secured debts. A secured debt is a debt for which you pledged some type of collateral (like a mortgage, consumer loan, car loan, etc.) or a debt based on a lien against your property (such as a judgment, tax, or mechanic's lien has been filed against property that you own). Even if a debt is only partially secured by collateral, you should list it here. If a creditor has more than one claim, such as debts arising from separate transactions, list each claim separately. You may have these debts canceled, but you will be required to either give up the collateral or buy it back from the court for its market value. Use the official Continuation Sheet if necessary. Please note that if you have a consumer debt secured by collateral, you must also file Chapter 7 Individual Debtor's Statement of Intention (Official Form 8) [see later instructions]. If you wish to keep such property, you should see an attorney.

In re: Enter your full name. If you're filing jointly, include your spouse's name.

Case No.: Leave this blank if filed with your petition. The court clerk will assign you a case number.

Check this box if debtor has no creditors holding secured claims to report on this Schedule D. If so, check box and go to Schedule E.

Creditor's Name, Mailing Address Including Zip Code, and Account Number: Fill in the complete name and address of each creditor (in alphabetical order). Include only the last four digits of an account number if there is one. If a minor child is the creditor, do not disclose the child's name or address. Simply state "a minor child."

Codebtor: If someone else cosigned the debt documents, is a non-filing spouse or joint owner, or otherwise can be held liable for the debt, place an X in this box. In community property states, non-filing spouses are generally liable for debts undertaken during a marriage. In common-law states, non-filing spouses are generally liable for debts for necessities (food, clothing, shelter, etc.).

Husband, Wife, Joint, or Community: If you are single, enter N/A. If you are married, enter H, W, J, or C, depending if the particular debt is owed individually by the husband or wife, is owed jointly by both (as joint tenants or tenants-by-the-entireties), or is owed as a community debt in a community property state. Check the language on the debt document. In common-law states, the liability for the debt generally depends on the names on the debt document. In most states, debts that were individually undertaken prior to a marriage are considered individual debts during the marriage.

Date Claim Was Incurred, Nature of Lien, and Description and Market Value of Property Subject to Lien: List all pertinent information about each secured debt. List the date that you signed the debt documents or that the lien was recorded. The nature of lien is either a *lien* or a *tax, judgment, child support*, or *mechanic's lien*. For debts, each debt is either a *purchase money debt* (the property purchased is the collateral), *non-purchase money debt* (the property purchased was not the collateral), or *possessory non-purchase money debt* (you obtained a loan on property that the creditor has possession of, such as a pawn-shop loan). To describe the property and market value of the collateral for any debt or lien, use the description and value from Schedule A or B.

Contingent, Unliquidated, or Disputed: "Contingent" means the debt is based on an event that has not yet occurred. "Unliquidated" means an outstanding loan whose amount has not yet been determined, such as the amount of damages in a car accident that has not yet been established by court action. "Disputed" means that you dispute either the amount or even the existence of the debt. You may check more than one box.

Amount of Claim without Deducting Value of Collateral: List the amount required to pay off the entire debt or lien.

Unsecured portion, If Any: If the value of the collateral is less than the amount of the debt, enter the difference here. If the collateral is worth more than the debt, enter $0.

Subtotal and Total: Subtotal the amounts in the "Amount of Claim Without Deducting Value of Collateral" column on each page and enter the total on the last page and also on the Summary of Schedules form. Also enter the amount of continuation sheets used, if any. If applicable, also total the amounts in the "Unsecured Portion, if Any" column on each page and enter the total of the last page and also on the Summary of Certain of Statistical Liabilities and Related Data.

B 6D (Official Form 6D) (12/07)

In re Mary Ellen and John Alan Smith _____,   Case No. _(supplied by clerk)_____
        Debtor   **(If known)**

SCHEDULE D - CREDITORS HOLDING SECURED CLAIMS

    State the name, mailing address, including zip code, and last four digits of any account number of all entities holding claims secured by property of the debtor as of the date of filing of the petition. The complete account number of any account the debtor has with the creditor is useful to the trustee and the creditor and may be provided if the debtor chooses to do so. List creditors holding all types of secured interests such as judgment liens, garnishments, statutory liens, mortgages, deeds of trust, and other security interests.

    List creditors in alphabetical order to the extent practicable. If a minor child is the creditor, state the child's initials and the name and address of the child's parent or guardian, such as "A.B., a minor child, by John Doe, guardian." Do not disclose the child's name. See, 11 U.S.C. §112 and Fed. R. Bankr. P. 1007(m). If all secured creditors will not fit on this page, use the continuation sheet provided.

    If any entity other than a spouse in a joint case may be jointly liable on a claim, place an "X" in the column labeled "Codebtor," include the entity on the appropriate schedule of creditors, and complete Schedule H – Codebtors. If a joint petition is filed, state whether the husband, wife, both of them, or the marital community may be liable on each claim by placing an "H," "W," "J," or "C" in the column labeled "Husband, Wife, Joint, or Community."

    If the claim is contingent, place an "X" in the column labeled "Contingent." If the claim is unliquidated, place an "X" in the column labeled "Unliquidated." If the claim is disputed, place an "X" in the column labeled "Disputed." (You may need to place an "X" in more than one of these three columns.)

    Total the columns labeled "Amount of Claim Without Deducting Value of Collateral" and "Unsecured Portion, if Any" in the boxes labeled "Total(s)" on the last sheet of the completed schedule. Report the total from the column labeled "Amount of Claim Without Deducting Value of Collateral" also on the Summary of Schedules and, if the debtor is an individual with primarily consumer debts, report the total from the column labeled "Unsecured Portion, if Any" on the Statistical Summary of Certain Liabilities and Related Data.

☐   Check this box if debtor has no creditors holding secured claims to report on this Schedule D.

CREDITOR'S NAME AND MAILING ADDRESS INCLUDING ZIP CODE AND AN ACCOUNT NUMBER *(See Instructions Above.)*	CODEBTOR	HUSBAND, WIFE, JOINT, OR COMMUNITY	DATE CLAIM WAS INCURRED, NATURE OF LIEN , AND DESCRIPTION AND VALUE OF PROPERTY SUBJECT TO LIEN	CONTINGENT	UNLIQUIDATED	DISPUTED	AMOUNT OF CLAIM WITHOUT DEDUCTING VALUE OF COLLATERAL	UNSECURED PORTION, IF ANY
ACCOUNT NO. 987654321 Centerville Savings & Loan 169 Front St. Centerville, IL 61111	x	J	mortgage on personal home at 16 Main St. Centerville, IL VALUE $ 148,000.00		X		137,000.00	
ACCOUNT NO. VALUE $								
ACCOUNT NO. VALUE $								
___ continuation sheets attached			Subtotal ▶ (Total of this page)				$ 137,000.00	$
			Total ▶ (Use only on last page)				$ 137,000.00	$
							(Report also on Summary of Schedules.)	(If applicable, report also on Statistical Summary of Certain Liabilities and Related Data.)

B 6D (Official Form 6D) (12/07) – Cont.   2

In re Mary Ellen and John Alan Smith   ,   Case No.   (supplied by clerk)
                    Debtor   **(if known)**

SCHEDULE D - CREDITORS HOLDING SECURED CLAIMS
(Continuation Sheet)

CREDITOR'S NAME AND MAILING ADDRESS INCLUDING ZIP CODE AND AN ACCOUNT NUMBER *(See Instructions Above.)*	CODEBTOR	HUSBAND, WIFE, JOINT, OR COMMUNITY	DATE CLAIM WAS INCURRED, NATURE OF LIEN , AND DESCRIPTION AND VALUE OF PROPERTY SUBJECT TO LIEN	CONTINGENT	UNLIQUIDATED	DISPUTED	AMOUNT OF CLAIM WITHOUT DEDUCTING VALUE OF COLLATERAL	UNSECURED PORTION, IF ANY
ACCOUNT NO.								
			VALUE $					
ACCOUNT NO.								
			VALUE $					
ACCOUNT NO.								
			VALUE $					
ACCOUNT NO.								
			VALUE $					
ACCOUNT NO.								
			VALUE $					

Sheet no._____of_____continuation sheets attached to Schedule of Creditors Holding Secured Claims

Subtotal (s)▶
(Total(s) of this page) $ $

Total(s) ▶
(Use only on last page) $ $

(Report also on Summary of Schedules.)   (If applicable, report also on Statistical Summary of Certain Liabilities and Related Data.)

Schedule E: Creditors Holding Unsecured Priority Claims

Unsecured priority claims are certain debts that are given priority in being paid off in a bankruptcy, but that have no collateral pledged. They include taxes that you might owe, wages you may owe to employees, alimony, child support, and certain other claims. Even if a debt is only partially subject to priority, you should only list it here. If a creditor has more than one claim, such as debts arising from separate transactions, list each claim separately. Use the official *Schedule E Continuation Sheet* if necessary.

In re: Enter your full name. If you're filing jointly, include your spouse's name.

Case No.: Leave this blank if filed with your petition. The court clerk will assign you a case number.

Check this box if debtor has no creditors holding unsecured priority claims to report on this Schedule E: If so, check the box and go on to *Schedule F*.

Type of Priority Claims: Read through each definition of the various priority claims carefully and check them against the debts that you have. The most likely unsecured priority claim will be for back taxes owed. Place an *X* before any of your debts that are considered priority claims. Unsecured priority claims fall into the following categories: Domestic support obligations (alimony or child support), extensions of credit in an involuntary bankruptcy, wages and salaries owed to employee of the debtor up to $10,950.00 money owed to employee benefit plans by the debtor, debts of up to $5,400.00 to certain farmers and fisherman, deposits of up to $2,425.00 for purchase, lease or rental of property or services from the debtor that were not delivered, any to taxes owed, certain commitments insured financial institutions, and claims against the debtor for death or personal injury resulting from an accident in which the debtor was intoxicated. The amounts listed above will be adjusted on April 1, 2010 and every three years thereafter.

Schedule E: Creditors Holding Unsecured Priority Claims Continuation Sheet Instructions

In re: Enter your full name. If you're filing jointly, include your spouse's name.

Case No.: Leave this blank if filed with your petition. The court clerk will assign you a case number.

Type of Priority: Enter the type of priority claim that was checked off on *Schedule E* for the claims that are listed on each continuation sheet.

Creditor's Name, Mailing Address Including Zip Code, and Account Number: Fill in the complete name and address of each creditor (in alphabetical order). Include the last four digits of account number if there is one. If a creditor is a minor child, do not include the child's name or address. Simply state "a minor child."

Codebtor: If someone else has cosigned the debt documents, is a non-filing spouse or joint owner, or otherwise can be held liable for the debt, place an *X* in this box. In community-property states, debts undertaken during a marriage are generally considered community debts, and non-filing spouses are liable. In common-law states, non-filing spouses are generally only liable for debts for necessities (food, clothing, shelter, etc.).

Husband, Wife, Joint, or Community: If you are single, enter *N/A*. If you are married, enter *H*, *W*, *J*, or *C*, depending if the particular debt is owed individually by the husband or wife, is owed jointly by both (as joint tenants or tenants-by-the-entireties), or is owed as a community debt in a community property state. Check the language on the debt document. In common-law states, the liability for the debt generally depends on the names on the debt document. In most states, debts that were individually undertaken prior to a marriage are considered individual debts during the marriage.

Date Claim Was Incurred and Consideration For Claim: List the date that the debt was incurred and a description of the debt or claim, including what you received in exchange for the debt, such as "goods purchased, "hours worked," or "cash deposited."

Contingent, Unliquidated, or Disputed: "Contingent" means the debt is based on an event that has not yet occurred. "Unliquidated" means an outstanding loan whose amount has not yet been determined, such as the amount of damages in a car accident that has not yet been established by court action. "Disputed" means that you dispute either the amount or even the existence of the debt. You may check more than one box.

Amount of Claim: List the total amount of the claimed debt, including any amount over the actual priority amount limit listed under "Types of Priority Claims" on the first page of *Schedule E*. Note that these amounts may change on April 1, 2010. Check with the court clerk for current amount limits.

Amount Entitled to Priority: List the lesser of the total amount of claims or the maximum priority amount from the list under "Types of Priority Claims."

Amount Not Entitled to Priority, if Any: List any amounts of the claims that are not entitled to priority (amounts of any claim that is over the maximum amounts for priority listed under "Types of Priority Claims" on the first two pages of Schedule E.

Subtotal and Total: Subtotal the amounts in the "Amount of Claim" column on each page and enter the total on the last page and also on the *Summary of Schedules* and if applicable, on the *Statistical Summary of Certain Liabilities and Related Data* form. Subtotal the amounts in the "Amount Not Entitled to Priority, if Any" column and enter the total on the last page and, if applicable, on the *Statistical Summary of Certain Liabilities and Related Data* form. Also enter the number of each sheet attached to the *Schedule E: Schedule of Creditors Holding Priority Claims* and the total number of sheets attached (if any).

B 6E (Official Form 6E) (12/07)

In re <u>Mary Ellen and John Alan Smith</u>,   Case No. <u>(supplied by clerk)</u>
                    Debtor   **(if known)**

SCHEDULE E - CREDITORS HOLDING UNSECURED PRIORITY CLAIMS

A complete list of claims entitled to priority, listed separately by type of priority, is to be set forth on the sheets provided. Only holders of unsecured claims entitled to priority should be listed in this schedule. In the boxes provided on the attached sheets, state the name, mailing address, including zip code, and last four digits of the account number, if any, of all entities holding priority claims against the debtor or the property of the debtor, as of the date of the filing of the petition. Use a separate continuation sheet for each type of priority and label each with the type of priority.

The complete account number of any account the debtor has with the creditor is useful to the trustee and the creditor and may be provided if the debtor chooses to do so. If a minor child is a creditor, state the child's initials and the name and address of the child's parent or guardian, such as "A.B., a minor child, by John Doe, guardian." Do not disclose the child's name. See, 11 U.S.C. §112 and Fed. R. Bankr. P. 1007(m).

If any entity other than a spouse in a joint case may be jointly liable on a claim, place an "X" in the column labeled "Codebtor," include the entity on the appropriate schedule of creditors, and complete Schedule H-Codebtors. If a joint petition is filed, state whether the husband, wife, both of them, or the marital community may be liable on each claim by placing an "H," "W," "J," or "C" in the column labeled "Husband, Wife, Joint, or Community."   If the claim is contingent, place an "X" in the column labeled "Contingent." If the claim is unliquidated, place an "X" in the column labeled "Unliquidated." If the claim is disputed, place an "X" in the column labeled "Disputed." (You may need to place an "X" in more than one of these three columns.)

Report the total of claims listed on each sheet in the box labeled "Subtotals" on each sheet. Report the total of all claims listed on this Schedule E in the box labeled "Total" on the last sheet of the completed schedule. Report this total also on the Summary of Schedules.

Report the total of amounts entitled to priority listed on each sheet in the box labeled "Subtotals" on each sheet. Report the total of all amounts entitled to priority listed on this Schedule E in the box labeled "Totals" on the last sheet of the completed schedule. Individual debtors with primarily consumer debts report this total also on the Statistical Summary of Certain Liabilities and Related Data.

Report the total of amounts <u>not</u> entitled to priority listed on each sheet in the box labeled "Subtotals" on each sheet. Report the total of all amounts not entitled to priority listed on this Schedule E in the box labeled "Totals" on the last sheet of the completed schedule. Individual debtors with primarily consumer debts report this total also on the Statistical Summary of Certain Liabilities and Related Data.

☐ Check this box if debtor has no creditors holding unsecured priority claims to report on this Schedule E.

TYPES OF PRIORITY CLAIMS (Check the appropriate box(es) below if claims in that category are listed on the attached sheets.)

☐ **Domestic Support Obligations**

Claims for domestic support that are owed to or recoverable by a spouse, former spouse, or child of the debtor, or the parent, legal guardian, or responsible relative of such a child, or a governmental unit to whom such a domestic support claim has been assigned to the extent provided in 11 U.S.C. § 507(a)(1).

☐ **Extensions of credit in an involuntary case**

Claims arising in the ordinary course of the debtor's business or financial affairs after the commencement of the case but before the earlier of the appointment of a trustee or the order for relief. 11 U.S.C. § 507(a)(3).

☐ **Wages, salaries, and commissions**

Wages, salaries, and commissions, including vacation, severance, and sick leave pay owing to employees and commissions owing to qualifying independent sales representatives up to $10,950* per person earned within 180 days immediately preceding the filing of the original petition, or the cessation of business, whichever occurred first, to the extent provided in 11 U.S.C. § 507(a)(4).

☐ **Contributions to employee benefit plans**

Money owed to employee benefit plans for services rendered within 180 days immediately preceding the filing of the original petition, or the cessation of business, whichever occurred first, to the extent provided in 11 U.S.C. § 507(a)(5).

B 6E (Official Form 6E) (12/07) – Cont.

In re Mary Ellen and John Alan Smith_____,   Case No._(supplied by clerk)_____
                        Debtor   **(if known)**

☐ **Certain farmers and fishermen**

   Claims of certain farmers and fishermen, up to $5,400* per farmer or fisherman, against the debtor, as provided in 11 U.S.C. § 507(a)(6).

☐ **Deposits by individuals**

   Claims of individuals up to $2,425* for deposits for the purchase, lease, or rental of property or services for personal, family, or household use, that were not delivered or provided. 11 U.S.C. § 507(a)(7).

☑ **Taxes and Certain Other Debts Owed to Governmental Units**

   Taxes, customs duties, and penalties owing to federal, state, and local governmental units as set forth in 11 U.S.C. § 507(a)(8).

☐ **Commitments to Maintain the Capital of an Insured Depository Institution**

   Claims based on commitments to the FDIC, RTC, Director of the Office of Thrift Supervision, Comptroller of the Currency, or Board of Governors of the Federal Reserve System, or their predecessors or successors, to maintain the capital of an insured depository institution. 11 U.S.C. § 507 (a)(9).

☐ **Claims for Death or Personal Injury While Debtor Was Intoxicated**

   Claims for death or personal injury resulting from the operation of a motor vehicle or vessel while the debtor was intoxicated from using alcohol, a drug, or another substance. 11 U.S.C. § 507(a)(10).

* Amounts are subject to adjustment on April 1, 2010, and every three years thereafter with respect to cases commenced on or after the date of adjustment.

_____ continuation sheets attached

B 6E (Official Form 6E) (12/07) – Cont.

In re <u>Mary Ellen and John Alan Smith</u>, Case No. <u>(supplied by clerk)</u>
　　　　　　Debtor　　　　　　　　　　　　　　　　　(if known)

SCHEDULE E - CREDITORS HOLDING UNSECURED PRIORITY CLAIMS
(Continuation Sheet)

Type of Priority for Claims Listed on This Sheet

CREDITOR'S NAME, MAILING ADDRESS INCLUDING ZIP CODE, AND ACCOUNT NUMBER (See instructions above.)	CODEBTOR	HUSBAND, WIFE, JOINT, OR COMMUNITY	DATE CLAIM WAS INCURRED AND CONSIDERATION FOR CLAIM	CONTINGENT	UNLIQUIDATED	DISPUTED	AMOUNT OF CLAIM	AMOUNT ENTITLED TO PRIORITY	AMOUNT NOT ENTITLED TO PRIORITY, IF ANY
Account No. 555-12-5656 Internal Revenue Service Kansa City, MO 64999		J	Federal income tax due on joint return filed February 15, 2007, for 2006.	X			850.00	850.00	
Account No.									
Account No.									
Account No.									

Sheet no. ____ of ____ continuation sheets attached to Schedule of Creditors Holding Priority Claims

Subtotals➤ (Totals of this page) | $ 850.00 | $ 850.00 |

Total➤ (Use only on last page of the completed Schedule E. Report also on the Summary of Schedules.) | $ 850.00 |

Totals➤ (Use only on last page of the completed Schedule E. If applicable, report also on the Statistical Summary of Certain Liabilities and Related Data.) | | $ 850.00 | $

Schedule F: Creditors Holding Unsecured Nonpriority Claims

Unsecured nonpriority claims are any other debts that you owe, other than leases or contractual obligations (that is, any debts that are not secured debts or unsecured priority debts). This includes, generally, all of your bills, including credit cards, medical bills, utility bills, personal loans with no collateral, and bills owed to stores. These debts will usually be canceled by your bankruptcy. Every debt must be listed, even those that you dispute are actually valid debts, those you wish to pay off, and those that are non-dischargeable (such as a student loan or court-ordered fine). If a creditor has more than one claim, such as debts arising from separate transactions, list each claim separately. You must list your debts accurately for them to be discharged. Do not include any debts that were already listed on *Schedules D* or *E*.

In re: Enter your full name. If you're filing jointly, include your spouse's name.

Case No.: Leave this blank if filed with your petition. The court clerk will assign you a case number.

Check this box if debtor has no creditors holding unsecured claims to report on this Schedule F: If so, check the box and go on to *Schedule G*.

Creditor's Name, Mailing Address Including Zip Code, and Account Number: Fill in the complete name and address of each creditor (in alphabetical order). Include only the last four digits of an account number if there is one. Include all collection agencies and attorneys who have contacted you regarding a debt, all cosigners on a debt you owe, all debtors with whom you have cosigned for a debt, and anyone who has sued you for a monetary amount. If you list multiple addresses for a single debt (such as if you list a credit card company and a collection agency for the same debt), do not repeat the description or amount of the debt, but note "same as above." If a creditor is a minor child, do not include the child's name or address. Simply state "a minor child."

Codebtor: If someone else has cosigned the debt documents, is a non-filing spouse or joint owner, or otherwise can be held liable for the debt, place an *X* in this box. In community-property states, debts undertaken during a marriage are generally considered community debts, and non-filing spouses are liable. In common-law states, non-filing spouses are generally liable for debts for necessities.

Husband, Wife, Joint, or Community: If you are single, enter *N/A*. If you are married, enter *H*, *W*, *J*, or *C*, depending if the particular debt is owed individually by the husband or wife, is owed jointly by both (as joint tenants or tenants-by-the-entireties), or is owed as a community debt in a community-property state. Check the language on the debt document. In common-law states, the liability for the debt generally depends on the names on the debt document. In most states, debts that were individually undertaken prior to a marriage are considered individual debts during the marriage.

Date Claim Was Incurred and Consideration for Claim. If Claim Subject to Setoff, So State: List the date that the debt was incurred and a brief but clear description of the debt or claim. A *setoff* means that the creditor owes you money and will apply it to a debt. If there is a setoff, state the amount and reason for the setoff.

Contingent, Unliquidated, or Disputed: "Contingent" means the debt is based on an event that has not yet occurred. "Unliquidated" means an outstanding loan whose amount has not yet been determined, such as the amount of damages in a car accident that has not yet been established by court action. "Disputed" means that you dispute either the amount or even the existence of the debt. You may check more than one box.

Amount of Claim: List the total amount of the claimed debt. If there are multiple creditors for the same amount (as when a collection agency has taken over a debt) only list the total amount for one creditor (preferably the original creditor). If the amount is approximate, add "approx." after the amount.

Subtotal and Total: Subtotal the amounts in the "Amount of Claim" column of each page (and any continuation sheets) and enter the total on the last page of the form and also on the *Summary of Schedules* form. Add the number of the sheet attached to the *Schedule of Creditors Holding Priority Claims* and the total number of sheets attached (if any).

B 6F (Official Form 6F) (12/07)

In re Mary Ellen and John Alan Smith_____,   Case No. (supplied by clerk)_____
               Debtor   **(if known)**

SCHEDULE F - CREDITORS HOLDING UNSECURED NONPRIORITY CLAIMS

State the name, mailing address, including zip code, and last four digits of any account number, of all entities holding unsecured claims without priority against the debtor or the property of the debtor, as of the date of filing of the petition. The complete account number of any account the debtor has with the creditor is useful to the trustee and the creditor and may be provided if the debtor chooses to do so. If a minor child is a creditor, state the child's initials and the name and address of the child's parent or guardian, such as "A.B., a minor child, by John Doe, guardian." Do not disclose the child's name. See, 11 U.S.C. §112 and Fed. R. Bankr. P. 1007(m). Do not include claims listed in Schedules D and E. If all creditors will not fit on this page, use the continuation sheet provided.

If any entity other than a spouse in a joint case may be jointly liable on a claim, place an "X" in the column labeled "Codebtor," include the entity on the appropriate schedule of creditors, and complete Schedule H - Codebtors. If a joint petition is filed, state whether the husband, wife, both of them, or the marital community may be liable on each claim by placing an "H," "W," "J," or "C" in the column labeled "Husband, Wife, Joint, or Community."

If the claim is contingent, place an "X" in the column labeled "Contingent." If the claim is unliquidated, place an "X" in the column labeled "Unliquidated." If the claim is disputed, place an "X" in the column labeled "Disputed." (You may need to place an "X" in more than one of these three columns.)

Report the total of all claims listed on this schedule in the box labeled "Total" on the last sheet of the completed schedule. Report this total also on the Summary of Schedules and, if the debtor is an individual with primarily consumer debts, report this total also on the Statistical Summary of Certain Liabilities and Related Data..

☐　Check this box if debtor has no creditors holding unsecured claims to report on this Schedule F.

CREDITOR'S NAME, MAILING ADDRESS INCLUDING ZIP CODE, AND ACCOUNT NUMBER *(See instructions above.)*	CODEBTOR	HUSBAND, WIFE, JOINT, OR COMMUNITY	DATE CLAIM WAS INCURRED AND CONSIDERATION FOR CLAIM. IF CLAIM IS SUBJECT TO SETOFF, SO STATE.	CONTINGENT	UNLIQUIDATED	DISPUTED	AMOUNT OF CLAIM
ACCOUNT NO. 1234567							
American Bank 1234 First Bank Chicago, IL 60606		J			X		3,500.00
ACCOUNT NO. 87654321							
Barker Bank 654321 66th Street Springfield, IL 62700		J			X		5,800.00
ACCOUNT NO. none							
Carter Car Repair 345 Oak Street Centerville, IL 61111		H				X	600.00
ACCOUNT NO. 123-456							
Centerville Bank 9876 Main Street Centerville, IL 61111		W			X		5,000.00
					Subtotal▶	$	14,900.00

____continuation sheets attached

                                                Total▶　$

(Use only on last page of the completed Schedule F.)
(Report also on Summary of Schedules and, if applicable, on the Statistical Summary of Certain Liabilities and Related Data.)

B 6F (Official Form 6F) (12/07) - Cont.

In re   Mary Ellen and John Alan Smith_____ ,   Case No.   (supplied by clerk)_____
                    Debtor   **(if known)**

SCHEDULE F - CREDITORS HOLDING UNSECURED NONPRIORITY CLAIMS
(Continuation Sheet)

CREDITOR'S NAME, MAILING ADDRESS INCLUDING ZIP CODE, AND ACCOUNT NUMBER (See instructions above.)	CODEBTOR	HUSBAND, WIFE, JOINT, OR COMMUNITY	DATE CLAIM WAS INCURRED AND CONSIDERATION FOR CLAIM. IF CLAIM IS SUBJECT TO SETOFF, SO STATE.	CONTINGENT	UNLIQUIDATED	DISPUTED	AMOUNT OF CLAIM
ACCOUNT NO. 567890 Centerville Hospital 3 Hospital Lane Centerville, IL 61111		H	hospital bills		X		12,000.00
ACCOUNT NO. 34567 Dwight Furniture 7878 Second Street Centerville, IL 61111		J	furniture, November 2006		X		1,000.00
ACCOUNT NO. none Dr. William Fredricks 35 Doctors Court Centerville, IL 61111		H	doctor's bills 2000-2007		X		4,300.00
ACCOUNT NO. 246810 Mobil Oil Company Box 1234 Houston, TX 77777		J	gas compny credit card 2000-2007		X		1,235.00
ACCOUNT NO. A-234 Personal Finance Company 6666 Lasalle Street Chicago, IL 60606		J	personal loan, December 2004		X		3,590.00

Sheet no._____ of_____ continuation sheets attached
to Schedule of Creditors Holding Unsecured
Nonpriority Claims

Subtotal➤ $ 22,125.00

Total➤ $ 37,025.00
(Use only on last page of the completed Schedule F.)
(Report also on Summary of Schedules and, if applicable on the Statistical
Summary of Certain Liabilities and Related Data.)

Schedule G: Executory Contracts and Unexpired Leases

Executory contracts are contracts that are still in force and contain obligations that you or another party must still fulfill. *Unexpired leases* are leases that are still in force, either for residential or business property. These include any type of contract or lease that you have signed and is still in force, including insurance contracts and business contracts. Examples might be timeshare interests, orders for furniture, or layaway arrangements at clothing stores. If you are past due on payments on a lease or contract, that should be listed as a debt on *Schedules D, E,* or *F. Schedule G* is a master list of all leases and contracts that are outstanding, whether or not you are delinquent in payments. This includes leases where someone leases property from you.

In re: Enter your full name. If you're filing jointly, include your spouse's name.

Case No.: Leave this blank if filed with your petition. The court clerk will assign you a case number.

Check this box if debtor has no executory contracts or unexpired leases: If so, check the box and continue to *Schedule H*.

Name and Mailing Address, Including Zip Code, of Other Parties to Lease or Contract: List the name and address of every person who is a party to any current lease or contract. This will include anyone who signed the lease or contract and every company that is involved with the lease or contract. State whether you are the *lessor* (landlord) or *lessee* (tenant) of any lease. If a minor child is a party to one of the leases or contracts listed, do not list the child's name or address. Simply state "a minor child."

Description of Contract or Lease and Nature of Debtor's Interest: State whether lease is for non-residential real property. State the date the lease or contract was signed and give a brief general description of the type of lease or contract that is included. In addition, briefly describe what the lease or contract requires of each party. If the contract is with any government agency or authority, list the contract number.

B 6G (Official Form 6G) (12/07)

In re Mary Ellen and John Alan Smith   ,   Case No. (supplied by clerk)
                    Debtor   **(if known)**

SCHEDULE G - EXECUTORY CONTRACTS AND UNEXPIRED LEASES

Describe all executory contracts of any nature and all unexpired leases of real or personal property. Include any timeshare interests. State nature of debtor's interest in contract, i.e., "Purchaser," "Agent," etc. State whether debtor is the lessor or lessee of a lease. Provide the names and complete mailing addresses of all other parties to each lease or contract described. If a minor child is a party to one of the leases or contracts, state the child's initials and the name and address of the child's parent or guardian, such as "A.B., a minor child, by John Doe, guardian." Do not disclose the child's name. See, 11 U.S.C. §112 and Fed. R. Bankr. P. 1007(m).

☐ Check this box if debtor has no executory contracts or unexpired leases.

NAME AND MAILING ADDRESS, INCLUDING ZIP CODE, OF OTHER PARTIES TO LEASE OR CONTRACT.	DESCRIPTION OF CONTRACT OR LEASE AND NATURE OF DEBTOR'S INTEREST. STATE WHETHER LEASE IS FOR NONRESIDENTIAL REAL PROPERTY. STATE CONTRACT NUMBER OF ANY GOVERNMENT CONTRACT.
Centerville Business Products 234 Business Lane Centerville, IL 61111	Co-signor with brother, William David Smith, on contract dated September 15, 2006 to buy computer

Schedule H: Codebtors

This schedule is a master list of all of the codebtors (other than a spouse who is jointly filing with you) that you have listed on *Schedules D, E,* and *F.* Codebtors may be cosignors, guarantors, and non-filing spouses who may be liable on a consumer debt. Review those forms and enter all of the codebtors again on this form.

Note for residents of community property states: If you (the debtor) reside or have previously resided in a community property state or territory (Arizona, California, Idaho, Louisiana, Nevada, New Mexico, Texas, Washington, or Wisconsin) within the eight years immediately preceding the filing for bankruptcy, then you should also include the name of the your spouse (or any former spouse within the last eight years). The spouse or former spouse must be listed even if you are filing as an individual and not jointly with your spouse. For the spouse or former spouse, be sure to include all names (including maiden names) used within the last eight years. *Note:* Spouses in Alaska can designate in writing that certain property is to be considered "community property."

In re: Enter your full name. If you're filing jointly, include your spouse's name.

Case No.: Leave this blank if filed with your petition. The court clerk will assign you a case number.

Check this box if debtor has no codebtors: If so, check the box and continue to *Schedule I.*

Name and Address of Codebtor: Enter the name and address of each codebtor listed on *Schedules D, E,* or *F.* If any of the Codebtors are minor children, do not list the name or address of the child. Simply state "a minor child."

Name and Address of Creditor: Enter the name and address of each creditor for each of the codebtors listed in the first column. This should be identical to the information for creditors that you listed on *Schedules D, E,* or *F* where there were codebtors indicated. If any of the creditors are minor children, do not list the name or address of the child. Simply state "a minor child."

B 6H (Official Form 6H) (12/07)

In re Mary Ellen and John Alan Smith   ,   Case No. (supplied by clerk)
                    Debtor   **(if known)**

SCHEDULE H - CODEBTORS

Provide the information requested concerning any person or entity, other than a spouse in a joint case, that is also liable on any debts listed by the debtor in the schedules of creditors. Include all guarantors and co-signers. If the debtor resides or resided in a community property state, commonwealth, or territory (including Alaska, Arizona, California, Idaho, Louisiana, Nevada, New Mexico, Puerto Rico, Texas, Washington, or Wisconsin) within the eight-year period immediately preceding the commencement of the case, identify the name of the debtor's spouse and of any former spouse who resides or resided with the debtor in the community property state, commonwealth, or territory. Include all names used by the nondebtor spouse during the eight years immediately preceding the commencement of this case. If a minor child is a codebtor or a creditor, state the child's initials and the name and address of the child's parent or guardian, such as "A.B., a minor child, by John Doe, guardian." Do not disclose the child's name. See, 11 U.S.C. §112 and Fed. R. Bankr. P. 1007(m).

☐ Check this box if debtor has no codebtors.

NAME AND ADDRESS OF CODEBTOR	NAME AND ADDRESS OF CREDITOR
William David Smith 567 Elm Street Centerville, IL 61111	Centerville Business Products 234 Business Lane Centerville, IL 61111

Schedule I: Current Income of Individual Debtor(s)

This form contains information on all of your current income, whether from wages, salary, self-employment, farming, real estate, investments, alimony, Social Security, pensions, or any other source. You will calculate your income on a monthly basis. Include a copy of your latest tax return with *Schedule I* when you file it with the court. If you are filing jointly, you must included your spouse's information. If you are married but not filing jointly, you must also include your spouse's information, unless you are separated from your spouse. Do not state the name of any minor child.

In re: Enter your full name. If you're filing jointly, include your spouse's name.

Case No.: Leave this blank if filed with your petition. The court clerk will assign you a case number.

Debtor's Marital Status: Indicate whether you are single, married, divorced, or widowed.

Dependents of Debtor and Spouse: Enter the ages and relationships of dependent children and others for whom you provide over half of the support. Do not state the name of any minor child.

Employment of Debtor and Spouse: Enter your occupation, name of employer, length of employment, and address of employer. Enter whether you are retired, disabled, or unemployed, if applicable.

Income: Line #1: For you and your spouse (if [1] filing jointly or [2] if married and not filing jointly and not separated), enter your total average *gross* (before taxes) monthly income from a regular job, or projected income from an anticipated future job.

Line #2: Enter your average monthly overtime, if applicable. If your income varies monthly or seasonally, divide the last full year's income by 12. Subtotal these amounts.

Line #3: Total the amounts on Lines 1 and 2 for you and your spouse (if applicable).

Less Payroll Deductions: Line #4: List the average monthly amount of all taxes, Social Security/Medicare, insurance, pensions, union dues, or other deductions that are taken out of your paycheck.

Line #5: Subtotal these payroll deduction amounts.

Total Net Monthly Take Home Pay: Line #6: Deduct Line #5 "Subtotal of Payroll Deductions" from Line #3 "Subtotal" of monthly wages and enter here.

Regular income from operation of business or profession or farm: Line #7: Enter the average monthly amount of income from a farm, business, or self-employment. Divide the last year's total income (taken from your latest tax return) by 12. Attach detailed statement on a continuation sheet.

Income from real property: Line #8: List the average monthly income that you make from rental of real estate, either commercial or residential.

Interest and dividends: Line #9: Enter the average monthly income from stocks, bank accounts, or other income-producing investments.

Alimony, maintenance or support payments payable: Line #10: Enter the monthly average amount that you receive for yourself or the support of any dependent child.

Social security or other government assistance: Line #11: List the monthly amount of any social security, unemployment, worker's compensation, disability, aid to families with dependent children, food stamps, veteran's benefits, or other government assistance. Specify the type of assistance.

Pension or retirement income: Line #12: Enter the average monthly amount of any retirement benefits, including IRAs, KEOGHs, or annuities. Specify the type.

Other monthly income: Line #13: Include the average monthly amount of any other type of income that you receive on a regular basis. Specify the source of the income.

Subtotal of Lines 7 through 13: Line #14: Subtotal Lines #7 through #13 for you and your spouse (if applicable).

Total Average Monthly Income: Line #15: Add Line #6 "Total Net Monthly Take Home Pay" amount and Line #14 and enter here.

Total Average Combined Monthly Income: **Line #16:** Add together both "Total Monthly Income" amounts for you and your spouse (on line #15) and enter on this line and on the *Summary of Schedules* and, if applicable, on the *Statistical Summary of Certain Liabilities and Related Data* form.

Describe any increase or decrease in income reasonably anticipated to occur within the year following the filing of this document: **Line #17:** If you know or anticipate any reason why your income will change in the next 12 months after you file your petition, explain here.

l6l (Official Form 6I) (12/07)

In re __Mary Ellen and John Alan Smith_____ ,   Case No. __(supplied by clerk)_____
                    Debtor   **(if known)**

SCHEDULE I - CURRENT INCOME OF INDIVIDUAL DEBTOR(S)

The column labeled "Spouse" must be completed in all cases filed by joint debtors and by every married debtor, whether or not a joint petition is filed, unless the spouses are separated and a joint petition is not filed. Do not state the name of any minor child. The average monthly income calculated on this form may differ from the current monthly income calculated on Form 22A, 22B, or 22C.

Debtor's Marital Status: Married	DEPENDENTS OF DEBTOR AND SPOUSE	
	RELATIONSHIP(S): none	AGE(S):

Employment:	DEBTOR	SPOUSE
Occupation	Teacher	Mechanic
Name of Employer	Centerville Elementary School	Centerville Auto Repair
How long employed	3 yrs	2 yrs
Address of Employer	987 West Mian Street Centerville, IL 61111	765 Elm Street, Centerville, IL 61111

INCOME: (Estimate of average or projected monthly income at time case filed)

	DEBTOR	SPOUSE
1. Monthly gross wages, salary, and commissions (Prorate if not paid monthly)	$ 1,000.00	$ 2,000.00
2. Estimate monthly overtime	$	$
3. SUBTOTAL	$ 1,000.00	$ 2,000.00
4. LESS PAYROLL DEDUCTIONS		
a. Payroll taxes and social security	$ 127.00	$ 234.00
b. Insurance	$	$
c. Union dues	$ 23.00	$
d. Other (Specify): _____	$	$
5. SUBTOTAL OF PAYROLL DEDUCTIONS	$ 150.00	$ 234.00
6. TOTAL NET MONTHLY TAKE HOME PAY	$ 850.00	$ 1,766.00
7. Regular income from operation of business or profession or farm (Attach detailed statement)	$	$
8. Income from real property	$	$
9. Interest and dividends	$	$
10. Alimony, maintenance or support payments payable to the debtor for the debtor's use or that of dependents listed above	$	$
11. Social security or government assistance (Specify):_____	$	$
12. Pension or retirement income	$	$
13. Other monthly income (Specify):_____	$	$
14. SUBTOTAL OF LINES 7 THROUGH 13	$ 850.00	$ 1,766.00
15. AVERAGE MONTHLY INCOME (Add amounts on lines 6 and 14)	$	$

16. COMBINED AVERAGE MONTHLY INCOME: (Combine column totals from line 15) $ 2,616.00

(Report also on Summary of Schedules and, if applicable, on Statistical Summary of Certain Liabilities and Related Data)

17. Describe any increase or decrease in income reasonably anticipated to occur within the year following the filing of this document:
    none

_____

Schedule J: Current Expenditures of Individual Debtor(s)

On this schedule, you will estimate your average monthly expenses. The amounts you list will be for your entire family's expenses, whether you are filing jointly, or are married and filing alone. If you are filing jointly, but you and your spouse do not live together, see below under "Check this Box." For all amounts, determine the average monthly expense amount at the time your case is filed.. For expenditures that are made on a weekly, quarterly, or annual basis, calculate the monthly amount and enter.

In re: Enter your full name. If you're filing jointly, include your spouse's name.

Case No.: Leave this blank if filed with your petition. The court clerk will assign you a case number.

Check this box if a joint petition is filed and debtor's spouse maintains a separate household: Do so if you and your spouse are separated but are filing a joint petition. You will then need to complete separate *Schedule J*s for you and your spouse. Clearly label your spouse's *Schedule J* as "Spouse."

Expenditures: Lines #1 – 17: For each of the listed expense items, list your average monthly amount. If the amount is paid other than monthly (i.e., weekly, annually, etc.), calculate the monthly average amount. Include any types of expenses not listed under "Other."

Total Monthly Expenses: Line #18: Total all expenses from Lines #1 – 17 and list this amount also on your *Summary of Schedules* and, if applicable, on the *Statistical Summary of Certain Liabilities and Related Data* form.

Describe any increase or decrease in expenditures reasonably anticipated to occur within the year following the filing of this document: Line #19: If you know or anticipate any reason why your expenses will change in the next 12 months after you file your petition, explain here.

Statement of Monthly Net Income: Line #20(a): list the amount from Line #16 on *Schedule I (Current Income of Individual Debtor[s])*.

Line #20(b): List the total monthly expenses from Line #18 on this form, above.

Line #20(c): Subtract Line #20(b) from Line #20(a) and enter the amount here. This is your monthly net income for bankruptcy purposes.

B6J (Official Form 6J) (12/07)

In re Mary Ellen and John Alan Smith   ,   Case No. (supplied by clerk)
            Debtor   **(if known)**

SCHEDULE J - CURRENT EXPENDITURES OF INDIVIDUAL DEBTOR(S)

Complete this schedule by estimating the average or projected monthly expenses of the debtor and the debtor's family at time case filed. Prorate any payments made bi-weekly, quarterly, semi-annually, or annually to show monthly rate. The average monthly expenses calculated on this form may differ from the deductions from income allowed on Form22A or 22C.

☐ Check this box if a joint petition is filed and debtor's spouse maintains a separate household. Complete a separate schedule of expenditures labeled "Spouse."

1. Rent or home mortgage payment (include lot rented for mobile home)	$	650.00
a. Are real estate taxes included? Yes ✔ No _____		
b. Is property insurance included? Yes ✔ No _____		
2. Utilities: a. Electricity and heating fuel	$	175.00
b. Water and sewer	$	78.00
c. Telephone	$	109.00
d. Other __cable TV__	$	45.00
3. Home maintenance (repairs and upkeep)	$	375.00
4. Food	$	200.00
5. Clothing	$	50.00
6. Laundry and dry cleaning	$	35.00
7. Medical and dental expenses	$	160.00
8. Transportation (not including car payments)	$	100.00
9. Recreation, clubs and entertainment, newspapers, magazines, etc.	$	1,200.00
10.Charitable contributions	$	
11.Insurance (not deducted from wages or included in home mortgage payments)		
a. Homeowner's or renter's	$	
b. Life	$	35.00
c. Health	$	60.00
d. Auto	$	117.00
e. Other _____	$	
12. Taxes (not deducted from wages or included in home mortgage payments) (Specify) _____	$	
13. Installment payments: (In chapter 11, 12, and 13 cases, do not list payments to be included in the plan)		
a. Auto	$	240.00
b. Other __personal loan__	$	345.00
c. Other _____	$	
14. Alimony, maintenance, and support paid to others	$	
15. Payments for support of additional dependents not living at your home	$	
16. Regular expenses from operation of business, profession, or farm (attach detailed statement)	$	
17. Other _____	$	
18. AVERAGE MONTHLY EXPENSES (Total lines 1-17. Report also on Summary of Schedules and, if applicable, on the Statistical Summary of Certain Liabilities and Related Data.)	$	3,974.00

19. Describe any increase or decrease in expenditures reasonably anticipated to occur within the year following the filing of this document:

20. STATEMENT OF MONTHLY NET INCOME

a. Average monthly income from Line 15 of Schedule I	$	2,616.00
b. Average monthly expenses from Line 18 above	$	3,974.00
c. Monthly net income (a. minus b.)	$	-1,358.00

Instructions for Continuation Sheet

You will use this unofficial form if you need to include any additional information on any of your schedules. If you use this form, it will be considered a continuation sheet and should be counted as a sheet when you need to list the total number of sheets for each schedule and on your *Summary of Schedules* (later in this chapter).

In re: Enter your full name. If you're filing jointly, include your spouse's name.

Case No.: Leave this blank. The court clerk will assign you a case number.

Continuation Sheet to Schedule or Form: Here list the letter of the schedule or form number which the sheet will supplement (for example, *Schedule A or Form 3*).

On the rest of the sheet include any information which you may need to add in order to complete or explain anything on the official schedule.

Note: Use only the official continuation sheets for *Schedules D, E, F* and *Form 8.*

In re: <u>Mary Ellen and John Alan Smith</u>   Case No. <u>(supplied by clerk)</u>
      Debtor

CONTINUATION SHEET TO SCHEDULE ____ OR FORM ____

Instructions for the Summary of Schedules (Official Form 6-Summary)

Here you will enter information from all schedules to act as a summary for the court.

Court Name: Fill in the full name of the judicial district in which you will be filing (as listed on your *Voluntary Petition*).

In re: Enter your full name. If you're filing jointly, include your spouse's name.

Case No.: Leave this line blank if filed with your petition. The court clerk will assign you a case number.

Chapter: Here list "7" for Chapter 7.

Attached (Yes/No): Indicate with a "yes" or "no" which schedules are attached. You should attach all schedules listed on the summary, even if one or some of the schedules do not apply to your situation.

No. of Sheets: For each schedule, count the number of pages. Include any continuation pages that you have used.

Amounts Scheduled: Enter asset totals from *Schedules A* and *B*; liability totals from *Schedules D, E,* and *F*; and income and expenditure totals from *Schedules I* and *J*. No amounts are listed for *Schedules G* and *H*. (**Note: For Schedule E, only enter total from "amount of claim" column.**)

Totals: Total the columns for the "Total Assets," and "Total Liabilities."

Instructions for the Statistical Summary of Certain Liabilities and Related Data: Official Form 6-Statistical Summary

All individual debtors are required to complete this form. If you are an individual debtor whose debts are not primarily consumer debts (for example, if your debts are primarily from medical bills), you should check the box located after the title of this form and you are not required to report any information on this form. You must, however, file this form with your other forms.

Court Name: Fill in the full name of the judicial district in which you will be filing (as listed on your *Voluntary Petition*).

In re: Enter your full name. If you're filing jointly, include your spouse's name.

Case No.: Leave this line blank if filed with your petition. The court clerk will assign you a case number.

Chapter: Here list "7" for Chapter 7.

Type of Liability and Amount: Insert the amounts requested from *Schedules E* or *F* and total on the last line.

State the Following: Insert the amounts requested from *Schedules I* and *J*, and from *Form 22A*.

State the Following: On Lines 1, 2, and 3, insert the amounts requested from *Schedules D, E,* and *F*. On Line 4, insert the total from *Schedule F*. On Line 5, total the amounts listed on Lines 1, 3, and 4.

B6 Summary (Official Form 6 - Summary) (12/07)

United States Bankruptcy Court

Northern District of Illinois

In re Mary Ellen and John Alan Smith   ,   Case No. (supplied by clerk)
                    Debtor

Chapter 7

SUMMARY OF SCHEDULES

Indicate as to each schedule whether that schedule is attached and state the number of pages in each. Report the totals from Schedules A, B, D, E, F, I, and J in the boxes provided. Add the amounts from Schedules A and B to determine the total amount of the debtor's assets. Add the amounts of all claims from Schedules D, E, and F to determine the total amount of the debtor's liabilities. Individual debtors also must complete the "Statistical Summary of Certain Liabilities and Related Data" if they file a case under chapter 7, 11, or 13.

NAME OF SCHEDULE	ATTACHED (YES/NO)	NO. OF SHEETS	ASSETS	LIABILITIES	OTHER
A - Real Property	Yes	1	$		
B - Personal Property	Yes	3	$		
C - Property Claimed as Exempt	Yes	1			
D - Creditors Holding Secured Claims	Yes	1		$ 137,000.00	
E - Creditors Holding Unsecured Priority Claims (Total of Claims on Schedule E)	Yes	3		$ 850.00	
F - Creditors Holding Unsecured Nonpriority Claims	Yes	2		$ 37,025.00	
G - Executory Contracts and Unexpired Leases	Yes	1			
H - Codebtors	Yes	1			
I - Current Income of Individual Debtor(s)	Yes	1			$ 2,616.00
J - Current Expenditures of Individual Debtors(s)	Yes	1			$ 3,974.00
TOTAL			$ 168,967.00	$ 74,875.00	

B 6 Summary (Official Form 6 - Summary) (12/07)

United States Bankruptcy Court

Northern District of Illinois

In re _Mary Ellen and John Alan Smith_____,   Case No. _(supplied by clerk)_
         Debtor

                      Chapter _7_____

STATISTICAL SUMMARY OF CERTAIN LIABILITIES AND RELATED DATA (28 U.S.C. § 159)

If you are an individual debtor whose debts are primarily consumer debts, as defined in § 101(8) of the Bankruptcy Code (11 U.S.C. § 101(8)), filing a case under chapter 7, 11 or 13, you must report all information requested below.

☐ Check this box if you are an individual debtor whose debts are NOT primarily consumer debts. You are not required to report any information here.

This information is for statistical purposes only under 28 U.S.C. § 159.

Summarize the following types of liabilities, as reported in the Schedules, and total them.

Type of Liability	Amount	
Domestic Support Obligations (from Schedule E)	$	850.00
Taxes and Certain Other Debts Owed to Governmental Units (from Schedule E)	$	
Claims for Death or Personal Injury While Debtor Was Intoxicated (from Schedule E) (whether disputed or undisputed)	$	
Student Loan Obligations (from Schedule F)	$	
Domestic Support, Separation Agreement, and Divorce Decree Obligations Not Reported on Schedule E	$	
Obligations to Pension or Profit-Sharing, and Other Similar Obligations (from Schedule F)	$	
TOTAL	$	850.00

State the following:

Average Income (from Schedule I, Line 16)	$	2,616.00
Average Expenses (from Schedule J, Line 18)	$	3,974.00
Current Monthly Income (from Form 22A Line 12; **OR**, Form 22B Line 11; **OR**, Form 22C Line 20)	$	4,300.00

State the following:

1. Total from Schedule D, "UNSECURED PORTION, IF ANY" column		$
2. Total from Schedule E, "AMOUNT ENTITLED TO PRIORITY" column.	$ 850.00	
3. Total from Schedule E, "AMOUNT NOT ENTITLED TO PRIORITY, IF ANY" column		$
4. Total from Schedule F		$ 149,000.00
5. Total of non-priority unsecured debt (sum of 1, 3, and 4)		$ 149,000.00

Instructions for the Declaration Concerning Debtor's Schedules (Official Form 6-Decl.)

This form is where you state that everything that you entered on all of the schedules is true and correct to the best of your knowledge. Everything that you enter on your bankruptcy forms must be absolutely true and you must be able to prove it with documents, receipts, bills, or other paper records. Keep in mind that the penalty for making a false statement on a bankruptcy form is a fine of up to $500,000.00 and imprisonment for up to five years, or both, and, of course, denial of your request to discharge your debts in bankruptcy.

In re: Enter your full name. If you're filing jointly, include your spouse's name.

Case No.: Leave this blank if filed with your petition. The court clerk will assign you a case number.

Declaration Under Penalty of Perjury by Individual Debtor: List the total number of sheets from your *Summary of Schedules* plus add one (for the *Summary of Schedules* itself). Date and sign (if joint, both spouses must sign).

Declaration and Signature of Non-Attorney Bankruptcy Petition Preparer: Enter *N/A* on the signature line, unless you are using a bankruptcy petition preparer.

Declaration Under Penalty of Perjury on Behalf of a Corporation or Partnership: Enter *N/A* on the signature line.

B6 Declaration (Official Form 6 - Declaration) (12/07)

In re __Mary Ellen & John Alan Smith__ ,   Case No. __(supplied by clerk)__
                    Debtor   (if known)

DECLARATION CONCERNING DEBTOR'S SCHEDULES

DECLARATION UNDER PENALTY OF PERJURY BY INDIVIDUAL DEBTOR

I declare under penalty of perjury that I have read the foregoing summary and schedules, consisting of __17__ sheets, and that they are true and correct to the best of my knowledge, information, and belief.

Date __03/15/2008_____   Signature: __handwritten signature_____
                                                                                      Debtor

Date __03/15/2008_____   Signature: __handwritten signature_____
                                                                              (Joint Debtor, if any)

[If joint case, both spouses must sign.]

DECLARATION AND SIGNATURE OF NON-ATTORNEY BANKRUPTCY PETITION PREPARER (See 11 U.S.C. § 110)

I declare under penalty of perjury that: (1) I am a bankruptcy petition preparer as defined in 11 U.S.C. § 110; (2) I prepared this document for compensation and have provided the debtor with a copy of this document and the notices and information required under 11 U.S.C. §§ 110(b), 110(h) and 342(b); and, (3) if rules or guidelines have been promulgated pursuant to 11 U.S.C. § 110(h) setting a maximum fee for services chargeable by bankruptcy petition preparers, I have given the debtor notice of the maximum amount before preparing any document for filing for a debtor or accepting any fee from the debtor, as required by that section.

_____   _____
Printed or Typed Name and Title, if any,   Social Security No.
of Bankruptcy Petition Preparer   *(Required by 11 U.S.C. § 110.)*

If the bankruptcy petition preparer is not an individual, state the name, title (if any), address, and social security number of the officer, principal, responsible person, or partner who signs this document.

_____
_____
_____
Address

x __n/a_____   _____
Signature of Bankruptcy Petition Preparer   Date

Names and Social Security numbers of all other individuals who prepared or assisted in preparing this document, unless the bankruptcy petition preparer is not an individual:

If more than one person prepared this document, attach additional signed sheets conforming to the appropriate Official Form for each person.

A bankruptcy petition preparer's failure to comply with the provisions of title 11 and the Federal Rules of Bankruptcy Procedure may result in fines or imprisonment or both. 11 U.S.C. § 110; 18 U.S.C. § 156.

DECLARATION UNDER PENALTY OF PERJURY ON BEHALF OF A CORPORATION OR PARTNERSHIP

I, the _____ [the president or other officer or an authorized agent of the corporation or a member or an authorized agent of the partnership] of the _____ [corporation or partnership] named as debtor in this case, declare under penalty of perjury that I have read the foregoing summary and schedules, consisting of __17__ sheets (*Total shown on summary page plus 1*), and that they are true and correct to the best of my knowledge, information, and belief.

Date _____

                    Signature: __n/a_____

                                        _____
                                        [Print or type name of individual signing on behalf of debtor.]

[An individual signing on behalf of a partnership or corporation must indicate position or relationship to debtor.]

Penalty for making a false statement or concealing property: Fine of up to $500,000 or imprisonment for up to 5 years or both. 18 U.S.C. §§ 152 and 3571.

Instructions for the Statement of Financial Affairs (Official Form 7)

This form is used to describe your financial transactions over the last two years. You must truthfully answer all questions on this form. *Note*: For some questions, the answers require information going back ten full years. The answers on this form will be checked very carefully by the court. In certain cases, the bankruptcy court may void certain transactions and take control of money or property that you transferred to others before you filed for bankruptcy. If you are filing jointly, list the information for each of you separately. If your answer for any question is "None," check the box to the left of the question. You can amend this statement at any time before your case is closed, but you must notify the bankruptcy trustee and any creditors of any changes. Do not disclose the name of any minor child on this form. Simply state "a minor child" where necessary for identification.

Note: You are considered to be "in business" if you have been (1) an officer, director, managing executive or owner [of 5% or more] of a corporation, or (2) a partner [other than a limited partner] of a partnership, or (3) a sole proprietor or self-employed, whether full or part-time, or (4) engaged in any trade or business to supplement your primary employment income.

Court Name: Fill in the full name of the judicial district in which you will be filing (as listed on your *Voluntary Petition*).

In re: Enter your full name. If you're filing jointly, include your spouse's name.

Case No.: Leave this blank if filed with your petition. The court clerk will assign you a case number.

1. Income from employment or operation of business: Two amounts are required. First, list all income from your job or business for this calendar year. Then, also list the total amount of income from your job or business during the two years prior to this calendar year. Use your tax returns to complete this section. Indicate the source used, such as your 2008 federal tax return.

2. Income other than from employment or operation of business: List all other income you have received from any source in the two years prior to filing for bankruptcy (tax refunds, alimony, bank account interest, for example). Use your tax returns to complete this section. Indicate the source used, such as your 2008 federal tax return.

3. Payments to creditors: **Line #3(a):** If you are a debtor with primarily consumer-related debts (as opposed to business debts), list any payments totaling over $600.00 that you have made on any loans or debts within the 90 days prior to filing for bankruptcy.

Line #3(b): If your debts are not primarily consumer-related, list any payments or transfers to any creditor made in the 90 days prior to filing for bankruptcy that totaled over $5,475.00 per creditor. Use an asterisk to indicate any payments made for domestic support or as part of an alternative repayment schedulee as noted on form.

Line #3(c): All debtors must list any payments for any amount made within one year prior to filing that were made to creditors who were or are *insiders* (relatives, business partners, or other closely related parties).

4. Suits and administrative proceedings, executions, garnishments and attachments: Under (a) list any lawsuits that you or your spouse were parties to within one year prior to filing for bankruptcy. Under (b) list any property that has been garnished, attached, or seized within one year prior to filing.

5. Repossessions, foreclosures and returns: Enter any property that was repossessed, foreclosed, or voluntarily returned to a seller within one year prior to filing.

6. Assignments and receiverships: Under (a) list any assignment of property made within 120 days prior to filing. Under (b) list any property held by a receiver or other court official within one year prior to filing.

7. Gifts: List every gift (cash or property) that you or your spouse made within one year prior to filing if the gifts total over $200.00 worth per family member or over $100.00 worth to any single charity.

8. Losses: List all fire, theft, gambling, or other losses within one year prior to filing or since filing for bankruptcy (Note: you may amend this form after your initial filing if you have later losses).

9. Payments related to debt counseling or bankruptcy: List any payments or property transferred to any party for any bankruptcy or debt counseling or assistance (including to lawyers) within one year prior to filing.

10. Other transfers: Under (a) list any other property that was transferred to anyone else within one year prior to filing, except ordinary business or financial transactions. Under (b) list any property transferred within the last 10 years to a 'living trust', revocable trust, or similar trust of which the debtor is also the beneficiary.

11. Closed financial accounts: List information regarding any financial or bank accounts that were closed or transferred within one year prior to filing for bankruptcy.

12. Safe deposit boxes: List all safe deposit boxes in which you or your spouse held any valuables within one year prior to filing.

13. Setoffs: List any setoffs made against a debt by a creditor or bank within 90 days prior to filing. *Setoffs* are money that a creditor owes you which the creditor has applied against a debt that you owe the creditor.

14. Property held for another person: List any property that you or your spouse are currently holding for someone else.

15. Prior address of debtor: List any addresses where you or your spouse have lived within the last three years.

16. Spouses and Former Spouses: Complete only if you have resided with a spouse in a community-property state at any time during the past eight years (Alaska, Arizona, California, Idaho, Louisiana, Nevada, New Mexico, Puerto Rico, Texas, Washington, or Wisconsin). Otherwise check the "None" box. If "yes," list the name of any spouse or former spouse with whom you lived in any of these states within the last eight years.

17. Environmental Information: Under (a) list the name and address for any location or property, whether or not presently owned, for which you have received any notice from any governmental agency that there may be liability or a violation under any federal, state, or local environmental law or regulation. List the site name and address, the name and address of the government unit, the date of the notice, and the environmental law that applies. Under (b), for any site for which you provided a release of hazardous material to any government unit, list the site name and address, the name and address of the government unit, the date of the notice, and the environmental law that applies. Under (c), if you have been a party to any lawsuit or administrative proceeding, including any settlements or order relating to any environmental law, you must list the name and address of the governmental unit involved, the docket number of the case, and the status of the case.

18. Nature, location and name of business: Under (a) list name, taxpayer I.D. number (FEIN or Social Security number), address, nature of the business, and the beginning and ending dates of every business that you or your spouse owned five percent or more of within the six years prior to filing for bankruptcy. Under (b) enter name and address of any property listed as a business under (a) that consists of a single piece of real estate.

Note: Questions 19 through 25 should only be answered if you or your spouse have been in business (or owned five percent or more of a business) within the past six years; either as a corporation, partnership, sole proprietorship, or otherwise self-employed. These questions must be answered even if you are no longer in business at the time you file for bankruptcy. If you or a spouse have not been in business in the last six years, check the "None" box, skip these questions, and go directly to the signature page.

19. Books, records and financial statements: Under (a) list the names and addresses of any bookkeepers and accountants who handled any of your business records within the two years prior to filing for bankruptcy. Under (b) list any person or firm who has audited or prepared financial records for your business within the two years prior to filing. Under (c) list any person or firm who had possession of any books or records of your business on the date of filing for bankruptcy. Under (d) list any financial institution or creditor to whom the business gave a financial statement within the two years prior to filing for bankruptcy.

20. Inventories: Under (a) list the dates and amounts for each of the last two business inventories. Also list the name of the person who supervised each inventory. Under (b) enter the name and address of the person who has possession of the records of those inventories.

21. Current Partners, Officers, Directors and Shareholders: Under (a) and (b) check the "None" box and enter *N/A*.

22. Former partners, officers, directors and shareholders: Under (a) and (b) check the "None" box and enter *N/A*.

23. Withdrawals from a partnership or distributions by a corporation: Enter *N/A*.

24. Tax consolidation group: Check the "None" box and enter *N/A*.

25. Pension Funds: Check the "None" box and enter *N/A*.

If completed by an individual or individual and spouse: Date and sign. If a joint petition, your spouse must also sign and date.

If completed on behalf of a partnership or corporation: Enter *N/A*.

Declaration and Signature of Non-Attorney Bankruptcy Petition Preparer: Enter *N/A* on the signature line, unless you were assisted by a bankruptcy petition preparer.

B 7 (Official Form 7) (12/07)

UNITED STATES BANKRUPTCY COURT

Northern District of Illinois

In re: Mary Ellen and John Alan Smith   ,   Case No. (supplied by clerk)
          Debtor   (if known)

STATEMENT OF FINANCIAL AFFAIRS

This statement is to be completed by every debtor. Spouses filing a joint petition may file a single statement on which the information for both spouses is combined. If the case is filed under chapter 12 or chapter 13, a married debtor must furnish information for both spouses whether or not a joint petition is filed, unless the spouses are separated and a joint petition is not filed. An individual debtor engaged in business as a sole proprietor, partner, family farmer, or self-employed professional, should provide the information requested on this statement concerning all such activities as well as the individual's personal affairs. To indicate payments, transfers and the like to minor children, state the child's initials and the name and address of the child's parent or guardian, such as "A.B., a minor child, by John Doe, guardian." Do not disclose the child's name. See, 11 U.S.C. §112 and Fed. R. Bankr. P. 1007(m).

Questions 1 - 18 are to be completed by all debtors. Debtors that are or have been in business, as defined below, also must complete Questions 19 - 25. **If the answer to an applicable question is "None," mark the box labeled "None."** If additional space is needed for the answer to any question, use and attach a separate sheet properly identified with the case name, case number (if known), and the number of the question.

DEFINITIONS

"In business." A debtor is "in business" for the purpose of this form if the debtor is a corporation or partnership. An individual debtor is "in business" for the purpose of this form if the debtor is or has been, within six years immediately preceding the filing of this bankruptcy case, any of the following: an officer, director, managing executive, or owner of 5 percent or more of the voting or equity securities of a corporation; a partner, other than a limited partner, of a partnership; a sole proprietor or self-employed full-time or part-time. An individual debtor also may be "in business" for the purpose of this form if the debtor engages in a trade, business, or other activity, other than as an employee, to supplement income from the debtor's primary employment.

"Insider." The term "insider" includes but is not limited to: relatives of the debtor; general partners of the debtor and their relatives; corporations of which the debtor is an officer, director, or person in control; officers, directors, and any owner of 5 percent or more of the voting or equity securities of a corporate debtor and their relatives; affiliates of the debtor and insiders of such affiliates; any managing agent of the debtor. 11 U.S.C. § 101.

---

1. Income from employment or operation of business

None
☐

State the gross amount of income the debtor has received from employment, trade, or profession, or from operation of the debtor's business, including part-time activities either as an employee or in independent trade or business, from the beginning of this calendar year to the date this case was commenced. State also the gross amounts received during the **two years** immediately preceding this calendar year. (A debtor that maintains, or has maintained, financial records on the basis of a fiscal rather than a calendar year may report fiscal year income. Identify the beginning and ending dates of the debtor's fiscal year.) If a joint petition is filed, state income for each spouse separately. (Married debtors filing under chapter 12 or chapter 13 must state income of both spouses whether or not a joint petition is filed, unless the spouses are separated and a joint petition is not filed.)

AMOUNT   SOURCE

$8,000.00   Debtor - wages from Centerville Elementary School
                 (attach a separate sheet for co-debtor information)

2. Income other than from employment or operation of business

None
☑

State the amount of income received by the debtor other than from employment, trade, profession, operation of the debtor's business during the **two years** immediately preceding the commencement of this case. Give particulars. If a joint petition is filed, state income for each spouse separately. (Married debtors filing under chapter 12 or chapter 13 must state income for each spouse whether or not a joint petition is filed, unless the spouses are separated and a joint petition is not filed.)

AMOUNT   SOURCE

---

3. Payments to creditors

Complete a. or b., as appropriate, and c.

None
☐

a. *Individual or joint debtor(s) with primarily consumer debts:* List all payments on loans, installment purchases of goods or services, and other debts to any creditor made within **90 days** immediately preceding the commencement of this case unless the aggregate value of all property that constitutes or is affected by such transfer is less than $600. Indicate with an asterisk (*) any payments that were made to a creditor on account of a domestic support obligation or as part of an alternative repayment schedule under a plan by an approved nonprofit budgeting and credit counseling agency. (Married debtors filing under chapter 12 or chapter 13 must include payments by either or both spouses whether or not a joint petition is filed, unless the spouses are separated and a joint petition is not filed.)

NAME AND ADDRESS OF CREDITOR	DATES OF PAYMENTS	AMOUNT PAID	AMOUNT STILL OWING
American Bank 1234 First Ave Centerville IL (attach a separate sheet for addtional info)	01/15/2007	550.00	

None
☑

b. *Debtor whose debts are not primarily consumer debts: List each payment or other transfer to any creditor made* within **90 days** immediately preceding the commencement of the case unless the aggregate value of all property that constitutes or is affected by such transfer is less than $5,475. If the debtor is an individual, indicate with an asterisk (*) any payments that were made to a creditor on account of a domestic support obligation or as part of an alternative repayment schedule under a plan by an approved nonprofit budgeting and credit counseling agency. (Married debtors filing under chapter 12 or chapter 13 must include payments and other transfers by either or both spouses whether or not a joint petition is filed, unless the spouses are separated and a joint petition is not filed.)

NAME AND ADDRESS OF CREDITOR	DATES OF PAYMENTS/ TRANSFERS	AMOUNT PAID OR VALUE OF TRANSFERS	AMOUNT STILL OWING

3

None

c. *All debtors:* List all payments made within **one year** immediately preceding the commencement of this case to or for the benefit of creditors who are or were insiders. (Married debtors filing under chapter 12 or chapter 13 must include payments by either or both spouses whether or not a joint petition is filed, unless the spouses are separated and a joint petition is not filed.)

NAME AND ADDRESS OF CREDITOR AND RELATIONSHIP TO DEBTOR	DATE OF PAYMENT	AMOUNT PAID	AMOUNT STILL OWING

4. Suits and administrative proceedings, executions, garnishments and attachments

None

a. List all suits and administrative proceedings to which the debtor is or was a party within **one year** immediately preceding the filing of this bankruptcy case. (Married debtors filing under chapter 12 or chapter 13 must include information concerning either or both spouses whether or not a joint petition is filed, unless the spouses are separated and a joint petition is not filed.)

CAPTION OF SUIT AND CASE NUMBER	NATURE OF PROCEEDING	COURT OR AGENCY AND LOCATION	STATUS OR DISPOSITION

None
☑
b. Describe all property that has been attached, garnished or seized under any legal or equitable process within **one year** immediately preceding the commencement of this case. (Married debtors filing under chapter 12 or chapter 13 must include information concerning property of either or both spouses whether or not a joint petition is filed, unless the spouses are separated and a joint petition is not filed.)

NAME AND ADDRESS OF PERSON FOR WHOSE BENEFIT PROPERTY WAS SEIZED	DATE OF SEIZURE	DESCRIPTION AND VALUE OF PROPERTY

5. Repossessions, foreclosures and returns

None
☐
List all property that has been repossessed by a creditor, sold at a foreclosure sale, transferred through a deed in lieu of foreclosure or returned to the seller, within **one year** immediately preceding the commencement of this case. (Married debtors filing under chapter 12 or chapter 13 must include information concerning property of either or both spouses whether or not a joint petition is filed, unless the spouses are separated and a joint petition is not filed.)

NAME AND ADDRESS OF CREDITOR OR SELLER	DATE OF REPOSSESSION, FORECLOSURE SALE, TRANSFER OR RETURN	DESCRIPTION AND VALUE OF PROPERTY
Hunt Ford Company 444 Main St Centerville IL	06/09/2005	Ford truck $15,000

4

6. Assignments and receiverships

None ☑

a. Describe any assignment of property for the benefit of creditors made within **120 days** immediately preceding the commencement of this case. (Married debtors filing under chapter 12 or chapter 13 must include any assignment by either or both spouses whether or not a joint petition is filed, unless the spouses are separated and a joint petition is not filed.)

NAME AND ADDRESS OF ASSIGNEE	DATE OF ASSIGNMENT	TERMS OF ASSIGNMENT OR SETTLEMENT

None ☑

b. List all property which has been in the hands of a custodian, receiver, or court-appointed official within **one year** immediately preceding the commencement of this case. (Married debtors filing under chapter 12 or chapter 13 must include information concerning property of either or both spouses whether or not a joint petition is filed, unless the spouses are separated and a joint petition is not filed.)

NAME AND ADDRESS OF CUSTODIAN	NAME AND LOCATION OF COURT CASE TITLE & NUMBER	DATE OF ORDER	DESCRIPTION AND VALUE Of PROPERTY

7. Gifts

None ☐

List all gifts or charitable contributions made within **one year** immediately preceding the commencement of this case except ordinary and usual gifts to family members aggregating less than $200 in value per individual family member and charitable contributions aggregating less than $100 per recipient. (Married debtors filing under chapter 12 or chapter 13 must include gifts or contributions by either or both spouses whether or not a joint petition is filed, unless the spouses are separated and a joint petition is not filed.)

NAME AND ADDRESS OF PERSON OR ORGANIZATION	RELATIONSHIP TO DEBTOR, IF ANY	DATE OF GIFT	DESCRIPTION AND VALUE OF GIFT
First Church of God 34 Main Street, Centerville, IL			cash donation $100 monthly

8. Losses

None ☑

List all losses from fire, theft, other casualty or gambling within **one year** immediately preceding the commencement of this case **or since the commencement of this case**. (Married debtors filing under chapter 12 or chapter 13 must include losses by either or both spouses whether or not a joint petition is filed, unless the spouses are separated and a joint petition is not filed.)

DESCRIPTION AND VALUE OF PROPERTY	DESCRIPTION OF CIRCUMSTANCES AND, IF LOSS WAS COVERED IN WHOLE OR IN PART BY INSURANCE, GIVE PARTICULARS	DATE OF LOSS

5

9.   Payments related to debt counseling or bankruptcy

None
☑

List all payments made or property transferred by or on behalf of the debtor to any persons, including attorneys, for consultation concerning debt consolidation, relief under the bankruptcy law or preparation of a petition in bankruptcy within **one year** immediately preceding the commencement of this case.

NAME AND ADDRESS OF PAYEE	DATE OF PAYMENT, NAME OF PAYER IF OTHER THAN DEBTOR	AMOUNT OF MONEY OR DESCRIPTION AND VALUE OF PROPERTY

10. Other transfers

None
☐

a. List all other property, other than property transferred in the ordinary course of the business or financial affairs of the debtor, transferred either absolutely or as security within **two years** immediately preceding the commencement of this case. (Married debtors filing under chapter 12 or chapter 13 must include transfers by either or both spouses whether or not a joint petition is filed, unless the spouses are separated and a joint petition is not filed.)

NAME AND ADDRESS OF TRANSFEREE, RELATIONSHIP TO DEBTOR	DATE	DESCRIBE PROPERTY TRANSFERRED AND VALUE RECEIVED
William David Smith 567 Elm St Centerville, IL	01/15/2005	Boat and trailer $1,500.00

None
☑

b. List all property transferred by the debtor within **ten years** immediately preceding the commencement of this case to a self-settled trust or similar device of which the debtor is a beneficiary.

NAME OF TRUST OR OTHER DEVICE	DATE(S) OF TRANSFER(S)	AMOUNT OF MONEY OR DESCRIPTION AND VALUE OF PROPERTY OR DEBTOR'S INTEREST IN PROPERTY

11. Closed financial accounts

None
☐

List all financial accounts and instruments held in the name of the debtor or for the benefit of the debtor which were closed, sold, or otherwise transferred within **one year** immediately preceding the commencement of this case. Include checking, savings, or other financial accounts, certificates of deposit, or other instruments; shares and share accounts held in banks, credit unions, pension funds, cooperatives, associations, brokerage houses and other financial institutions. (Married debtors filing under chapter 12 or chapter 13 must include information concerning accounts or instruments held by or for either or both spouses whether or not a joint petition is filed, unless the spouses are separated and a joint petition is not filed.)

NAME AND ADDRESS OF INSTITUTION	TYPE OF ACCOUNT, LAST FOUR DIGITS OF ACCOUNT NUMBER, AND AMOUNT OF FINAL BALANCE	AMOUNT AND DATE OF SALE OR CLOSING
Credit Union, 56 Broadway Centerville, IL	Checking Account 2223 $12.00	4/05/2005

6

12. Safe deposit boxes

None
☑ List each safe deposit or other box or depository in which the debtor has or had securities, cash, or other valuables within **one year** immediately preceding the commencement of this case. (Married debtors filing under chapter 12 or chapter 13 must include boxes or depositories of either or both spouses whether or not a joint petition is filed, unless the spouses are separated and a joint petition is not filed.)

NAME AND ADDRESS OF BANK OR OTHER DEPOSITORY	NAMES AND ADDRESSES OF THOSE WITH ACCESS TO BOX OR DEPOSITORY	DESCRIPTION OF CONTENTS	DATE OF TRANSFER OR SURRENDER, IF ANY

13. Setoffs

None
☑ List all setoffs made by any creditor, including a bank, against a debt or deposit of the debtor within **90 days** preceding the commencement of this case. (Married debtors filing under chapter 12 or chapter 13 must include information concerning either or both spouses whether or not a joint petition is filed, unless the spouses are separated and a joint petition is not filed.)

NAME AND ADDRESS OF CREDITOR	DATE OF SETOFF	AMOUNT OF SETOFF

14. Property held for another person

None
☐ List all property owned by another person that the debtor holds or controls.

NAME AND ADDRESS OF OWNER	DESCRIPTION AND VALUE OF PROPERTY	LOCATION OF PROPERTY

15. Prior address of debtor

None
☑ If debtor has moved within **three years** immediately preceding the commencement of this case, list all premises which the debtor occupied during that period and vacated prior to the commencement of this case. If a joint petition is filed, report also any separate address of either spouse.

ADDRESS	NAME USED	DATES OF OCCUPANCY

16. Spouses and Former Spouses

None

If the debtor resides or resided in a community property state, commonwealth, or territory (including Alaska, Arizona, California, Idaho, Louisiana, Nevada, New Mexico, Puerto Rico, Texas, Washington, or Wisconsin) within **eight years** immediately preceding the commencement of the case, identify the name of the debtor's spouse and of any former spouse who resides or resided with the debtor in the community property state.

NAME

17. Environmental Information.

For the purpose of this question, the following definitions apply:

"Environmental Law" means any federal, state, or local statute or regulation regulating pollution, contamination, releases of hazardous or toxic substances, wastes or material into the air, land, soil, surface water, groundwater, or other medium, including, but not limited to, statutes or regulations regulating the cleanup of these substances, wastes, or material.

"Site" means any location, facility, or property as defined under any Environmental Law, whether or not presently or formerly owned or operated by the debtor, including, but not limited to, disposal sites.

"Hazardous Material" means anything defined as a hazardous waste, hazardous substance, toxic substance, hazardous material, pollutant, or contaminant or similar term under an Environmental Law.

None

a. List the name and address of every site for which the debtor has received notice in writing by a governmental unit that it may be liable or potentially liable under or in violation of an Environmental Law. Indicate the governmental unit, the date of the notice, and, if known, the Environmental Law:

SITE NAME AND ADDRESS	NAME AND ADDRESS OF GOVERNMENTAL UNIT	DATE OF NOTICE	ENVIRONMENTAL LAW

None

b. List the name and address of every site for which the debtor provided notice to a governmental unit of a release of Hazardous Material. Indicate the governmental unit to which the notice was sent and the date of the notice.

SITE NAME AND ADDRESS	NAME AND ADDRESS OF GOVERNMENTAL UNIT	DATE OF NOTICE	ENVIRONMENTAL LAW

None

c. List all judicial or administrative proceedings, including settlements or orders, under any Environmental Law with respect to which the debtor is or was a party. Indicate the name and address of the governmental unit that is or was a party to the proceeding, and the docket number.

NAME AND ADDRESS OF GOVERNMENTAL UNIT	DOCKET NUMBER	STATUS OR DISPOSITION

18. Nature, location and name of business

None

a. *If the debtor is an individual*, list the names, addresses, taxpayer-identification numbers, nature of the businesses, and beginning and ending dates of all businesses in which the debtor was an officer, director, partner, or managing executive of a corporation, partner in a partnership, sole proprietor, or was self-employed in a trade, profession, or other activity either full- or part-time within **six years** immediately preceding the commencement of this case, or in which the debtor owned 5 percent or more of the voting or equity securities within **six years** immediately preceding the commencement of this case.

If the debtor is a partnership, list the names, addresses, taxpayer-identification numbers, nature of the businesses, and beginning and ending dates of all businesses in which the debtor was a partner or owned 5 percent or more of the voting or equity securities, within **six years** immediately preceding the commencement of this case.

If the debtor is a corporation, list the names, addresses, taxpayer-identification numbers, nature of the businesses, and beginning and ending dates of all businesses in which the debtor was a partner or owned 5 percent or more of the voting or equity securities within **six years** immediately preceding the commencement of this case.

NAME	LAST FOUR DIGITS OF SOCIAL-SECURITY OR OTHER INDIVIDUAL TAXPAYER-I.D. NO. (ITIN)/ COMPLETE EIN	ADDRESS	NATURE OF BUSINESS	BEGINNING AND ENDING DATES

None   b. Identify any business listed in response to subdivision a., above, that is "single asset real estate" as defined in 11 U.S.C. § 101.

NAME   ADDRESS

The following questions are to be completed by every debtor that is a corporation or partnership and by any individual debtor who is or has been, within **six years** immediately preceding the commencement of this case, any of the following: an officer, director, managing executive, or owner of more than 5 percent of the voting or equity securities of a corporation; a partner, other than a limited partner, of a partnership, a sole proprietor, or self-employed in a trade, profession, or other activity, either full- or part-time.

*(An individual or joint debtor should complete this portion of the statement **only** if the debtor is or has been in business, as defined above, within six years immediately preceding the commencement of this case. A debtor who has not been in business within those six years should go directly to the signature page.)*

---

19. Books, records and financial statements

None   a. List all bookkeepers and accountants who within **two years** immediately preceding the filing of this bankruptcy case kept or supervised the keeping of books of account and records of the debtor.

NAME AND ADDRESS   DATES SERVICES RENDERED

None   b. List all firms or individuals who within **two years** immediately preceding the filing of this bankruptcy case have audited the books of account and records, or prepared a financial statement of the debtor.

NAME   ADDRESS   DATES SERVICES RENDERED

9

None ☑ c. List all firms or individuals who at the time of the commencement of this case were in possession of the books of account and records of the debtor. If any of the books of account and records are not available, explain.

NAME   ADDRESS

None ☑ d. List all financial institutions, creditors and other parties, including mercantile and trade agencies, to whom a financial statement was issued by the debtor within **two years** immediately preceding the commencement of this case.

NAME AND ADDRESS   DATE ISSUED

20. Inventories

None ☑ a. List the dates of the last two inventories taken of your property, the name of the person who supervised the taking of each inventory, and the dollar amount and basis of each inventory.

                DOLLAR AMOUNT
                OF INVENTORY
DATE OF INVENTORY INVENTORY SUPERVISOR (Specify cost, market or other basis)

None ☑ b. List the name and address of the person having possession of the records of each of the inventories reported in a., above.

                NAME AND ADDRESSES
                OF CUSTODIAN
DATE OF INVENTORY   OF INVENTORY RECORDS

21 . Current Partners, Officers, Directors and Shareholders

None ☑ a. If the debtor is a partnership, list the nature and percentage of partnership interest of each member of the partnership

NAME AND ADDRESS   NATURE OF INTEREST PERCENTAGE OF INTEREST

None ☑ b. If the debtor is a corporation, list all officers and directors of the corporation, and each stockholder who directly or indirectly owns, controls, or holds 5 percent or more of the voting or equity securities of the corporation.

                NATURE AND PERCENTAGE
NAME AND ADDRESS   TITLE   OF STOCK OWNERSHIP

10

22. Former partners, officers, directors and shareholders

None ☑

a. If the debtor is a partnership, list each member who withdrew from the partnership within **one year** immediately preceding the commencement of this case.

NAME   ADDRESS   DATE OF WITHDRAWAL

None ☑

b. If the debtor is a corporation, list all officers or directors whose relationship with the corporation terminated within **one year** immediately preceding the commencement of this case.

NAME AND ADDRESS   TITLE   DATE OF TERMINATION

---

23. Withdrawals from a partnership or distributions by a corporation

None ☑

If the debtor is a partnership or corporation, list all withdrawals or distributions credited or given to an insider, including compensation in any form, bonuses, loans, stock redemptions, options exercised and any other perquisite during **one year** immediately preceding the commencement of this case.

NAME & ADDRESS OF RECIPIENT, RELATIONSHIP TO DEBTOR	DATE AND PURPOSE OF WITHDRAWAL	AMOUNT OF MONEY OR DESCRIPTION AND VALUE OF PROPERTY

---

24. Tax Consolidation Group.

None ☑

If the debtor is a corporation, list the name and federal taxpayer-identification number of the parent corporation of any consolidated group for tax purposes of which the debtor has been a member at any time within **six years** immediately preceding the commencement of the case.

NAME OF PARENT CORPORATION   TAXPAYER-IDENTIFICATION NUMBER (EIN)

---

25. Pension Funds.

None ☑

If the debtor is not an individual, list the name and federal taxpayer-identification number of any pension fund to which the debtor, as an employer, has been responsible for contributing at any time within **six years** immediately preceding the commencement of the case.

NAME OF PENSION FUND   TAXPAYER-IDENTIFICATION NUMBER (EIN)

* * * * * *

11

[If completed by an individual or individual and spouse]

I declare under penalty of perjury that I have read the answers contained in the foregoing statement of financial affairs and any attachments thereto and that they are true and correct.

Date   03/15/2008   Signature of Debtor   handwritten signature

Date   03/15/2008   Signature of Joint Debtor (if any)   handwritten signature

[If completed on behalf of a partnership or corporation]

I declare under penalty of perjury that I have read the answers contained in the foregoing statement of financial affairs and any attachments thereto and that they are true and correct to the best of my knowledge, information and belief.

Date   Signature   n/a

         Print Name and Title

[An individual signing on behalf of a partnership or corporation must indicate position or relationship to debtor.]

____continuation sheets attached

Penalty for making a false statement: Fine of up to $500,000 or imprisonment for up to 5 years, or both. 18 U.S.C. §§ 152 and 3571

DECLARATION AND SIGNATURE OF NON-ATTORNEY BANKRUPTCY PETITION PREPARER (See 11 U.S.C. § 110)

I declare under penalty of perjury that: (1) I am a bankruptcy petition preparer as defined in 11 U.S.C. § 110; (2) I prepared this document for compensation and have provided the debtor with a copy of this document and the notices and information required under 11 U.S.C. §§ 110(b), 110(h), and 342(b); and, (3) if rules or guidelines have been promulgated pursuant to 11 U.S.C. § 110(h) setting a maximum fee for services chargeable by bankruptcy petition preparers, I have given the debtor notice of the maximum amount before preparing any document for filing for a debtor or accepting any fee from the debtor, as required by that section.

Printed or Typed Name and Title, if any, of Bankruptcy Petition Preparer   Social-Security No. (Required by 11 U.S.C. § 110.)

If the bankruptcy petition preparer is not an individual, state the name, title (if any), address, and social-security number of the officer, principal, responsible person, or partner who signs this document.

Address

n/a

Signature of Bankruptcy Petition Preparer   Date

Names and Social-Security numbers of all other individuals who prepared or assisted in preparing this document unless the bankruptcy petition preparer is not an individual:

If more than one person prepared this document, attach additional signed sheets conforming to the appropriate Official Form for each person

A bankruptcy petition preparer's failure to comply with the provisions of title 11 and the Federal Rules of Bankruptcy Procedure may result in fines or imprisonment or both. 18 U.S.C. § 156.

Instructions for the Statement of Social Security Number(s)

Court Name: Select the full name of the judicial district in which you will be filing (as listed on your Voluntary Petition).

In re: Enter your full name. If you're filing jointly, include your spouse's name. Include married, maiden, and any trade names used by you or your spouse within the last 8 years.

Address: Enter your address as listed on your Voluntary Petition.

Case No.: Leave this blank if filed with your Voluntary Petition. The Court Clerk will assign you a case number.

Chapter: Enter "7" here.

Last four digits of Social Security or Individual Taxpayer Identification No(s).: Enter your own and your spouse's if filing jointly.

Employer Tax Identification No(s) (if any): Enter if applicable.

Name of Debtor: Fill in the debtor's (your) name, last name first. Then check the appropriate box and complete.

Name of Joint Debtor: Complete the same for your spouse, if filing jointly.

Then you and your spouse should sign and date this form.

B 21 (Official Form 21) (12/07)

UNITED STATES BANKRUPTCY COURT

Northern District of Illinois

In re Mary Ellen and John Alan Smith_____,)
　[Set forth here all names including married, maiden,　)
　and trade names used by debtor within last 8 years]　)
　　　　　　　　　　　　　　　　　　　　　　　　　)
　　　　　　　　　　　　Debtor　　　　　　　　　)　Case No. if known_____
Address 16 Main Street, Centerville, IL 61111　　　)
　　　　　　　　　　　　　　　　　　　　　　　　　)　Chapter 7_____
　　　　　　　　　　　　　　　　　　　　　　　　　)
Last four digits of Social-Security or Individual Taxpayer-　)
Identification (ITIN) No(s).,(if any): _____　)
5555　　　　　　　　　　　　　　　　　　　　　　)
Employer Tax-Identification (EIN) No(s).(if any):　　　　)
　　　　　　　　　　　　　　　　　　　　　　　　　)

STATEMENT OF SOCIAL-SECURITY NUMBER(S)
(or other Individual Taxpayer-Identification Number(s) (ITIN(s)))[*]

1.Name of Debtor (Last, First, Middle): Smith, Mary Ellen_____
(Check the appropriate box and, if applicable, provide the required information.)

　　☑ Debtor has a Social-Security Number and it is: 555-55-5555
　　　　　(If more than one, state all.)
　　☐ Debtor does not have a Social-Security Number but has an Individual Taxpayer-Identification
　　　　Number (ITIN), and it is: _____
　　　　　(If more than one, state all.)
　　☐ Debtor does not have either a Social-Security Number or an Individual Taxpayer-Identification
　　　　Number (ITIN).

2.Name of Joint Debtor (Last, First, Middle): Smith, John Alan_____
(Check the appropriate box and, if applicable, provide the required information.)

　　☑ Joint Debtor has a Social-Security Number and it is: 888-88-8888
　　　　　(If more than one, state all.)
　　☐ Joint Debtor does not have a Social-Security Number but has an Individual Taxpayer-Identification
　　　　Number (ITIN) and it is: _____
　　　　　(If more than one, state all.)
　　☐ Joint Debtor does not have either a Social-Security Number or an Individual Taxpayer-Identification
　　　　Number (ITIN).

I declare under penalty of perjury that the foregoing is true and correct.

　　　X　handwritten signature and date_____
　　　　　Signature of Debtor　　　　　Date
　　　X　handwritten signature and date_____
　　　　　Signature of Joint Debtor　　　Date

_____

[*] *Joint debtors must provide information for both spouses.*

Penalty for making a false statement: Fine of up to $250,000 or up to 5 years imprisonment or both. 18 U.S.C. §§ 152 and 3571.

Instructions for the Chapter 7 Individual Debtor's Statement of Intention (Official Form 8)

This form is required if you have a *secured debt* (a debt for which you have pledged some type of collateral or which has a lien against it–listed on *Schedule D*) or are renting property under a lease that has not expired (listed on *Schedule F*). It is crucial if you wish to keep the collateral and/or eliminate the creditor's claims on the collateral. If you have secured debts, refer to your completed *Schedule D*. You must separate all debts listed on that *Schedule D* into two categories: (1) debts for which you will surrender the collateral and (2) debts for which you wish to keep the collateral. For those debts for which you wish to keep the collateral, there are three additional choices. (1) You may reaffirm the debt; (2) you can claim the property as exempt and redeem the property; or (3) you may claim the property as exempt and seek to eliminate the creditor's lien on the property. Note that you must perform your stated intentions within 45 days of filing Form 8 with the bankruptcy court. If you do not wish to surrender your collateral, you should seek legal advice or you may lose the property. NOTE: If you have a house listed on *Schedule D*, you are very strongly advised to seek the help of a competent bankruptcy attorney or you may lose your home. This form is also used to reaffirm and assume a lease that you listed on *Schedule F*.

Court Name: Fill in the full name of the judicial district in which you will be filing (as listed on your *Voluntary Petition*).

In re: Fill in your full name (last name first). If you are filing jointly, fill in both you and your spouse's names.

Case No.: Leave this line blank. The court clerk will assign you a case number.

PART A - Debts Secured by Property of the Estate: For each property that you have, complete the following information. If you have more than 2 properties, please use the continuation sheet that is provided (for both Parts A and B):

Creditors Name: Fill in the complete name of the creditor (as shown on your *Schedule D)* for each property.

Description of Property Securing Debt: Here describe each item of property listed on your *Schedule D* as collateral. Use the property descriptions as shown on your *Schedule D*. If you have no debts listed on *Schedule D*, enter *N/A* here and skip to PART B.

Property will be (check one): Here you are first given two choices:

Surrendered: If you choose to surrender the property that you pledged as collateral for the debt, check this box. Under this option, should you be granted a bankruptcy, you will be free from the debt entirely; however, you also lose the property.

Retained: If you wish to retain your secured property either by reaffirmation or redemption, you are very strongly advised to seek the assistance of a competent attorney. There are additional forms that must be prepared that are beyond the scope of this book. Be very careful not to reaffirm any of your debts without legal advice. Consult an attorney if you wish to pursue this option.

If Retaining the Property, I intend to (check at least one): If you wish to retain the property that you have pledged as collateral for the secured debt, you should check the box for "redeem the property". If you wish to reaffirm the debt, you are very strongly advised to seek the assistance of a competent attorney. If any other situation applies, you are also advised to seek the assistance of an attorney.

Property is (check one): If you claim that the property in question is exempt (on *Schedule C*), check the appropriate box. If there is an exemption for the property which is less than the claim against the property, the secured property will generally be surrendered to the bankruptcy trustee and sold. You will receive the amount of the exemption in cash and the remaining proceeds will be used to pay off the secured creditor.

PART B - Personal Property Subject to unexpired leases: For each property that you have, complete the following information. If you have more than 2 properties, please use the continuation sheet that is provided (for both Parts A and B):

Lessor's Name: Fill in the complete name of the lessor for any unexpired leases listed on *Schedule F*.

Describe Leased Property: Here list a description of the property that you listed on *Schedule F*. If you wish to assume the lease and continue to make your rental payments regardless of your bankruptcy, state "Yes" in the third column. If you do not have any leases listed on *Schedule F*, enter N/A under the first column, and skip to the signature line.

___**continuation sheets attached (if any):** Here list the number of any continuation pages added.

Date and Signature of Debtor: Date and sign the form. If filing jointly, spouse should also sign. Note that this signature is declared under penalty of perjury that the items on this form are your intentions.

B 8 (Official Form 8) (12/08)

UNITED STATES BANKRUPTCY COURT
Northern District of Illinois

In re <u>Mary Ellen & John Alan Smith</u> ,   Case No. <u>(supplied by clerk)</u>
            Debtor   Chapter 7

CHAPTER 7 INDIVIDUAL DEBTOR'S STATEMENT OF INTENTION

PART A – Debts secured by property of the estate. *(Part A must be fully completed for EACH debt which is secured by property of the estate. Attach additional pages if necessary.)*

Property No. 1	
Creditor's Name: Centerville Savings & Loan	**Describe Property Securing Debt:** primary residence

Property will be *(check one)*:
    ❏ Surrendered   ☑ Retained

If retaining the property, I intend to *(check at least one)*:
    ☑ Redeem the property
    ❏ Reaffirm the debt
    ❏ Other. Explain _____ (for example, avoid lien
using 11 U.S.C. § 522(f)).

Property is *(check one)*:
    ☑ Claimed as exempt   ❏ Not claimed as exempt

Property No. 2 *(if necessary)*	
Creditor's Name:	**Describe Property Securing Debt:**

Property will be *(check one)*:
    ❏ Surrendered   ❏ Retained

If retaining the property, I intend to *(check at least one)*:
    ❏ Redeem the property
    ❏ Reaffirm the debt
    ❏ Other. Explain _____ (for example, avoid lien
using 11 U.S.C. § 522(f)).

Property is *(check one)*:
    ❏ Claimed as exempt   ❏ Not claimed as exempt

B 8 (Official Form 8) (12/08)   Page 2

PART B – Personal property subject to unexpired leases. *(All three columns of Part B must be completed for each unexpired lease. Attach additional pages if necessary.)*

Property No. 1		
Lessor's Name:	**Describe Leased Property:**	Lease will be Assumed pursuant to 11 U.S.C. § 365(p)(2): ☐ YES ☐ NO

Property No. 2 *(if necessary)*		
Lessor's Name:	**Describe Leased Property:**	Lease will be Assumed pursuant to 11 U.S.C. § 365(p)(2): ☐ YES ☐ NO

Property No. 3 *(if necessary)*		
Lessor's Name:	**Describe Leased Property:**	Lease will be Assumed pursuant to 11 U.S.C. § 365(p)(2): ☐ YES ☐ NO

_____ continuation sheets attached *(if any)*

I declare under penalty of perjury that the above indicates my intention as to any property of my estate securing a debt and/or personal property subject to an unexpired lease.

Date: date signed _____

(handwritten signature) _____
Signature of Debtor

(handwritten signature) _____
Signature of Joint Debtor

B 8 (Official Form 8) (12/08) Page 3

CHAPTER 7 INDIVIDUAL DEBTOR'S STATEMENT OF INTENTION
(Continuation Sheet)

PART A - Continuation

Property No.	
Creditor's Name:	**Describe Property Securing Debt:**

Property will be *(check one)*:
❏ Surrendered   ❏ Retained

If retaining the property, I intend to *(check at least one)*:
❏ Redeem the property
❏ Reaffirm the debt
❏ Other. Explain _____ (for example, avoid lien using 11 U.S.C. § 522(f)).

Property is *(check one)*:
❏ Claimed as exempt   ❏ Not claimed as exempt

PART B - Continuation

Property No.		
Lessor's Name:	**Describe Leased Property:**	Lease will be Assumed pursuant to 11 U.S.C. § 365(p)(2): ❏ YES ❏ NO

Property No.		
Lessor's Name:	**Describe Leased Property:**	Lease will be Assumed pursuant to 11 U.S.C. § 365(p)(2): ❏ YES ❏ NO

Instructions for the Application to Pay Filing Fee in Installments (Official Form 3A)

Page 1

This form is used to request permission to pay your filing fees in installments. You have the right to request this under bankruptcy law. Using this form, you make an initial payment with the filing of your bankruptcy papers and then indicate that you will make up to three further installment payments over a period of up to 120 days in order to pay the filing fee in full. There are a few restrictions, however:

1. You must certify that you are unable to pay the entire fee at one time. Be certain that this request coincides with your description of your current financial situation. If your petition and schedules indicate that you have sufficient cash to pay the filing fee, your request will be denied.

2. If you have already paid an attorney or bankruptcy petition preparer for assistance with your case, you cannot request permission to pay your fee in installments.

3. If your request is granted, you may not pay anyone for any services or assistance related to your bankruptcy until you have first paid your filing fee in full. Additionally, by filing this form, you agree and affirm that you will not make any payment nor transfer any property to an attorney or anyone else as payment for services in connection with your bankruptcy until your entire filing fee is paid.

Court Name: Fill in the full name of the judicial district in which you will be filing (as listed on your *Voluntary Petition*).

In re: Fill in your full name (last name first) that you regularly use to sign checks, etc.

Case No.: Leave this line blank. The court clerk will assign you a case number.

Chapter: Here list "7" for Chapter 7.

Application to Pay Filing Fee in Installments: At the end of Line #1, enter the total amount of the filing fee ($299.00). You may request to pay the fee in up to four installments (The payment amount for each of four installments is $74.50). On Line #4, list first the amount that you will pay either with the filing of the petition itself (check the appropriate box) or within 15 days of filing (list the date in the space shown if you check "On or before"). On the next three lines, indicate the amount that you will pay for each installment and the date on or before which you will pay the installment. The final installment must be paid within 120 days of the filing of your petition, unless you can show the court extraordinary circumstances and they grant you an additional 60 days for final payment (for a total of 180 days).

Signature of Attorney and Date: Enter N/A

Signature of Debtor and Date: Sign and date the form. If filing jointly, spouse should also sign.

Declaration and Signature of Non-Attorney Bankruptcy Petition Preparer: Enter *N/A*, unless you were assisted by a bankruptcy petition preparer.

Page 2: Order Approving Payment of Filing Fee in Installments

Court Name: Fill in the name and state of the bankruptcy court

In re: Fill in your full name (last name first) that you regularly use to sign checks.

Case No.: Leave this line blank. The court clerk will assign you a number.

Chapter: Here list "7" for Chapter 7.

It is Ordered: Leave the rest of this form blank. It will be completed by the bankruptcy court judge if your request to pay the fee in installments is approved.

B 3A (Official Form 3A) (12/07)

UNITED STATES BANKRUPTCY COURT

Northern District of Illinois

In re Mary Ellen and John Alan Smith_____,   Case No. supplied by clerk_____
                    Debtor

                                                       Chapter 7_____

APPLICATION TO PAY FILING FEE IN INSTALLMENTS

1.   In accordance with Fed. R. Bankr. P. 1006, I apply for permission to pay the filing fee amounting to $ 299.00_____ in installments.

2.   I am unable to pay the filing fee except in installments.

3.   Until the filing fee is paid in full, I will not make any additional payment or transfer any additional property to an attorney or any other person for services in connection with this case.

4.   I propose the following terms for the payment of the Filing Fee.*

       $ _____74.75____ Check one ☑ With the filing of the petition, or
                                     ☐ On or before _____

       $ _____74.75____ on or before 04/01/2008_____

       $ _____74.75____ on or before 04/15/2008_____

       $ _____74.75____ on or before 04/30/2008_____

*   The number of installments proposed shall not exceed four (4), and the final installment shall be payable not later than 120 days after filing the petition. For cause shown, the court may extend the time of any installment, provided the last installment is paid not later than 180 days after filing the petition. Fed. R. Bankr. P. 1006(b)(2).

5.   I understand that if I fail to pay any installment when due, my bankruptcy case may be dismissed and I may not receive a discharge of my debts.

n/a_____   handwritten signature and date_____
Signature of Attorney   Date   Signature of Debtor   Date
                                             (In a joint case, both spouses must sign.)

_____   handwritten signature and date_____
Name of Attorney   Signature of Joint Debtor (if any)   Date

DECLARATION AND SIGNATURE OF NON-ATTORNEY BANKRUPTCY PETITION PREPARER (See 11 U.S.C. § 110)

   I declare under penalty of perjury that: (1) I am a bankruptcy petition preparer as defined in 11 U.S.C. § 110; (2) I prepared this document for compensation and have provided the debtor with a copy of this document and the notices and information required under 11 U.S.C. §§ 110(b), 110(h), and 342(b); (3) if rules or guidelines have been promulgated pursuant to 11 U.S.C. § 110(h) setting a maximum fee for services chargeable by bankruptcy petition preparers, I have given the debtor notice of the maximum amount before preparing any document for filing for a debtor or accepting any fee from the debtor, as required under that section; and (4) I will not accept any additional money or other property from the debtor before the filing fee is paid in full.

_____   _____
Printed or Typed Name and Title, if any, of Bankruptcy Petition Preparer   Social-Security No. (Required by 11 U.S.C. § 110.)
If the bankruptcy petition preparer is not an individual, state the name, title (if any), address, and social-security number of the officer, principal, responsible person, or partner who signs the document.

_____
Address

x n/a_____   _____
Signature of Bankruptcy Petition Preparer   Date

Names and Social-Security numbers of all other individuals who prepared or assisted in preparing this document, unless the bankruptcy petition preparer is not an individual:

If more than one person prepared this document, attach additional signed sheets conforming to the appropriate Official Form for each person.
A bankruptcy petition preparer's failure to comply with the provisions of title 11 and the Federal Rules of Bankruptcy Procedure may result in fines or imprisonment or both. 11 U.S.C. § 110; 18 U.S.C. § 156.

B 3A (Official Form 3A) (12/07) - Cont.

UNITED STATES BANKRUPTCY COURT

In re _Mary Ellen and John Alan Smith_____,
                      Debtor

Case No. _supplied by clerk___

Chapter _7_____

ORDER APPROVING PAYMENT OF FILING FEE IN INSTALLMENTS

☐   IT IS ORDERED that the debtor(s) may pay the filing fee in installments on the terms proposed in the foregoing application.

☐   IT IS ORDERED that the debtor(s) shall pay the filing fee according to the following terms:

$ _____   Check one ☐ With the filing of the petition, or
                                        ☐ On or before _____

$ _____ on or before _____

$ _____ on or before _____

$ _____ on or before _____

☐   IT IS FURTHER ORDERED that until the filing fee is paid in full the debtor(s) shall not make any additional payment or transfer any additional property to an attorney or any other person for services in connection with this case.

BY THE COURT

Date: _____

_____
United States Bankruptcy Judge

Instructions for the Mailing List of Creditors' Names and Addresses

You will need to prepare a mailing list of all of your creditors' names and addresses in all bankruptcy courts, to be used by the court to provide official notifications to each creditor or security holder that you have listed on your bankruptcy schedules. However, each bankruptcy court has its own specific instructions and forms for preparing mailing lists. Be sure to check with your particular court clerk for any specific instructions for preparing mailing lists and any required verification form to be filed with your list.

Instructions for the Application for Waiver of the Chapter 7 Filing Fee For Individuals Who Cannot Pay the Filing Fee in Full or in Installments (Official Form 3B)

Page 1

This form is used to request a waiver of the payment of all of your filing fees. You have the right to request this under bankruptcy law. Whether you are granted the requested waiver depends on your financial ability to pay, as determined by the income and expenses that you have reported on other bankruptcy forms. To complete this form, you will need to have already completed *Schedule I (Current Income of Individual Debtor[s])* and attach a copy of it to this *Application*. You will also either need to have already completed *Schedules A (Real Property)*, *Schedule B (Personal Property)*, and *Schedule J (Current Expenditures of Individual Debtor[s])* or have the information regarding your expenses and assets available to list on this form. If these forms are available, you will need to attach a copy of each of them to this Application.

Court Name: Fill in the full name of the judicial district in which you will be filing (as listed on your *Voluntary Petition*).

In re: Fill in your full name (last name first) that you regularly use to sign checks, etc.

Case No.: Leave this line blank. The court clerk will assign you a case number.

Part A. Family Size and Income

Line #1: Here list the number of people in your household as you have listed on *Schedule I*. Include children that live at home and any dependants. Include your wife (unless you are separated and not filing a joint bankruptcy petition).

Line #2: Here insert the information from Line #16 of *Schedule I*.

Line #3: If any of the dependants that are listed in Line #1 above had income that is *not* listed in Line #2, list that amount here. If none, enter $0.

Line #4: Add Lines #2 and 3 and enter the total here.

Line #5: If you expect the amount on Line #4 to increase or decrease by more than 10 percent in the next 6 months, check the 'yes' box and explain. If not, check "no."

Part B. Monthly Expenses

Line #6: If you have completed *Schedule J (Current Expenditures of Individual Debtor[s])*, attach it to the application and list the amount from Line #18 of *Schedule J* on Line #6. If you have not completed *Schedule J*, estimate your total monthly expenses and enter it here.

Line #7: If you expect the amount on Line #7 to increase or decrease by more than 10 percent in the next 6 months, check the 'yes' box and explain. If not, check "no."

Part C. Real and Personal Property

Lines #8-11: If you have completed *Schedules A* and *B*, attach them to the *Application* and skip Lines #8-11. If you have not completed these schedules, estimate the following amounts:

Line #8: Cash that you have on hand as of the date you complete the *Application*.

Line #9: Any money that you have in any bank account of any kind. List the name of the bank or financial institution, the type of account and the amount in each account.

Page 2

Line #10: Here you must list the large items that you own: your home, any other real estate, any motor vehicles, and any large items of personal property (such as expensive jewelry, a boat, etc.). You don't have to list ordinary household furnishings or clothing.

Line #11: If anyone or any business or government body, owes you any money (such as back pay, tax refunds, loans, etc.) list it here.

Part D. Additional Information

Lines #12-16: You must also answer the next five questions regarding any payments that you have made for any type of bankruptcy services (Note: you do not need to list the purchase of this book as a bankruptcy service).

Page 3

Line #17: If you have previously filed for bankruptcy within the past eight years, list the case, year, location, and result here.

Line #18: Here you can list any other reasons that you may have why you are unable to pay the filing fee in installments (such as: inability to work due to sickness or accident, overwhelming expenses, no income, etc.).

Line #19: Finally, you declare that everything that you entered on this *Application* is true and correct and that you cannot pay the filing fee at all. Then you (and your co-debtor if filing jointly) must sign and date the form.

Declaration and Signature of Non Attorney Bankruptcy Petition Preparer: Enter *N/A*, unless you were assisted by a bankruptcy petition preparer.

Page 4: Order Approving Payment of Filing Fee in Installments

Court Name: Fill in the name and state of the bankruptcy court

In re: Fill in your full name (last name first) that you regularly use to sign checks.

Case No.: Leave this line blank. The court clerk will assign you a number.

Upon consideration . . . : Leave the rest of this form blank. It will be completed by the bankruptcy court judge if your request to pay the fee in installments is approved.

Note: The Bankruptcy Judge may order a brief hearing to determine your ability to pay the filing fee in installments. If so, it will be listed on the bottom of Page 2 of this form. If you fail to show up at this hearing, you will be required to pay the bankruptcy filing fee.

B 3B (Official Form 3B) (12/07) -- Cont.

UNITED STATES BANKRUPTCY COURT

In re: Mary & John Smith _____   Case No. _(supplied by clerk)____
          Debtor(s)   (if known)

APPLICATION FOR WAIVER OF THE CHAPTER 7 FILING FEE
FOR INDIVIDUALS WHO CANNOT PAY THE FILING FEE IN FULL OR IN INSTALLMENTS

Part A. Family Size and Income

1. Including yourself, your spouse, and dependents you have listed or will list on Schedule I (Current Income of Individual Debtors(s)), how many people are in your family? (Do not include your spouse if you are separated AND are not filing a joint petition.) ____2____

2. Restate the following information that you provided, or will provide, on Line 16 of Schedule I. Attach a completed copy of Schedule I, if it is available.

   Total Combined Monthly Income (Line 16 of Schedule I): $ _____2,616.00___

3. State the monthly net income, if any, of dependents included in Question 1 above. Do not include any income already reported in Item 2. If none, enter $0.

                                                                                                $_____

4. Add the "Total Combined Monthly Income" reported in Question 2 to your dependents' monthly net income from Question 3.

                                                                                                $_____2,616.00___

5. Do you expect the amount in Question 4 to increase or decrease by more than 10% during the next 6 months? Yes ___ No ✔

   If yes, explain.

Part B. Monthly Expenses

6. EITHER (a) attach a completed copy of Schedule J (Schedule of Monthly Expenses), and state your total monthly expenses reported on Line 18 of that Schedule, OR (b) if you have not yet completed Schedule J, provide an estimate of your total monthly expenses.

                                                                                                $_____3,974.00___

7. Do you expect the amount in Question 6 to increase or decrease by more than 10% during the next 6 months? Yes ___ No ✔
   If yes, explain.

Part C. Real and Personal Property

EITHER (1) attach completed copies of Schedule A (Real Property) and Schedule B (Personal Property), OR (2) if you have not yet completed those schedules, answer the following questions.

8. State the amount of cash you have on hand. $ _____ 90.00___

9. State below any money you have in savings, checking, or other accounts in a bank or other financial institution.

Bank or Other Financial Institution:	Type of Account such as savings, checking, CD:	Amount:
First Bank of Centerville	checking	$_____137.00___
_____	_____	$_____

B 3B (Official Form 3B) (12/07) -- Cont.

10. State below the assets owned by you. **Do not list ordinary household furnishings and clothing.**

Home

Address:

16 Main Street
Centerville, IL 61111

Value: $ _____ 148,000.00

Amount owed on mortgages and liens: $ _____ 137,000.00

Other real estate

Address:

Value: $ _____

Amount owed on mortgages and liens: $ _____

Motor vehicle

Model/Year: _____
2001 Honda Accord

Value: $ _____ 9,000.00

Amount owed: $ _____ 0.00

Motor vehicle

Model/Year: _____
1999 Chevy Pickup

Value: $ _____ 4,000.00

Amount owed: $ _____ 0.00

Other

Description _____
Misc. Tools

Value: $ _____ 1,800.00

Amount owed: $ _____ 0.00

11. State below any person, business, organization, or governmental unit that owes you money and the amount that is owed.

Name of Person, Business, or Organization that Owes You Money	Amount Owed
_____	$ _____
_____	$ _____

Part D. Additional Information.

12. Have you paid an **attorney** any money for services in connection with this case, including the completion of this form, the bankruptcy petition, or schedules? Yes ___ No ✔
    If yes, how much have you paid? $ _____

13. Have you promised to pay or do you anticipate paying an **attorney** in connection with your bankruptcy case? Yes ___ No ✔
    If yes, how much have you promised to pay or do you anticipate paying? $ _____

14. Have you paid **anyone other than an attorney** (such as a bankruptcy petition preparer, paralegal, typing service, or another person) any money for services in connection with this case, including the completion of this form, the bankruptcy petition, or schedules? Yes ___ No ✔
    If yes, how much have you paid? $ _____

15. Have you promised to pay or do you anticipate paying **anyone other than an attorney** (such as a bankruptcy petition preparer, paralegal, typing service, or another person) any money for services in connection with this case, including the completion of this form, the bankruptcy petition, or schedules? Yes ___ No ✔
    If yes, how much have you promised to pay or do you anticipate paying? $ _____

16. Has anyone paid an attorney or other person or service in connection with this case, on your behalf? Yes ___ No ✔

    If yes, explain.

B 3B (Official Form 3B) (12/07) -- Cont.

17. Have you previously filed for bankruptcy relief during the past eight years? Yes ___ No ✔

Case Number (if known)	Year filed	Location of filing	Did you obtain a discharge? (if known)
_____	_____	_____	Yes _____ No _____ Don't know _____
_____	_____	_____	Yes _____ No _____ Don't know _____

18. Please provide any other information that helps to explain why you are unable to pay the filing fee in installments.

19. I (we) declare under penalty of perjury that I (we) cannot currently afford to pay the filing fee in full or in installments and that the foregoing information is true and correct.

Executed on: 03/15/2008
     Date
    03/15/2008
     Date

       handwritten signature
        Signature of Debtor
       handwritten signature
        Signature of Codebtor

DECLARATION AND SIGNATURE OF BANKRUPTCY PETITION PREPARER (See 11 U.S.C. § 110)

I declare under penalty of perjury that: (1) I am a bankruptcy petition preparer as defined in 11 U.S.C. § 110; (2) I prepared this document for compensation and have provided the debtor with a copy of this document and the notices and information required under 11 U.S.C. §§ 110(b), 110(h), and 342(b); and (3) if rules or guidelines have been promulgated pursuant to 11 U.S.C. § 110(h) setting a maximum fee for services chargeable by bankruptcy petition preparers, I have given the debtor notice of the maximum amount before preparing any document for filing for a debtor or accepting any fee from the debtor, as required under that section.

_____
Printed or Typed Name and Title, if any, of Bankruptcy Petition Preparer   Social-Security No. (Required by 11 U.S.C. §110.)

If the bankruptcy petition preparer is not an individual, state the name, title (if any), address, and social-security number of the officer, principal, responsible person, or partner who signs the document.

_____

Address

x n/a
_____   _____
Signature of Bankruptcy Petition Preparer   Date

Names and Social-Security numbers of all other individuals who prepared or assisted in preparing this document, unless the bankruptcy petition preparer is not an individual:

If more than one person prepared this document, attach additional signed sheets conforming to the appropriate Official Form for each person.
A bankruptcy petition preparer's failure to comply with the provisions of title 11 and the Federal Rules of Bankruptcy Procedure may result in fines or imprisonment or both. 11 U.S.C. § 110; 18 U.S.C. § 156.

B 3B (Official Form 3B) (12/07) -- Cont.

UNITED STATES BANKRUPTCY COURT

Northern District of Illinois

In re: Mary & John Smith
      Debtor(s)

Case No.   (supplied by clerk)

ORDER ON DEBTOR'S APPLICATION FOR WAIVER OF THE CHAPTER 7 FILING FEE

Upon consideration of the debtor's "Application for Waiver of the Chapter 7 Filing Fee," the court orders that the application be:

[ ] GRANTED.

> This order is subject to being vacated at a later time if developments in the administration of the bankruptcy case demonstrate that the waiver was unwarranted.

[ ] DENIED.

> The debtor shall pay the chapter 7 filing fee according to the following terms:
>
> $ _____ on or before _____
>
> $ _____ on or before _____
>
> $ _____ on or before _____
>
> $ _____ on or before _____
>
> Until the filing fee is paid in full, the debtor shall not make any additional payment or transfer any additional property to an attorney or any other person for services in connection with this case.
>
> IF THE DEBTOR FAILS TO TIMELY PAY THE FILING FEE IN FULL OR TO TIMELY MAKE INSTALLMENT PAYMENTS, THE COURT MAY DISMISS THE DEBTOR'S CASE.

[ ] SCHEDULED FOR HEARING.

> A hearing to consider the debtor's "Application for Waiver of the Chapter 7 Filing Fee" shall be held on _____ at _____ am/pm at _____.
>   (address of courthouse)
>
> IF THE DEBTOR FAILS TO APPEAR AT THE SCHEDULED HEARING, THE COURT MAY DEEM SUCH FAILURE TO BE THE DEBTOR'S CONSENT TO THE ENTRY OF AN ORDER DENYING THE FEE WAIVER APPLICATION BY DEFAULT.

BY THE COURT:

DATE: _____

_____
United States Bankruptcy Judge

Instructions for Debtor's Certification of Completion of Instructional Course Concerning Personal Financial Management (Official Form 23)

Every individual debtor is required to file this form. If a joint petition has been filed, each spouse must complete a copy of this form. This form is used to certify that you have completed the required course in Personal Financial Management that must be taken before your bankruptcy will be granted. Appendix D provides a listing of the non-profit agencies that provide such education. Contact them to determine the details of the required course. There are some very limited waivers of this requirement: if you are disabled, or if you are on active military duty in a combat zone, or if there are no adequate instructional courses in your area. If you are unsure about the adequacy of the instructional courses in your jurisdiction, contact you local bankruptcy court clerk for information. *(Note: This form must be filed within 45 days of the first date set for the creditor's meeting in your case. This form is NOT related to the credit counseling course that you should have taken prior to filing for bankruptcy.)*

Court Name: Fill in the name and state of the bankruptcy court.

In re: Fill in your full name. (If filing jointly use both spouse's names)

Case No.: Leave this line blank. The court clerk will assign you a number.

Chapter: Here list "7" for Chapter 7.

First Box: Check this box if you have completed an instructional course. List your name, the date that you completed the course, and the name of the approved course provider and the certificate number you received from your course provider. *(Note: Each joint debtor must complete a separate form 23)*. Skip to the signature section.

Second Box: If you believe that you qualify for a waiver of this requirement, list your name (and any joint debtor's name) and check whichever one of the next three boxes that apply.

Signatures: You must sign and date in the spaces provided. If you are filing jointy, each spouse must fill out and sign a separate form.

B 23 (Official Form 23) (12/08)

UNITED STATES BANKRUPTCY COURT

Northern District of Illinois

In re Mary Ellen and John Alan Smith _____ ,
    Debtor

Case No. (supplied by clerk) _____

Chapter 7 _____

DEBTOR'S CERTIFICATION OF COMPLETION OF POSTPETITION INSTRUCTIONAL COURSE CONCERNING PERSONAL FINANCIAL MANAGEMENT

Every individual debtor in a chapter 7, chapter 11 in which § 1141(d)(3) applies, or chapter 13 case must file this certification. If a joint petition is filed, each spouse must complete and file a separate certification. Complete one of the following statements and file by the deadline stated below:

☑ I, Mary Ellen and John Alan Smith _____ , the debtor in the above-styled case, hereby
        (Printed Name of Debtor)
certify that on March 13, 2007 _____ *(Date)*, I completed an instructional course in personal financial management

provided by Bankruptcy Management, Inc. _____ , an approved personal financial
            (Name of Provider)
management provider.

Certificate No. *(if any)*: 0-1234 _____ .

☐ I, _____ , the debtor in the above-styled case, hereby
        (Printed Name of Debtor)
certify that no personal financial management course is required because of *[Check the appropriate box.]*:

☐ Incapacity or disability, as defined in 11 U.S.C. § 109(h);

☐ Active military duty in a military combat zone; or

☐ Residence in a district in which the United States trustee *(or bankruptcy administrator)* has determined that the approved instructional courses are not adequate at this time to serve the additional individuals who would otherwise be required to complete such courses.

Signature of Debtor: handwritten signature (each sign separate form if filing jointly)

Date: date signed

Instructions: Use this form only to certify whether you completed a course in personal financial management. (Fed. R. Bankr. P. 1007(b)(7).) Do NOT use this form to file the certificate given to you by your prepetition credit counseling provider and do NOT include with the petition when filing your case.

Filing Deadlines: In a chapter 7 case, file within 45 days of the first date set for the meeting of creditors under § 341 of the Bankruptcy Code. In a chapter 11 or 13 case, file no later than the last payment made by the debtor as required by the plan or the filing of a motion for a discharge under § 1141(d)(5)(B) or § 1328(b) of the Code. (See Fed. R. Bankr. P. 1007(c).)

Instructions for Notice to Individual Consumer Debtor under Section 342(b) of the Bankruptcy Code (Official Form B201)

This form is used to provide each debtor that has mainly consumer debts with an explanation of the services provided by Credit Counseling Agencies, as well as an explanation of the different types of bankruptcies that are available and the various crimes that arise in bankruptcy proceedings. You should read this form carefully.

Certificate of [Non-Attorney] Bankruptcy Petition Preparer: Enter *N/A*, unless you were assisted by a bankruptcy petition preparer.

Certificate of Debtor: Sign your name (any joint debtor must also sign) and date the form.

Case No.: Leave this line blank. The court clerk will assign you a number.

B 201 (04/09/06)

UNITED STATES BANKRUPTCY COURT

NOTICE TO INDIVIDUAL CONSUMER DEBTOR UNDER § 342(b)
OF THE BANKRUPTCY CODE

In accordance with § 342(b) of the Bankruptcy Code, this notice: (1) Describes briefly the services available from credit counseling services; (2) Describes briefly the purposes, benefits and costs of the four types of bankruptcy proceedings you may commence; and (3) Informs you about bankruptcy crimes and notifies you that the Attorney General may examine all information you supply in connection with a bankruptcy case. You are cautioned that bankruptcy law is complicated and not easily described. Thus, you may wish to seek the advice of an attorney to learn of your rights and responsibilities should you decide to file a petition. Court employees cannot give you legal advice.

1. Services Available from Credit Counseling Agencies

With limited exceptions, § 109(h) of the Bankruptcy Code requires that all individual debtors who file for bankruptcy relief on or after October 17, 2005, receive a briefing that outlines the available opportunities for credit counseling and provides assistance in performing a budget analysis. The briefing must be given within 180 days **before** the bankruptcy filing. The briefing may be provided individually or in a group (including briefings conducted by telephone or on the Internet) and must be provided by a nonprofit budget and credit counseling agency approved by the United States trustee or bankruptcy administrator. The clerk of the bankruptcy court has a list that you may consult of the approved budget and credit counseling agencies.

In addition, after filing a bankruptcy case, an individual debtor generally must complete a financial management instructional course before he or she can receive a discharge. The clerk also has a list of approved financial management instructional courses.

2. The Four Chapters of the Bankruptcy Code Available to Individual Consumer Debtors

Chapter 7: Liquidation ($245 filing fee, $39 administrative fee, $15 trustee surcharge: Total fee $299)
1. Chapter 7 is designed for debtors in financial difficulty who do not have the ability to pay their existing debts. Debtors whose debts are primarily consumer debts are subject to a "means test" designed to determine whether the case should be permitted to proceed under chapter 7. If your income is greater than the median income for your state of residence and family size, in some cases, creditors have the right to file a motion requesting that the court dismiss your case under § 707(b) of the Code. It is up to the court to decide whether the case should be dismissed.
2. Under chapter 7, you may claim certain of your property as exempt under governing law. A trustee may have the right to take possession of and sell the remaining property that is not exempt and use the sale proceeds to pay your creditors.
3. The purpose of filing a chapter 7 case is to obtain a discharge of your existing debts. If, however, you are found to have committed certain kinds of improper conduct described in the Bankruptcy Code, the court may deny your discharge and, if it does, the purpose for which you filed the bankruptcy petition will be defeated.
4. Even if you receive a general discharge, some particular debts are not discharged under the law. Therefore, you may still be responsible for most taxes and student loans; debts incurred to pay nondischargeable taxes; domestic support and property settlement obligations; most fines, penalties, forfeitures, and criminal restitution obligations; certain debts which are not properly listed in your bankruptcy papers; and debts for death or personal injury caused by operating a motor vehicle, vessel, or aircraft while intoxicated from alcohol or drugs. Also, if a creditor can prove that a debt arose from fraud, breach of fiduciary duty, or theft, or from a willful and malicious injury, the bankruptcy court may determine that the debt is not discharged.

Chapter 13: Repayment of All or Part of the Debts of an Individual with Regular Income ($235 filing fee, $39 administrative fee: Total fee $274)
1. Chapter 13 is designed for individuals with regular income who would like to pay all or part of their debts in installments over a period of time. You are only eligible for chapter 13 if your debts do not exceed certain dollar amounts set forth in the Bankruptcy Code.

B 201   Page 2

2. Under chapter 13, you must file with the court a plan to repay your creditors all or part of the money that you owe them, using your future earnings. The period allowed by the court to repay your debts may be three years or five years, depending upon your income and other factors. The court must approve your plan before it can take effect.

3. After completing the payments under your plan, your debts are generally discharged except for domestic support obligations; most student loans; certain taxes; most criminal fines and restitution obligations; certain debts which are not properly listed in your bankruptcy papers; certain debts for acts that caused death or personal injury; and certain long term secured obligations.

Chapter 11: **Reorganization ($1000 filing fee, $39 administrative fee: Total fee $1039)**

Chapter 11 is designed for the reorganization of a business but is also available to consumer debtors. Its provisions are quite complicated, and any decision by an individual to file a chapter 11 petition should be reviewed with an attorney.

Chapter 12: **Family Farmer or Fisherman ($200 filing fee, $39 administrative fee: Total fee $239)**

Chapter 12 is designed to permit family farmers and fishermen to repay their debts over a period of time from future earnings and is similar to chapter 13. The eligibility requirements are restrictive, limiting its use to those whose income arises primarily from a family-owned farm or commercial fishing operation.

3. Bankruptcy Crimes and Availability of Bankruptcy Papers to Law Enforcement Officials

A person who knowingly and fraudulently conceals assets or makes a false oath or statement under penalty of perjury, either orally or in writing, in connection with a bankruptcy case is subject to a fine, imprisonment, or both. All information supplied by a debtor in connection with a bankruptcy case is subject to examination by the Attorney General acting through the Office of the United States Trustee, the Office of the United States Attorney, and other components and employees of the Department of Justice.

WARNING: Section 521(a)(1) of the Bankruptcy Code requires that you promptly file detailed information regarding your creditors, assets, liabilities, income, expenses and general financial condition. Your bankruptcy case may be dismissed if this information is not filed with the court within the time deadlines set by the Bankruptcy Code, the Bankruptcy Rules, and the local rules of the court.

Certificate of [Non-Attorney] Bankruptcy Petition Preparer

I, the [non-attorney] bankruptcy petition preparer signing the debtor's petition, hereby certify that I delivered to the debtor this notice required by § 342(b) of the Bankruptcy Code.

_____   _____
Printed name and title, if any, of Bankruptcy Petition Preparer   Social Security number (If the bankruptcy petition
                                                 preparer is not an individual, state the Social Security
Address: number of the officer, principal, responsible person, or
_____   partner of the bankruptcy petition preparer.) (Required
                                                 by 11 U.S.C. § 110.)

X_____
Signature of Bankruptcy Petition Preparer or officer,
principal, responsible person, or partner whose Social
Security number is provided above.

Certificate of the Debtor

I (We), the debtor(s), affirm that I (we) have received and read this notice.

Mary Ellen and John Alan Smith   X_____ handwritten signature and date
_____   _____
Printed Name(s) of Debtor(s)   Signature of Debtor   Date

Case No. (if known) _(supplied by clerk)___   X_____ handwritten signature and date
                                               _____
                                               Signature of Joint Debtor (if any)   Date

Instructions for Statement of Current Monthly Income and Means Test Calculation (Official Form B22A)

This new form is designed to determine whether you can afford to repay your debts, rather than have them discharged in bankruptcy. It will be used to determine if you can proceed with a Chapter 7 bankruptcy or will be forced to proceed with a Chapter 13 bankruptcy and attempt to pay back your creditors. This form is used to compute your monthly income, then deduct monthly expenses, and see what is left over to pay off your creditors. This sounds fairly simple and straightforward. This form is anything but. It is perhaps the most complicated form that the federal government has ever devised for use by the general public. It makes income tax returns look like child's play. It was designed, in part, to discourage people from using bankruptcy to eliminate their debts. It is a very complex form, with very difficult mathematical calculations. You will need to obtain various IRS and Census data to complete this form. The data is available either from the clerk of your local Bankruptcy Court or online from the U.S. Bankruptcy Trustee Service. Please check each section of the form for the applicable website information needed to complete this form. Note that websites are often changed and that you may need to go to the main U.S. Trustee Service website home page to find the essential information. That home page is **www.usdoj.gov/ust/.**

To complete this form, you will need to have completed the following schedules: *Schedule D (Creditors Holding Secured Claims), Schedule E (Creditors Holding Unsecured Priority Claims), Schedule F (Creditors Holding Unsecured Nonpriority Claims), Schedule I (Current Income of Individual Debtor[s])* and *Schedule J (Current Expenditures of Individual Debtor[s])*. It will also be helpful to have your bankruptcy questionnaire completed and before you as you work on this form. Using your computer, TAB through the form and complete each line very carefully according to the instructions explained below.

Warning: This is a very, very complicated form and will be the most difficult part of the bankruptcy process. Please take your time and try not to get frustrated as you work through the instructions and complete this form. Read the instructions very carefully and reread them if you get confused. Unfortunately, this form is required of every individual debtor.

Final Note Regarding this Form: If you feel that this form is unnecessarily difficult to complete, you may wish to send a copy of this form to your local representatives of the U.S. Congress and ask them to try and complete this form. Don't send these instructions to help them figure it out, because neither the Department of Justice nor the federal Bankruptcy Courts have provided any instructions to complete this form.

In Re: Enter your full name. If you're filing jointly, include your spouse's name.

Case No.: Leave this blank if filed with your petition. The court clerk will assign you a case number.

The Presumption Arises or The Presumption Does Not Arise Box:
You do not fill this box in until the form is completed. Also, note that this box must be filled in by hand using an ink pen. The box cannot be filled in using your computer.

Part I. Exclusion for Disabled Veterans:

Line #1A: If you are a disabled veteran and your indebtedness occurred while you were on active duty or performing homeland defense activities, you are excused from completing the remainder of this form. Check the box in Line #1A and go to the instructions for Section VIII of the form (Signatures and Verification).

Line # 1 B: If your debts are NOT primarily consumer debts (that is, your debts are mostly business-related debts), check the box for this line and go directly to Part VIII and complete the verification section.

Part II. Calculation of Monthly Income for Section 707(b)(7) Exclusion

Line #2: Check the marital status box that applies and then complete the columns noted. Note that the figures that you enter for Lines # 3-11 must be averages of the last six months of your (and your spouses' if you check boxes [c] or [d]) income. Note that the information required for this section of the form is the same information required to complete your annual income tax returns. Also note that each figure that you enter in this section of the form should be the average monthly amount, calculated for the last 6 months. In other words, add up your last 6 months information and then divide by 6. This final number is what you should enter on each line. **Note**: If you are married and not separated, you must include information for your spouse in Column B, even if you are not filing jointly for bankruptcy.

Line #3: Include the monthly average of all of your wages, salary, overtime, bonuses and commissions.

Line #4: Here you list the total monthly average income and expenses from any and all businesses that you operate. On line (a) list your total average monthly business receipts over the last 6 months from all businesses. On line (b) list your total average monthly business expenses over the last 6 months from all businesses. Line (c) is your net business income from all businesses. Note that the form will do the subtraction for you.

Line #5: Here you list the total average monthly income and expenses from any real estate or rental property that you own. On line (a) list your total average monthly business receipts over the last 6 months. On line (b) list your total average monthly business expenses over the last 6 months. Line (c) is your net business income. Note that the form will do the subtraction for you.

Line #6: Here list all of your monthly average income from interest, dividends, and royalties, if any.

Line #7: Here list your average monthly income from any pensions or retirement accounts.

Line #8: If you have any household members who are dependants and they receive any income that is used to pay your household expenses, the average monthly amount should be listed here. This includes any child support or alimony payments that are paid for the purpose of household expenses. Do not include alimony or separate maintenance payments paid by your spouse if Column B is completed (because you are filing jointly with your spouse), but do include any other alimony or separate maintenance that is paid for household expenses.

Line #9: Here list your average monthly unemployment compensation. If you believe that your unemployment compensation is a Social Security benefit, do not include it in Columns A or B. Rather list the amount in the smaller box where noted.

Line #10: Here include your average monthly income from all other sources. You must specify the source and the amount in (a) and/or (b). If you have more than 2 additional sources, list the sources on a Continuation sheet. Do not include any Social Security disability income or any payments as a war crime or terrorism victim. Do not include alimony or separate maintenance payments paid by your spouse if Column B is completed (because you are filing jointly with your spouse), but do include any other alimony or separate maintenance that is paid for other than household expenses and that you have not already included under Line #8.

Line #11: Subtotal all of the amounts in Lines #3-10.

Line #12: Total the amounts in Column A and Column B and enter here.

Part III. Application of the Section 707(b)(2) Exclusion

Line #13: Multiply the amount on Line # 12 by the number 12

Line #14: On line (a) enter the state in which you reside. On line (b) enter the number of people in your household, including any dependants. To obtain the amount to enter on Line #14, you will either need to take that information to the local Bankruptcy Court clerk or go to the following website:

www.usdoj.gov/ust/eo/bapcpa/bci_data/median_income_table.htm

This will take you to a chart titled: Census Bureau Median Family Income by Family Size. Find your state of residence in the right-hand column and your family size along the top of this chart. Note that if your family size is over four, you must add an additional amount (that is found on the bottom of the page) to the income figure. Enter the income amount.

Line #15: If the amount listed on Line #13 is less than (or equal to) the amount on Line #14, check the first box and skip to Section VIII of this form (Signatures and Verification). Also go back to the first page of the form and check the box in the upper right hand corner that "The presumption does not arise." This is good news and means that you may continue with Chapter 7 bankruptcy and that you will not be forced to attempt to repay your creditors (or complete the rest of this form).

If the amount on Line #13 is greater than the amount on Line #14, then you must complete the rest of this form.

Part IV. Calculation of Current Monthly Income for Section 707(b)(2)

Line #16: Enter the amount from Line #12.

Line #17: If you are married, but not filing jointly (and thus you checked the box on Line #2[c]), you can deduct the amount of your spouse's average monthly income (from Line 11, Column B) that was not used for your or any dependant's household expenses. In other words, any of your spouse's income that was spent only on your spouse's separate expenses may be deducted from your income at this point. On lines (a), (b), and (c), you must specify your reason for excluding this income and the amount excluded. Reasons for excluding your spouse's income might be 'used to pay spouse's tax liability' or 'used to support other persons'. If you did not check the box on Line #2(c), you should enter zero here.

Line #18: Subtract the amount on Line #17 from the amount on Line #18 and enter here.

Part V. Calculation of Deductions Allowed Under Section 707(b)(2)

Subpart A: Deductions under the Standards of the Internal Revenue Service (IRS)

From the Current Monthly Income (that is now listed on Line #18), you are allowed to deduct certain expenses. Note however that you do not deduct your own expense amounts. Rather, in this next section, you must deduct various local and national average expense amounts as computed by the IRS. This makes the next section of this form very difficult to complete, as you must obtain the expense information for each line either from your local Bankruptcy Court clerk or from the U.S. Bankruptcy Trustee's website. If you do not have access to a computer that is online, you should go through the rest of the form and make a list of all of the information that you will need to obtain from your local Bankruptcy Court clerk. Once you have obtained the correct information, enter it where required.

Line #19A: To complete this line, you must obtain information for "National Standards for food, clothing, household supplies, personal care, and miscellaneous expenses," based on your family size and income level from your local Bankruptcy Court clerk or from the following website:

www.usdoj.gov/ust/eo/bapcpa/meanstesting.htm

(**Note** that Alaska and Hawaii have their own charts. Also note that the chart for Hawaii may be used for all U.S. Territories). On the main page, you will need to click on "Data Required for Completing Form 22A and Form 22C" and "GO". Then go down the page that appears to: #2. National Standards: Food Clothing & Other Items and click again. You will find charts for the number of members of your family. On your correct family size chart, find the column that indicates your income level (the amount shown on Line #12). At the bottom of this column, you will find the correct amount. (**Note**: if your family has more than 4 members, at the bottom of this page is a chart for "More Than Four Persons." Add this additional figure to your amount for each additional person in your family over four). Enter the figure that you obtain in the right hand column.

Line 19B: To complete this line, you must obtain information for "National Standards: health care," based on your family size and income level from your local Bankruptcy Court clerk or from the following website:

www.usdoj.gov/ust/eo/bapcpa/meanstesting.htm

(**Note** that Alaska and Hawaii have their own charts. Also note that the chart for Hawaii may be used for all U.S. Territories). On the main page, you will need to click on "Data Required for Completing Form 22A and Form 22C" and "GO". Then go down the page that appears to: # 3. National Standards: Out-of-Pocket Health Care Expenses. and click again. You will find a chart that notes the amount for health care costs for "Under 65" and for "65 and Older". Enter the correct figures in Lines 19B, Lines (a1), (b1), (c1) for household members under age 65 and in lines (a2), (b2), (c2) for household members who are 65 and older. To obtain the subtotal for Line (c1) you will need to multiply the amount in Line (a1) by the amount in Line (b1). To obtain the subtotal for Line (c2) you will need to multiply the amount in Line (a2) by the amount in Line (b2). Enter the total of Lines (c1) and (c2) in the far right hand column. (NOTE: The total number of household members (the sum of Lines (b1) and (b2)) must be the same as the number you entered earlier in Line 14B).

Line #20A: To complete this line, you must obtain information for "Local Standards: housing and utilities; non-mortgage expenses," based on your county of residence and family size from your local Bankruptcy Court clerk or from the following website:

www.usdoj.gov/ust/eo/bapcpa/meanstesting.htm

On the main page, you will need to click on "Data Required for Completing Form 22A and Form 22C" and "GO". Then go down the page that appears to #4(a) Local Housing and Utility and Expense Standards. Here enter your state of residence where indicated and click on "GO". You will be taken to a chart that has 'family size' across the top and 'county' down the side. Find the correct column and row and enter the "Non-mortgage" figure that you obtain.

Line #20B: This is a particularly complex line to complete. To complete this line, you must obtain information for "Local Standards housing and utilities; mortgage/rent expenses," based on your county of residence and family size from your local Bankruptcy Court clerk or from the following website:

www.usdoj.gov/ust/eo/bapcpa/meanstesting.htm

On the main page, you will need to click on "Data Required for Completing Form 22A and Form 22C" and "GO". Then go down the page that appears to #4(a) Local Housing and Utility and Expense Standards. Here enter your state of residence where indicated and click on "GO". You will be taken to a chart that has 'family size' across the top and 'county' down the side. Find the correct column and row and enter the "Mortgage/rent" figure that you obtain in the box on Line (a). To complete the box on Line (b), you must first determine how the amount of your average monthly mortgage payment. This is computed on Line #42 of this form.

Note: You will need to complete Line #42 out of the normal sequence of completing a normal form, but of course, this is anything but a normal form. On your form, use the TAB to move ahead to Line #42 and follow these instructions:

Line #42: This box is where you compute your mortgage and car payment deductions. A secured claim is a debt that is secured by collateral of some type. For most people, this is either just their home mortgage or, perhaps, a car loan, also. These debts will be listed on your Schedule D Creditors Holding Secured Claims. You will need to determine the total amount of payments for each debt for the next 60 months. Then you divide this total by 60 to determine the average future monthly payments that are due. For each creditor, on line (a), (b), and (c) list the name of the creditor, the property that is used as collateral, and the average monthly payment, and whether the payment includes taxes and/or insurance. For Line #42, total the amounts on (a), (b) and (c) and enter it.

To complete Line #20B(b), follow these additional instructions. Now, using your TAB, tab all the way through the form without filling out any more information, back to the beginning, and continue tabbing until you are back to Line #20B(b). Here on line (b) you enter any amounts listed on Line #42 for which your home is collateral, that is, the amounts of your average monthly mortgage payments. BUT, you must not enter an amount that is greater than the amount listed on Line (a). For Line (c), you subtract Line (b) from Line (a) and enter this amount in the right-hand column.

Line #21: On this line you may make an adjustment to the amount computed on Lines #20A and 20B if you believe that the method that the IRS used to determine the housing, utility, and rent expenses is not fair in your case. If so, state in simple terms why you should be allowed a higher deduction and enter the additional amount that you feel that you should be entitled to on Line #21. Reasons why you may feel that the amount is unfair may be that your actual utility costs are higher than the average amount that the IRS uses, or that your rent is higher than the average because you need to rent a home that is handicapped accessible, or some other reason that makes the average amounts unfair in your specific circumstances.

Line #22A: This is where the first of a three-part section where average transportation expenses are deducted. You are allowed this deduction even if you do not use public transportation and even if you do not own a car. Check the box that indicates the number of vehicles that you operate. Then you must obtain a figure for "Local Standards: transportation; vehicle operation/public transportation expense," from the clerk of your local Bankruptcy Court or from the following website:

www.usdoj.gov/ust/eo/bapcpa/meanstesting.htm

On the main page, you will need to click on "Data Required for Completing Form 22A and Form 22C" and "GO". Then go down the page that appears to #4 (b) Local Transportation Expense Standards. Here enter area of the country that you live in (for example: "Midwest census region") where indicated and click on "GO". (**Note**: if you are unsure which area you live in, pick the most likely region and click "GO" and the top of the chart will indicate which states are in that region.) You will be taken to a chart that has lists Metropolitan Statistical Areas and the counties that are included in those areas. Find the county that you live in if you are near a major city and go to the next chart down (the Operating Costs and Public Transportation Costs chart). If you do not live near a major city, go to that chart also. On this chart: if you found your county on the previous chart (Metropolitan Statistical Areas) go to that row, and enter the amount listed for the number of cars you own (or 'no car' if you do not own a car). If your county was not listed in the Metropolitan Statistical Areas chart, use the top line of this Operating Costs and Public Transportation Costs chart (that is just labeled with your region of the country, such as "Midwest region) to obtain your figure and enter it on Line #22A.

Line #22B: On this line you may make an adjustment to the amount computed on Line #22A if you believe that the method that the IRS used to determine the local transportation expenses is not fair in your case. If so, state in simple terms why you should be allowed a higher deduction and enter the additional amount that you feel that you should be entitled to on Line #21. Reasons why you may feel that the amount is unfair may be that your actual transportation costs are higher than the average amount that the IRS uses, or that your costs are higher than the average because you need handicapped accessible transport, or some other reason that makes the average amounts unfair in your specific circumstances.

Line #23: This is the second part of the transportation deduction. You are only allowed this deduction if you actually own and pay expenses for one or more cars. Check the box that indicates the number of vehicles that you operate and pay expenses for. Then you must obtain a figure for "Local Standards: transportation ownership/lease expenses Vehicle 1," from the clerk of your local Bankruptcy

Court or from the following website:

www.usdoj.gov/ust/eo/bapcpa/meanstesting.htm

On the main page, you will need to click on "Data Required for Completing Form 22A and Form 22C" and "GO". Then go down the page that appears to #4 (b): Local Standards. Find (b) Local Transportation Expense Standards. Here enter area of the country that you live in (for example: "Midwest census region") where indicated and click on "GO". (**Note**: if you are unsure which area you live in, pick the most likely region and click "GO" and the top of the chart will indicate which states are in that region.) You will be taken to a chart that has lists Metropolitan Statistical Areas and the counties that are included in those areas. Skip this chart and the next chart and go to the bottom of the page to the chart entitled "Ownership Costs." For your first car, enter the amount on Line (a). For Line (b), enter any amount of average monthly expenses that you filled in the boxes on Line #42 that are for car payments. BUT, you must not enter an amount on Line (b) that is greater than the amount on Line (a). Finally, subtract Line (b) from Line (a) and enter the amount.

Line #24: This is the third part of the transportation deduction. You will only complete this line if you checked the box for 2 or more vehicles under line #23. You complete this line just like Line #23 above. You must obtain a figure for "Local Standards: transportation ownership/lease expense Vehicle 2," from the clerk of your local Bankruptcy Court or from the following website:

www.usdoj.gov/ust/eo/bapcpa/meanstesting.htm

On the main page, you will need to click on "Data Required for Completing Form 22A and Form 22C" and "GO". Then go down the page that appears to #4 (b): Local Standards. Find (b) Local Transportation Expense Standards. Here enter area of the country that you live in (for example: "Midwest census region") where indicated and click on "GO". (**Note**: if you are unsure which area you live in, pick the most likely region and click "GO" and the top of the chart will indicate which states are in that region.) You will be taken to a chart that has lists Metropolitan Statistical Areas and the counties that are included in those areas. Skip this chart and the next chart and go to the bottom of the page to the chart entitled "Ownership Costs." For your second car, enter the amount on Line (a). For Line (b), enter any amount of average monthly expenses that you filled in the boxes on Line #42 that are for car payments. BUT, you must not enter an amount on Line (b) that is greater than the amount on Line (a). Finally, subtract Line (b) from Line (a) and enter the amount.

Line #25: Here list the average monthly amount of taxes that you pay (other than real estate taxes and sales taxes). This line would include income taxes, self employment taxes, Social Security taxes, and Medicare taxes, including those that are paid when you pay your income taxes and those that are taken out of your paycheck. You will need to figure the amount that will be due for the next 6 months and divide that amount by 6 and enter the monthly average here.

Line #26: Here is where you will list any other mandatory payroll deductions, such as mandatory retirement deductions, union dues, uniform costs etc. Remember this is the monthly average amount of such deductions. Don't include non-mandatory amounts such as voluntary donations to a retirement account.

Line #27: List your monthly average "term" life insurance premiums here if the insurance is on your life. Do not list insurance on your dependants or "whole" life, or any other type of insurance.

Line #28: Here you should list the monthly average of any court-ordered child support or alimony payments. If you have been ordered to make any other type of court-ordered payments, list that amount here also.

Line #29: This line is a listing for two separate expenses. First, you may list the monthly average cost that you pay for any education that is required by your employer. Second, you may list the average monthly cost of any educational services for a physically or mentally challenged child, if those services are not available through your public education system. Total the amounts and list here.

Line #30: List the average monthly amounts for any childcare expenses for your children (such as baby-sitting, daycare, nursery or preschool expenses), but not expenses for other educational expenses. Those will be entered on Line #38.

Line #31: List here the monthly average of all of your healthcare costs and/or helath savings account costs that are required for the health and welfare of yourself and your dependents that are not covered by insurance or a health care savings plan. Don't include health insurance costs. Those will be reported on Line #34.

Line #32: Enter the monthly average total cost of cell phones, pagers, call waiting, internet services, or special long distance services, as long as you can justify that these devices are for necessary for the health and welfare of you and your children. Cell phones, for example, can be considered necessary in order to be able to contact your children at home if you must be at work. Internet services may be necessary to be able to check on health issues on the internet if you or a child have any health care issues. Do not include expenses for your basic local telephone expenses or any amounts that may have been previously deducted.

Line #33: Total the amounts on Lines #19 through 33 and enter the amount here. This amount is your "Total Expenses Allowed under IRS Standards."

Subpart B: Additional Expense Deductions Under Section 707(b)

For this section do not list any expenses that you have listed previously.

Line #34: Here is where you will include your monthly average costs for any health or disability insurance or health savings account expenses for yourself, your spouse and/or your dependents. On Line (a) list monthly average costs for health insurance. Line (b) should have monthly average costs for any disability insurance, and Line (c) should be your monthly average contributions to any health savings accounts. Total the amounts and enter. If you do not actually spend this total amount state your total average monthly health expenses in the space noted (but not in the right hand column).

Line #35: Here you may list the monthly average expenses that you may incur for the care of any elderly, chronically ill or otherwise disabled. The person in question need not be a dependant for tax purposes, but must be a member of your household (that is, they must live with you).

Line #36: If you have any expenses to maintain the safety of your family against family violence under the Family Violence Prevention and Services Act, you should enter the monthly average here. **Note**: the nature of any expenses that you list here are required to be kept confidential by the Bankruptcy Court.

Line #37: Here you may include any home energy costs that exceed the amount that you entered on Line #20A for "non-mortgage expenses." Total your home energy costs for 6 months, divide that amount by 6. If that amount is greater than the amount listed on Line #20A, deduct the amount listed on Line #20A from your average monthly energy costs, and list that figure here.

(**Note**: you will need to provide your Bankruptcy Trustee with documentation [receipts and records] and also demonstrate that the amount claimed is reasonable).

Line #38: Here is where you will enter educational expenses for all of your children under the age of 18 for their attendance at any public or private elementary or secondary schools. Enter the average monthly expenses (up to the amount of $137.50 per child) that you actually pay for educational expenses. (**Note**: you will need to provide documentation [records and receipts] to your Bankruptcy Trustee that any educational expenses listed here are reasonable and not already included in the IRS Standards. You may wish to argue that educational expenses do not appear to be accounted for anywhere in the IRS Standards. Private or parochial school expenses may be listed here and should be considered reasonable and necessary).

Line #39: Here is where you may include any actual food and clothing costs that exceed the amount that you entered in Line 19A (which was taken from the IRS standards chart on the Internet). You may claim up to 5 percent more than the amount allowed in Line 19A.

[**Note**: you will need to provide your Bankruptcy Trustee with documentation [receipts and records] and also demonstrate that the amount claimed is reasonable).

Line #40: Here enter your monthly average continuing charitable contribution amount, such as monthly average church donations or a monthly average of any annual charitable contributions to non-profit organizations.

Line #41: Total Lines #34 through 40 here. This is total is your Additional Expense Deductions under Section 707(b).

Subpart C: Deductions for Debt Payment

Line #42: You should have already completed Line #42 when you worked on Line #20B. If not, refer back to the instructions under Line #20B to complete this line.

Line #43: If any of the debts that you listed on Line #42 are past due, and the property that is the collateral for the debt is used for your support or the support of your family, you will need to complete this line. Your main house or car should be considered as necessary for the support of your family. From each creditor for which an amount is past due, enter on lines (a), (b) or (c) the following: name of the creditor, a brief description of the property held as collateral (such as 'house' or 'car'). Finally, you will need to obtain from each creditor, the amount necessary to keep possession of the collateral and avoid foreclosure of your home or repossession of your car or other necessary property. This is the "cure amount". It may, in some cases, be necessary to pay off the entire loan to "cure" the default. In any event, divide the "cure amount" that was obtained from the creditor by 60 and enter it on the proper line in the last column of the chart. Total any amounts on Lines (a), (b) and (c) and enter it in the right-hand column.

Line #44: From your Schedule E Creditors Holding Unsecured Priority Claims (such as tax, child support, or alimony claims), you should find the total of all the claims. Divide this number by 60 and enter it here. (**Note:** do not include any current obligations, such as any that are already included on Line 28).

Line #45: Since you are attempting to file under Chapter 7, do not enter any amount for this line.

Line #46: Total the amounts on Lines #42 through 45 and enter here. This amount is your Total Deductions for Debt Payment.

Subpart D: Total Deductions Allowed under Section 707(b)(2)

Line #47: Here total the amounts on Lines #33, 41 and 46 and enter here.

Part VI. Determination of the Section 707(b)(2) Presumption

Line #48: Here enter the amount from Line #18.

Line #49: Here enter the amount from Line #47.

Line #50: Subtract the amount on Line #49 from the amount on Line #48 and enter here.

Line #51: Multiply the amount on Line #50 by 60 and enter the amount here.

Line #52: Using the amount shown on Line #51, determine which of the three boxes to check. If the amount is less than $6,575.00, check the first box and then go back to the first page of this form and check the box "The Presumption Does Not Arise." This is good news and means that you may proceed with a Chapter 7 Bankruptcy and have most of your debts eliminated. Do not complete Lines #53, 54, 55 and 56. Skip to Line #57 to sign and date this form.

If the amount on Line #51 is over $10,950.00, check the second box and then go back to the first page of this form and check the box "The Presumption Arises." This, unfortunately, is bad news and means that you will not be allowed to continue with a Chapter 7 bankruptcy and will be forced to proceed under Chapter 13 and develop a plan to pay off your creditors. At this point, you may wish to consult with a competent bankruptcy attorney and review your options. In any event, there is no point in filing for Chapter 7 Bankruptcy as you will not be allowed to proceed.

If the amount on Line #51 is between $6,575.00 and $10,950.00, you must complete Lines #53, 54, 55, and 56. Line #53: From your Schedule E Creditors Holding Unsecured Priority Claims, enter the total amount of all such claims on this line.

Line #54: Multiply the amount on Line #53 by 0.25.

Line #55: If the amount on Line #51 is less than the amount on Line #54, check the first box and then go back to the first page of this form and check the box "The Presumption Does Not Arise." This is good news and means that you may proceed with a Chapter 7 Bankruptcy and have most of your debts eliminated. Go to Line #57 to sign and date this form.

If the amount on Line #51 is equal to or greater than the amount on Line #54, check the second box and then go back to the first page of this form and check the box "The Presumption Arises." This, unfortunately, is bad news and means that you will not be allowed to continue with a Chapter 7 bankruptcy and will be forced to proceed under Chapter 13 and develop a plan to pay off your creditors. At this point, you may wish to consult with a competent bankruptcy attorney and review your options. In any event, there is no point in filing for Chapter 7 Bankruptcy as you will not be allowed to proceed.

Part VII: Additional Expense Claims

Line #56: If you checked the second box in Line #55, you may wish to enter any additional expenses that were not already accounted for in this form. However, if you checked the second box, you are very strongly advised to seek legal help before proceeding. It is unlikely that you will be allowed to proceed under Chapter 7 without the assistance of an attorney to help you with the process.

Part VII: Verification

Line #57: You should sign and date this form and have your spouse (if filing jointly) also sign and date this form. File this form with the clerk of the Bankruptcy Court when you file your other bankruptcy paperwork.

B 22A (Official Form 22A) (Chapter 7) (01/08)

In re	Mary Ellen & John Alan Smith
	Debtor(s)

Case Number: (supplied by clerk)
(If known)

According to the calculations required by this statement:

☐ **The presumption arises.**
☐ **The presumption does not arise.**

(Check the box as directed in Parts I, III, and VI of this statement)

CHAPTER 7 STATEMENT OF CURRENT MONTHLY INCOME AND MEANS-TEST CALCULATION

In addition to Schedules I and J, this statement must be completed by every individual chapter 7 debtor, whether or not filing jointly. Joint debtors may complete one statement only.

	Part I. EXCLUSION FOR DISABLED VETERANS AND NON-CONSUMER DEBTORS
1A	If you are a disabled veteran described in the Veteran's Declaration in this Part I, (1) check the box at the beginning of the Veteran's Declaration, (2) check the box for "The presumption does not arise" at the top of this statement, and (3) complete the verification in Part VIII. Do not complete any of the remaining parts of this statement. ☐ **Veteran's Declaration.** By checking this box, I declare under penalty of perjury that I am a disabled veteran (as defined in 38 U.S.C. § 3741(1)) whose indebtedness occurred primarily during a period in which I was on active duty (as defined in 10 U.S.C. § 101(d)(1)) or while I was performing a homeland defense activity (as defined in 32 U.S.C. §901(1)).
1B	If your debts are not primarily consumer debts, check the box below and complete the verification in Part VIII. Do not complete any of the remaining parts of this statement. ☐ **Declaration of non-consumer debts.** By checking this box, I declare that my debts are not primarily consumer debts.

	Part II. CALCULATION OF MONTHLY INCOME FOR § 707(b)(7) EXCLUSION
2	**Marital/filing status.** Check the box that applies and complete the balance of this part of this statement as directed. a. ☐ Unmarried. **Complete only Column A ("Debtor's Income") for Lines 3-11.** b. ☐ Married, not filing jointly, with declaration of separate households. By checking this box, debtor declares under penalty of perjury: "My spouse and I are legally separated under applicable non-bankruptcy law or my spouse and I are living apart other than for the purpose of evading the requirements of § 707(b)(2)(A) of the Bankruptcy Code." **Complete only Column A ("Debtor's Income") for Lines 3-11.** c. ☐ Married, not filing jointly, without the declaration of separate households set out in Line 2.b above. **Complete both Column A ("Debtor's Income") and Column B ("Spouse's Income") for Lines 3-11.** d. ☑ Married, filing jointly. **Complete both Column A ("Debtor's Income") and Column B ("Spouse's Income") for Lines 3-11.**

		Column A Debtor's Income	Column B Spouse's Income
	All figures must reflect average monthly income received from all sources, derived during the six calendar months prior to filing the bankruptcy case, ending on the last day of the month before the filing. If the amount of monthly income varied during the six months, you must divide the six-month total by six, and enter the result on the appropriate line.		
3	**Gross wages, salary, tips, bonuses, overtime, commissions.**	$ 2,000.00	$ 1,000.00

4	**Income from the operation of a business, profession or farm.** Subtract Line b from Line a and enter the difference in the appropriate column(s) of Line 4. If you operate more than one business, profession or farm, enter aggregate numbers and provide details on an attachment. Do not enter a number less than zero. **Do not include any part of the business expenses entered on Line b as a deduction in Part V.**			
	a.	Gross receipts	$ 1,000.00	
	b.	Ordinary and necessary business expenses	$ 300.00	
	c.	Business income	Subtract Line b from Line a	$ 700.00	$
5	**Rent and other real property income.** Subtract Line b from Line a and enter the difference in the appropriate column(s) of Line 5. Do not enter a number less than zero. **Do not include any part of the operating expenses entered on Line b as a deduction in Part V.**			
	a.	Gross receipts	$ 500.00	
	b.	Ordinary and necessary operating expenses	$ 100.00	
	c.	Rent and other real property income	Subtract Line b from Line a	$ 400.00	$
6	**Interest, dividends and royalties.**		$	$
7	**Pension and retirement income.**		$	$
8	**Any amounts paid by another person or entity, on a regular basis, for the household expenses of the debtor or the debtor's dependents, including child support paid for that purpose.** Do not include alimony or separate maintenance payments or amounts paid by your spouse if Column B is completed.		$	$
9	**Unemployment compensation.** Enter the amount in the appropriate column(s) of Line 9. However, if you contend that unemployment compensation received by you or your spouse was a benefit under the Social Security Act, do not list the amount of such compensation in Column A or B, but instead state the amount in the space below: Unemployment compensation claimed to be a benefit under the Social Security Act Debtor $ _____ Spouse $ _____		$	$
10	**Income from all other sources.** Specify source and amount. If necessary, list additional sources on a separate page. **Do not include alimony or separate maintenance payments paid by your spouse if Column B is completed, but include all other payments of alimony or separate maintenance.** Do not include any benefits received under the Social Security Act or payments received as a victim of a war crime, crime against humanity, or as a victim of international or domestic terrorism.			
	a.		$ 200.00	
	b.		$	
	Total and enter on Line 10		$	$ 200.00
11	**Subtotal of Current Monthly Income for § 707(b)(7).** Add Lines 3 thru 10 in Column A, and, if Column B is completed, add Lines 3 through 10 in Column B. Enter the total(s).		$ 3,100.00	$ 1,200.00
12	**Total Current Monthly Income for § 707(b)(7).** If Column B has been completed, add Line 11, Column A to Line 11, Column B, and enter the total. If Column B has not been completed, enter the amount from Line 11, Column A.			$ 4,300.00

Part III. APPLICATION OF § 707(b)(7) EXCLUSION

13	**Annualized Current Monthly Income for § 707(b)(7).** Multiply the amount from Line 12 by the number 12 and enter the result.	$ 51,600.00

14	**Applicable median family income.** Enter the median family income for the applicable state and household size. (This information is available by family size at www.usdoj.gov/ust/ or from the clerk of the bankruptcy court.) a. Enter debtor's state of residence: __Illinois__ b. Enter debtor's household size: _____2	$ 39,755.00

15	**Application of Section 707(b)(7).** Check the applicable box and proceed as directed. ☐ **The amount on Line 13 is less than or equal to the amount on Line 14.** Check the box for "The presumption does not arise" at the top of page 1 of this statement, and complete Part VIII; do not complete Parts IV, V, VI or VII. ☑ **The amount on Line 13 is more than the amount on Line 14.** Complete the remaining parts of this statement.

Complete Parts IV, V, VI, and VII of this statement only if required. (See Line 15.)

Part IV. CALCULATION OF CURRENT MONTHLY INCOME FOR § 707(b)(2)

16	**Enter the amount from Line 12.**	$ 4,300.00
17	**Marital adjustment.** If you checked the box at Line 2.c, enter on Line 17 the total of any income listed in Line 11, Column B that was NOT paid on a regular basis for the household expenses of the debtor or the debtor's dependents. Specify in the lines below the basis for excluding the Column B income (such as payment of the spouse's tax liability or the spouse's support of persons other than the debtor or the debtor's dependents) and the amount of income devoted to each purpose. If necessary, list additional adjustments on a separate page. If you did not check box at Line 2.c, enter zero. <table><tr><td>a.</td><td></td><td>$</td></tr><tr><td>b.</td><td></td><td>$</td></tr><tr><td>c.</td><td></td><td>$</td></tr></table> Total and enter on Line 17.	$ 200.00
18	**Current monthly income for § 707(b)(2).** Subtract Line 17 from Line 16 and enter the result.	$ 4,100.00

Part V. CALCULATION OF DEDUCTIONS FROM INCOME

Subpart A: Deductions under Standards of the Internal Revenue Service (IRS)

19A	**National Standards: food, clothing and other items.** Enter in Line 19A the "Total" amount from IRS National Standards for Food, Clothing and Other Items for the applicable household size. (This information is available at www.usdoj.gov/ust/ or from the clerk of the bankruptcy court.)	$ 857.00
19B	**National Standards: health care.** Enter in Line a1 below the amount from IRS National Standards for Out-of-Pocket Health Care for persons under 65 years of age, and in Line a2 the IRS National Standards for Out-of-Pocket Health Care for persons 65 years of age or older. (This information is available at www.usdoj.gov/ust/ or from the clerk of the bankruptcy court.) Enter in Line b1 the number of members of your household who are under 65 years of age, and enter in Line b2 the number of members of your household who are 65 years of age or older. (The total number of household members must be the same as the number stated in Line 14b.) Multiply Line a1 by Line b1 to obtain a total amount for household members under 65, and enter the result in Line c1. Multiply Line a2 by Line b2 to obtain a total amount for household members 65 and older, and enter the result in Line c2. Add Lines c1 and c2 to obtain a total health care amount, and enter the result in Line 19B. <table><tr><td colspan="3">Household members under 65 years of age</td><td colspan="3">Household members 65 years of age or older</td></tr><tr><td>a1.</td><td>Allowance per member</td><td>57.00</td><td>a2.</td><td>Allowance per member</td><td></td></tr><tr><td>b1.</td><td>Number of members</td><td>2</td><td>b2.</td><td>Number of members</td><td></td></tr><tr><td>c1.</td><td>Subtotal</td><td>114.00</td><td>c2.</td><td>Subtotal</td><td></td></tr></table>	$ 114.00

B 22A (Official Form 22A) (Chapter 7) (01/08)   4

20A	**Local Standards: housing and utilities; non-mortgage expenses.** Enter the amount of the IRS Housing and Utilities Standards; non-mortgage expenses for the applicable county and household size. (This information is available at www.usdoj.gov/ust/ or from the clerk of the bankruptcy court).			$	301.00

20B	**Local Standards: housing and utilities; mortgage/rent expense.** Enter, in Line a below, the amount of the IRS Housing and Utilities Standards; mortgage/rent expense for your county and household size (this information is available at www.usdoj.gov/ust/ or from the clerk of the bankruptcy court); enter on Line b the total of the Average Monthly Payments for any debts secured by your home, as stated in Line 42; subtract Line b from Line a and enter the result in Line 20B. **Do not enter an amount less than zero.**				
	a.	IRS Housing and Utilities Standards; mortgage/rental expense	$ 611.00		
	b.	Average Monthly Payment for any debts secured by your home, if any, as stated in Line 42	$		
	c.	Net mortgage/rental expense	Subtract Line b from Line a.	$	611.00

21	**Local Standards: housing and utilities; adjustment.** If you contend that the process set out in Lines 20A and 20B does not accurately compute the allowance to which you are entitled under the IRS Housing and Utilities Standards, enter any additional amount to which you contend you are entitled, and state the basis for your contention in the space below: _____ _____ _____		$

22A	**Local Standards: transportation; vehicle operation/public transportation expense.** You are entitled to an expense allowance in this category regardless of whether you pay the expenses of operating a vehicle and regardless of whether you use public transportation. Check the number of vehicles for which you pay the operating expenses or for which the operating expenses are included as a contribution to your household expenses in Line 8. ☐ 0 ☐ 1 ☑ 2 or more. If you checked 0, enter on Line 22A the "Public Transportation" amount from IRS Local Standards: Transportation. If you checked 1 or 2 or more, enter on Line 22A the "Operating Costs" amount from IRS Local Standards: Transportation for the applicable number of vehicles in the applicable Metropolitan Statistical Area or Census Region. (These amounts are available at www.usdoj.gov/ust/ or from the clerk of the bankruptcy court.)	$ 336.00

22B	**Local Standards: transportation; additional public transportation expense.** If you pay the operating expenses for a vehicle and also use public transportation, and you contend that you are entitled to an additional deduction for your public transportation expenses, enter on Line 22B the "Public Transportation" amount from IRS Local Standards: Transportation. (This amount is available at www.usdoj.gov/ust/ or from the clerk of the bankruptcy court.)	$

23	**Local Standards: transportation ownership/lease expense; Vehicle 1.** Check the number of vehicles for which you claim an ownership/lease expense. (You may not claim an ownership/lease expense for more than two vehicles.) ☐ 1 ☐ 2 or more. Enter, in Line a below, the "Ownership Costs" for "One Car" from the IRS Local Standards: Transportation (available at www.usdoj.gov/ust/ or from the clerk of the bankruptcy court); enter in Line b the total of the Average Monthly Payments for any debts secured by Vehicle 1, as stated in Line 42; subtract Line b from Line a and enter the result in Line 23. **Do not enter an amount less than zero.**				
	a.	IRS Transportation Standards, Ownership Costs	$ 475.00		
	b.	Average Monthly Payment for any debts secured by Vehicle 1, as stated in Line 42	$ 250.00		
	c.	Net ownership/lease expense for Vehicle 1	Subtract Line b from Line a.	$	225.00

B 22A (Official Form 22A) (Chapter 7) (01/08)   5

24	**Local Standards: transportation ownership/lease expense; Vehicle 2.** Complete this Line only if you checked the "2 or more" Box in Line 23. Enter, in Line a below, the "Ownership Costs" for "One Car" from the IRS Local Standards: Transportation (available at www.usdoj.gov/ust/ or from the clerk of the bankruptcy court); enter in Line b the total of the Average Monthly Payments for any debts secured by Vehicle 2, as stated in Line 42; subtract Line b from Line a and enter the result in Line 24. **Do not enter an amount less than zero.**		
	a.	IRS Transportation Standards, Ownership Costs	$ 338.00
	b.	Average Monthly Payment for any debts secured by Vehicle 2, as stated in Line 42	$
	c.	Net ownership/lease expense for Vehicle 2	Subtract Line b from Line a. $ 338.00
25	**Other Necessary Expenses: taxes.** Enter the total average monthly expense that you actually incur for all federal, state and local taxes, other than real estate and sales taxes, such as income taxes, self-employment taxes, social-security taxes, and Medicare taxes. **Do not include real estate or sales taxes.**		$ 156.00
26	**Other Necessary Expenses: involuntary deductions for employment.** Enter the total average monthly payroll deductions that are required for your employment, such as retirement contributions, union dues, and uniform costs. **Do not include discretionary amounts, such as voluntary 401(k) contributions.**		$ 129.00
27	**Other Necessary Expenses: life insurance.** Enter total average monthly premiums that you actually pay for term life insurance for yourself. **Do not include premiums for insurance on your dependents, for whole life or for any other form of insurance.**		$ 112.00
28	**Other Necessary Expenses: court-ordered payments.** Enter the total monthly amount that you are required to pay pursuant to the order of a court or administrative agency, such as spousal or child support payments. **Do not include payments on past due obligations included in Line 44.**		$
29	**Other Necessary Expenses: education for employment or for a physically or mentally challenged child.** Enter the total average monthly amount that you actually expend for education that is a condition of employment and for education that is required for a physically or mentally challenged dependent child for whom no public education providing similar services is available.		$
30	**Other Necessary Expenses: childcare.** Enter the total average monthly amount that you actually expend on childcare—such as baby-sitting, day care, nursery and preschool. **Do not include other educational payments.**		$
31	**Other Necessary Expenses: health care.** Enter the total average monthly amount that you actually expend on health care that is required for the health and welfare of yourself or your dependents, that is not reimbursed by insurance or paid by a health savings account, and that is in excess of the amount entered in Line 19B. **Do not include payments for health insurance or health savings accounts listed in Line 34.**		$ 89.00
32	**Other Necessary Expenses: telecommunication services.** Enter the total average monthly amount that you actually pay for telecommunication services other than your basic home telephone and cell phone service—such as pagers, call waiting, caller id, special long distance, or internet service—to the extent necessary for your health and welfare or that of your dependents. **Do not include any amount previously deducted.**		$ 45.00
33	**Total Expenses Allowed under IRS Standards.** Enter the total of Lines 19 through 32.		$ 3,199.00

Subpart B: Additional Living Expense Deductions

Note: Do not include any expenses that you have listed in Lines 19-32

34	**Health Insurance, Disability Insurance, and Health Savings Account Expenses.** List the monthly expenses in the categories set out in lines a-c below that are reasonably necessary for yourself, your spouse, or your dependents.		
	a.	Health Insurance	$ 221.00
	b.	Disability Insurance	$
	c.	Health Savings Account	$

	Total and enter on Line 34	$ 221.00
	If you do not actually expend this total amount, state your actual total average monthly expenditures in the space below: $ _____	

35	**Continued contributions to the care of household or family members.** Enter the total average actual monthly expenses that you will continue to pay for the reasonable and necessary care and support of an elderly, chronically ill, or disabled member of your household or member of your immediate family who is unable to pay for such expenses.	$
36	**Protection against family violence.** Enter the total average reasonably necessary monthly expenses that you actually incurred to maintain the safety of your family under the Family Violence Prevention and Services Act or other applicable federal law. The nature of these expenses is required to be kept confidential by the court.	$
37	**Home energy costs.** Enter the total average monthly amount, in excess of the allowance specified by IRS Local Standards for Housing and Utilities, that you actually expend for home energy costs. **You must provide your case trustee with documentation of your actual expenses, and you must demonstrate that the additional amount claimed is reasonable and necessary.**	$
38	**Education expenses for dependent children less than 18.** Enter the total average monthly expenses that you actually incur, not to exceed $137.50 per child, for attendance at a private or public elementary or secondary school by your dependent children less than 18 years of age. **You must provide your case trustee with documentation of your actual expenses, and you must explain why the amount claimed is reasonable and necessary and not already accounted for in the IRS Standards.**	$
39	**Additional food and clothing expense.** Enter the total average monthly amount by which your food and clothing expenses exceed the combined allowances for food and clothing (apparel and services) in the IRS National Standards, not to exceed 5% of those combined allowances. (This information is available at www.usdoj.gov/ust/ or from the clerk of the bankruptcy court.) **You must demonstrate that the additional amount claimed is reasonable and necessary.**	$ 31.00
40	**Continued charitable contributions.** Enter the amount that you will continue to contribute in the form of cash or financial instruments to a charitable organization as defined in 26 U.S.C. § 170(c)(1)-(2).	$ 80.00
41	**Total Additional Expense Deductions under § 707(b).** Enter the total of Lines 34 through 40	$ 332.00

Subpart C: Deductions for Debt Payment

B 22A (Official Form 22A) (Chapter 7) (01/08)   7

42	**Future payments on secured claims.** For each of your debts that is secured by an interest in property that you own, list the name of the creditor, identify the property securing the debt, state the Average Monthly Payment, and check whether the payment includes taxes or insurance. The Average Monthly Payment is the total of all amounts scheduled as contractually due to each Secured Creditor in the 60 months following the filing of the bankruptcy case, divided by 60. If necessary, list additional entries on a separate page. Enter the total of the Average Monthly Payments on Line 42.				

	Name of Creditor	Property Securing the Debt	Average Monthly Payment	Does payment include taxes or insurance?
a.	Car Lot Inc.	2000 Chevy Nova	$ 250.00	☑ yes ☐ no
b.			$	☐ yes ☐ no
c.			$	☐ yes ☐ no
			Total: Add Lines a, b and c.	

		$ 250.00

43	**Other payments on secured claims.** If any of debts listed in Line 42 are secured by your primary residence, a motor vehicle, or other property necessary for your support or the support of your dependents, you may include in your deduction 1/60th of any amount (the "cure amount") that you must pay the creditor in addition to the payments listed in Line 42, in order to maintain possession of the property. The cure amount would include any sums in default that must be paid in order to avoid repossession or foreclosure. List and total any such amounts in the following chart. If necessary, list additional entries on a separate page.		

	Name of Creditor	Property Securing the Debt	1/60th of the Cure Amount
a.			$
b.			$
c.			$
		Total: Add Lines a, b and c	$

44	**Payments on prepetition priority claims.** Enter the total amount, divided by 60, of all priority claims, such as priority tax, child support and alimony claims, for which you were liable at the time of your bankruptcy filing. **Do not include current obligations, such as those set out in Line 28.**	$ 185.00

45	**Chapter 13 administrative expenses.** If you are eligible to file a case under chapter 13, complete the following chart, multiply the amount in line a by the amount in line b, and enter the resulting administrative expense.	

a.	Projected average monthly chapter 13 plan payment.	$	
b.	Current multiplier for your district as determined under schedules issued by the Executive Office for United States Trustees. (This information is available at www.usdoj.gov/ust/ or from the clerk of the bankruptcy court.)	x	
c.	Average monthly administrative expense of chapter 13 case	Total: Multiply Lines a and b	$

46	**Total Deductions for Debt Payment.** Enter the total of Lines 42 through 45.	$ 435.00

Subpart D: Total Deductions from Income

47	**Total of all deductions allowed under § 707(b)(2).** Enter the total of Lines 33, 41, and 46.	$ 3,996.00

	Part VI. DETERMINATION OF § 707(b)(2) PRESUMPTION		
48	Enter the amount from Line 18 (Current monthly income for § 707(b)(2))	$	4,100.00
49	Enter the amount from Line 47 (Total of all deductions allowed under § 707(b)(2))	$	3,966.00
50	Monthly disposable income under § 707(b)(2). Subtract Line 49 from Line 48 and enter the result	$	134.00
51	60-month disposable income under § 707(b)(2). Multiply the amount in Line 50 by the number 60 and enter the result.	$	8,040.00
52	**Initial presumption determination.** Check the applicable box and proceed as directed. ☐ **The amount on Line 51 is less than $6,575** Check the box for "The presumption does not arise" at the top of page 1 of this statement, and complete the verification in Part VIII. Do not complete the remainder of Part VI. ☐ **The amount set forth on Line 51 is more than $10,950.** Check the box for "The presumption arises" at the top of page 1 of this statement, and complete the verification in Part VIII. You may also complete Part VII. Do not complete the remainder of Part VI. ☑ **The amount on Line 51 is at least $6,575, but not more than $10,950.** Complete the remainder of Part VI (Lines 53 through 55).		
53	Enter the amount of your total non-priority unsecured debt	$	34,987.00
54	Threshold debt payment amount. Multiply the amount in Line 53 by the number 0.25 and enter the result.	$	8,746.75
55	**Secondary presumption determination.** Check the applicable box and proceed as directed. ☐ **The amount on Line 51 is less than the amount on Line 54.** Check the box for "The presumption does not arise" at the top of page 1 of this statement, and complete the verification in Part VIII. ☐ **The amount on Line 51 is equal to or greater than the amount on Line 54.** Check the box for "The presumption arises" at the top of page 1 of this statement, and complete the verification in Part VIII. You may also complete Part VII.		

	Part VII: ADDITIONAL EXPENSE CLAIMS		
56	**Other Expenses.** List and describe any monthly expenses, not otherwise stated in this form, that are required for the health and welfare of you and your family and that you contend should be an additional deduction from your current monthly income under § 707(b)(2)(A)(ii)(I). If necessary, list additional sources on a separate page. All figures should reflect your average monthly expense for each item. Total the expenses.		

	Expense Description	Monthly Amount
a.		$
b.		$
c.		$
	Total: Add Lines a, b and c	$

	Part VIII: VERIFICATION
57	I declare under penalty of perjury that the information provided in this statement is true and correct *(If this is a joint case, both debtors must sign.)* Date: 03/15/2008 Signature: handwritten signature (Debtor) Date: 03/15/2008 Signature: handwritten signature (Joint Debtor, if any)

Chapter 6

Completing Your Bankruptcy

Once you have completed filling in your official bankruptcy forms, you are ready to complete your bankruptcy. There are five basic steps left. First, you must complete a credit counseling course prior to filing your bankruptcy paperwork. Then, you must file the original and copies of your complete set of papers with the bankruptcy court in your area and pay the required fees. Next, you will be required to attend a creditors' meeting and surrender any non-exempt property. Then, before a bankruptcy judge will grant your discharge, you must complete a personal financial management course. Finally, you will receive a discharge in bankruptcy which will officially eliminate your dischargeable debts and leave you with full possession of your exempt property. These five steps are not difficult to complete. From start to finish, the entire process will take around four to six months to complete. You may wish to review the two checklists located at the end of Chapter 2 for an overview of the needed actions and the necessary items to file.

Filing Your Bankruptcy Papers

There are several steps you should take prior to actually filing your papers with the bankruptcy court.

Complete a Credit Counseling Course: Consult the listing of approved credit counseling agencies in Appendix C. You may also wish to check for updates on this listing that are posted on the U.S. Bankruptcy Trustee Service website (the website address is shown in Appendix C). Contact the agency that you have chosen and complete the required course prior to filing your *Voluntary Petition* and other paperwork with the Bankruptcy Court. You will certify that you have completed such course on your V*oluntary Petition*.

Determine Which Bankruptcy Court: You should determine which bankruptcy court is the correct court for you to use. Appendix B contains a listing of the names, addresses, and phone numbers of all of the federal bankruptcy courts. You should file your bankruptcy papers in the federal district where you have lived or conducted your business for the last six months. If you are in doubt as to which court, call and ask the clerk of the bankruptcy court. Although court employees are prohibited from giving you legal advice, they should be able to answer basic informational questions.

Contact the Bankruptcy Court Clerk: You will also need to contact the clerk of your local bankruptcy court to determine if there are any additional local forms which may be required. The official forms in this book are acceptable in all bankruptcy courts in the United States. However, each federal district can also require its own local forms for organizational purposes. These generally consist of cover sheets or other forms to assist the court employees in filing the forms. When you check with the court clerk, you will also need to ask how many copies of your bankruptcy papers will be required. You will generally be required to file the original and at least two sets of photocopies of all of your papers. In addition, you will need to have a copy for yourself. Also, ask the court clerk for a list of the order in which they prefer the papers to be filed. If no particular order is required, file your papers with the cover sheet first and then in the order listed on your cover sheet.

Emergency Filing: If you have decided to pursue an emergency filing, you will only need to file your *Voluntary Petition*, any additional required local court forms (check with the court clerk), and a complete *Mailing List* with your creditors' names

> **☼ Toolkit Tip!**
>
> You will need to check with the Clerk of the proper Bankruptcy Court regarding any additional forms that may be necessary. A local cover sheet may be required for filing your paperwork.

and addresses with verification. You will also need to either pay the filing fees in full or file an application to pay your filing fee in installments, if you desire. You will have 15 days to file all of the additional required forms. If you miss the 15-day deadline, your case will likely be dismissed and you won't be able to file again for six months. You may also be unable to discharge the debts you owed at the time of your emergency filing. Follow the rest of the instructions for filing your forms.

Check Your Papers Carefully: Go over each of the official documents which you have filled in. Carefully check every item for accuracy, particularly the names and addresses of your creditors. These names and addresses will be used for notifying the creditors of your bankruptcy. If the creditors are not notified properly, your debt to them may not be erased by your bankruptcy. Your creditors must have an opportunity to attend the creditors' meeting or challenge your bankruptcy (although this seldom happens). Also be very certain that you have included every item of property that you own and every debt you owe, regardless how small. Check also that each continuation sheet that you may have used is properly completed. Any required local forms should also be filled in and checked.

Toolkit Tip!

Make certain that you (and your spouse if you are filing jointly) have signed the originals of each of the required forms where indicated.

Once you have determined that all of your forms are neatly and properly filled in, you should sign and date the originals of each form where indicated. If you are filing jointly, your spouse must also sign the forms. After signing, you should make certain that you have all of the sheets in proper order. Where indicated on each form, note if any continuation sheets are included. *Schedules D, E, F* and your *Statement of Financial Affairs* have lines on the lower left-hand side of their first page for this information. On your *Summary of Schedules*, note the number of total pages you are filing.

Make Copies of Your Bankruptcy Papers: You will now need to make several copies of your complete set of bankruptcy papers. Check with the court clerk to determine how many copies are required to be filed. Using your original, you will need to make the required number of copies plus an additional one for yourself. Your additional copy should be taken with you to the court when you file all of your papers. Have the court clerk stamp this copy with a dated "Filed" stamp to indicate that you have filed your bankruptcy papers. All copies and the original of your bankruptcy papers should be two-hole punched at the top. You can have a quick-print shop do the copying and hole punching if you desire. Be certain that you have your forms in the correct order. If you have debts secured by property listed on *Schedule D* and you are filing a *Chapter 7 Individual Debtor's Statement of Intention* for those debts, you will need to also make an additional copy of your *Chapter 7 Individual Debtor's Statement of Intention* for each creditor listed on this form and one for the bankruptcy trustee. Please see "Sending Your *Chapter 7 Individual Debtor's Statement of Intention*" on the next page for further instructions. Note: you will not file your *Debtor's Certification of Completion of Instructional Course Concerning Personal Financial Management* (Official Form 23) until you have actually completed such a course.

File Your Papers and Pay Your Fees: You should now either mail the papers listed below or go in person to the correct bankruptcy court armed with the following items:

> ⚡ **Warning!**
> Make certain that all of the information on your forms as up-to-date as possible before you file your paperwork.

- The complete set of the originals of all of your official bankruptcy forms (except your *Chapter 7 Individual Debtor's Statement of Intention* and your *Debtor's Certification of Completion of Instructional Course Concerning Personal Financial Management* (Official Form 23))

- The required number of copies of your full set of bankruptcy forms (except your *Chapter 7 Individual Debtor's Statement of Intention* and your *Debtor's Certification of Completion of Instructional Course Concerning Personal Financial Management* (Official Form 23))

- Your own copy of the full set of bankruptcy forms (except your *Chapter 7 Individual Debtor's Statement of Intention* and your *Debtor's Certification of Completion of Instructional Course Concerning Personal Financial Management* (Official Form 23))

- A completed original and the required copies of your *Application to Pay Filing Fees in Installments* or *Application for Waiver of the Chapter 7 Filing Fee* (if you are requesting either of these actions from the Court)

• A money order or certified bank check for $299.00 made out to the "U.S. Bankruptcy Court." If you are asking for permission to pay your filing fee in installments, make the check out for the down payment amount which you have listed on your *Application to Pay Filing Fees in Installments.*

Either in person or by mail, ask that the original and copies of your bankruptcy papers be filed. Pay your fee. Ask the court clerk to "File" stamp your own copy of your bankruptcy papers. Request the name and address of the bankruptcy trustee for your case.

Automatic Stay: Once you have filed your bankruptcy papers, the automatic stay goes into effect. The bankruptcy court will notify each of the creditors that you have listed of your filing and of the automatic stay. However, if you are in an emergency situation, you yourself can notify any creditors, collection agencies, landlords, police, or others. To do this, simply make a copy of the file-stamped version of all three pages of your *Voluntary Petition* (Official Form 1) for each person whom you wish to notify. Using your creditor mailing list, mail a copy of the file-stamped *Voluntary Petition* to each person whom you wish to immediately notify. This will prevent any further action on their part to evict you, shut off your utilities, harass you, or take any actions to collect on any of your debts. These creditors, however, have the right to ask the bankruptcy court to lift the automatic stay for their particular situation. If they do petition the court to lift the stay, you will be notified by the court.

Sending Your *Chapter 7 Individual Debtor's Statement of Intention*: If you have any secured debts listed on *Schedule D* and you have completed a *Chapter 7 Individual Debtor's Statement of Intention* with regard to those debts, you have one more step to complete in filing your papers. If you did not list any debts on *Schedule D*, skip the following steps.

You must personally notify each of your secured creditors of your intentions with regard to their debt. To do this, follow these simple steps:

• Within 30 days of filing your papers with the court, you will need to mail a copy of your *Chapter 7 Individual Debtor's*

☀ Toolkit Tip!

If you have any secured debts (like a mortgage), you will need to take 3 more steps: (1) mail a copy of your 'Statement of Intention' to each secured creditor, (2) Prepare a Proof of Service by Mail for each creditor, and (3) File the Statement and Proofs with the Court Clerk.

Statement of Intention to each creditor listed on Schedule D and also to your bankruptcy trustee and complete a Proof of Service by Mail form

- You will need to obtain a *Proof of Service by Mail* form from your local bankruptcy court which lists the names and addresses of all of the creditors from your Schedule D and of your bankruptcy trustee

- Mail or take your signed original individual debtor's statement of intention and the signed original *Proof of Service by Mail* to the bankruptcy court within 30 days of filing your other papers. File these two documents with the bankruptcy court clerk and ask the clerk to "file-stamp" your copies of these two forms.

The Creditors' Meeting

The next step in your bankruptcy is the creditors' meeting. After you have filed your bankruptcy papers, the court assigns a bankruptcy trustee to handle your case. The trustee sends notices of your bankruptcy, the automatic stay, and a creditors' meeting to all of the creditors which you have listed on your mailing list. You will also be notified of the time and place of this meeting. It will usually be held about a month after the filing of your papers. You must attend this meeting. If you do not, you may be fined, your bankruptcy may be dismissed, and you may be prevented from filing again for six months. Both you and your spouse must attend if you filed jointly. If you have a major schedule conflict, you may be able to contact the court and reschedule the meeting.

Unless you have significant non-exempt assets which can be sold or a creditor suspects you of fraudulent activities with regard to your bankruptcy, creditors rarely attend the meeting. The meeting should take about a half-hour. Generally, at the meeting, the bankruptcy trustee goes over your papers and may question you regarding specific debts or property. The trustee will also likely ask you questions regarding your understanding of bankruptcy. He or she is supposed to be certain that you understand the effect of bankruptcy on your credit, the consequences of a bankruptcy discharge, the availability of other types of bankruptcies, and the

> **⊘ Definition:**
>
> **Creditors' Meeting:** This is a brief meeting with your creditor's (and the bankruptcy trustee who is assigned to your case) that will be held about a month after you file for bankruptcy. **Note:** You MUST attend this meeting.

effect of reaffirming a debt. If you have read this entire book, you should have no difficulty in answering these questions. Prior to the meeting, review this book and look over your bankruptcy papers so that you will be able to honestly and easily answer any questions regarding your financial circumstances. You should also bring with you any of your financial records that you used to fill in your bankruptcy questionnaire and official forms. The meeting should be relatively brief and businesslike. If you feel that you are being intimidated by the trustee or a creditor, you have the right to stop the meeting and ask for a court hearing.

Within 30 days of your creditors' meeting, the bankruptcy trustee or your creditors can object to your listing certain property as exempt. They must do so in writing and a court hearing will be scheduled. Generally, you need not attend the court hearing unless you wish to contest their claim that the property should not be exempt. Additionally, creditors can specifically object to the discharge of a particular debt. This may be done if they claim it is a non-dischargeable debt or if they feel that you incurred the debt by fraud or dishonesty of some kind. If a creditor challenges the discharge of a particular debt, you will be served court papers informing you of this challenge. If you wish to defend the dischargeability of the debt, you will need to seek the advice of a competent attorney. Finally, a creditor, on rare occasions, can seek to prevent you from obtaining a bankruptcy at all on the basis that you have incurred the bulk of your debts by fraud. If this happens, you will be notified and you should immediately seek the assistance of an attorney skilled in bankruptcy law.

Surrendering Your Property

♀ Toolkit Tip!
After your creditor's meeting, you will be notified when and how to surrender any non-exempt property to the court.

After your creditors' meeting, your bankruptcy trustee will notify you which of your non-exempt property will have to be surrendered to the court. Excess cash and any valuable property which could be sold to pay your creditors will likely be the only non-exempt property you will need to surrender. You may also be able to negotiate with your trustee to buy back any non-exempt property for cash or trade some of your exempt property for particular non-exempt property which you wish to keep. Most trustees are flexible, as long as they are able to collect property with an equivalent value. You must deal with any secured property (collateral) in the manner in which you have indicated on your *Chapter 7 Individual Debtor's Statement of Intention*. You have 45 days from the date you filed your bankruptcy papers with the court to complete your stated intentions. If you indicated on your *Chapter 7 Individual Debtor's Statement of Intention* that you would surrender secured property, it is up to your creditor to repossess the property.

Complete a Personal Financial Management Course

Consult the listing of approved debtor education agencies in Appendix D. You may also wish to check for updates on this listing that are posted on the U.S. Bankruptcy Trustee Service website (the website address is shown in Appendix D). Contact the agency that you have chosen and complete the required course at any time after filing for bankruptcy and before your final discharge. You must then file your *Debtor's Certification of Completion of Instructional Course Concerning Personal Financial Management* (Official Form 23). This form must be filed before a Bankruptcy Court judge will grant your final discharge.

Your Final Discharge

The final step in your bankruptcy will come about three months after your creditors' meeting. Generally, you will be notified by the court of the scheduling of a very brief court hearing. At this quick hearing, the bankruptcy judge will determine that all of the proper steps have been taken and that your bankruptcy should be approved. The judge will then also generally inform you of the effects of bankruptcy. Finally, the judge will issue an order of discharge and your bankruptcy will be over. All of your dischargeable debts will be forever wiped clean. You will receive a final notice of your discharge in the mail a few weeks later.

Congratulations: your dischargeable debts have now been officially cancelled.

> ## ☼ Toolkit Tip!
>
> Before the Court will order a Final Discharge of your debts, you *must* attend complete a Personal Financial Management course. Please see Appendix D for a list of agencies that provide such courses.

After Your Bankruptcy

Once your bankruptcy is over, all of the debts listed on your bankruptcy papers that were not successfully challenged by a creditor are wiped out. You are not liable to pay them in any way. Debts that are non-dischargeable are still valid. If a creditor claims you still owe them, write them and state that your bankruptcy has discharged your debt. There are, of course, several other consequences to your bankruptcy:

Your Credit Record: By law, the fact that you have obtained a personal bankruptcy can remain on your credit record for up to 10 years.

Filing Another Bankruptcy: Once you have obtained a personal bankruptcy, you will not be allowed to file another bankruptcy for a period of eight years.

Discrimination: All governmental agencies are prohibited from taking action against you based on your bankruptcy. This includes firing you, evicting you, refusing to issue you a license, or other discriminatory actions. In addition, private employers are prohibited from firing you or otherwise discriminating against you because of your bankruptcy.

If You Made a Mistake on Your Bankruptcy Papers: If, after your final discharge, you discover that you have made a mistake on the bankruptcy papers that you filed, you must notify the bankruptcy trustee. This is particularly important if you neglected to include non-exempt property that might have been sold to pay your creditors. The bankruptcy trustee has the power to reopen your case and seek recovery of any non-exempt property that you owned at the time of your discharge and which was not included on your bankruptcy papers. Generally, this will not be done for small amounts of property. If you neglected to list a creditor, unfortunately, the debt you owe to that creditor will not be discharged unless you can show that the creditor actually knew of your bankruptcy in time to file a claim. If the debt is substantial, you may need to seek legal assistance.

> **⎯☼⎯Toolkit Tip!**
>
> Once you have obtained your bankruptcy, be very careful about getting back into debt over your head. You will not be allowed to file for another bankruptcy for eight years.

If You Receive an Inheritance, Divorce Settlement, or Insurance Proceeds: If within six months of the date when you filed for bankruptcy (not the date of your discharge) you receive or are informed of an inheritance, or divorce or insurance settlement, you must notify your bankruptcy trustee. In the situation of such windfalls that you receive shortly after your bankruptcy, the bankruptcy trustee also has the power to reopen your case and seek to claim such property.

Rebuilding Your Credit: Once you have eliminated your debts through a bankruptcy, you must then begin the process of rebuilding your credit rating. If you have a steady job and are able to build a record of making on-time rental or utility payments, it should take only a few years to be eligible for credit of some kind. The first credit that will generally be available to you will be collateralized consumer loans or credit for consumer goods. Next, within as little as three to four years, credit cards and auto loans may become available. Finally, if you maintain a clear financial record, home mortgages will again be available to you. Be very careful, however, about once again getting into the credit traps which caused your first bankruptcy. Good credit is a valuable asset that can assist you in reaching your goals and achieving a better life. Bankruptcy will have given you a new start on the road to that life.

> **☼ Toolkit Tip!**
>
> For six months after the date on which you originally filed for bankruptcy, you will need to notify your bankruptcy trustee of any inheritance, or divorce or insurance settlement. This is true even *after* your final discharge.

Appendix A

State and Federal Bankruptcy Exemptions

On the following pages, you will find an alphabetical state-by-state listing of state bankruptcy exemptions. In addition, at the end of this appendix you will find a listing for federal bankruptcy exemptions and federal non-bankruptcy exemptions.

In all states, you can use both the state and federal non-bankruptcy exemptions. In addition, residents of Arkansas, Connecticut, the District of Columbia, Hawaii, Massachusetts, Michigan, Minnesota, New Jersey, New Mexico, Pennsylvania, Rhode Island, South Carolina, Texas, Vermont, Washington, and Wisconsin have a choice. They may choose to use either their state exemptions and the federal non-bankruptcy exemptions or they can choose to use only the federal bankruptcy exemptions as listed at the end of the appendix of state exemptions. If residents of these states choose to use the federal bankruptcy exemptions, they cannot use the state exemptions or the federal non-bankruptcy exemptions. The first item in each listing will explain whether you can use the state exemptions and federal non-bankruptcy exemptions only or can choose between those and the federal bankruptcy exemptions. California residents may choose between two different state exemption systems and can use the federal non-bankruptcy exemptions with either state system.

You should read through the entire listing for your state. Using your completed Schedules A: Real Property and B: Personal Property, determine which of your property falls into any of the categories. On a separate worksheet, list the property that you feel is exempt under your state's laws. Then do the same for the federal non-bankruptcy exemptions. If your state does not allow a choice, fill in the property that you have determined is exempt on your Schedule C: Property Claimed as Exempt. If your state allows a choice, make another listing for the federal bankruptcy exemptions. Now, compare the state/federal non-bankruptcy exemption list with the federal bankruptcy exemption list. Decide which exemption list allows you to retain the most property and list that property on Schedule C.

Appendix A: State and Federal Bankruptcy Exemptions

In general, all of your property is either personal property or real estate. Real estate includes all land and the buildings or improvements that are permanently attached to the land. All of the rest of your property is considered personal property. Personal property can be divided further into two categories: *tangible property* (property you can see and touch, such as artwork or a car) and *intangible property* (property that represents some type of ownership, such as stocks, bonds, copyrights, etc.). If you are unclear of the meaning of the language in the statute, check the Glossary. The following explains the various exemptions that are listed:

Benefits: This listing contains various governmental benefits that are exempt from bankruptcy. This may include workers' compensation, unemployment payments, welfare payments, veterans' benefits and other government benefits. Private benefits are listed under either "Insurance" or "Pensions."

Insurance: Under this listing you will find any insurance-related property, including the cash value of your insurance policies, private annuity and disability proceeds, and various other insurance-based assets.

Miscellaneous: This listing includes those types of property that are not listed elsewhere. This category most often includes property of a business partnership and exemption amounts that may be applied to any property (whether real estate or personal property).

Pensions: Under this list are those items of property that are related to retirement. Various pensions, IRAs, KEOGHs, and other retirement plans are included. Also listed are certain profit-sharing plans that are exempt.

Personal Property: This listing contains all of the personal property that is specifically exempt from bankruptcy. It is under this listing that you will most likely find property that you can keep after your bankruptcy. Every item listed as a state exemption (or federal, if allowed) can be retained.

Real Estate: Listed here are the real estate exemptions. These may also be referred to as homestead exemptions. In general, these allow the exemption of a fixed value amount of the worth of your personal residence. In some states, this amount is very substantial and will allow you to retain your entire house. In other states, the actual size of the property determines the exemption. Note: The 2005 Bankruptcy Act limits homestead exemptions to $136,875.00 if you have lived in the state where you are attempting to claim the exemption for less than 40 months (1215 days). This is true even if your state homestead exemption allows for a higher amount.

Wages: Under this listing are both general and specific wage exemptions for certain professions. Generally, 75 percent of general wages are exempt from creditors. However, check your specific state listing.

NOTE FOR SPOUSES: Most states allow spouses who are filing jointly to each claim a complete set of exemptions. In other words, for joint filers, you can list exemptions for double the amounts that are shown under your state's listing. There are a few exceptions to this. Check your specific state's listings. If in doubt, claim double the exemption amount if filing jointly.

Alabama

Alabama residents cannot use the Federal Bankruptcy Exemptions, but may use the Federal Non-Bankruptcy Exemptions listed at the end of this Appendix and the following state exemptions:

Benefits: Aid to aged, blind, disabled, and families with dependent children (unlimited amount): Alabama Code 38-4-8; Coal miners pneumoconiosis benefits (unlimited amount): Alabama Code 25-5-179; Southeast Asian War POW benefits (unlimited amount): Alabama Code 31-7-2; Unemployment compensation (unlimited amount): Alabama Code 25-4-140; Workers compensation (unlimited amount): Alabama Code 25-5-86.

Insurance: Annuity proceeds (up to $250 per month): Alabama Code 27-14-32; Disability proceeds (up to an average of $250 per month): Alabama Code 27-14-31; Fraternal society benefits (unlimited amount): Alabama Code 27-34-27; Life insurance proceeds if beneficiary is insured's spouse or child (unlimited amount): Alabama Code 6-10-8 & 27-14-29; Life insurance proceeds if policy prohibits use to pay creditors (unlimited amount): Alabama Code 27-15-26; Mutual aid association benefits (unlimited amount): Alabama Code 27-30-25.

Pensions: Judges (75% of salary prescribed by law): Alabama Code 12-18-10(a-b); Law enforcement officers (unlimited amount): Alabama Code 36-21-77; State employees (unlimited amount): Alabama Code 36-27-28; Teachers (unlimited amount): Alabama Code 16-25-23.

Personal Property: Any personal property not listed below, except life insurance (up to $3,000 total): Alabama Code 6-10-6; Arms, uniforms, and equipment required for military use (unlimited amount): Alabama Code 31-2-78; Books (unlimited amount): Alabama Code 6-10-6; Burial lot (unlimited amount): Alabama Code 6-10-5; Church pew (unlimited amount): Alabama Code 6-10-5; Clothing needed (unlimited amount): Alabama Code 6-10-6; Crops (unlimited amount): Alabama Code 6-9-41; Family portraits or pictures (unlimited amount): Alabama Code 6-10-6.

Real Estate: Real property or mobile home (up to $5,000): Alabama Code 6-10-2; up to 160 acres, husband and wife may double the amount, must file homestead exemption with Probate Court to be effective: Alabama Code 6-10-2.

Wages: 75% of earned but unpaid wages (judge may allow more for low-income debtors): Alabama Code 6-10-7.

Alaska

Alaska residents cannot use the Federal Bankruptcy Exemptions, but may use the Federal Non-Bankruptcy Exemptions listed at the end of this Appendix and the following state exemptions. Amounts may be revised by the state in even-numbered years.

Benefits: Aid to aged, blind, disabled, and families with dependent children (unlimited amount): Alaska Statutes 47.25.210 & 47.25.550; Alaska longevity bonus (unlimited amount): Alaska Statutes 9.38.015(a)(5); Crime victims compensation (unlimited amount): Alaska Statutes 9.38.015 (a)(4); Federally exempt benefits (unlimited amount): Alaska Statutes 9.38.015(a)(6); General relief assistance (unlimited amount): Alaska Statutes 47.25.210; Permanent fund dividends (20% of amount): Alaska Statutes 43.23.065; Tuition credits under an advance college tuition payment contract (unlimited amount): Alaska Statutes 9.38.015(a)(9); Unemployment compensation (unlimited amount): Alaska Statutes 9.38.015(b) & 23.20.405; Workers compensation (unlimited amount): Alaska Statutes 23.30.160.

Insurance: Disability benefits (unlimited amount): Alaska Statutes 9.38.015(b) & 9.38.030 (e)(1), (5); Fraternal society benefits (unlimited amount): Alaska Statutes 21.84.240; Insurance proceeds or recoveries for personal injury or wrongful death (up to wage exemption amount): Alaska Statutes 9.38.030(e)(3) & 9.38.050(a); Unmatured life insurance or annuity contract loan (up to $12,500); Alaska Statutes 9.38.017 & 9.38.025; Life insurance proceeds if beneficiary is insured's spouse or dependent (up to wage exemption amount): Alaska Statutes 9.38.030(e)(4); Medical, surgical, or hospital benefits (unlimited amount): Alaska Statutes 9.38.015(a)(3).

Miscellaneous: Alimony (up to wage exemption amount): Alaska Statutes 9.38.030(e)(2); Child support payments held in an agency (unlimited amount): Alaska Statutes 25.27.095; Liquor licenses (unlimited amount): Alaska Statutes 9.38.015(a)(7); Permits for limited entry into Alaska Fisheries (unlimited amount): Alaska Statutes 9.38.015(a)(8); Property of business partnership (unlimited amount): Alaska Statutes 9.38.100(b).

Pensions: Elected public officers (unpaid benefits only): Alaska Statutes 9.38.015(b); Judicial employees (unpaid benefits only): Alaska Statutes 9.38.015(b); Other pensions (up to wage exemption amount and only for payments being paid): Alaska Statutes 9.38.030(e)(5); Public employees (unpaid benefits only): Alaska Statutes 9.38.015(b) & 39.35.505; Retirement benefits deposited more than 120 days before filing bankruptcy (unlimited amount): Alaska Statutes 9.38.017; Teachers (unpaid benefits only): Alaska Statutes 9.38.015(b).

Personal Property: Books, clothing, family portraits, heirlooms, household goods, and musical instruments (up to $3,750 total): Alaska Statutes 9.38.020(a); Building materials (unlimited amount): Alaska Statutes 34.35.105; Burial plot (unlimited amount): Alaska Statutes 9.38.015(a)(1); Health aids (unlimited amount): Alaska Statutes 9.38.015(a)(2); Implements, books, or tools of a trade (up to $3,500): Alaska Statutes 9.38.020(c); Jewelry (up to $1,250): Alaska Statutes 9.38.020(b); Motor vehicle (up to $3,750, vehicle's market value cannot exceed $20,000): Alaska Statutes 9.38.020(e); Pets (up to $1,250): Alaska Statutes 9.38.020(d); Proceeds for lost, damaged, or destroyed exempt property (up to exemption amount): Alaska Statutes 9.38.060.

Real Estate: Real property used as a residence (up to $67,500): Alaska Statutes 9.38.010.

Wages: If paid weekly, then net earnings up to $438, unless sole wage earner in household, then up to $688; if paid monthly or semi-monthly, then up to $1,750 in cash or liquid assets paid in any month, unless sole wage earner in household, then up to $2,750: Alaska Statutes 9.38.030 (a)(b) & 9.38.050(b).

Arizona

Arizona residents cannot use the Federal Bankruptcy Exemptions, but may use the Federal Non-Bankruptcy Exemptions listed at the end of this Appendix and the following state exemptions. Wife and husband may double all exemption amounts, except real estate exemption.

Benefits: Unemployment compensation (unlimited amount): Arizona Revised Statutes 23-783; Welfare benefits (unlimited amount): Arizona Revised Statutes 46-208; Workers compensation (unlimited amount): Arizona Revised Statutes 23-1068; State employee long-term disability benefits: Arizona Revised Statutes 38-791(D); Wrongful death awards: Arizona Revised Statutes 12-592.

Insurance: Fraternal society benefits (unlimited amount): Arizona Revised Statutes 20-877; Group life insurance policy or proceeds (unlimited amount): Arizona Revised Statutes 20-1132; Health, accident, or disability benefits (unlimited amount): Arizona Revised Statutes 33-1126(A)(4); Life insurance cash value (up to $1,000 per dependent, $25,000 total): Arizona Revised Statutes 33-1126(A)(6); Life insurance proceeds (up to $20,000 if beneficiary is spouse or child): Arizona Revised Statutes 33-1126(A)(1); Husband and wife may double: Arizona Revised Statutes 33-1121.01.

Miscellaneous: Property of business partnership (unlimited amount): Arizona Revised Statutes 29-225; Child support or spousal maintenance (alimony): Arizona Revised Statutes 33-1126(A)(3).

Pensions: Board of regents members, faculty, and administration under the jurisdiction of Board of Regents (unlimited amount): Arizona Revised Statutes 15-1628; Firefighters and police officers (unlimited amount): Arizona Revised Statutes 9-968 & 9-931; Rangers (unlimited amount): Arizona Revised Statutes 41-955; State employees: Arizona Revised Statutes 38-792; Retirement benefits from a qualified plan deposited more than 120 days before filing bankruptcy (unlimited amount): Arizona Revised Statutes 33-1126(B).

Personal Property: Appliances, furniture, household goods, and paintings (up to $4,000 total for all listed): Arizona Revised Statutes 33-1123; Arms, uniforms, and equipment required for military use (unlimited amount): Arizona Revised Statutes 33-1130(3); Bank deposit (up to $150 in 1 account, must file notice with bank): Arizona Revised Statutes 33-1126(A)(9); Bible, bicycle, sewing machine, typewriter, burial plot, rifle, pistol, or shotgun (up to $500 total): Arizona Revised Statutes 33-1125; Books (up to $250), clothing (up to $500), wedding and engagement rings (up to $1,000), watch (up to $100), pets, horses, milk cows, and poultry (up to $500), and musical instruments (up to $250): Arizona Revised Statutes 33-1125; Farm machinery and equipment, utensils, seed, feed, grain, and animals (up to $2,500 total): Arizona Revised Statutes 33-1130(2); Food and fuel (amount to last 6 months): Arizona Revised Statutes 33-1124; Health aids (unlimited amount): Arizona Revised Statutes 33-1125; Motor vehicle (up to $5,000; up to $10,000, if disabled): 33-1125(8); Prepaid rent or security deposit (up to $1,000 or 1-1/2 times rent, whichever is less, instead of real estate exemption): Arizona Revised Statutes 33-1126(C); Proceeds for sold or damaged exempt property (up to exemption amount): Arizona Revised Statutes 33-1126(A)(4), (6); Tools, equipment, instruments, and books, except vehicle driven to work (up to $2,500): Arizona Revised Statutes 33-1130(1); Teaching aids of teacher (unlimited amount): Arizona Revised Statutes 33-1127; Pre-arranged funeral trust: Arizona Revised Statutes 32-1391.05.

Real Estate: Real estate, apartment, or mobile home used as residence (up to $150,000);

sale proceeds are exempt for 18 months or until new home is purchased, whichever occurs first; must record homestead declaration: Arizona Revised Statutes 33-1101(A), 33-1102.
Wages: Minor child's earnings, unless debt is for child (unlimited amount): Arizona Revised Statutes 33-1126(A)(2); 75% of earned but unpaid wages or pension payments (judge may allow more for low-income debtors): Arizona Revised Statutes 33-1131.

Arkansas

Arkansas residents may use either the Federal Bankruptcy Exemptions listed at the end of this Appendix or the state exemptions listed below. If state exemptions are used, then Federal Non-Bankruptcy Exemptions listed at the end of this Appendix can also be used.
Benefits: Crime victims compensation ($10,000 limit): Arkansas Code Annotated 16-90-716(a)(1); Crime victims compensation for total and permanent disability ($25,000 limit): Arkansas Code Annotated 16-90-716(a)(2); Unemployment compensation (unlimited amount): Arkansas Code Annotated 11-10-109; Workers compensation (unlimited amount): Arkansas Code Annotated 11-9-110.
Insurance: Annuity contract (unlimited amount): Arkansas Code Annotated 23-79-134; Disability benefits (unlimited amount): Arkansas Code Annotated 23-79-133; Fraternal society benefits (unlimited amount): Arkansas Code Annotated 23-74-403; Group life insurance (unlimited amount): Arkansas Code Annotated 23-79-132; Life, health, accident, or disability cash value, or proceeds paid or due (limited to $500 personal property exemption provided by 9-1 and 9-2 of the Arkansas Constitution): Arkansas Code Annotated 16-66-209; Life insurance proceeds if policy prohibits proceeds from being used to pay creditors (unlimited amount): Arkansas Code Annotated 23-79-131; Life insurance proceeds if beneficiary is not the insured (unlimited amount): Arkansas Code Annotated 23-79-131; Mutual life or disability benefits (up to $1,000): Arkansas Code Annotated 23-72-114; Stipulated insurance premiums (unlimited amount): Arkansas Code Annotated 23-71-112.
Miscellaneous: Any property (up to $800 if single, up to $1,250 if married): Arkansas Code Annotated 16-66-218(a)(1); Property of business partnership (unlimited amount): Arkansas Code Annotated 4-46-501 - 4-46-504.
Pensions: Firefighters (unlimited amount): Arkansas Code Annotated 24-11-814; Police officers (unlimited amount): Arkansas Code Annotated 24-11-417; Firefighters (unlimited amount): Arkansas Code Annotated 24-10-616; IRA deposits (up to $20,000 if deposited at least 1 year before filing for bankruptcy): Arkansas Code Annotated 16-66-218(b)(16); Police officers (unlimited amount): Arkansas Code Annotated 24-10-616; School employees (unlimited amount): Arkansas Code Annotated 24-7-715; State police officers (unlimited amount): Arkansas Code Annotated 24-6-223.
Personal Property: Any personal property (up to $500 if married or head of household, otherwise up to $200): Arkansas Constitution 9-1 & 9-2; Arkansas Code Annotated 16-66-218(b)(1) & (2); Burial plot (up to 5 acres, instead of real estate option #2): Arkansas Code Annotated 16-66-207 & 16-66-218(a)(1); Prepaid funeral trust (unlimited amount) Arkansas Code 23-40-117; Clothing (unlimited amount): Arkansas Constitution 9-1 & 9-2; Implements, books, and tools of a trade (up to $750): Arkansas Code Annotated 16-66-218(a)(4). Motor vehicle (up to $1,200): Arkansas Code Annotated 16-66-218(a)(2); Wedding bands (unlimited amount, diamond cannot exceed ½ carat): Arkansas Code Annotated 16-66-218(a)(3).
Real Estate: Real or personal property used as residence by head of family; if property is

up to 1/4 acre in city, town, village, or 80 acres elsewhere (unlimited value is exempt); if property is between 1/4 to 1 acre in city, town, or village, or 80 to 160 acres elsewhere (up to $2,500 is exempt); no homestead may exceed 1 acre in city, town, or village, or 160 acres elsewhere: Arkansas Constitution 9-3, 9-4, & 9-5; Arkansas Code Annotated 16-66-210 & 16-66-218(b)(3). (Note 1: Husband and wife may not double the real estate exemption) (Note 2: The 2005 Bankruptcy Act limits homestead exemptions to $136,875.00 if you have lived in the state where you are attempting to claim the exemption for less than 40 months (1215 days). This is true even if your state homestead exemption allows for a higher amount.)

Wages: Earned but unpaid wages due for 60 days (up to $500 if married or head of household, or up to $200 otherwise): Arkansas Code Annotated 16-66-208 & 16-66-218(b)(6).

California

California residents cannot use the Federal Bankruptcy Exemptions, but may use the Federal Non-Bankruptcy Exemptions listed at the end of this Appendix and one of the following state exemption options only. Married couples cannot double any exemptions under Option #2.

California OPTION #1

Benefits: Aid to aged, blind, disabled, and families with dependent children (unlimited amount): California Code of Civil Procedure 704.170; Financial aid to students (unlimited amount): California Code of Civil Procedure 704.190; Relocation benefits (unlimited amount): California Code of Civil Procedure 704.180; Direct-deposited Social Security and/or public benefit payments (unlimited amount): California Code of Civil Procedure704.080(c); Unemployment benefits (unlimited amount): California Code of Civil Procedure 704.120; Union benefits due to labor dispute (unlimited amount): California Code of Civil Procedure 704.120(b)(5); Workers compensation (unlimited amount): California Code of Civil Procedure 704.160.

Insurance: Disability or health benefits (unlimited amount): California Code of Civil Procedure 704.130; Fidelity bonds (unlimited amount): California Code-Labor 404; Fraternal unemployment benefits (unlimited amount): California Code of Civil Procedure 704.120; Homeowners insurance proceeds up to 6 months after receipt (up to real estate exemption amount): California Code of Civil Procedure 704.720(b); Life insurance proceeds if policy prohibits proceeds from being used to pay creditors (unlimited amount): California Code-Insurance 10171; Matured life insurance benefits (amount needed for support): California Code of Civil Procedure 704.100(c); Unmatured life insurance policy loan value (up to $9,700, husband and wife may double): California Code of Civil Procedure 704.100(b).

Miscellaneous: Business or professional licenses, except liquor licenses (unlimited amount): California Code of Civil Procedure 695.060 & 708.630; Inmate's trust funds (up to $1,225): California Code of Civil Procedure 704.090(a); Inmate's trust account where judgment is for restitution fine or order (up to $300): California Code of Civil Procedure 704.090(b); Property of business partnership (unlimited amount): California Code-Corporations 16504(d).

Pensions: County employees, firefighters, and peace officers (unlimited amount): California Code-Government 31452, 31913, & 32210; Public and private retirement benefits (unlimited amount): California Code of Civil Procedure 704.110 & 704.115, Government 21201.

Personal Property: Appliances, clothing, food, and furnishings (amount needed): California Code of Civil Procedure 704.020; Bank deposits from Social Security (up to $2,700 for single and $4,050 for husband and wife); Bank deposits from other public benefits (up to $1,350 for single and $2,025 for husband and wife): California Code of Civil Procedure 704.080; Books, equipment, furnishings, materials, tools, uniforms, and vessel (up to $6,750 if single and $13,475 if husand and wife use tools in same profession); Commercial motor vehicle if not claimed otherwise (up to $4,850 if single and $9,700 if husand and wife and use vehicle in same profession: California Code of Civil Procedure 704.060; Building materials to repair or improve home (up to $2,700, but husband and wife can not double this amount): California Code of Civil Procedure 704.030; Burial plot and health aids (unlimited amount): California Code of Civil Procedure 704.050 & 704.200; Jewelry, heirlooms or art (up to $6,750 total, but husband and wife can not double this amount): California Code of Civil Procedure 704.040; Motor vehicles or auto insurance proceeds if vehicle lost, damaged, or destroyed (up to $2,550, but husband and wife can not double this amount): California Code of Civil Procedure 704.010; Personal injury causes of action or recovery (amount needed for support): California Code of Civil Procedure 704.140; Wrongful death causes of action or recovery (amount needed for support): California Code of Civil Procedure 704.150.

Real Estate: Real or personal property used as residence (up to $50,000 if single and not disabled, up to $75,000 for families if no other member has a homestead; up to $150,000 if: [a] 65 or older, or physically or mentally disabled; [b] 55 or older, single, earn under $15,000, and creditors seek to force the sale of your home; or [c] 55 or older, married, earn under $20,000, and creditors seek to force the sale of your home); proceeds from sale of home exempt for 6 months (husband and wife may not double): California Code of Civil Procedure 704.710, 704.720, & 704.730; California case law.

Wages: Public employee vacation credits (unlimited amount): California Code of Civil Procedure 704.113; 75% of wages paid within 30 days of filing for bankruptcy: California Code of Civil Procedure 704.070.

California OPTION #2:
Benefits: Crime victims compensation (unlimited amount): California Code of Civil Procedure 703.140(b)(11)(A); Public assistance (unlimited amount): California Code of Civil Procedure 703.140(b)(10)(A); Social Security (unlimited amount): California Code of Civil Procedure 703.140(b)(10)(A); Unemployment compensation (unlimited amount): California Code of Civil Procedure 703.140(b)(10)(A); Veterans benefits (unlimited amount): California Code of Civil Procedure 703.140(b)(10)(B).

Insurance: Disability benefits (unlimited amount): California Code of Civil Procedure 703.140(b)(10)(C); Life insurance proceeds (reasonable amount): California Code of Civil Procedure 703.140(b)(11)(C); Unmatured life insurance contract (up to $9,300): California Code of Civil Procedure 703.140(b)(8); Unmatured life insurance policy other than credit (unlimited amount): California Code of Civil Procedure 703.140(b)(7).

Miscellaneous: Alimony and child support (amount needed for support): California Code of Civil Procedure 703.140(b)(10)(D); Any property (up to $925): California Code of Civil Procedure 703.140 (b)(5); Unused portion of real estate or burial exemption (can be used with any property): California Code of Civil Procedure 703.140(b)(5).

Pensions: Retirement benefits (amount needed for support): California Code of Civil Procedure 703.140(b)(10)(E).

Personal Property: Animals, appliances, books, clothing, crops, furnishings, household goods, and musical instruments (up to $525 per item): California Code of Civil Procedure 703.140(b)(3); Burial plot (up to $20,735, if used instead of real estate exemption): California Code of Civil Procedure 703.140(b)(1); Health aids (unlimited amount): California Code of Civil

Procedure 703.140 (b)(9); Implements, books, and tools of a trade (up to $2,075): California Code of Civil Procedure 703.140(b)(6); Jewelry (up to $1,350): California Code of Civil Procedure 703.140(b)(4); Motor vehicle (up to $3,300): California Code of Civil Procedure 703.140 (b)(2); Personal injury recoveries (up to $20,725, but not pain and suffering or pecuniary loss): California Code of Civil Procedure 703.140(b)(11)(D), (E); Wrongful death recoveries (amount needed for support): California Code of Civil Procedure 703.140(b)(11)(B).
Real Estate: Real or personal property, including co-op, used as residence (up to $20,725); unused portion of real estate or burial exemption may be applied to any property: California Code of Civil Procedure 703.140(b)(1).
Wages: No exemption.

Colorado

Colorado residents cannot use the Federal Bankruptcy Exemptions, but may use the Federal Non-Bankruptcy Exemptions listed at the end of this Appendix and the following state exemptions:
Benefits: Aid to aged, blind, disabled, and families with dependent children (unlimited amount): Colorado Revised Statutes 26-2-131; Crime victims compensation (unlimited amount): Colorado Revised Statutes 13-54-102(1)(q); Unemployment compensation (unlimited amount): Colorado Revised Statutes 8-80-103; Veterans benefits if war veteran (unlimited amount): Colorado Revised Statutes 13-54-102(1)(h); Workers compensation (unlimited amount): Colorado Revised Statutes 8-42-124.
Insurance: Disability benefits (up to $200 per month, entire amount if received as a lump sum): Colorado Revised Statutes 10-16-212; Fraternal society benefits (unlimited amount): Colorado Revised Statutes 10-14-403; Group life insurance policy or proceeds (unlimited amount): Colorado Revised Statutes 10-7-205; Homeowners insurance proceeds for 1 year after received (up to real estate exemption amount): Colorado Revised Statutes 38-41-209; Life insurance cash value or proceeds (up to $50,000): Colorado Revised Statutes 13-54-102(1)(k); Life insurance proceeds if policy prohibits proceeds from being used to pay creditors (unlimited amount): Colorado Revised Statutes 10-7-106.
Miscellaneous: Property of a business partnership (unlimited amount): Colorado Revised Statutes 7-60-125; Income tax credit refund (unlimited amount): Colorado Revised Statutes 13-54-102(1)(o).
Pensions: Firefighters (unlimited amount): Colorado Revised Statutes 31-30-1117; Police officers (unlimited amount): Colorado Revised Statutes 31-30.5-208; Public employees (unlimited amount): Colorado Revised Statutes 24-51-212 & 24-52-105; Retirement benefits, including IRAs (unlimited amount): Colorado Revised Statutes 13-54-102(1)(s); Teachers (unlimited amount): Colorado Revised Statutes 22-64-120; Veterans (unlimited amount): Colorado Revised Statutes 13-54-102(1)(h) & 13-54-104.
Personal Property: Library of professional person (up to $3,000 total): Colorado Revised Statutes 13-54-102(1)(k); Business materials, supplies, machines, tools, equipment, or books (up to $20,000): Colorado Revised Statutes 13-54-102; Clothing (up to $1,500): Colorado Revised Statutes 13-54-102(1)(a); Motor vehicles or bicycles used for work (up to $5,000, up to $10,000 if debtor a dependant is 60 or over or disabled): Colorado Revised Statutes 13-54-102(j)(1)(II)(a); Appliances or household goods (up to $3,000): Colorado Revised Statutes 13-54-102(1)(e); Health aids (unlimited amount): Colorado Revised Statutes 13-

54-102(1)(p); Livestock, poultry, or other animals and agricultural machinery, equipment, and tools (up to $50,000 total): Colorado Revised Statutes 13-54-102(1)(g); Jewelry and/or watches (up to $2,000): Colorado Revised Statutes 13-54-102(1)(b); Food and fuel (up to $600): Colorado Revised Statutes 13-54-102(1)(f); Personal injury recoveries, unless debt is related to injury (unlimited amount): Colorado Revised Statutes 13-54-102(1)(n); Library, family pictures, and books (up to $1,500): Colorado Revised Statutes 13-54-102 (1)(c); Proceeds for damaged exempt property (up to exemption amount): Colorado Revised Statutes 13-54-102(1)(m); Burial plot (unlimited amount): Colorado Revised Statutes 13-54-102(1)(d); Security deposit (unlimited amount): Colorado Revised Statutes 13-54-102(1)(r); Military equipment owned by member of National Guard (unlimited amount): Colorado Revised Statutes 13-54-102(1)(h.5).

Real Estate: Real property, mobile home, or manufactured home (up to $60,000, or up to $90,000 if owner, spouse, or dependant is disabled or 60 or over); proceeds from sale exempt for 2 years after received; must file exemption with county: Colorado Revised Statutes 38-41-201, 38-41-201.6, 38-41-203, 38-41-202, & 38-41-207; Mobile home used as residence (up to $6,000): Colorado Revised Statutes 13-54-102(1)(o)(II).

Wages: 75% of earned but unpaid wages or pension payments; 50% where supporting spouse; 60% if single (judge may allow more for low-income debtors): Colorado Revised Statutes 13-54-104.

Connecticut

Connecticut residents may use either the Federal Bankruptcy Exemptions listed at the end of this Appendix or the state exemptions listed below. If state exemptions are used, then Federal Non-Bankruptcy Exemptions listed at the end of this Appendix can also be used.

Benefits: Aid to aged, blind, disabled, and families with dependent children (unlimited amount): Connecticut General Statutes Annotated 52-352b(d); Crime victims compensation (unlimited amount): Connecticut General Statutes Annotated 52-352b(o) & 54-213; Social Security (unlimited amount): Connecticut General Statutes Annotated 52-352b(g); Unemployment compensation (unlimited amount): Connecticut General Statutes Annotated 31-272(c) & 52-352b(g); Veterans benefits (unlimited amount): Connecticut General Statutes Annotated 52-352b(g); Wages from earnings incentive program (unlimited amount): Connecticut General Statutes Annotated 52-352b(d); Workers compensation (unlimited amount): Connecticut General Statutes Annotated 52-352b(g).

Insurance: Disability benefits paid by association (unlimited amount): Connecticut General Statutes Annotated 52-352b(p); Fraternal society benefits (unlimited amount): Connecticut General Statutes Annotated 38a-637; Health or disability benefits (unlimited amount): Connecticut General Statutes Annotated 52-352b(e); Life insurance proceeds (unlimited amount): Connecticut General Statutes Annotated 38a-453, 454; Unmatured life insurance policy loan value (up to $4,000): Connecticut General Statutes Annotated 52-352b(s).

Miscellaneous: Alimony (up to amount of wage exemption): Connecticut General Statutes Annotated 52-352b(n); Animals and livestock feed for farm partnership (with at least 50% same family members): Connecticut General Statutes Annotated 52-352d; Any property (up to $1,000): Connecticut General Statutes Annotated 52-352b(r); Child support (unlimited amount): Connecticut General Statutes Annotated 52-352b(h); Liquor licenses (unlimited amount): Connecticut General Statutes Annotated 30-14.

Pensions: Municipal employees (unlimited amount): Connecticut General Statutes Annotated 7-446; Probate judges and employees (unlimited amount): Connecticut General Statutes Annotated 45a-48; Retirement benefits (amounts being received): Connecticut General Statutes Annotated 52-352b(m); State employees (unlimited amount): Connecticut General Statutes Annotated 5-171 & 5-192w; Teachers (unlimited amount): Connecticut General Statutes Annotated 10-183q.

Personal Property: Property of any type, may be applied to real estate or personal property (up to $1,000): Connecticut General Statutes Annotated 2-35(b)r; Appliances, food, clothing, furniture, and bedding (amounts needed): Connecticut General Statutes Annotated 52-352b(a); Arms, equipment, uniforms, or musical instruments required for military use (unlimited amount): Connecticut General Statutes Annotated 52-352b(i); Burial plot (unlimited amount): Connecticut General Statutes Annotated 52-352b(c); Health aids (unlimited amount): Connecticut General Statutes Annotated 52-352b(f); Motor vehicle (up to $3,500): Connecticut General Statutes Annotated 52-352b(j); Proceeds for damaged exempt property (up to exemption amount): Connecticut General Statutes Annotated 52-352b(q); Tools, books, instruments, and farm animals (amounts needed): Connecticut General Statutes Annotated 52-352b(b). Utility and security deposits for residence (unlimited amount): Connecticut General Statutes Annotated 52-352b(l); Wedding and engagement rings (unlimited amount): Connecticut General Statutes Annotated 52-352b(k).

Real Estate: Real property, including mobile or manufactured home (up to $75,000): Connecticut General Statutes Annotated 52-352b(t).

Wages: 75% of earned but unpaid wages (judge may allow more for low-income debtors): Connecticut General Statutes Annotated 52-36la(f)(1).

Delaware

Delaware residents cannot use the Federal Bankruptcy Exemptions, but may use the Federal Non-Bankruptcy Exemptions listed at the end of this Appendix and the following state exemptions. Wife and husband may double exemption amounts. However, an individual is limited to a total exemption amount of $25,000 and a husband and wife are limited to a total exemption of $50,000 (not including retirement plan exemptions): Delaware Code Annotated 10-4914.

Benefits: Aid to aged, blind, disabled, families with dependent children, and general assistance (up to exemption limit): Delaware Code Annotated 31-513 & 31-2309; Unemployment compensation (up to exemption limit): Delaware Code Annotated 19-3374; Workers compensation (up to exemption limit): Delaware Code Annotated 19-2355.

Insurance: Annuity contract proceeds (up to $350 per month): Delaware Code Annotated 18-2728; Group life insurance policy or proceeds (up to exemption limit): Delaware Code Annotated 18-2727; Health or disability benefits (up to exemption limit): Delaware Code Annotated 18-2726; Life insurance proceeds if policy prohibits proceeds from being used to pay creditors (up to exemption limit): Delaware Code Annotated 18-2729; Life insurance proceeds (up to exemption limit): Delaware Code Annotated 18-2725.

Miscellaneous: Property of business partnership (unlimited amount): Delaware Code Annotated 6-15-504(f).

Pensions: Kent County employees (up to exemption limit): Delaware Code Annotated 9-4316;

Police and fire officers (up to exemption limit): Delaware Code Annotated 11-8803; State employees (up to exemption limit): Delaware Code Annotated 29-5503; Volunteer firefighters (up to exemption limit): Delaware Code Annotated 16-6653.

Personal Property: Any personal property, except tools of a trade, if debtor is head of family (up to $500): Delaware Code Annotated 10-4903; Bible, books, and family pictures (up to exemption limit): Delaware Code Annotated 10-4902(a); Burial plot (up to exemption limit): Delaware Code Annotated 10-4902(a); Church pew or seat in public place of worship (up to exemption limit): Delaware Code Annotated 10-4902(a); Clothing, includes jewelry (up to exemption limit): Delaware Code Annotated 10-4902(a); Pianos and leased organs (up to exemption limit): Delaware Code Annotated 10-4902(d); Tools or vehicles of a trade (up to 15,000): Delaware Code Annotated 10-4914(c); Sewing machines (up to exemption limit): Delaware Code Annotated 10-4902(c); Tools, implements, and fixtures (up to $75 in New Castle and Sussex Counties, up to $50 in Kent County): Delaware Code Annotated 10-4902(b).

Real Estate: No exemption.

Wages: 85% of earned but unpaid wages: Delaware Code Annotated 10-4913.

District Of Columbia (Washington D.C.)

District of Columbia residents may use either the Federal Bankruptcy Exemptions listed at the end of this Appendix or the district exemptions listed below. If district exemptions are used, then Federal Non-Bankruptcy Exemptions at the end of this Appendix may also be used.

Benefits: Aid to aged, blind, disabled, families with dependent children, and general assistance (unlimited amount): District of Columbia Code 4-215.01; Crime victims compensation (unlimited amount): District of Columbia Code 4-507(e), & 15-501(a)(11)(A); Wrongful death award: District of Columbia Code 15-501(a)(11)(B); Disability, illness, or unemployment compensation (unlimited amount): District of Columbia Code 15-501(a)(7)(C); Unemployment compensation (unlimited amount) District of Columbia Code 51-118(b); Workers compensation (unlimited amount): District of Columbia Code 32-1517; Social Security benefits (unlimited amount): District of Columbia Code 15-501(a)(7)(A); Veteran's benefits (unlimited amount): District of Columbia Code 15-501(a)(7)(B).

Insurance: Disability benefits: District of Columbia Code 31-4716.01; Fraternal society benefits (unlimited amount): District of Columbia Code 31-5315; Group life insurance policy or proceeds (unlimited amount): District of Columbia Code 31-4717; Life insurance proceeds if policy prohibits proceeds from being used to pay creditors (unlimited amount): District of Columbia Code 31-4719; Unmatured life insurance policy, other than a credit life insurance contract (unlimited amount): District of Columbia Code 15-501(a)5; Life insurance proceeds: District of Columbia Code 31-4716; Life insurance proceeds from a person whom the debtor was a dependent of (amount reasonably necessary for support): District of Columbia Code 15-501(a)(11)(C); Other insurance proceeds (up to $60 per month, for 2 months, if head of family, then up to $200 per month): District of Columbia Code 15-503(a) & (b); Payments for pain and suffering, actual loss, or future earnings: District of Columbia Code 15-501(a)(11)(D) & (E).

Miscellaneous: Alimony, support, or separate maintenance (amount reasonably necessary for support): District of Columbia Code 15-501(a)(7)(D).

Pensions: Payment under a stock, bonus, pension, profit-sharing, annuity, or similar plan or contract on account of disability, death, age, or length of service, unless established by a relative when the debtor was employed by the relative and does not qualify under IRS sections 401(a) or 403(b) (amount reasonably necessary for support): District of Columbia Code 15-501(a)(7)(E); Benefits under a retirement plan qualified under IRS sections 401(a), 403(a) or (b), 408, 408(A), 414(d) or (e) [*Note*: there are other complex provisions regarding pension plans. Check Code directly]: District of Columbia Code 15-501(a)(9); Judges (unlimited amount): District of Columbia Code 11-1570(f); Public school teachers (unlimited amount): District of Columbia Code 38-2001.17 & 38-2021.17.

Personal Property: Household furnishings, household goods, wearing apparel, appliances, books, crops, or musical instruments (up to $425 per item and $8,625 total): District of Columbia Code 15-501(a)(2); Professionally prescribed health aids: District of Columbia Code 15-501(a)(6); Books and family pictures (up to $400): District of Columbia Code 15-501(a)(8); Clothing (up to $300): District of Columbia Code 15-503(b); Cooperative association holdings (up to $50): District of Columbia Code 29-928; Provisions for support, such as food, utilities, etc. (amount to last 3 months): District of Columbia Code 15-501(a)(12), (4); Library, furniture, and tools of professional person or artist (up to $300): District of Columbia Code 15-501(a)(13); Implements, professional books, or tools of a trade or business of debtor or dependent (up to $1,625): District of Columbia Code 15-501(a)(4); Mechanic's tools (up to $200): District of Columbia Code 15-503(b); Motor vehicle (up to $2,575): District of Columbia Code 15-501(a)(1); Residential condominium deposit (unlimited amount): District of Columbia Code 42-1904.09; Cemetery or burial funds (unlimited amount): District of Columbia Code 15-501(a)(14); Seal and documents of notary public (unlimited amount): District of Columbia Code 1-1206; any other property (up to $850, plus up to $8,075 additional property if you do not use the real estate exemption listed below): District of Columbia Code 15-501(a)(3).

Real Estate: Any residence or property in a cooperative that is used as a residence of debtor or debtor's dependent or a burial plot of debtor or dependent (unlimited amount): District of Columbia Code 15-501(a)(14). (Note: The 2005 Bankruptcy Act limits homestead exemptions to $136,875.00 if you have lived in the state where you are attempting to claim the exemption for less than 40 months (1215 days). This is true even if your state homestead exemption allows for a higher amount.)

Wages: 75% of earned but unpaid wages or the amount by which his or her disposable wages for that week exceed 30 times the federal minimum hourly wage, whichever is less is the amount subject to use by creditors; in other words, 75% of the wages are exempt up 30 times minimum hourly wage (judge may allow more for low-income debtors): District of Columbia Code 16-572; Non-wage earnings, including insurance, annuity, pension, or retirement benefits (up to $60 per month for 2 months; if head of family, then up to $200 per month for 2 months): District of Columbia Code 15-503(a) & (b); the wages of any person not residing in the District of Columbia who does not earn the majority of wages in the District (exempt up to limits allowed in home state): District of Columbia Code 15-503(c).

Florida

Florida residents cannot use the Federal Bankruptcy Exemptions, but may use the Federal Non-Bankruptcy Exemptions listed at the end of this Appendix and the following state exemptions:

Benefits: Crime victims compensation unless for injury incurred during the crime (unlimited amount): Florida Statutes Annotated 960.14; Public assistance (unlimited amount): Florida Statutes Annotated 222.201; Social Security (unlimited amount): Florida Statutes Annotated 222.201; Unemployment compensation (unlimited amount): Florida Statutes Annotated 222.201 & 443.051(2), (3); Veterans benefits (unlimited amount): Florida Statutes Annotated 222.201 & 744.626; Workers compensation (unlimited amount): Florida Statutes Annotated 440.22.

Insurance: Annuity contract proceeds (unlimited amount): Florida Statutes Annotated 222.14; Death benefits if not payable to the deceased's estate (unlimited amount): Florida Statutes Annotated 222.13; Disability or illness benefits (unlimited amount): Florida Statutes Annotated 222.18; Fraternal society benefits (unlimited amount): Florida Statutes Annotated 632.619; Life insurance cash surrender value (unlimited amount): Florida Statutes Annotated 222.14.

Miscellaneous: Alimony and child support (amount needed for support): Florida Statutes Annotated 222.201; Damages to employees for injuries in hazardous occupations (unlimited amount): Florida Statutes Annotated 769.05; Property of business partnership (unlimited amount): Florida Statutes Annotated 620.8501.

Pensions: County officers or employees (unlimited amount): Florida Statutes Annotated 122.15; Federal employee pension payments (amounts needed for support and received at least 3 months before filing for bankruptcy): Florida Statutes Annotated 222.21; Firefighters (unlimited amount): Florida Statutes Annotated 175.241; Police officers (unlimited amount): Florida Statutes Annotated 185.25; Retirement benefits (unlimited amount): Florida Statutes Annotated 222.21(2); State officers or employees (unlimited amount): Florida Statutes Annotated 121.131; Teachers (unlimited amount): Florida Statutes Annotated 238.15.

Personal Property: Any personal property (up to $1,000): Florida Constitution 10-4; Health aids (unlimited amount): Florida Statutes Annotated 222.25; Motor vehicle (up to $1,000): Florida Statutes Annotated 222.25; Pre-paid college trust fund: Florida Statutes Annotated 222.22(1); Pre-paid hurricane savings account: Florida Statutes Annotated 222.22(4); Pre-paid medical savings account: Florida Statutes Annotated 222.22(2).

Real Estate: Real or personal property used as residence including mobile or modular home (unlimited value, property cannot exceed 160 contiguous acres); must file exemption in Circuit Court: Florida Constitution 10-4 & Florida Statutes Annotated 222.01, 222.02, 222.03, & 222.05. (Note: The 2005 Bankruptcy Act limits homestead exemptions to $136,875.00 if you have lived in the state where you are attempting to claim the exemption for less than 40 months (1215 days). This is true even if your state homestead exemption allows for a higher amount.)

Wages: 100% of wages for heads of family (up to $500 per week either unpaid or paid and deposited into bank account for up to 6 months): Florida Statutes Annotated 222.11.

Georgia

Georgia residents cannot use the Federal Bankruptcy Exemptions, but may use the Federal Non-Bankruptcy Exemptions listed at the end of this Appendix and the following state exemptions:

Benefits: Aid to aged, blind, or disabled (unlimited amount): Code of Georgia Annotated 49-4-35, 49-4-58, 49-4-84, & 44-13-100(a)(2)(C); Crime victims compensation (unlimited amount): Code of Georgia Annotated 44-13-100(a)(11)(A); Local public assistance (unlimited amount): Code of Georgia Annotated 44-13-100(a)(2)(A); Social Security (unlimited amount): Code of Georgia Annotated 44-13-100 (a)(2)(A); Unemployment compensation (unlimited amount): Code of Georgia Annotated 44-13-100(a)(2)(A); Veterans benefits (unlimited amount): Code of Georgia Annotated 44-13-100 (a)(2)(B); Workers compensation (unlimited amount): Code of Georgia Annotated 34-9-84; Compensation for loss of future earnings (up to $7,500): Code of Georgia Annotated 44-13-100(a)(11)(E); Compensation for personal bodily injury (up to $10,000): Code of Georgia Annotated 44-13-100(a)(11)(D) .

Insurance: Annuity contract benefits (unlimited amount): Code of Georgia Annotated 33-28-7; Payments under a pension, annuity, or similar contract (unlimited amount): Code of Georgia Annotated 44-13-100(a)(2)(E); Disability or health benefits (up to $250 per month): Code of Georgia Annotated 33-29-15; Fraternal society benefits (unlimited amount): Code of Georgia Annotated 33-15-62; Group insurance (unlimited amount): Code of Georgia Annotated 33-30-10; Industrial life insurance if policy needed for support (unlimited amount): Code of Georgia Annotated 33-26-5; Life insurance proceeds if policy needed for support (unlimited amount): Code of Georgia Annotated 44-13-100(a)(11)(C); Unmatured life insurance contract (unlimited amount): Code of Georgia Annotated 44-13-100(a)(8); Unmatured life insurance dividends, interest, loan value, or cash value (up to $2,000): Code of Georgia Annotated 44-13-100(a)(9).

Miscellaneous: Alimony or child support (amount needed for support): Code of Georgia Annotated 44-13-100(a)(2)(D); Any property (up to $600 plus any unused portion of real estate exemption): Code of Georgia Annotated 44-13-100(a)(6).

Pensions: Any pensions or retirement benefits (unlimited amount): Code of Georgia Annotated 18-4-22, 44-13-100(a)(2)(E), & 44-13-100(a)(2.1)(C); Employees of non-profit corporations (unlimited amount): Code of Georgia Annotated 44-13-100(a)(2.1)(B); Public employees (unlimited amount): Code of Georgia Annotated 44-13-100 (a)(2.1)(A) & 47-2-332.

Personal Property: Any property up to $600 (exemption may be applied to either personal property or real estate): Code of Georgia Annotated 44-13-100(a)(6); Animals, appliances, books, clothing, crops, furnishings, household goods, and musical instruments (up to $300 per item and up to $5,000 total): Code of Georgia Annotated 44-13-100(a)(4); Burial plot (if taken instead of real estate exemption): Code of Georgia Annotated 44-13-100(a)(1); Health aids (unlimited amount): Code of Georgia Annotated 44-13-100(a)(10); Implements, books, or tools of a trade (up to $1,500): Code of Georgia Annotated 44-13-100(a)(7); Jewelry (up to $500): Code of Georgia Annotated 44-13-100(a)(5); Lost future earnings (amount needed for support): Code of Georgia Annotated 44-13-100(a)(11)(E); Motor vehicles (up to $3,500): Code of Georgia Annotated 44-13-100(a)(3); Personal injury recoveries (up to $10,000, but not for pain and suffering): Code of Georgia Annotated 44-13-100(a)(11)(D); Wrongful death recoveries (amount needed for support): Code of Georgia Annotated 44-13-100(a)(11)(B).

Real Estate: Real or personal property used as residence and burial plot (up to $10,000, or up to $20,000 if debtor is married, regardless of whether spouse is also filing for bankruptcy; in addition, unused portion of real estate exemption may be used with any property): Code of Georgia Annotated 44-13-100(a)(1) & 44-13-100(a)(6).

Wages: 75% of earned but unpaid wages (judge may allow more for low-income debtors): Code of Georgia Annotated 18-4-20 & 18-4-21.

Hawaii

Hawaii residents may use either the Federal Bankruptcy Exemptions listed at the end of this Appendix or the state exemptions listed below. If state exemptions are used, then Federal Non-Bankruptcy Exemptions at the end of this Appendix may also be used.

Benefits: Public assistance for work done in home or workshop (unlimited amount): Hawaii Revised Statutes 346-33; Unemployment compensation (unlimited amount): Hawaii Revised Statutes 383-163; Unemployment work relief funds (up to $60 per month): Hawaii Revised Statutes 653-4; Workers compensation (unlimited amount): Hawaii Revised Statutes 386-57; Crime victim's compensation and special account to limit commercial exploitation of crimes (unlimited amount): Hawaii Revised Statutes 351-66.

Insurance: Annuity contract if beneficiary is insured's spouse, child, or parent (unlimited amount): Hawaii Revised Statutes 431:10-232(b); Disability benefits (unlimited amount): Hawaii Revised Statutes 431:10-231; Fraternal society benefits (unlimited amount): Hawaii Revised Statutes 432:2-403; Group life insurance policy or proceeds (unlimited amount): Hawaii Revised Statutes 431:10-233; Life insurance proceeds if policy prohibits proceeds from being used to pay creditors (unlimited amount): Hawaii Revised Statutes 431:10-D: 112; Life or health insurance policy for spouse or child (unlimited amount): Hawaii Revised Statutes 431:10-234.

Miscellaneous: Property of business partnership (unlimited amount): Hawaii Revised Statutes 425-125.

Pensions: Firefighters (unlimited amount): Hawaii Revised Statutes 88-169; Police officers (unlimited amount): Hawaii Revised Statutes 88-169; Public officers and employees (unlimited amount): Hawaii Revised Statutes 88-91 & 653-3; Retirement benefits paid in at least 3 years before filing for bankruptcy (unlimited amount): Hawaii Revised Statutes 651-124.

Personal Property: Appliances and furnishings (amounts needed for support): Hawaii Revised Statutes 651-121(1); Books (unlimited amount): Hawaii Revised Statutes 651-121(1); Burial plot not exceeding 250 square feet and tombstones (unlimited amount): Hawaii Revised Statutes 651-121(4); Clothing (unlimited amount): Hawaii Revised Statutes 651-121(1); Jewelry (up to $1,000): Hawaii Revised Statutes 651-121(1); Motor vehicle (up to $2,575): Hawaii Revised Statutes 651-121(2); Proceeds from sold or damaged exempt property within last 6 months (up to exemption amount): Hawaii Revised Statutes 651-121(5); Tools, books, uniforms, furnishings, fishing equipment, motor vehicle, and other personal property (amount needed for work): Hawaii Revised Statutes 651-121(3).

Real Estate: Real estate if used as a residence (up to 1 acre and up to $30,000 for head of family or if over 65, otherwise up to $20,000)(husband and wife may not double exemption); sale proceeds exempt for 6 months: Hawaii Revised Statutes 651-91, 651-92(a)(2) & 651-96.

Wages: Prisoner's wages (unlimited amount): Hawaii Revised Statutes 353-22; Unpaid wages due for work of past 31 days; Wages due for over 31 days, then 95% of 1st $100, 90% of 2nd $100, and 80% of remainder: Hawaii Revised Statutes 651-121(6) & 652-1.

Idaho

Idaho residents cannot use the Federal Bankruptcy Exemptions, but may use the Federal Non-Bankruptcy Exemptions listed at the end of this Appendix and the following state exemptions:

Benefits: Aid to aged, blind, disabled, and families with dependent children (unlimited amount): Idaho Code 56-223; Federal, state, or local public assistance (unlimited amount): Idaho Code 11-603(4); General assistance (unlimited amount): Idaho Code 56-223; Social Security (unlimited amount): Idaho Code 11-603(3); Unemployment compensation (unlimited amount): Idaho Code 11-603(6); Veterans benefits (unlimited amount): Idaho Code 11-603(3); Workers compensation (unlimited amount): Idaho Code 72-802.

Insurance: Annuity proceeds (up to $1,250 per month): Idaho Code 41-1836; Death or disability benefits (unlimited amount): Idaho Code 11-604(1)(a) & 41-1834; Fraternal society benefits (unlimited amount): Idaho Code 41-3218; Group life insurance benefits (unlimited amount): Idaho Code 41-1835; Homeowners insurance proceeds (up to amount of real estate exemption): Idaho Code 55-1008; Life insurance proceeds if policy prohibits proceeds from being used to pay creditors (unlimited amount): Idaho Code 41-1930; Life insurance proceeds for beneficiary other than the insured (unlimited amount): Idaho Code 11-604(1)(d) & 41-1833; Medical, surgical, or hospital care benefits (unlimited amount): Idaho Code 11-603(5).

Miscellaneous: Alimony or child support (amount needed for support): Idaho Code 11-604(1)(b); Liquor licenses (unlimited amount): Idaho Code 23-514.

Pensions: Firefighters (unlimited amount): Idaho Code 72-1422; Police officers (unlimited amount): Idaho Code 50-1517; Public employees (unlimited amount): Idaho Code 59-1317; Retirement benefits (unlimited amount): Idaho Code 55-1011.

Personal Property: Appliances, books, clothing, family portraits, 1 firearm, furnishings, musical instruments, pets, and sentimental heirlooms (up to $500 per item, and up to $5,000 total): Idaho Code 11-605(1) & (7); Arms, uniforms, and equipment required for peace officer, national guard, or military personnel (unlimited amount): Idaho Code 11-605(5); Building materials (unlimited amount): Idaho Code 45-514; Burial plot (unlimited amount): Idaho Code 11-603(1); Crops on up to 50 acres (up to $1,000): Idaho Code 11-605(6); Health aids (unlimited amount): Idaho Code 11-603(2); Implements, books, and tools of a trade (up to $1,500): Idaho Code 11-605(3); Any personal property (up to $800): Idaho Code 11-605(10); Jewelry (up to $1,000): Idaho Code 11-605(2); Motor vehicle (up to $5,000): Idaho Code 11-605(3); Personal injury recoveries (unlimited amount): Idaho Code 11-604(1)(c); Proceeds for damaged exempt property within last 3 months (up to amount of exemption): Idaho Code 11-606; Water rights (up to 160 inches): Idaho Code 11-605(6); Wrongful death recoveries (unlimited amount): Idaho Code 11-604(1)(c).

Real Estate: Real property or mobile home used as residence (up to $100,000); proceeds from sale are exempt for 6 months; must record homestead exemption; husband and wife may not double real estate exemption: Idaho Code 55-1003, 55-1004, & 55-1113.

Wages: 75% of earned but unpaid wages or pension payments (judge may allow more for low-income debtors): Idaho Code 11-207.

Illinois

Illinois residents cannot use the Federal Bankruptcy Exemptions, but may use the Federal Non-Bankruptcy Exemptions listed at the end of this Appendix and the following state exemptions. Wife and husband may double the real estate exemption.

Benefits: Aid to aged, blind, disabled, and families with dependent children (unlimited amount): Illinois Annotated Statutes 305-5/11-3; Crime victims compensation (unlimited amount): Illinois Annotated Statutes 735-5/12-1001(h)(1); Social Security (unlimited amount): Illinois Annotated Statutes 735-5/12-1001(g)(1); Unemployment compensation (unlimited amount): Illinois Annotated Statutes 735-5/12-1001(g)(1), (3); Veterans benefits (unlimited amount): Illinois Annotated Statutes 735-5/12-1001(g)(2); Workers compensation (unlimited amount): Illinois Annotated Statutes 820-305/21; Workers occupational disease compensation (unlimited amount): Illinois Annotated Statutes 820-310/21.

Insurance: Annuity, life insurance proceeds, or cash value if beneficiary is insured's child, parent, spouse, or other dependent (unlimited amount): Illinois Annotated Statutes 215-5/238; Fraternal society benefits (unlimited amount): Illinois Annotated Statutes 215-5/299.1a; Health or disability benefits (unlimited amount): Illinois Annotated Statutes 735-5/12-1001(g)(3); Homeowners insurance proceeds (up to $15,000): Illinois Annotated Statutes 735-5/12-907; Life insurance policy if beneficiary is insured's spouse or child (unlimited amount). Illinois Annotated Statutes 735-5/12-1001(f); Life insurance proceeds if policy prohibits proceeds from being used to pay creditors (unlimited amount): Illinois Annotated Statutes 215-5/238; Life insurance proceeds (amount needed for support): Illinois Annotated Statutes 735-5/12-1001(f) & (h)(3).

Miscellaneous: Alimony and child support (needed for support): Illinois Annotated Statutes 735-5/12-1001(g)(4); Any property (up to $4,000): Illinois Annotated Statutes 735-5/12-1001(b); Property of a business partnership (unlimited amount): Illinois Annotated Statutes 805-205/25.

Pensions: Civil service employees (unlimited amount): Illinois Annotated Statutes 40-5/11-223; Correction employees (unlimited amount): Illinois Annotated Statutes 40-5/19-117; Firefighters, disabled firefighters, and widows and children of firefighters (unlimited amount): Illinois Annotated Statutes 40-5/4-135 & 40-5/6-213; General assembly members (unlimited amount): Illinois Annotated Statutes 40-5/2-154; Judges (unlimited amount): Illinois Annotated Statutes 40-5/18-161; Park employees (unlimited amount): Illinois Annotated Statutes 40-5/12-190; Police officers (unlimited amount): Illinois Annotated Statutes 40-5/3-144.1 & 40-5/5-218; Public, public library, municipal, county, and state employees (unlimited amount): Illinois Annotated Statutes 40-5/7-217(a), 40-5/8-244, 40-5/9-228, 40-5/14-147, & 735-5/12-1006; Retirement benefits (unlimited amount): Illinois Annotated Statutes 735-5/12-1006; Sanitation district employees (unlimited amount): Illinois Annotated Statutes 40-5/13-805; State university employees (unlimited amount): Illinois Annotated Statutes 40-5/15-185; Teachers (unlimited amount): Illinois Annotated Statutes 40-5/16-190 & 40-5/17-151.

Personal Property: Bible, family pictures, and schoolbooks (unlimited amount) and clothing (amount needed): Illinois Annotated Statutes 735-5/12-1001(a); Health aids (unlimited amount): Illinois Annotated Statutes 735-5/12-1001(e); Implements, books, and tools of a trade (up to $1,500): Illinois Annotated Statutes 735-5/12-1001(d); Motor vehicle (up to $2,400 per person): Illinois Annotated Statutes 735-5/12-1001(c); Personal injury recoveries (up to $15,000): Illinois Annotated Statutes 735-5/12-1001(h)(4); Proceeds from sale of exempt property (up to exemption amount): Illinois Annotated Statutes 735-5/12-1001; Wrongful death recoveries (amount needed for support): Illinois Annotated Statutes 735-5/12-1001(h)(2); Pre-paid cemetery funds (unlimited amount): Illinois Annotated Statutes 225-45/4a & 815-390/16; Liquor permits (unlimited amount): Illinois Annotated Statutes 235-5/6-1; Cemetery care fund: (unlimited amount): Illinois Annotated Statutes 760-100/4.

Real Estate: Real or personal property used as a residence including a farm, building, condominium, co-op, or mobile home (up to $15,000); proceeds from sale are exempt for up to 1 year from sale; must file exemption with county: Illinois Annotated Statutes 735-5/12-901, 735-5/12-902, & 735-5/12-906.

Wages: 85% of earned but unpaid wages (judge may allow more for low-income debtors): Illinois Annotated Statutes 740-170/4.

Indiana

Indiana residents cannot use the Federal Bankruptcy Exemptions, but may use the Federal Non-Bankruptcy Exemptions listed at the end of this Appendix and the following state exemptions. Wife and husband may double the real estate exemption.

Benefits: Crime victims compensation except for treatment of injury incurred during the crime (unlimited amount): Indiana Statutes Annotated 5-2-6.1-38; Unemployment compensation (unlimited amount): Indiana Statutes Annotated 22-4-33-3; Workers compensation (unlimited amount): Indiana Statutes Annotated 22-3-2-17.

Insurance: Fraternal society benefits (unlimited amount): Indiana Statutes Annotated 27-11-6-3; Group life insurance policy (unlimited amount): Indiana Statutes Annotated 27-1-12-29; Life insurance policy, proceeds, or cash value if beneficiary is insured's spouse or dependent (unlimited amount): Indiana Statutes Annotated 27-1-12-14; Life insurance proceeds if policy prohibits proceeds to be used to pay creditors (unlimited amount): Indiana Statutes Annotated 27-2-5-1; Mutual life or accident insurance proceeds (unlimited amount): Indiana Statutes Annotated 27-8-3-23.

Miscellaneous: Any real estate or tangible personal property (up to $8,000): Indiana Statutes Annotated 34-55-10-2(c)(2); Property of a business partnership (unlimited amount): Indiana Statutes Annotated 23-4-1-25.

Pensions: Firefighters (unlimited amount): Indiana Statutes Annotated 36-8-7-22 & 36-8-8-17; Police officers (only unpaid benefits): Indiana Statutes Annotated 36-8-8-17; Retirement benefits (unlimited amount): Indiana Statutes Annotated 5-10.3-8-9; Sheriffs (only unpaid benefits): Indiana Statutes Annotated 36-8-10-19; State teachers (unlimited amount): Indiana Statutes Annotated 21-6.1-5-17; Contributions made to retirement plan; any rollovers of such and any earnings made on such: Indiana Statutes Annotated 34-55-10-2(b)(6)(A), (B), & (C).

Personal Property: Any intangible personal property, except money that is owed to debtor (up to $300): Indiana Statutes Annotated 34-55-10-2(c)(3); Professionally prescribed health aids (unlimited amount): Indiana Statutes Annotated 34-55-10-2(c)(4); National guard uniforms, arms, and equipment (unlimited amount): Indiana Statutes Annotated 10-16-10-3; Medical care savings account: Indiana Statutes Annotated 34-55-10-2(c)(7); Other personal property (see below under "Real Estate").

Real Estate: Real estate or personal property used as residence (up to $15,000): Indiana Statutes Annotated 34-55-10-2(c)(1); Other real estate or tangible personal property (amount up to $8,000) Indiana Statutes Annotated 34-55-10-2(c)(2); Property owned as tenancy-by-the-entireties: Indiana Statutes Annotated 34-55-10-2(c)(5).

Wages: 75% of earned but unpaid wages (judge may allow more for low-income debtors): Indiana Statutes Annotated 24-4.5-5-105.

Iowa

Iowa residents cannot use the Federal Bankruptcy Exemptions, but may use the Federal Non-Bankruptcy Exemptions listed at the end of this Appendix and the following state exemptions:

Benefits: Adopted child assistance (unlimited amount): Iowa Code Annotated 627.19; Aid to Families with Dependent Children (unlimited amount): Iowa Code Annotated 627.6(8)(a); Disability or illness benefits (unlimited amount): Iowa Code Annotated 627.6(8)(c); Local public assistance (unlimited amount): Iowa Code Annotated 627.6(8)(a); Social Security (unlimited amount): Iowa Code Annotated 627.6(8)(a); Unemployment compensation (unlimited amount): Iowa Code Annotated 627.6(8)(a); Veterans benefits (unlimited amount): Iowa Code Annotated 627.6(8)(b); Workers compensation (unlimited amount): Iowa Code Annotated 627.13.

Insurance: Accident, disability, health, illness, or life insurance proceeds (unlimited, but only up to $10,000, if paid to a surviving spouse, child, or other dependent within 2 years of filing for bankruptcy): Iowa Code Annotated 627.6(6); Fraternal benefit society benefits: Iowa Code Annotated 512B.18; Employee group insurance policy or proceeds (unlimited amount): Iowa Code Annotated 509.12; Life insurance cash value or proceeds (up to $10,000, if acquired within 2 years of filing for bankruptcy, and if paid to spouse, child, or other dependent): Iowa Code Annotated 627.6(6).

Miscellaneous: Alimony or child support (amount needed for support): Iowa Code Annotated 627.6(8)(d); Liquor licenses (unlimited amount): Iowa Code Annotated 123.38; Property of a business partnership (unlimited amount): Iowa Code Annotated 410.11.

Pensions: Federal government pensions (payments being received): Iowa Code Annotated 627.8; Firefighters or police officers (payments being received): Iowa Code Annotated 410.11; Firefighters (unlimited amount): Iowa Code Annotated 411.13; Other pensions (payments being received): Iowa Code Annotated 627.6(8)(e); Peace officers (unlimited amount): Iowa Code Annotated 97A.12; Police officers (unlimited amount): Iowa Code Annotated 411.13; Public employees (unlimited amount): Iowa Code Annotated 97B.39; Retirement plan savings: Iowa Code Annotated 627.6(8)(f).

Personal Property: Any personal property, including cash (up to $1,000): Iowa Code Annotated 627.6(14); Appliances, furnishings, household goods, musical instruments, and tax refund (up to $7,000 total, only up to $1,000 may be from tax refund): Iowa Code Annotated 627.6(5); Bibles, books, paintings, pictures, and portraits (up to $1,000): Iowa Code Annotated 627.6(3); Burial plot (up to 1 acre): Iowa Code Annotated 627.6(4); Clothing, engagement, or wedding rings (up to $7,000 plus receptacles to hold clothing): Iowa Code Annotated 627.6(1); Farm equipment, including livestock and feed (up to $10,000): Iowa Code Annotated 627.6(11); Health aids (unlimited amount): Iowa Code Annotated 627.6(7); Motor vehicle (up to $7,000): Iowa Code Annotated 627.6(9) & 9; Musket, rifle, or shotgun (unlimited amount): Iowa Code Annotated 627.6(2); Non-farm business books, equipment, and tools (up to $10,000): Iowa Code Annotated 627.6(11).

Real Estate: Real property or an apartment used as a residence (unlimited value, property cannot exceed ½ acre in town or city, or 40 acres elsewhere): Iowa Code Annotated 561.2 & 561.16. (Note: The 2005 Bankruptcy Act limits homestead exemptions to $136,875.00 if you have lived in the state where you are attempting to claim the exemption for less than 40 months (1215 days). This is true even if your state homestead exemption allows for a higher amount.)

Wages: If annual wage income is less than $12,000, then $250 for each judgment creditor, otherwise depending on income made within 1 year: $12,000-$16,000 = $400/creditor; $16,001-$24,000 = $800/creditor; $24,001-$35,000 = $1,500/creditor; $35,001-$50,000 = $2,000/creditor; over $50,000 = 10% of expected earnings: Iowa Code Annotated 642.21; Wages or salary of prisoner (unlimited amount): Iowa Code Annotated 356.29.

Kansas

Kansas residents cannot use the Federal Bankruptcy Exemptions, but may use the Federal Non-Bankruptcy Exemptions listed at the end of this Appendix and the following state exemptions:

Benefits: Social Security, unemployment compensation, aid to families with dependent children, general assistance, and welfare (unlimited amount): 11 United States Code 522(d)(10)(A through E); Crime victims compensation (unlimited amount): Kansas Statutes Annotated 60-2313(a)(5); Workers compensation (unlimited amount): Kansas Statutes Annotated 44-514.

Insurance: Fraternal life insurance benefits (unlimited amount): Kansas Statutes Annotated 60-2313(a)(8); Life insurance cash value if bankruptcy filed at least 1 year after policy issued (unlimited amount): Kansas Statutes Annotated 60-2313(a)(7); Life insurance proceeds if policy prohibits proceeds from being used to pay creditors (unlimited amount): Kansas Statutes Annotated 60-2313(a)(7).

Miscellaneous: Liquor licenses (unlimited amount): Kansas Statutes Annotated 650-2313(a)(6).

Pensions: Elected and appointed officials in cities with populations between 120,000 and 200,000 (unlimited amount): Kansas Statutes Annotated 13-14,102; Federal government pension payments paid within 3 months of filing for bankruptcy (unlimited amount): Kansas Statutes Annotated 60-2308(a); Firefighters (unlimited amount): Kansas Statutes Annotated 12-5005(e); Judges (unlimited amount): Kansas Statutes Annotated 20-2618; Police officers (unlimited amount): Kansas Statutes Annotated 12-5005(e); Public employees (unlimited amount): Kansas Statutes Annotated 74-4923; Retirement benefits (unlimited amount): Kansas Statutes Annotated 60-2308(b); State highway patrol officers (unlimited amount): Kansas Statutes Annotated 74-4978g; State school employees (unlimited amount): Kansas Statutes Annotated 72-5526.

Personal Property: Books, documents, furniture, instruments, equipment, breeding stock, seed, grain, and livestock used in farm business (up to $7,500 total): Kansas Statutes Annotated 60-2304(e); Burial plot or crypt (unlimited amount): Kansas Statutes Annotated 60-2304(d); Clothing (amount to last 1 year): Kansas Statutes Annotated 60-2304(a); Food and fuel (amount to last 1 year): Kansas Statutes Annotated 60-2304(a); Funeral plan prepayments (unlimited amount): Kansas Statutes Annotated 60-2313(a)(10); Cemetery trust fund: Kansas Statutes Annotated 60-2313(a)(9); Household furnishings and equipment (unlimited amount): Kansas Statutes Annotated 60-2304(a); Jewelry (up to $1,000): Kansas Statutes Annotated 60-2304(b); Motor vehicle (up to $20,000; unlimited amount if equipped for disabled person): Kansas Statutes Annotated 60-2304(c); National Guard uniforms, arms, and equipment (unlimited amount): Kansas Statutes Annotated 48-245.

Real Estate: Real property or mobile home used as residence (unlimited value, up to 1 acre in town or city, or 160 acres on farm): Kansas Statutes Annotated 60-2301 & Kansas Constitution 15-9. (Note: The 2005 Bankruptcy Act limits homestead exemptions to $136,875.00 if you have lived in the state where you are attempting to claim the exemption for less than 40 months (1215 days). This is true even if your state homestead exemption allows for a higher amount.)

Wages: 75% of earned but unpaid wages (judge may allow more for low-income debtors): Kansas Statutes Annotated 60-2310.

Kentucky

Kentucky residents cannot use the Federal Bankruptcy Exemptions, but may use the Federal Non-Bankruptcy Exemptions listed at the end of this Appendix and the following state exemptions:

Benefits: Aid to aged, blind, disabled, and families with dependent children (unlimited amount): Kentucky Revised Statutes 205.220; Crime victims compensation (unlimited amount): Kentucky Revised Statutes 427.150(2)(a); Unemployment compensation (unlimited amount): Kentucky Revised Statutes 341.470; Workers compensation (unlimited amount): Kentucky Revised Statutes 342.180.

Insurance: Annuity contract proceeds (up to $350 per month): Kentucky Revised Statutes 304.14-330; Cooperative life or casualty insurance benefits (unlimited amount): Kentucky Revised Statutes 427.110(1); Fraternal society benefits (unlimited amount): Kentucky Revised Statutes 427.110(2); Group life insurance proceeds (unlimited amount): Kentucky Revised Statutes 304.14-320; Health or disability benefits (unlimited amount): Kentucky Revised Statutes 304.14-310; Life insurance policy if beneficiary is a married woman (unlimited amount): Kentucky Revised Statutes 304.14-340; Life insurance proceeds if policy prohibits proceeds from being used to pay creditors (unlimited amount): Kentucky Revised Statutes 304.14-350; Life Insurance proceeds or cash value if beneficiary is someone other than insured (unlimited amount): Kentucky Revised Statutes 304.14-300.

Miscellaneous: Alimony or child support (amount needed for support): Kentucky Revised Statutes 427.150(1); Any property (real estate or personal property [up to $1,000]): Kentucky Revised Statutes 427.160; Property of a business partnership (unlimited amount): Kentucky Revised Statutes 362.270.

Pensions: Firefighters and police officers (unlimited amount): Kentucky Revised Statutes 67A.620, 95.878, 427.120, & 427.125; Other pensions (unlimited amount): Kentucky Revised Statutes 427.150(2)(e); State employees (unlimited amount): Kentucky Revised Statutes 61.690; Teachers (unlimited amount): Kentucky Revised Statutes 161.700; Urban county government employees (unlimited amount): Kentucky Revised Statutes 67A.350.

Personal Property: Burial plot (up to $5,000, if used instead of real estate exemption): Kentucky Revised Statutes 427.060; Clothing, jewelry, or furnishings (up to $3,000 total): Kentucky Revised Statutes 427.010(1); Health aids (unlimited amount): Kentucky Revised Statutes 427.010(1); Library, equipment, instruments, and furnishings (up to $1,000) and motor vehicle (up to $2,500) of minister, attorney, physician, surgeon, chiropractor, veterinarian, or dentist (vehicle exemption also valid for mechanic or mechanical or electrical equipment servicer): Kentucky Revised Statutes 427.030 & 427.040; Lost earnings payments (amount needed for support): Kentucky Revised Statutes 427.150(2)(d); Medical expenses benefits received under Kentucky motor vehicle reparation law (unlimited amount): Kentucky Revised Statutes 304.39-260; Motor vehicle (up to $2,500): Kentucky Revised Statutes 427.010(1); Personal injury recoveries (up to $7,500, not including pain and suffering or pecuniary loss): Kentucky Revised Statutes 427.150(2)(c); Tools of a non-farmer (up to $300): Kentucky Revised Statutes 427.30; Tools, equipment, livestock, and poultry of a farmer (up to $3,000): Kentucky Revised Statutes 427.010(1); Wrongful death recoveries (unlimited amount): Kentucky Revised Statutes 427.150(2)(b); Prepaid tuition account: Kentucky Revised Statutes Annotated 164A.707.

Real Estate: Real or personal property used as residence (up to $5,000); proceeds from sale are also exempt: Kentucky Revised Statutes 427.060 & 427.090.

Wages: 75% of earned but unpaid wages (judge may allow more for low-income debtors): Kentucky Revised Statutes 427.010(2) & (3).

Louisiana

Louisiana residents cannot use the Federal Bankruptcy Exemptions, but may use the Federal Non-Bankruptcy Exemptions listed at the end of this Appendix and the following state exemptions:

Benefits: Aid to aged, blind, disabled, and families with dependent children (unlimited amount): Louisiana Revised Statutes Annotated 46:111; Crime victims compensation (unlimited amount): Louisiana Revised Statutes Annotated 46:1811; Unemployment compensation (unlimited amount): Louisiana Revised Statutes Annotated 23:1693; Workers compensation (unlimited amount): Louisiana Revised Statutes Annotated 23:1205.

Insurance: Fraternal society benefits (unlimited amount): Louisiana Revised Statutes Annotated 22:558; Group insurance policies or proceeds (unlimited amount): Louisiana Revised Statutes Annotated 22:649; Health, accident, or disability proceeds (unlimited amount): Louisiana Revised Statutes Annotated 22:646; Life insurance proceeds (unlimited amount, unless policy was issued within 9 months of bankruptcy filing, then exempt only up to $35,000): Louisiana Revised Statutes Annotated 22:647.

Miscellaneous: Personal Property of a minor child (unlimited amount): Louisiana Revised Statutes Annotated 13:3881A(3) & Louisiana Civil Code 223.

Pensions: Gratuitous payments to an employee or heirs (unlimited amount): Louisiana Revised Statutes Annotated 20:33(2); Retirement benefits (unlimited amount if contribution was made over 1 year before bankruptcy filed): Louisiana Revised Statutes Annotated 13:3881D(1) & 20:33(1).

Personal Property: Arms, bedding, chinaware, clothing, cow (1), family portraits, freezer, glassware, heating and cooling equipment, household pets, linens and bedroom furniture, living room and dining room furniture, military equipment, musical instruments, poultry, pressing irons, refrigerator, sewing machine, silverware (if non-sterling), stove, utensils, washer, and dryer: Louisiana Revised Statutes Annotated 13:3881A(4); Cemetery plot and monuments (unlimited amount): Louisiana Revised Statutes Annotated 8:313; Engagement and wedding rings (up to $5,000): Louisiana Revised Statutes Annotated 13:3881A(5); Tools, instruments, books, pickup truck (up to 3 tons), auto (non-luxury), or utility trailer (amount needed for work): Louisiana Revised Statutes Annotated 3:3881A(2).

Real Estate: Real estate used as residence (up to $25,000 and up to 200 acres; however, unlimited amount If debts are the result of catastrophic or terminal illnes or injury; value is based on market value 1 year prior to filing for bankruptcy), spouse or child of deceased owner may claim homestead exemption: Louisiana Revised Statutes Annotated 20:1. (Note: The 2005 Bankruptcy Act limits homestead exemptions to $136,875.00 if you have lived in the state where you are attempting to claim the exemption for less than 40 months (1215 days). This is true even if your state homestead exemption allows for a higher amount.)

Wages: 75% of earned but unpaid wages (judge may allow more for low-income debtors): Louisiana Revised Statutes Annotated 13:3881A(1)(a).

Maine

Maine residents cannot use the Federal Bankruptcy Exemptions, but may use the Federal Non-Bankruptcy Exemptions listed at the end of this Appendix and the following state exemptions:

Benefits: Aid to needy and needy families or dependent children (unlimited amount): Maine Revised Statutes Annotated 22-3180 & 22-3766; Crime victims compensation (unlimited amount): Maine Revised Statutes Annotated 14-4422(14)A; Social Security (unlimited amount): Maine Revised Statutes Annotated 14-4422(13)A; Unemployment compensation (unlimited amount): Maine Revised Statutes Annotated 14-4422(13)A & C; Veterans benefits (unlimited amount): Maine Revised Statutes Annotated 14-4422(13)B; Workers compensation (unlimited amount): Maine Revised Statutes Annotated 24A-2431; Compensation for personal bodily injury (amount up to $12,500): Maine Revised Statutes Annotated 14-4422(14(D).

Insurance: Annuity proceeds (up to $450 per month): Maine Revised Statutes Annotated 24-A-2431; Disability or health insurance proceeds (unlimited amount): Maine Revised Statutes Annotated 14-4422(13)A, C, & 24-A-2429; Fraternal society benefits (unlimited amount): Maine Revised Statutes Annotated 24-A-4118; Group health or life insurance policy or proceeds (unlimited amount): Maine Revised Statutes Annotated 24-A-2430; Life, endowment, annuity, or accident policy or proceeds (unlimited amount): Maine Revised Statutes Annotated 14-4422(14)C & 24-A-2428; Life insurance policy, proceeds, or loan value (up to $4,000): Maine Revised Statutes Annotated 14-4422(11); Unmatured life insurance policy except credit insurance policy (unlimited amount): Maine Revised Statutes Annotated 14-4422(10); Death benefits of police, fire, or emergency personnel who die in the line of duty (unlimited amount): Maine Revised Statutes Annotated 25-1612.

Miscellaneous: Alimony/child support (amount needed for support): Maine Revised Statutes Annotated 14-4422(13)D; Any additional property (up to $400): Maine Revised Statutes Annotated 14-4422(15); Property of a business partnership (unlimited amount): Maine Revised Statutes Annotated 31-1051 through 31-1054; Maintenance under the Maine Rehabilitation Act (unlimited amount): Maine Revised Statutes Annotated 26-1411-H.

Pensions: Judges, legislators, and state employees (unlimited amount): Maine Revised Statutes Annotated 3-703, 4-1203, & 5-17054; Retirement benefits (unlimited amount): Maine Revised Statutes Annotated 14-4422(13)E.

Personal Property: Animals, appliances, books, clothing, crops, furnishings, household goods, and musical instruments (up to $200 per item): Maine Revised Statutes Annotated

14-4422(3); Boat used in commercial fishing (up to 5 tons): Maine Revised Statutes Annotated 14-4422(9); Burial plot (instead of real estate exemption): Maine Revised Statutes Annotated 14-4422(1); Business books, materials, and stock (up to $5,000): Maine Revised Statutes Annotated 14-4422(5); Cooking or heating stove or furnaces and fuel (unlimited amount and up to 10 cords of wood, 5 tons of coal, or 1,000 gallons of petroleum): Maine Revised Statutes Annotated 14-4422(6)A-C; Food (amount to last 6 months): Maine Revised Statutes Annotated 14-4422(7)A; Health aids (unlimited amount): Maine Revised Statutes Annotated 14-4422(12); Jewelry (up to $750, no limit for wedding/engagement ring): Maine Revised Statutes Annotated 14-4422(4); Lost earnings payments (unlimited amount): Maine Revised Statutes Annotated 14-4422(14)E; Military uniforms, arms, and equipment (unlimited amount): Maine Revised Statutes Annotated 37-B-262; Motor vehicle (up to $5,000): Maine Revised Statutes Annotated 14-4422(2); Personal injury recoveries (up to $12,500, but not pain and suffering): Maine Revised Statutes Annotated 14-4422(14)D; Tools, seeds, fertilizer, and equipment (amount to raise and harvest food for 1 season) and farm implements needed to harvest and raise crops (1 of each type): Maine Revised Statutes Annotated 14-4422(7-8); Unused portion of real estate exemption (up to $6,000 may be used any personal property) and any unsed portion of exemptions for animals, appliances, books, clothing, crops, furnishings, household goods, musical instruments, personal injury recoveries up to $12,500, and tools of a trade of up to $5,000 may be used for any other personal property): Maine Revised Statutes Annotated 14-4422(16); Wrongful death recoveries (unlimited amount): Maine Revised Statutes Annotated 14-4422(14)B.

Real Estate: Real or personal property (including co-op) used as residence and burial plot (up to $35,000, up to $70,000 if debtor lives with any dependent, and up to $70,000 if debtor is over age 60 or physically or mentally disabled); joint debtors may double exemption amount: Sale proceeds are exempt for up to 6 months: Maine Revised Statutes Annotated 14-4422(1).

Wages: None.

Maryland

Maryland residents cannot use the Federal Bankruptcy Exemptions, but may use the Federal Non-Bankruptcy Exemptions listed at the end of this Appendix and the following state exemptions:

Benefits: Aid to families with dependent children and general assistance (unlimited amount): Annotated Code of Maryland 88A-73; Crime victims compensation (unlimited amount): Annotated Code of Maryland-Civil Procedure-11-816; Unemployment compensation (unlimited amount): Annotated Code of Maryland-Labor and Employment-8-106b; Workers compensation (unlimited amount): Annotated Code of Maryland-Labor and Employment-9-732.

Insurance: Disability and health benefits, court awards, and settlements (unlimited amount): Annotated Code of Maryland-Courts and Judicial Proceedings-11-504(b)(2); Fraternal society benefits (unlimited amount): Annotated Code of Maryland-Insurance-8-431; Medical benefits that are deducted from wages (unlimited amount): Annotated Code of Maryland-Commercial-15-601.1.

Miscellaneous: Any property, including a car or real estate (up to $6,000 if exemption is claimed within 30 days of attachment or levy): Annotated Code of Maryland-Courts and Judicial Proceedings-11-504(b)(5) & (f); Partnership property: Annotated Code of Maryland-Corporations and Associations-9A-501; Any additional personal property or real estate (up to $5,000): Annotated Code of Maryland 11-504(f).

Pensions: State employees (unlimited amount): Annotated Code of Maryland-State Personnel and Pensions-21-502; Retirement benefits, except IRAs (unlimited amount): Annotated Code of Maryland-Courts and Judicial Proceedings-11-504(h); Death benefits for Baltimore city police: Annotated Code of Maryland 24-16-103.

Personal Property: Appliances, books, clothing, furnishings, household goods, and pets (up to $1,000 total): Annotated Code of Maryland-Courts and Judicial Proceedings-11-504(b)(4); Clothing, books, tools, instruments, and appliances (up to $5,000): Annotated Code of Maryland-Courts and Judicial Proceedings-11-504(b)(1); Health aids (unlimited amount): Annotated Code of Maryland-Courts and Judicial Proceedings-11-504(b)(3); Lost future earnings recoveries (unlimited amount): Annotated Code of Maryland-Courts and Judicial Proceedings-11-504(b)(2); Perpetual care fund (unlimited amount): Annotated Code of Maryland-Business Regulation-5-602; Pre-paid college trust benefits: Annotated Code of Maryland-Education-18-1913.

Real Estate: None, specifically, but may use both the $6,000 and the $5,000 exemptions noted under "Miscellaneous" for real estate, if desired.

Wages: Earned but unpaid wages (up to the greater of 75% or $145 per week; except in Kent, Caroline, and Queen Anne's of Worcester Counties; up to the greater of 75% of actual wages or 30% of federal minimum wage): Annotated Code of Maryland-Commercial Law-15-601.1.

Massachusetts

Massachusetts residents may use either the Federal Bankruptcy Exemptions listed at the end of this Appendix or the state exemptions listed below. If state exemptions are used, then the Federal Non-Bankruptcy Exemptions at the end of this Appendix may also be used.

Benefits: Aid to families with dependent children (unlimited amount): Massachusetts General Laws Annotated 118-10; Aid to aged/disabled or public assistance (unlimited amount): Massachusetts General Laws Annotated 235-34; Unemployment compensation (unlimited amount): Massachusetts General Laws Annotated 151A-36; Veterans benefits (unlimited amount): Massachusetts General Laws Annotated 115-5; Workers compensation (unlimited amount): Massachusetts General Laws Annotated 152-47.

Insurance: Disability benefits (up to $400 per week): Massachusetts General Laws Annotated 175-110A; Fraternal society benefits (unlimited amount): Massachusetts General Laws Annotated 176-22; Group annuity policy or proceeds (unlimited amount): Massachusetts General Laws Annotated 175-132C; Group life insurance policy (unlimited amount): Massachusetts General Laws Annotated 175-135; Life or endowment policy, proceeds, or cash value (unlimited amount): Massachusetts General Laws Annotated 175-125; Life insurance annuity contract if contract states that it is exempt (unlimited amount): Massachusetts General Laws Annotated 175-125; Life insurance policy if beneficiary is married woman (unlimited amount): Massachusetts General Laws Annotated 175-126; Life insurance proceeds if policy prohibits proceeds from being used to pay creditors (unlimited amount): Massachusetts General Laws Annotated 175-119A; Medical malpractice self-insurance (unlimited amount): Massachusetts General Laws Annotated 175F-15.

Miscellaneous: Property of business partnership (unlimited amount): Massachusetts General Laws Annotated 108A-25.

Pensions: Private retirement benefits (unlimited amount): Massachusetts General Laws Annotated 32-41; Public employees (unlimited amount): Massachusetts General Laws Annotated 32-19; Retirement benefits (unlimited amount): Massachusetts General Laws Annotated 235-34A & 246-28; Savings bank employees (unlimited amount): Massachusetts General Laws Annotated 168-41 & 168-44.

Personal Property: Arms, equipment, and uniforms required for military use (unlimited amount): Massachusetts General Laws Annotated 235-34; Beds, bedding, and heating unit (unlimited amount); clothing (amount needed): Massachusetts General Laws Annotated 235-34; Bibles and books (up to $200 total): Massachusetts General Laws Annotated 235-34; Boats, tackle, and nets of a fisherman (up to $500 total): Massachusetts General Laws Annotated 235-34; Burial plots, tombs, and church pew (unlimited amount): Massachusetts General Laws Annotated 235-34; Cash for fuel, heat, water, or light (up to $75 per month): Massachusetts General Laws Annotated 235-34; Cash for rent (up to $200 per month; instead of real estate exemption): Massachusetts General Laws Annotated 235-34; Cash or bank deposits (up to $500): Massachusetts General Laws Annotated 246-28A; Additional bank deposit (up to $125): Massachusetts General Laws Annotated 235-34; Cooperative association shares (up to $100): Massachusetts General Laws Annotated 235-34; Cows (2), sheep (12), swine (2), and hay (4 tons): Massachusetts General Laws Annotated 235-34; Food or cash for food (up to $300): Massachusetts General Laws Annotated 235-34; Furniture (up to $3,000): Massachusetts General Laws Annotated 235-34; Materials used in business (up to $500): Massachusetts General Laws Annotated 235-34; Motor vehicle (up to $700): Massachusetts General Laws Annotated 235-34; Sewing machine (up to $200): Massachusetts General Laws Annotated 235-34; Tools, implements, and fixtures of business (up to $500 total): Massachusetts General Laws Annotated 235-34.

Real Estate: Property used as a residence (up to $500,000; Note: special rules apply if debtor is over 65 or disabled) must record homestead declaration before filing bankruptcy: Massachusetts General Laws Annotated 188-1, 188-1A, & 188-2. (Note: The 2005 Bankruptcy Act limits homestead exemptions to $136,875.00 if you have lived in the state where you are attempting to claim the exemption for less than 40 months (1215 days). This is true even if your state homestead exemption allows for a higher amount.)

Wages: Earned but unpaid wages (up to $125 per week): Massachusetts General Laws Annotated 246-28; Seaman's wages (unlimited amount): Massachusetts General Laws Annotated 246-32(7).

Michigan

Michigan residents may use either the Federal Bankruptcy Exemptions listed at the end of this Appendix or the state exemptions listed below. If state exemptions are used, then the Federal Non-Bankruptcy Exemptions at the end of this Appendix may also be used.

Benefits: Aid to families with dependent children (unlimited amount): Michigan Compiled Laws Annotated 330.1158a; Crime victims compensation (unlimited amount): Michigan Compiled Laws Annotated 18.362; Unemployment compensation (unlimited amount): Michigan Compiled Laws Annotated 421.30; Veterans benefits for war veterans (unlimited amount): Michigan Compiled Laws Annotated 35.926, 35.977 & 35.1027; Welfare benefits (unlimited amount): Michigan Compiled Laws Annotated 400.63; Workers compensation (unlimited amount): Michigan Compiled Laws Annotated 418.821.

Insurance: Disability, mutual life, or health insurance benefits (unlimited amount): Michigan Compiled Laws Annotated 600.6023(1)(f); Fraternal society benefits (unlimited amount): Michigan Compiled Laws Annotated 500.8181; Life, endowment, or annuity proceeds if policy prohibits proceeds from being used to pay creditors (unlimited amount): Michigan Compiled Laws Annotated 500.4054; Employer-sponsored life insurance policy or trust fund (unlimited amount): Michigan Compiled Laws Annotated 500-2210.

Miscellaneous: Property of a business partnership (unlimited amount): Michigan Compiled Laws Annotated 449.25.

Pensions: Firefighters (unlimited amount): Michigan Compiled Laws Annotated 38.559(6); Police officers (unlimited amount): Michigan Compiled Laws Annotated 38.559(6); Retirement benefits (unlimited amount): Michigan Compiled Laws Annotated 600.6023(1)(l); IRAs (unlimited amount): Michigan Compiled Laws Annotated 600.6023 (1)(k); Legislators (unlimited amount): Michigan Compiled Laws Annotated 38.1057; Public school employees (unlimited amount): Michigan Compiled Laws Annotated 38.1346; State employees (unlimited amount): Michigan Compiled Laws Annotated 38.1683.

Personal Property: Arms and equipment required for military use (unlimited amount): Michigan Compiled Laws Annotated 600.6023(1)(a); Appliances, books, furniture, household goods, and utensils ($525 each item, up to $3,450 total): Michigan Compiled Laws Annotated 600.6023(1)(b); Building and loan association shares (up to $1,150 par value, instead of real estate): Michigan Compiled Laws Annotated 600.6023(1)(g); Burial plots or church pew (up to $575): Michigan Compiled Laws Annotated 600.6023(1)(c); Clothing (unlimited amount):

Michigan Compiled Laws Annotated 600.6023(1)(a); Cows (2), hens (100), roosters (5), sheep (10), swine (5), and feed to last 6 months (up to $2,300): Michigan Compiled Laws Annotated 600.6023(1)(d); Family pictures (unlimited amount): Michigan Compiled Laws Annotated 600.6023(1)(a); Food and fuel (amount to last 6 months): Michigan Compiled Laws Annotated 600.6023(1)(a); Tools, implements, materials, stock, apparatus, team, horse, and harness used in a business (up to $2,300 total): Michigan Compiled Laws Annotated 600.6023(1)(e); Motor vehicle (up to $3,175) Michigan Compiled Laws Annotated 600.6023(1)(g); Computer and accessories (up to $575): Michigan Compiled Laws Annotated 600.6023(1)(h); Household pets (up to $575): Michigan Compiled Laws Annotated 600.6023(1)(f); Professionally pre-scribed health aids (unlimited amount) Michigan Compiled Laws Annotated 600.5451(a).

Real Estate: Real estate, including condominium unit occupied as homestead (up to $34,450 or $51,650 if 65 or disabled, can be up to 1 lot in town, village, city, or 40 acres elsewhere) husand and wife may not double real estate exemption: Michigan Compiled Laws Annotated 559.214, 600.6023 (1)(h) & (i) & (j), 600.6023(3), & 600.6027.

Wages: 60% of earned but unpaid wages (head of household only), otherwise 40%; head of household may keep at least $15 per week plus $2 per week per non-spouse dependent; others at least $10 per week: Michigan Compiled Laws Annotated 600.5311.

Minnesota

Minnesota residents may use either the Federal Bankruptcy Exemptions listed at the end of this Appendix or the state exemptions listed below. If state exemptions are used, then Federal Non-Bankruptcy Exemptions at the end of this Appendix may also be used. Certain state exemptions are adjusted for inflation on July 1st of even-numbered years. The exemptions noted below are current as of July 1, 2008. The next scheduled adjustment is July 1, 2010.

Benefits: Aid to families with dependent children, supplemental and general assistance, and supplemental security income (unlimited amount): Minnesota Statutes Annotated 550.37(14); Crime victims compensation (unlimited amount): Minnesota Statutes Annotated 611A.60; Unemployment compensation (unlimited amount): Minnesota Statutes Annotated 268.192; Veterans benefits (unlimited amount): Minnesota Statutes Annotated 550.38; Workers com-pensation (unlimited amount): Minnesota Statutes Annotated 176.175.

Insurance: Accident or disability insurance proceeds (unlimited amount): Minnesota Stat-utes Annotated 550.39; Fraternal society benefits (unlimited amount): Minnesota Statutes Annotated 64B.18; Life insurance proceeds if beneficiary is spouse or child of insured (up to $20,000, plus $5,000 per dependent): Minnesota Statutes Annotated 550.37(10); Police, fire, or beneficiary association benefits (unlimited amount): Minnesota Statutes Annotated 550.37(11); Unmatured life insurance contract dividends, interest, or loan value (up to $4,000 if insured is debtor or dependent): Minnesota Statutes Annotated 550.37(23).

Miscellaneous: Property of a business partnership (unlimited amount): Minnesota Statutes Annotated 323A.0501 through 323A.0504.

Pensions: Retirement benefits and IRAs (up to $30,000 in present value): Minnesota Statutes Annotated 550.37(24); State employees (unlimited amount): Minnesota Statutes Annotated 352.96; State troopers (unlimited amount): Minnesota Statutes Annotated 352B.071.

Personal Property: Appliances, furniture, phonographs, radio, and TV (up to $9,000 total): Minnesota Statutes Annotated 550.37(4)(b); Bible, books, and musical instruments (unlim-ited amount): Minnesota Statutes Annotated 550.37(2); Burial plot and church pew seat (unlimited amount): Minnesota Statutes Annotated 550.37(3); Clothing, food, utensils, and watch (reasonable amount for a family): Minnesota Statutes Annotated 550.37(4)(a); Farm machines, implements, livestock, farm produce, and crops (up to $13,000 total; total farm tools and other tools exemption cannot exceed $13,000): Minnesota Statutes Annotated 550.37(5); Motor vehicle (up to $4,000, up to $40,000 if modified for disability): Minnesota Statutes Annotated 550.37(12a); Personal injury recoveries (unlimited amount): Minnesota Statutes Annotated 550.37(22); Proceeds for damaged exempt property (up to exemption amount): Minnesota Statutes Annotated 550.37(9) & (16); Teaching materials of public school teacher (unlimited amount): Minnesota Statutes Annotated 550.37(8); Tools, implements, machines, business furniture, stock-in-trade, and library used in business (up to $10,000 total): Minnesota Statutes Annotated 550.37(6); Wedding ring (up to $2,250): Minnesota Statutes Annotated 550.37(4)(c); Wrongful death recoveries (unlimited amount): Minnesota Statutes Annotated 550.37(22).

Real Estate: Real property, mobile home, or manufactured home ($300,000 for non-farmland, $750,000 for farmland, up to ½ acre in city or 160 acres elsewhere): Minnesota Statutes Annotated 510.01, 510.02, & 550.37(12). (Note: The 2005 Bankruptcy Act limits homestead exemptions to $136,875.00 if you have lived in the state where you are attempting to claim the exemption for less than 40 months (1215 days). This is true even if your state homestead exemption allows for a higher amount.)

Wages: Earned but unpaid wages (unlimited amount if paid within 6 months of returning to work and if debtor has ever received welfare): Minnesota Statutes Annotated 550.37(13); Earnings of a minor child (unlimited amount): Minnesota Statutes Annotated 550.37(15); Wages when supporting a dependent (50%): Minnesota Statutes Annotated 550.136(3)(2)(1); Wages deposited into bank accounts for 20 days after deposit: Minnesota Statutes Annotated 550.37(13); Wages of released inmates paid within 6 months of release (unlimited amount): Minnesota Statutes Annotated 550.37(14); 75% of earned but unpaid wages (judge may allow more for low-income debtors): Minnesota Statutes Annotated 571.922.

Mississippi

Mississippi residents cannot use the Federal Bankruptcy Exemptions, but may use the Federal Non-Bankruptcy Exemptions listed at the end of this Appendix and the following state exemptions:

Benefits: Assistance to aged, blind, and disabled (unlimited amount): Mississippi Code 43-9-19, 43-3-71, & 43-29-15; Crime victims compensation (unlimited amount): Mississippi Code 99-41-23(7); Social Security (unlimited amount): Mississippi Code 25-11-129; Unemployment compensation (unlimited amount): Mississippi Code 71-5-539; Workers compensation (unlimited amount): Mississippi Code 71-3-43.

Insurance: Disability benefits (unlimited amount): Mississippi Code 85-3-1(b)(ii); Fraternal society benefits (unlimited amount): Mississippi Code 83-29-39; Homeowners insurance proceeds (up to $75,000): Mississippi Code 85-3-23; Life insurance cash value (up to $50,000): Mississippi Code 85-3-11; Life insurance proceeds if policy prohibits proceeds from being used to pay creditors (unlimited amount): Mississippi Code 83-7-5.

Miscellaneous: Property of a business partnership (unlimited amount): Mississippi Code 79-13-501 through 79-13-504; If debtor is 70 or older, any personal property or real estate (up to $50,000): Mississippi Code 85-7-1(h).

Pensions: Firefighters (unlimited amount): Mississippi Code 21-29-257; Highway patrol officers (unlimited amount): Mississippi Code 25-13-31; IRAs (unlimited amount if deposited over 1 year before filing for bankruptcy): Mississippi Code 85-3-1; Keogh (unlimited amount if deposited over 1 year before filing for bankruptcy): Mississippi Code 85-3-1; Private retirement benefits (unlimited amount to the extent they are tax-deferred): Mississippi Code 71-1-43; Police officers (unlimited amount): Mississippi Code 21-29-257; Public employees retirement and disability benefits (unlimited amount): Mississippi Code 25-11-129; Retirement benefits (unlimited amount if deposited over 1 year before filing for bankruptcy): Mississippi Code 85-3-1; State employees (unlimited amount): Mississippi Code 25-14-5; Teachers (unlimited amount): Mississippi Code 25-11-201(1)(d); Pension, profit-sharing, stock bonus plan, deferred compensation plan, or retirement account (unlimited amount): Mississippi Code 85-3-1.

Personal Property: Personal injury recoveries (up to $10,000): Mississippi Code 85-3-17; Proceeds from sale of exempt property (up to exemption amount): Mississippi Code 85-3-1(b)(i); Tangible personal property of any type (up to $10,000): Mississippi Code 85-3-1(a). Any individual items of personal property worth less that $200 each: Mississippi 85-3-1(a).

Real Estate: Proceeds from real estate insurance (up to exemption amount): Mississippi Code 85-3-23; Property used as residence (up to $75,000 and up to 160 acres): Mississippi Code 85-3-21; Mobile home (up to $30,000): Mississippi Code 85-3-1(d).

Wages: Earned but unpaid wages owed for 30 days; after 30 days, 75% of wages due (judge may allow more for low-income debtors): Mississippi Code 85-3-4.

Missouri

Missouri residents cannot use the Federal Bankruptcy Exemptions, but may use the Federal Non-Bankruptcy Exemptions listed at the end of this Appendix and the following state exemptions:

Benefits: Aid to families with dependent children (unlimited amount): Missouri Annotated Statutes 513.430(10)(a); Social Security (unlimited amount): Missouri Annotated Statutes 513.430(10)(a); Unemployment compensation (unlimited amount): Missouri Annotated Statutes 288.380(10)(1) & 513.430(10)(c); Veterans benefits (unlimited amount): Missouri Annotated Statutes 513.430(10)(b); Workers compensation (unlimited amount): Missouri Annotated Statutes 287.260; Crime victim's compensation: Missouri Annotated Statutes 595.025.

Insurance: Disability or illness benefits (unlimited amount): Missouri Annotated Statutes 513.430(10)(c); Fraternal society benefits (up to $5,000 if purchased over 6 months before filing for bankruptcy): Missouri Annotated Statutes 513.430(8); Insurance premium proceeds (unlimited amount): Missouri Annotated Statutes 377.090; Life insurance dividends, loan value, or interest (up to $5,000 if purchased over 6 months before filing for bankruptcy): Missouri Annotated Statutes 513.430(8); Unmatured life insurance policy (unlimited amount): Missouri Annotated Statutes 513.430(7).

Miscellaneous: Alimony or child support (up to $750 per month): Missouri Annotated Statutes 513.430(10)(d); Any property (up to $1,250 plus $350 per child if head of family, otherwise up to $600): Missouri Annotated Statutes 513.430(3) & 513.440; Property of a business partnership (unlimited amount): Missouri Annotated Statutes 358.250(3).

Pensions: Employees of municipalities (unlimited amount): Missouri Annotated Statutes 71.207; Firefighters (unlimited amount): Missouri Annotated Statutes 87.090, 87.365, & 87.485; Police department employees (unlimited amount): Missouri Annotated Statutes 86.190, 86.353, 86.493, & 86.780; Political officials and employees (unlimited amount): Missouri Annotated Statutes 70.695; Retirement benefits (amount needed for support and only payments being received): Missouri Annotated Statutes 513.430(10)(e); State employees (unlimited amount): Missouri Annotated Statutes 104.540(2); Teachers (unlimited amount): Missouri Annotated Statutes 169.090; Employee benefit spendthrift trust: Missouri Annotated Statutes 456.014.

Personal Property: Animals, appliances, books, clothing, crops, furnishings, household goods, and musical instruments (up to $3,000 total): Missouri Annotated Statutes 513.430(1); Burial grounds (up to 1 acre or $100): Missouri Annotated Statutes 214.190; Health aids (unlimited amount): Missouri Annotated Statutes 513.430(9); Implements, books, and tools of a trade (up to $3,000): Missouri Annotated Statutes 513.430(4); Wedding ring (up to $1,500) any other jewelry (up to $500): Missouri Annotated Statutes 513.430(2); Motor vehicle (up to $3,000): Missouri Annotated Statutes 513.430(5); Wrongful death recoveries (unlimited amount): Missouri Annotated Statutes 513.430(11).

Real Estate: Real property (up to $15,000) or mobile home (up to $5,000); joint owners may not double: Missouri Annotated Statutes 513.430(6) & 513.475.

Wages: 75% of earned but unpaid wages (90% if head of family and judge may allow more for low-income debtors): Missouri Annotated Statutes 525.030; Wages of servant or common laborer (up to $90): Missouri Annotated Statutes 513.470.

Montana

Montana residents cannot use the Federal Bankruptcy Exemptions, but may use the Federal Non-Bankruptcy Exemptions listed at the end of this Appendix and the following state exemptions:

Benefits: Aid to aged, blind, disabled, and families with dependent children (unlimited amount): Montana Code Annotated 53-2-607; Crime victims compensation (unlimited amount): Montana Code Annotated 53-9-129; Local public assistance (unlimited amount): Montana Code Annotated 25-13-608(1)(b); Silicosis benefits (unlimited amount): Montana Code Annotated 39-73-110; Social Security (unlimited amount): Montana Code Annotated 25-13-608(1)(b); Unemployment compensation (unlimited amount): Montana Code Annotated 31-2-106(2) & 39-51-3105; Veterans benefits (unlimited amount): Montana Code Annotated 25-13-608 (1)(c); Workers compensation (unlimited amount): Montana Code Annotated 39-71-743.

Insurance: Annuity contract proceeds (up to $350 per month): Montana Code Annotated 33-15-514; Disability, illness, medical, surgical, or hospital proceeds or benefits (unlimited amount): Montana Code Annotated 25-13-608(1)(d) & (f), & 33-15-513; Fraternal society benefits (unlimited amount): Montana Code Annotated 33-7-522; Group life insurance policy or proceeds (unlimited amount): Montana Code Annotated 33-15-512; Hail insurance benefits (unlimited amount): Montana Code Annotated 80-2-245; Life insurance proceeds if policy prohibits proceeds from being used to pay creditors (unlimited amount): Montana Code Annotated 33-20-120; Medical, surgical, or hospital care benefits (unlimited amount): Montana Code Annotated 25-13-608(1)(e).

Miscellaneous: Alimony or child support (unlimited amount): Montana Code Annotated 25-13-608(1)(g).

Pensions: Firefighters (unlimited amount): Montana Code Annotated 19-18-612(1); Police officers (unlimited amount): Montana Code Annotated 19-19-504(1); Public employees (unlimited amount): Montana Code Annotated 19-2-1004; Retirement benefits (unlimited amount; amount in excess of 15% of debtor's yearly income must have been deposited over 1 year before filing for bankruptcy): Montana Code Annotated 31-2-106; Teachers (unlimited amount): Montana Code Annotated 19-20-706(2); University system employees (unlimited amount): Montana Code Annotated 19-21-212.

Personal Property: Animals, appliances, books, clothing, crops, firearms, household furnishings, jewelry, musical instruments, and sporting goods (up to $600 per item, $4,500 total): Montana Code Annotated 25-13-609(1); Arms and equipment required for military use (unlimited amount): Montana Code Annotated 25-13-613(b); Burial plot (unlimited amount): Montana Code Annotated 25-13-608(1)(h); Cooperative association shares (up to $500): Montana Code Annotated 35-15-404; Health aids (unlimited amount): Montana Code Annotated 25-13-608(1)(a); Implements, books, and tools of a trade (up to $3,000): Montana Code Annotated 25-13-609(3); Motor vehicle (up to $2,500): Montana Code Annotated 25-13-609(2); Proceeds for damaged or lost exempt property for 6 months after received (up to exemption amount): Montana Code Annotated 25-13-610.

Real Estate: Real property or mobile home used as a residence (up to $250,000); proceeds from sale, condemnation, or insurance are exempt for 18 months; must record homestead declaration before filing for bankruptcy: Montana Code Annotated 70-32-104, 70-32-105, 70-32-201, & 70-32-216.

Wages: 75% of earned but unpaid wages (judge may allow more for low-income debtors): Montana Code Annotated 25-13-614.

Nebraska

Nebraska residents cannot use the Federal Bankruptcy Exemptions, but may use the Federal Non-Bankruptcy Exemptions listed at the end of this Appendix and the following state exemptions:

Benefits: Aid to aged, blind, disabled, poor persons, and families with dependent children (unlimited amount): Revised Statutes of Nebraska 68-1013 & 68-148; Unemployment compensation (unlimited amount): Revised Statutes of Nebraska 48-647; Workers compensation (unlimited amount): Revised Statutes of Nebraska 48-149; Deferred compensation (unlimited amount): Revised Statutes of Nebraska 48-1401.

Insurance: Fraternal society benefits (up to $100,000 loan value): Revised Statutes of Nebraska 44-1089; Life insurance or annuity contract proceeds (up to $100,000 loan value): Revised Statutes of Nebraska 44-371.

Miscellaneous: None.

Pensions: County employees (unlimited amount): Revised Statutes of Nebraska 23-2322; Military disability benefits (up to $2,000): Revised Statutes of Nebraska 25-1559; Retirement benefits (amount needed for support): Revised Statutes of Nebraska 25-1563.01; School employees (unlimited amount): Revised Statutes of Nebraska 79-948; State employees (unlimited amount): Revised Statutes of Nebraska 84-1324.

Personal Property: Any personal property, except wages (up to $2,500 if taken instead of real estate exemption): Revised Statutes of Nebraska 25-1552; Burial plot, crypts, lots, tombs, and vaults (unlimited amount): Revised Statutes of Nebraska 12-517 & 12-605; Clothing (amount needed): Revised Statutes of Nebraska 25-1556; Equipment or tools for professional use (husband and wife may double exemption amount (up to $2,400 each): Revised Statutes of Nebraska 25-1556; Food and fuel (amount to last 6 months): Revised Statutes of Nebraska 25-1556; Furniture, kitchen utensils, computers, books, or musical instruments (up to $1,500): Revised Statutes of Nebraska 25-1556; Health aids (unlimited amount): Revised Statutes of Nebraska 25-1556; Medical or health care savings accounts (up to $25,000): Revised Statutes of Nebraska 8-1, 131(2)(b); Perpetual care funds (unlimited amount): Revised Statutes of Nebraska 12-511; Personal injury recoveries (unlimited amount): Revised Statutes of Nebraska 25-1563.02; Personal possessions (unlimited amount): Revised Statutes of Nebraska 25-1556.

Real Estate: Real estate used as residence (up to $60,000 for head of household or married couple and may include up to 2 lots in city or village, 160 acres elsewhere) husand and wife may not double exemption for real estate; sale proceeds exempt for 6 months after sale: Revised Statutes of Nebraska 40-101, 40-111, & 40-113.

Wages: Earned but unpaid wages or pension payments (85% for head of family, 75% for others; judge may allow more for low-income debtors): Revised Statutes of Nebraska 25-1558.

Nevada

Nevada residents cannot use the Federal Bankruptcy Exemptions, but may use the Federal Non-Bankruptcy Exemptions listed at the end of this Appendix and the following state exemptions:

Benefits: Aid to aged, blind, disabled, children, and families with dependent children (unlimited amount): Nevada Revised Statutes Annotated 422.291 & 432.036; Industrial insurance [workers compensation] (unlimited amount): Nevada Revised Statutes Annotated 616C.205; Unemployment compensation (unlimited amount): Nevada Revised Statutes Annotated 612.710; Vocational rehabilitation benefits (unlimited amount): Nevada Revised Statutes Annotated 615.270.

Insurance: Annuity contract proceeds (up to $350 per month): Nevada Revised Statutes Annotated 687B.290; Fraternal society benefits (unlimited amount): Nevada Revised Statutes Annotated 695A.220; Group life or health policy or proceeds (amount of life insurance bought not to exceed $1,000 annual premium): Nevada Revised Statutes Annotated 687B.280; Health proceeds (unlimited amount): Nevada Revised Statutes Annotated 687B.270; Life insurance policy or proceeds (unlimited): Nevada Revised Statutes Annotated 21.090(1)(k); Life insurance proceeds if debtor is not the insured (unlimited amount): Nevada Revised Statutes Annotated 687B.260.

Miscellaneous: Alimony or child support (unlimited amount): Nevada Revised Statutes Annotated 21.090(1)(r) & (s); Property of a business partnership (unlimited amount): Nevada Revised Statutes Annotated 87.250.

Pensions: Public employees (unlimited amount): Nevada Revised Statutes Annotated 286.670; Retirement benefits (up to $500,000): Nevada Revised Statutes Annotated 21.090; Simplified Employee Pension Plan (up to $500,000): Nevada Revised Statutes Annotated 21-090; Cash or deferred arrangement (up to $500,00): Nevada Revised Statutes Annotated 21.090; Trust forming part of a stock bonus, pension, or profit-sharing plan (up to $500,00): Nevada Revised Statutes Annotated 21.090.

Personal Property: Any personal property (up to $1,000): Nevada Revised Statutes Annotated 21.090(1)(z); Appliances, furniture, home and yard equipment, and household goods (up to $12,000 total): Nevada Revised Statutes Annotated 21.090(1)(b); Arms, uniforms, and equipment required for military use (unlimited amount): Nevada Revised Statutes Annotated 21.090(1)(i); Books (up to $5,000): Nevada Revised Statutes Annotated 21.090(1)(a); Cabin or dwelling of miner or prospector, cars and equipment for mining, and mining claim (up to $4,500): Nevada Revised Statutes Annotated 121.090(1)(e); Farm trucks, stock, tools, equipment, and seed (up to $4,500): Nevada Revised Statutes Annotated 21.090(1)(c); Funeral service money held in trust (unlimited amount): Nevada Revised Statutes Annotated 689.700; Geological specimens, art curiosities, or paleontological remains (unlimited amount, if catalogued and numbered): Nevada Revised Statutes Annotated 21.100; Gun (1 only): Nevada Revised Statutes Annotated 21.090(1)(i); Health aids (unlimited amount): Nevada Revised Statutes Annotated 21.090 (1)(q); Keepsakes and pictures (unlimited amount): Nevada Revised Statutes Annotated 21.090(1)(a); Library, equipment, supplies, tools, and materials for business (up to $10,000): Nevada Revised Statutes Annotated 21.090(1)(d); Motor vehicle (if debtor's equity does not exceed $15,000, unlimited amount if equipped for disabled person): Nevada Revised Statutes Annotated 21.090(1)(f), (o); Personal injury recoveries (up to $16,500): Nevada Revised Statutes Annotated 21.090(1)(c).

Real Estate: Real property or mobile home used as a residence (if amount of equity in the property does not exceed $550,000 in value, husband and wife may not double); must record homestead declaration before filing for bankruptcy: Nevada Revised Statutes Annotated 21.090(1)(l) & (m), 115.010, & 115.020.

Wages: 75% of earned but unpaid wages (judge may allow more for low-income debtors): Nevada Revised Statutes Annotated 21.090(1)(g).

New Hampshire

New Hampshire residents cannot use the Federal Bankruptcy Exemptions, but may use the Federal Non-Bankruptcy Exemptions listed at the end of this Appendix and the following state exemptions:

Benefits: Aid to aged, blind, disabled, and families with dependent children (unlimited amount): New Hampshire Revised Statutes Annotated 167:25; Unemployment compensation (unlimited amount): New Hampshire Revised Statutes Annotated 282-A:159; Workers compensation (unlimited amount): New Hampshire Revised Statutes Annotated 281-A:52.

Insurance: Firefighters insurance (unlimited amount): New Hampshire Revised Statutes Annotated 402:69; Fraternal society benefits (unlimited amount): New Hampshire Revised Statutes Annotated 418:24; Homeowners insurance proceeds (up to $5,000): New Hampshire Revised Statutes Annotated 512:21(VIII).

Miscellaneous: Any property whether personal property or real estate (up to $1,000): New Hampshire Revised Statutes Annotated 512:21(III); Child support (unlimited amount): New Hampshire Revised Statutes Annotated 161-C:11; Jury and witness fees (unlimited amount): New Hampshire Revised Statutes Annotated 512:21(VI); Property of a business partnership (unlimited amount): New Hampshire Revised Statutes Annotated 304-A:25.

Pensions: Federal pension (unpaid benefits only): New Hampshire Revised Statutes Annotated 512:21(IV); Firefighters (unlimited amount): New Hampshire Revised Statutes Annotated 102:23; Firemen's retirement (unlimited amount): New Hampshire Revised Statutes Annotated 102:23; Public employees (unlimited amount): New Hampshire Revised Statutes Annotated 100-A:26.

Personal Property: Auto (up to $4,000): New Hampshire Revised Statutes Annotated 511:2(XVI); Beds, bedding, and cooking utensils (amount needed): New Hampshire Revised Statutes Annotated 511:2(II); Bibles and books (up to $800): New Hampshire Revised Statutes Annotated 511:2(VIII); Burial plot or lot, or church pew (unlimited amount): New Hampshire Revised Statutes Annotated 511:2(XIV) & 511:2(XV); Clothing (amount needed): New Hampshire Revised Statutes Annotated 511:2(I); Cooking and heating stoves, and refrigerator (unlimited amount): New Hampshire Revised Statutes Annotated 511:2(IV); Cow (1), sheep and fleece (6), and hay (4 tons): New Hampshire Revised Statutes Annotated 511:2(XI), (XII); Food and fuel (up to $400): New Hampshire Revised Statutes Annotated 511:2(VI); Fowl (up to $300): New Hampshire Revised Statutes Annotated 511:2(XIII); Furniture (up to $3,500): New Hampshire Revised Statutes Annotated 511:2(III); Jewelry (up to $500): New Hampshire Revised Statutes Annotated 511:2(XVII); Pork (1, if already slaughtered): New Hampshire Revised Statutes Annotated 511:2(X); Proceeds for lost or destroyed exempt property (up to exemption amount): New Hampshire Revised Statutes Annotated 512:21; Sewing machine (unlimited amount): New Hampshire Revised Statutes Annotated 511:2(V); Tools of a trade (up to $5,000): New Hampshire Revised Statutes Annotated 511:2(IX); Uniforms, arms, and equipment required for military use (unlimited amount): New Hampshire Revised Statutes Annotated 511:2(VII); Yoke of oxen or horse (1, if needed for farming): New Hampshire Revised Statutes Annotated 511:2(XII). May use up to $7,000 of unused exemptions for books, food, fuel, furniture, jewelry, motor vehicle and tools for any other personal property: New Hampshire Revised Statutes Annotated 512:21(XVIII).

Real Estate: Real property or manufactured housing, if located on land owned by debtor (up to $100,000): New Hampshire Revised Statutes Annotated 480:4.

Wages: Earned but unpaid wage (judge decides amount of exemption): New Hampshire Revised Statutes Annotated 512:21(II); Earned but unpaid wages of spouse (unlimited amount): New Hampshire Revised Statutes Annotated 512:21 (III); Wages of a minor child (unlimited amount): New Hampshire Revised Statutes Annotated 512:21 (III).

New Jersey

New Jersey residents may use either the Federal Bankruptcy Exemptions listed at the end of this Appendix or the state exemptions listed below. If state exemptions are used, then the Federal Non-Bankruptcy Exemptions at the end of this Appendix may also be used.

Benefits: Aid to aged and permanent disability assistance (unlimited amount): New Jersey Statutes Annotated 44:7-35; Crime victims compensation (unlimited amount): New Jersey Statutes Annotated 52:4B-18; Unemployment compensation (unlimited amount): New Jersey Statutes Annotated 43:21-53; Workers compensation (unlimited amount): New Jersey Statutes Annotated 34:15-29.

Insurance: Annuity contract proceeds (up to $500 per month): New Jersey Statutes Annotated 17B:24-7; Group life or health policy or proceeds (unlimited amount): New Jersey Statutes Annotated 17B:24-9; Health or disability benefits (unlimited amount): New Jersey Statutes Annotated 17:18-12 & 17B:24-8; Life insurance proceeds if debtor is not the insured (unlimited amount): New Jersey Statutes Annotated 17B:24-(6b); Life insurance proceeds if policy prohibits proceeds from being used to pay creditors (unlimited amount): New Jersey Statutes Annotated 17B:24-10; Military disability or death benefits (unlimited amount): New Jersey Statutes Annotated 38A:4-8.

Miscellaneous: None.

Pensions: Alcohol beverage control officers (unlimited amount): New Jersey Statutes Annotated 43:8A-20; City board of health employees (unlimited amount): New Jersey Statutes Annotated 43:18-12; Civil defense workers (unlimited amount): New Jersey Statutes Annotated A:9-57.6; County employees (unlimited amount): New Jersey Statutes Annotated 43:10-57 & 43:10-105; Firefighters (unlimited amount): New Jersey Statutes Annotated 43:16-7; Judges (unlimited amount): New Jersey Statutes Annotated 43:6A-41; Municipal employees (unlimited amount): New Jersey Statutes Annotated 43:13-44; Police officers (unlimited amount): New Jersey Statutes Annotated 43:16-7; Prison employees (unlimited amount): New Jersey Statutes Annotated 43:7-13; Public employees (unlimited amount): New Jersey Statutes Annotated 43:15A-53; Retirement benefits (unlimited amount): New Jersey Statutes Annotated 43:13-9; School district employees (unlimited amount): New Jersey Statutes Annotated 18A:66-116; State police (unlimited amount): New Jersey Statutes Annotated 53:5A-45; Street and water department employees (unlimited amount): New Jersey Statutes Annotated 43:19-17; Teachers (unlimited amount): New Jersey Statutes Annotated 18A:66-51; Traffic officers (unlimited amount): New Jersey Statutes Annotated 43:16A-17.

Personal Property: Any personal property or stock in corporation (up to $1,000 total): New Jersey Statutes Annotated 2A:17-19; Clothing (unlimited amount): New Jersey Statutes Annotated 2A:17-19; Furniture and household goods (up to $1,000): New Jersey Statutes Annotated 2A:26-4.
Real Estate: None.
Wages: Military wages or allowances (unlimited amount): New Jersey Statutes Annotated 38A:4-8; 90% of earned but unpaid wages (if income under $7,500; if income over $7,500, judge decides wage exemption amount): New Jersey Statutes Annotated 2A:17-56.

New Mexico

New Mexico residents may use either the Federal Bankruptcy Exemptions listed at the end of this Appendix or the state exemptions listed below. If state exemptions are used, then the Federal Non-Bankruptcy Exemptions at the end of this Appendix may also be used.
Benefits: Aid to families with dependent children and general assistance (unlimited amount): New Mexico Statutes Annotated 27-2-21; Crime victims compensation if paid before July 1, 1993 (unlimited amount until July 1, 2001): New Mexico Statutes Annotated 31-22-15; Occupational disease disability benefits (unlimited amount): New Mexico Statutes Annotated 52-3-37; Unemployment compensation (unlimited amount): New Mexico Statutes Annotated 51-1-37; Workers compensation (unlimited amount): New Mexico Statutes Annotated 52-1-52.
Insurance: Benevolent association benefits (up to $5,000): New Mexico Statutes Annotated 42-10-4; Fraternal society benefits (unlimited amount): New Mexico Statutes Annotated 59A-44-18; Life, accident, health or annuity benefits, or cash value, if beneficiary is a New Mexico citizen (unlimited amount): New Mexico Statutes Annotated 42-10-3 & 42-10-5.
Miscellaneous: Any property (up to $5,000, if taken instead of real estate exemption): New Mexico Statutes Annotated 42-10-10; Ownership in an unincorporated association (unlimited amount): New Mexico Statutes Annotated 53-10-2.
Pensions: Pension or retirement benefits (unlimited amount): New Mexico Statutes Annotated 42-10-1 & 42-10-2; Public school employees (unlimited amount): New Mexico Statutes Annotated 22-11-42.
Personal Property: Any personal property (up to $500): New Mexico Statutes Annotated 42-10-1; Books, furniture, and health equipment (unlimited amount): New Mexico Statutes Annotated 42-10-1 & 42-10-2; Books, implements, and tools of a trade (up to $1,500): New Mexico Statutes Annotated 42-10-1 & 42-10-2; Building materials (unlimited amount): New Mexico Statutes Annotated 48-2-15; Clothing (unlimited amount): New Mexico Statutes Annotated 42-10-1 & 42-10-2; Cooperative association shares (minimum amount needed to be member): New Mexico Statutes Annotated 53-4-28; Health aids (unlimited amount): New Mexico Statutes Annotated 42-10-1 & 42-10-2; Jewelry (up to $2,500): New Mexico Statutes Annotated 42-10-1 & 42-10-2; Materials, tools, and machinery to drill, complete, operate, or repair oil line, gas well, or pipeline (unlimited amount): New Mexico Statutes Annotated 70-4-12; Motor vehicle (up to $4,000): New Mexico Statutes Annotated 42-10-1 & 42-10-2.
Real Estate: Real property (up to $60,000; joint owners may double): New Mexico Statutes Annotated 42-10-9.
Wages: 75% of earned but unpaid wages (judge may allow more for low-income debtors): New Mexico Statutes Annotated 35-12-7.

New York

New York residents cannot use the Federal Bankruptcy Exemptions, but may use the Federal Non-Bankruptcy Exemptions listed at the end of this Appendix and the following state exemptions:

Benefits: Aid to aged, blind, disabled, and families with dependent children (unlimited amount): Consolidated Laws of New York: Debtor and Creditor Article 10-A 282(2)(c); Crime victims compensation (unlimited amount): Consolidated Laws of New York: Debtor and Creditor Article 10-A 282(3)(i); Disability, illness, or unemployment benefits, local public assistance, and social security (unlimited amount): Consolidated Laws of New York: Debtor and Creditor Article 10-A 282(2)(a) & (c); Veterans benefits (unlimited amount): Consolidated Laws of New York: Debtor and Creditor Article 10-A 282(2)(b); Workers compensation (unlimited amount): Consolidated Laws of New York: Debtor and Creditor Article 10-A 282(2)(c).

Insurance: Annuity contract benefits (unlimited amount, unless purchased within 6 months of filing for bankruptcy and not tax-deferred, then up to $5,000): Insurance Article 32-3212(d), Consolidated Laws of New York: Debtor and Creditor Article 10-A 283(1); Disability or illness benefits (up to $400 per month): Consolidated Laws of New York: Insurance Article 32-3212(c); Life insurance proceeds if beneficiary is the spouse of the insured (unlimited amount): Consolidated Laws of New York: Insurance Article 32-3212(b)(2); Life insurance proceeds if policy prohibits proceeds from being used to pay creditors (unlimited amount): Consolidated Laws of New York: Estates, Powers, and Trusts Article 7-1.5(a)(2).

Miscellaneous: Alimony and child support (amount needed for support): Consolidated Laws of New York: Debtor and Creditor Article 10-A 282(2)(d); New York State College State tuition savings program (100% or an amount not exceeding $10,000): Consolidated Laws of New York: Civil Practice Laws and Rules Article 52-5205(j); Property of a business partnership (unlimited amount): Consolidated Laws of New York: Partnership Article 5-51; Trust fund principal and 90% of income: Consolidated Laws of New York: Civil Practice Laws and Rules Article 52 Section 5205(c) & (d).

Pensions: Public retirement benefits (unlimited amount): Consolidated Laws of New York: Insurance 4607; Retirement benefits, IRAs, and Keogh (amount needed for support): Consolidated Laws of New York: Debtor and Creditor 282(2)(e) & Civil Practice Law and Rules Article 52 Sec.5205(c); State employees (unlimited amount): Consolidated Laws of New York: Retirement and Social Security 110.

Personal Property: Bible, books (up to $50), church pew or seat, clothing, cooking utensils, crockery, food (amount to last 60 days), furniture, pet (with food to last 60 days, up to $450), pictures, radio, refrigerator, schoolbooks, sewing machine, stoves and fuel (to last 60 days), tableware, TV, watch (up to $35), and wedding ring: Consolidated Laws of New York: Civil Practice Law and Rules Article 52-5205(1)-(6); Burial plot (up to 1/4 acre): Consolidated Laws of New York: Civil Practice Law and Rules Article 52-5206(f); Cash (the lesser of either $2,500 or $5,000 as an annuity, to be taken instead of real estate): Consolidated Laws of New York: Debtor and Creditor Article 10-A 283(2); Farm machinery, team (with food for 60 days), business furniture, books, and instruments (up to $600 total): Consolidated Laws of New York: Civil Practice Law and Rules Article 52-5205(a)(7); Health aids (unlimited amount): Consolidated Laws of New York: Civil Practice Law and Rules Article 52-5205(h); Lost earnings recoveries (amount needed for support): Consolidated Laws of New York: Debtor and Creditor Article 10-A 282(3)(iv); Motor vehicle (up to $2,400): Consolidated Laws of New York: Debtor and

Creditor Article 10-A 282(1); Personal injury recoveries (up to $7,500): Consolidated Laws of New York: Debtor and Creditor Article 10-A 282(3)(iii); Savings and loan deposits (up to $600): Consolidated Laws of New York: Banking 407Security deposits (unlimited amount): Consolidated Laws of New York: Civil Practice Law and Rules Article 52-5205(g); Uniforms, arms, and equipment required for military use (unlimited amount): Consolidated Laws of New York: Civil Practice Law and Rules Article 52-5205(e); Wrongful death recoveries (amount needed for support): Consolidated Laws of New York: Debtor and Creditor Article 10-A 282(3)(ii).

Real Estate: Real property used as residence including co-op, condo, or mobile home (up to $50,000): Consolidated Laws of New York: Civil Practice Law and Rules Article 52-5206(a).

Wages: 90% of earned but unpaid wages (if received within 60 days of filing for bankruptcy): Consolidated Laws of New York: Civil Practice Law and Rules Article 52-5205(d), (e).

North Carolina

North Carolina residents cannot use the Federal Bankruptcy Exemptions, but may use the Federal Non-Bankruptcy Exemptions listed at the end of this Appendix and the following state exemptions:

Benefits: Aid to blind, families with dependent children, special adult assistance, and assistance under the Work First Program (unlimited amount): General Statutes of North Carolina 108A-36 & 111-18; Crime victims compensation (unlimited amount): General Statutes of North Carolina 15B-17; Unemployment compensation (unlimited amount): General Statutes of North Carolina 96-17; Workers compensation (unlimited amount): General Statutes of North Carolina 97-21.

Insurance: Employee group life policy or proceeds (unlimited amount): General Statutes of North Carolina 58-58-165; Fraternal society benefits (unlimited amount): General Statutes of North Carolina 58-24-85; Life insurance policy or proceeds (unlimited amount): General Statutes of North Carolina 1C-1601(a)(6).

Miscellaneous: Any property (up to $5,000, if taken instead of real estate or burial plot exemption): General Statutes of North Carolina 1C-1601(a)(2); Property of a business partnership (unlimited amount): General Statutes of North Carolina 59-55; Support for surviving spouse for 1 year (up to $10,000): General Statutes of North Carolina 30-15.

Pensions: Firefighters and rescue squad workers (unlimited amount): General Statutes of North Carolina 58-86-90; IRAs (unlimited amount): General Statutes of North Carolina 1C-1601(a)(9); Law enforcement officers (unlimited amount): General Statutes of North Carolina 143-166.30(g); Legislators (unlimited amount): General Statutes of North Carolina 120-4.29; Municipal, city, and county employees (unlimited amount): General Statutes of North Carolina 128-31; Teachers and state employees (unlimited amount): General Statutes of North Carolina 135-9 & 135-95.

Personal Property: Animals, appliances, books, clothing, crops, furnishings, household goods, and musical instruments (up to $5,000 total, plus up to $1,000 additional per dependent, not to exceed $4,000 for dependents; all items must have been purchased more then 90 days prior to filing for bankruptcy to be exempt): General Statutes of North Carolina 1C-1601(a)(4); Burial plot (up to $18,500, if taken instead of real estate): General Statutes of North Carolina 1C-1601(a)(1); College savings accounts (up to $25,000): General Statutes of North Carolina 1C-1601 (a)(7); Health aids (unlimited amount): General Statutes of North

Carolina 1C-1601 (a)(7); Implements, books, and tools of a trade (up to $2,000): General Statutes of North Carolina 1C-1601(a)(5); Motor vehicle (up to $3,500): General Statutes of North Carolina 1C-1601 (a)(3); Personal injury recoveries (unlimited amount): General Statutes of North Carolina 1C-1601(a)(8); Wrongful death recoveries (unlimited amount): General Statutes of North Carolina 1C-1601(a)(8).

Real Estate: Real or personal property, including co-op, used as residence (up to $18,500): General Statutes of North Carolina 1C-1601(a)(1).

Wages: Earned but unpaid wages (amount needed for support and if received 60 days before filing for bankruptcy): General Statutes of North Carolina 1-362.

North Dakota

North Dakota residents cannot use the Federal Bankruptcy Exemptions, but may use the Federal Non-Bankruptcy Exemptions listed at the end of this Appendix and the following state exemptions:

Benefits: Aid to families with dependent children (unlimited amount): North Dakota Century Code 28-22-19(3); Armed conflict veterans benefits (unlimited amount): North Dakota Century Code 37-27-06; Crime victims compensation (unlimited amount): North Dakota Century Code 28-22-19(2); Desert Storm veterans benefits (unlimited amount): North Dakota Century Code 37-26-06; Social Security (unlimited amount): North Dakota Century Code 28-22-03.1 (4)(c); Unemployment compensation (unlimited amount): North Dakota Century Code 52-06-30; Workers compensation (unlimited amount): North Dakota Century Code 65-05-29; Old age and survivor insurance program benefits (unlimited amount): North Dakota Century Code 59-09-22; Deferred compensation program benefits for public employees: North Dakota Century Code 54-52.2-06.

Insurance: Fraternal society benefits (unlimited amount): North Dakota Century Code 26.1-15.1-18 & 26.1-33-40; Life insurance if beneficiary is insured's relative and policy was owned over 1 year before filing for bankruptcy (up to $100,000 per policy and up to $200,000 total life insurance and retirement, IRA, or Keogh; unlimited life insurance if needed for support): North Dakota Century Code 28-22-03.1(3); Life insurance proceeds payable to deceased's estate (unlimited amount): North Dakota Century Code 26.1-33-40.

Miscellaneous: None.

Pensions: Disabled veterans benefits, except military retirement pay (unlimited amount): North Dakota Century Code 28-22-03.1(4)(d); Public employees (unlimited amount): North Dakota Century Code 28-22-19(1); Retirement benefits, IRAs, and Keogh (up to $100,000 per plan and up to $200,000 total life insurance and retirement, IRA, or Keogh; unlimited if needed for support): North Dakota Century Code 28-22-03.1(3).

Personal Property: Any personal property (up to $7,500, if taken instead of real estate exemption): North Dakota Century Code 28-22-03 & 28-22-03.1(1); Bible and books (up to $100): North Dakota Century Code 28-22-02(4); Burial plots and church pew (unlimited amount): North Dakota Century Code 28-22-02(2) & (3); Crops (amount raised on debtor's land of up to 160 acres; if this exemption is used, debtor may not take advantage of any other alternative exemptions): North Dakota Century Code 28-22-02(8); Food and fuel (amount to last 1 year): North Dakota Century Code 28-22-02(6); Motor vehicle (up to $1,200): North Dakota Century Code 28-22-03.1(2); Personal injury recoveries (up to $15,000; but not for pain and suffering): North Dakota Century Code 28-22-03.1(4)(b); Pictures and clothing (unlimited amount): North Dakota Century Code 28-22-02(1) & (5); Wrongful death recoveries (up to $15,000): North Dakota Century Code 28-22-03.1(4)(a); [*Note*: Any non-head of household who does not claim a crops exemption may claim an additional $2,500 of any Personal Property: North Dakota Century Code 28-22-05. Any head of household who does not claim a crops exemption may claim an additional $5,000 of any personal property or all of the following: North Dakota Century Code 28-22-03: Books and musical instruments (up to $1,500): North Dakota Century Code 28-22-04(1); Furniture and bedding (up to $1,000): North Dakota Century Code 28-22-04(2); Library and professional tools (up to $1,000): North Dakota Century Code 28-22-04(4); Livestock and farm implements (up to $4,500): North Dakota Century Code 28-22-04(3); Tools of a mechanic and business inventory (up to $1,000): North Dakota Century Code 28-22-04(4).]

Real Estate: Real property, house trailer, or mobile home used as a residence (up to $80,000) (husband and wife may not double real estate exemption); proceeds for sale of exempt real estate are exempt: North Dakota Century Code 28-22-02(10) & 47-18-01.

Wages: 75% of earned but unpaid pensions or wages (judge may allow more for low-income debtors): North Dakota Century Code 32-09.1-03.

Ohio

Ohio residents cannot use the Federal Bankruptcy Exemptions, but may use the Federal Non-Bankruptcy Exemptions listed at the end of this Appendix and the following state exemptions:

Benefits: Aid to families with dependent children and public assistance benefits (unlimited amount): Ohio Revised Code 2329.66(A)(9)(d), 5107.12, & 5108.08; Crime victims compensation (unlimited amount if received during 12 months before filing for bankruptcy): Ohio Revised Code 2329.66(A)(12)(a) & 2743.66; Disability assistance payments (unlimited amount): Ohio Revised Code 2329.66 (A)(9)(e) & 5115.07; Living maintenance benefits (unlimited amount): Ohio Revised Code 2329.66 (A)(16) & 3304.19; Tuition credit (unlimited amount): Ohio Revised Code 2329.66(A)(16); Unemployment compensation (unlimited amount): Ohio Revised Code 2329.66 (A)(9)(c) & 4141.32; Workers compensation (unlimited amount): Ohio Revised Code 2329.66(A) (9)(b) & 4123.67.

Insurance: Benevolent society benefits (up to $5,000): Ohio Revised Code 2329.63 & 2329.66(A)(6)(a); Disability benefits (up to $600 per month): Ohio Revised Code 2329.66 (A)(6)(e) & 3923.19; Fraternal society benefits (unlimited amount): Ohio Revised Code 2329.66 (A)(6)(d) & 3921.18; Group life insurance policy or proceeds (unlimited amount): Ohio Revised Code 2329.66(A)(6)(c) & 3917.05; Life, endowment, or annuity contract benefits for spouse, child, or dependent (unlimited amount): Ohio Revised Code 2329.66(A)(6)(b) & 3911.10; Life insurance proceeds for spouse (unlimited amount): Ohio Revised Code 3911.12; Life insurance proceeds if policy prohibits proceeds from being used to pay creditors (unlimited amount): Ohio Revised Code 3911.14.

Miscellaneous: Alimony or child support (amount needed for support): Ohio Revised Code 2329.66(A)(11); Any property, real estate or personal property (up to $400): Ohio Revised Code 2329.66(A)(17); Property of a business partnership (unlimited amount): Ohio Revised Code 1775.24 & 2329.66(A)(14).

Pensions: Firefighters and police officers pensions or death benefits (unlimited amount): Ohio Revised Code 742.47 & 2329.66(A)(10)(a); Public employees (unlimited amount): Ohio Revised Code 145.56 & 2329.66 (A)(10)(a); Public school employees (unlimited amount): Ohio Revised Code 3307.71 & 3309.66; Retirement benefits, IRAs, and Keogh (amount needed for support): Ohio Revised Code 2329.66(A)(10)(b) & (c); State highway patrol employees (unlimited amount): Ohio Revised Code 2329.66 (A)(10)(a) & 5505.22; Volunteer firefighters dependents (unlimited amount): Ohio Revised Code 146.13 & 2329.66(A)(10)(a).

Personal Property: Animals, appliances, books, crops, firearms, furnishings, household goods, hunting and fishing equipment, jewelry (up to $400 per item and $1,500 total), musical instruments (up to $200 per item), refrigerator and stove (up to $300 each) [total exemption for this category is $2,000 if no real estate exemption is taken]: Ohio Revised Code 2329.66(A)(3), 2329.66(A)(4)(b) & (d), & 2329.66(A)(c) & (d); Bank deposits, cash, money due within 90 days, security deposits, and tax refunds (up to $400 total): Ohio Revised Code 2329.66(4)(a); Beds, bedding, and clothing (up to $200 per item): Ohio Revised Code 2329.66(A)(3); Burial plot (unlimited amount): Ohio Revised Code 517.09 & 2329.66(A)(8); Health aids (unlimited amount): Ohio Revised Code 2329.66(A)(7); Implements, books, and tools of a trade (up to $750): Ohio Revised Code 2329.66(A)(5); Lost future earnings (amount needed for support if received during 12 months before filing for bankruptcy): Ohio Revised Code 2329.66(A)(12)(d); Motor vehicle (up to $1,000): Ohio Revised Code 2329.66(A)(2); Personal injury recoveries (up to $5,000 if received during 12 months before filing for bankruptcy, but not for pain and suffering): Ohio Revised Code 2329.66(A)(12)(c); Wrongful death recoveries (amount needed for support if received during 12 months before filing): Ohio Revised Code 2329.66(A)(12)(b).

Real Estate: Real or personal property used as a residence (up to $5,000): Ohio Revised Code 2329.66(A)(1)(b).

Wages: 75% of earned but unpaid wages that are due for 30 days (judge may allow more for low-income debtors): Ohio Revised Code 2329.66 (A)(13).

Oklahoma

Oklahoma residents cannot use the Federal Bankruptcy Exemptions, but may use the Federal Non-Bankruptcy Exemptions listed at the end of this Appendix and the following state exemptions:

Benefits: Aid to the aged, blind, disabled, and families with dependent children (unlimited amount): Oklahoma Statutes Annotated 56-173; Crime victims compensation (unlimited amount): Oklahoma Statutes Annotated 21-142.13; Social Security (unlimited amount): Oklahoma Statutes Annotated 56-173; Unemployment compensation (unlimited amount): Oklahoma Statutes Annotated 40-2-303; Workers compensation (unlimited amount): Oklahoma Statutes Annotated 85-48.

Insurance: Fraternal society benefits (unlimited amount): Oklahoma Statutes Annotated 36-2718.1; Funeral benefits (if prepaid and placed in trust; unlimited amount): Oklahoma Statutes Annotated 36-6125; Group life policy or proceeds (unlimited amount): Oklahoma Statutes Annotated 36-3632; Limited stock insurance benefits (unlimited amount): Oklahoma Statutes Annotated 36-2510; Mutual benefits (unlimited amount): Oklahoma Statutes Annotated 36-2410.

Miscellaneous: Alimony and child support (unlimited amount): Oklahoma Statutes Annotated 31-1(A)(19); Partnership property (unlimited amount): Oklahoma Statutes Annotated 16-1-

Appendix Standard 13.6; Limited liability company property (unlimited amount): Oklahoma Statutes Annotated 16-1-Appendix Standard 14.6.

Pensions: County employees (unlimited amount): Oklahoma Statutes Annotated 19-959; Disabled veterans (unlimited amount): Oklahoma Statutes Annotated 31-7; Firefighters (unlimited amount): Oklahoma Statutes Annotated 11-49-126; Law enforcement employees (unlimited amount): Oklahoma Statutes Annotated 47-2-303.3; Police officers (unlimited amount): Oklahoma Statutes Annotated 11-50-124; Public employees (unlimited amount): Oklahoma Statutes Annotated 74-923; Retirement benefits (unlimited amount): Oklahoma Statutes Annotated 31-1 (A)(20); Tax exempt benefits (unlimited amount): Oklahoma Statutes Annotated 60-328); Funds in individual development account (unlimited amount): Oklahoma Statutes Annotated 31-1(A)(22); Funds in Roth individual retirement account (unlimited amount): Oklahoma Statutes Annotated 31-1(A)(23); Funds in individual education retirement account (unlimited amount): Oklahoma Statutes Annotated 31-1(A)(24).

Personal Property: Books, gun (1, up to $2,000), pictures, and portraits (unlimited amount): Oklahoma Statutes Annotated 31-1(A)(14); Bridles and saddles (2 each total): Oklahoma Statutes Annotated 31-1 (A)(12); Burial plots (unlimited amount): Oklahoma Statutes Annotated 31-1(A)(4); Chickens (100), dairy cows and calves under 6 months (5), hogs (10), horses (2), sheep (20), and feed to last 1 year: Oklahoma Statutes Annotated 31-1(A)(10), (11), (15), (16), (17); Clothing (up to $4,000): Oklahoma Statutes Annotated 31-1(A)(7); Farm implements to farm homestead (up to $10,000 total): Oklahoma Statutes Annotated 31-1(A)(5); Tools, books, and business equipment (up to $10,000 total): Oklahoma Statutes Annotated 31-1(A)(5); Food (amount to last 1 year): Oklahoma Statutes Annotated 31-1(A)(17); Furniture and health aids (unlimited amount): Oklahoma Statutes Annotated 31-1-(A)(3), (9); Motor vehicle (up to $7,500): Oklahoma Statutes Annotated 31-1(A)(13); Personal injury, wrongful death, and workers compensation recoveries (up to $50,000 total; but not punitive damages): Oklahoma Statutes Annotated 31-1(A)(21); Federal earned income tax credit (unlimited amount): Oklahoma Statutes Annotated 31-1(A)(23); Liquor license (unlimited amount): Oklahoma Statutes Annotated 37-532; Statutory support trusts (unlimited amount): Oklahoma Statutes Annotated 6-3010; Prepaid funeral benefits (unlimited amount): Oklahoma Statutes Annotated 36-6125; Prepaid dental plan deposits (unlimited amount): Oklahoma Statutes Annotated 36-6146; Wedding and/or anniversary ring (up to $3,000): Oklahoma Statutes Annotated 31-1-(A)(8).

Real Estate: Real property or manufactured home (unlimited value for up to 1 acre in city, town, or village, or up to 160 acres elsewhere): Oklahoma Statutes Annotated 31-1(A)(1), (2), & 31-2. (Note: The 2005 Bankruptcy Act limits homestead exemptions to $136,875.00 if you have lived in the state where you are attempting to claim the exemption for less than 40 months (1215 days). This is true even if your state homestead exemption allows for a higher amount.)

Wages: 75% of wages earned in the 90 days before filing for bankruptcy (judge may allow more for hardship): Oklahoma Statutes Annotated 12-1171.1 & 31-1(A)(18).

Oregon

Oregon residents cannot use the Federal Bankruptcy Exemptions, but may use the Federal Non-Bankruptcy Exemptions listed at the end of this Appendix and the following state exemptions:

Benefits: Civil defense and disaster relief (up to $7,500): Oregon Revised Statutes 401.405; Crime victims compensation (up to $7,500): Oregon Revised Statutes 18.345 & 147.325; General assistance (up to $7,500): Oregon Revised Statutes 411.760; Inmates injury benefits (up to $7,500): Oregon Revised Statutes 655.530; Medical assistance (up to $7,500): Oregon Revised Statutes 414.095; Unemployment compensation (up to $7,500): Oregon Revised Statutes 657.855; Vocational rehabilitation (up to $7,500): Oregon Revised Statutes 344.580; Workers compensation (up to $7,500): Oregon Revised Statutes 656.234; Veteran's benefits and loans (unlimited amount): Oregon Revised Statutes 18.345(1)(m).

Insurance: Annuity contract benefits (up to $500 per month): Oregon Revised Statutes 743.049; Fraternal society benefits (unlimited amount): Oregon Revised Statutes 748.207; Group life policy or proceeds not payable to the insured (unlimited amount): Oregon Revised Statutes 743.047; Health or disability proceeds (unlimited amount): Oregon Revised Statutes 743.050; Life insurance proceeds or cash value if debtor is not the insured (unlimited amount): Oregon Revised Statutes 743.046.

Miscellaneous: Alimony and child support (amount needed for support): Oregon Revised Statutes 18.345(1)(i); Liquor licenses (unlimited amount): Oregon Revised Statutes 471.292.

Pensions: Public officials and employees (unlimited amount): Oregon Revised Statutes 237.980, 238.445, & 746.147.

Personal Property: Any personal property not listed below (up to $400): Oregon Revised Statutes 18.345(1)(o); Bank deposits (up to $7,500, if from exempt wages or pension): Oregon Revised Statutes 18.348; Books, pictures, and musical instruments (up to $600 total): Oregon Revised Statutes 18.345(1)(a); Burial plot (unlimited amount): Oregon Revised Statutes 65.870; Clothing, jewelry, and personal items (up to $1,800 total): Oregon Revised Statutes 18.345(1)(b); Domestic animals and poultry, with food to last 60 days (up to $1,000): Oregon Revised Statutes 18.345(1)(e); Food and fuel (amount to last 60 days): Oregon Revised Statutes 18.345(1)(f); Furniture, household items, radios, TVs, and utensils (up to $3,000 total): Oregon Revised Statutes 18.345(1)(f); Health aids (unlimited amount): Oregon Revised Statutes 18.345(1)(h); Lost future earnings payments (amount needed for support): Oregon Revised Statutes 18.345(1)(L); Motor vehicle (up to $2,150): Oregon Revised Statutes 18.345(1)(d); Personal injury recoveries (up to $10,000): Oregon Revised Statutes 18.345(1)(k); Compensation for lost future earnings (up to $10,000): Oregon Revised Statutes 18.345(1)(L); Pistol, rifle, or shotgun (up to $1,000): Oregon Revised Statutes 18.362; Proceeds from sale of exempt property (up to exemption amount): Oregon Revised Statutes 18.428; Tools, business equipment, library, and team with food to last 60 days (up to $3,000): Oregon Revised Statutes 18.345(1)(c); Earned income tax credit: Oregon Revised Statutes 18.345(1)(n); Building materials for construction or improvement (unlimited amount): Oregon Revised Statutes 87.075; Tuition savings program account (unlimited amount): Oregon Revised Statutes 348.863; Real estate client's trust account (unlimited amount): Oregon Revised Statutes 696.241; Real estate escrow funds (unlimited amount): Oregon Revised Statutes 696.579; Trust funds maintained by a debt consolidation agency (unlimited amount): Oregon Revised Statutes 697.722.

Real Estate: Real property, mobile home, or houseboat used as a residence (up to $30,000, $39,000 for joint owners, only $23,000 if mobile home, and $30,000 for joint mobile home owners if debtors own the property on which the mobile home sits, otherwise only $20,000 and $27,000 for joint mobile home owners; property may be up to 1 block in town or city or 160 acres elsewhere; sale proceeds are exempt for 1 year if held to purchase another home): Oregon Revised Statutes 18.428, 18.395, & 18.402; All real estate of soldeirs and sailors during wartime is exempt: Oregon Revised Statutes 408.440.

Wages: 75% of earned but unpaid wages (judge may allow more for low-income debtors): Oregon Revised Statutes 18.385; Wages withheld in state employees bond savings accounts: Oregon Revised Statutes 292.070.

Pennsylvania

Pennsylvania residents may use either the Federal Bankruptcy Exemptions listed at the end of this Appendix or the state exemptions listed below. If state exemptions are used, then the Federal Non-Bankruptcy Exemptions at the end of this Appendix may also be used.

Benefits: Unemployment compensation (unlimited amount): Pennsylvania Consolidated Statutes Annotated 42-8124(c)(10) & 43-863; Veterans benefits (unlimited amount): Pennsylvania Consolidated Statutes Annotated 51-20012 & 51-20098; Workers compensation (unlimited amount): Pennsylvania Consolidated Statutes Annotated 42-8124(c)(2).

Insurance: Accident or disability benefits (unlimited amount): Pennsylvania Consolidated Statutes Annotated 42-8124(c)(7); Fraternal society benefits (unlimited amount): Pennsylvania Consolidated Statutes Annotated 42-8124(c)(8); Group life policy or proceeds (unlimited amount): Pennsylvania Consolidated Statutes Annotated 42-8124(c)(5); Insurance annuity policy, cash value, or proceeds if beneficiary is insured's dependent, child, or spouse (unlimited amount): Pennsylvania Consolidated Statutes Annotated 42-8124(c)(6); Insurance or annuity payments, if insured is beneficiary, (up to $100 per month): Pennsylvania Consolidated Statutes Annotated 42-8124(c)(3); Life insurance proceeds if policy prohibits proceeds from being used to pay creditors (unlimited amount): Pennsylvania Consolidated Statutes Annotated 42-8124(c)(4); No-fault automobile insurance proceeds (unlimited amount): Pennsylvania Consolidated Statutes Annotated 42-8124(c)(9).

Miscellaneous: Any property (up to $300): Pennsylvania Consolidated Statutes Annotated 42-8123; Property of a business partnership (unlimited amount): Pennsylvania Consolidated Statutes Annotated 15-8341.

Pensions: City employees (unlimited amount): Pennsylvania Consolidated Statutes Annotated 53-13445, 53-23572, & 53-39383; County employees (unlimited amount): Pennsylvania Consolidated Statutes Annotated 16-4716; Municipal employees (unlimited amount): Pennsylvania Consolidated Statutes Annotated 53-881.115; Police officers (unlimited amount): Pennsylvania Consolidated Statutes Annotated 53-764, 53-776, & 53-23666; Private retirement benefits if deposited for over 1 year before filing for bankruptcy and if policy prohibits proceeds from being used to pay creditors (up to $15,000): Pennsylvania Consolidated Statutes Annotated 42-8124(b); Public school employees (unlimited amount): Pennsylvania Consolidated Statutes Annotated 24-8533; State employees (unlimited amount): Pennsylvania Consolidated Statutes Annotated 71-5953.

Personal Property: Bibles, schoolbooks, and sewing machines (unlimited amount): Pennsylvania Consolidated Statutes Annotated 42-8124(a)(2), (3); Clothing (unlimited amount):

Pennsylvania Consolidated Statutes Annotated 42-8124(a)(1); Personal property located at a U.S. government international exhibit (unlimited amount): Pennsylvania Consolidated Statutes Annotated 42-8125; Uniform and equipment required for military use (unlimited amount): Pennsylvania Consolidated Statutes Annotated 42-8124(a)(4).
Real Estate: None.
Wages: Earned but unpaid wages (unlimited amount): Pennsylvania Consolidated Statutes Annotated 42-8127; Wages of abused person or victim: Pennsylvania Consolidated Statutes Annotated 42-8127(F).

Rhode Island

Rhode Island residents may use either the Federal Bankruptcy Exemptions listed at the end of this Appendix or the state exemptions listed below. If state exemptions are used, then the Federal Non-Bankruptcy Exemptions at the end of this Appendix may also be used.
Benefits: Aid to aged, blind, disabled, families with dependent children, and general assistance (unlimited amount): General Laws of Rhode Island 40-5.1-15 & 40-6-14; Disability benefits (unlimited amount): General Laws of Rhode Island 28-41-32; Unemployment compensation (unlimited amount): General Laws of Rhode Island 28-44-58; Veterans disability or death benefits (unlimited amount): General Laws of Rhode Island 30-7-9; Workers compensation (unlimited amount): General Laws of Rhode Island 28-33-27; Crime victim's compensation: General Laws of Rhode Island 12-25.1-3.
Insurance: Accident or sickness proceeds or benefits (unlimited amount): General Laws of Rhode Island 27-18-24; Fraternal society benefits (unlimited amount): General Laws of Rhode Island 27-25-18; Life insurance proceeds if policy prohibits proceeds from being used to pay creditors (unlimited amount): General Laws of Rhode Island 27-4-12; Temporary disability insurance (unlimited amount): General Laws of Rhode Island 28-41-32.
Miscellaneous: Property of business partnership: General Laws of Rhode Island 7-12-36.
Pensions: Firefighters (unlimited amount): General Laws of Rhode Island 9-26-5; IRAs (unlimited amount): General Laws of Rhode Island 9-26-4(11); Police officers (unlimited amount): General Laws of Rhode Island 9-26-5; Private employees (unlimited amount): General Laws of Rhode Island 28-17-4; Retirement benefits (unlimited amount): General Laws of Rhode Island 9-26-4 (12); State and municipal employees (unlimited amount): General Laws of Rhode Island 36-10-34.
Personal Property: Beds, bedding, furniture, and household goods (up to $8,600 total): General Laws of Rhode Island 9-26-4(3); Bibles and books (up to $300): General Laws of Rhode Island 9-26-4(4); Burial plot (unlimited amount): General Laws of Rhode Island 9-26-4(5); Clothing (unlimited amount): General Laws of Rhode Island 9-26-4(1); Cooperative association holdings (up to $50): General Laws of Rhode Island 7-8-25; Debt secured by promissory note (unlimited amount): General Laws of Rhode Island 9-26-4(7); Library of a professional in practice (unlimited amount): General Laws of Rhode Island 9-26-4(2); Tools used for work (up to $1,200): General Laws of Rhode Island 9-26-4(2); Motor vehicle (up to $10,000): General Laws of Rhode Island 9-26-4(13): Jewelry (up to $1,000): General Laws of Rhode Island 9-26-4(14); Prepaid tuition or tuition savings program (unlimited amount): General Laws of Rhode Island 9-26-4(15).
Real Estate: Real estate if occupied or intended to be occupied as a principal residence (up to $30,000) husband and wife may not double: General Laws of Rhode Island 9-26-4.

Wages: Earned but unpaid wages (up to $50): General Laws of Rhode Island 9-26-4(8)(iii); Earned but unpaid wages due military member on active duty (unlimited amount): General Laws of Rhode Island 30-7-9; Earned but unpaid wages due seaman (unlimited amount): General Laws of Rhode Island 9-26-4(6); Earned but unpaid wages if debtor received welfare during the year before filing for bankruptcy (unlimited amount): General Laws of Rhode Island 9-26-4(8)(ii); Earnings of a minor child (unlimited amount): General Laws of Rhode Island 9-26-4(9); Wages of spouse (unlimited amount): General Laws of Rhode Island 9-26-4(9); Wages to the needy if paid by a charitable organization (unlimited amount): General Laws of Rhode Island 9-26-4(8).

South Carolina

South Carolina residents may use either the Federal Bankruptcy Exemptions listed at the end of this Appendix or the state exemptions listed below. If state exemptions are used, then the Federal Non-Bankruptcy Exemptions at the end of this Appendix may also be used.

Benefits: Aid to aged, blind, disabled, families with dependent children, and general relief (unlimited amount): Code of Laws of South Carolina 43-5-190; Crime victims compensation (unlimited amount): Code of Laws of South Carolina 15-41-30(11)(A) & 16-3-1300; Local public assistance (unlimited amount): Code of Laws of South Carolina 15-41-30(10)(A); Social Security (unlimited amount): Code of Laws of South Carolina 15-41-30 (10)(A); Unemployment compensation (unlimited amount): Code of Laws of South Carolina 15-41-30(10)(A); Veterans benefits (unlimited amount): Code of Laws of South Carolina 15-41-30(10)(B); Workers compensation (unlimited amount): Code of Laws of South Carolina 42-9-360.

Insurance: Disability, illness, or unemployment benefits (unlimited amount): Code of Laws of South Carolina 15-41-30(10)(C); Life insurance benefits if proceeds left with insurance company (up to $50,000 cash value): Code of Laws of South Carolina 38-63-40; Life insurance proceeds (up to $4,000): Code of Laws of South Carolina 15-41-30(8) & 15-41-30(11)(C); Unmatured life insurance contract (unlimited amount): Code of Laws of South Carolina 15-41-30(7).

Miscellaneous: Alimony and child support (unlimited amount): Code of Laws of South Carolina 15-41-30(10)(D); Property of a business partnership (unlimited amount): Code of Laws of South Carolina 33-41-720.

Pensions: Firefighters (unlimited amount): Code of Laws of South Carolina 9-13-230; General assembly members (unlimited amount): Code of Laws of South Carolina 9-9-180; Judges and solicitors (unlimited amount): Code of Laws of South Carolina 9-8-190; Police officers (unlimited amount): Code of Laws of South Carolina 9-11-270; Public employees (unlimited amount): Code of Laws of South Carolina 9-1-1680; Retirement benefits (unlimited amount): Code of Laws of South Carolina 15-41-30(10)(E).

Personal Property: Animals, appliances, books, clothing, crops, furnishings, household goods, and musical instruments (up to $2,500): Code of Laws of South Carolina 15-41-30(3); Burial plot (up to $50,000, if taken instead of real estate exemption): Code of Laws of South Carolina 15-41-30(1); Cash and other liquid assets (up to $1,000, if taken instead of burial or real estate exemption): Code of Laws of South Carolina 15-41-30(5); Health aids (unlimited amount): Code of Laws of South Carolina 15-41-30(9); Implements, books, and tools of a trade (up to $750): Code of Laws of South Carolina 15-41-30(6); Jewelry (up to $500): Code of Laws of South Carolina 15-41-30(4); Motor vehicle (up to $1,200): Code of Laws of South

Carolina 15-41-30(2); Personal injury recoveries (unlimited amount): Code of Laws of South Carolina 15-41-30(11)(B); Wrongful death recoveries (unlimited amount): Code of Laws of South Carolina 15-41-30(11)(B).

Real Estate: Real property used as a residence, including a co-op (up to $50,000): Code of Laws of South Carolina 15-41-30(1).

Wages: Earnings from personal service: Code of Laws of South Carolina 15-39-410.

South Dakota

South Dakota residents cannot use the Federal Bankruptcy Exemptions, but may use the Federal Non-Bankruptcy Exemptions listed at the end of this Appendix and the following state exemptions:

Benefits: Aid to families with dependent children and public assistance (unlimited amount): South Dakota Codified Laws 28-7A-18; Unemployment compensation (unlimited amount): South Dakota Codified Laws 61-6-28; Workers compensation (unlimited amount): South Dakota Codified Laws 62-4-42; Crime victim's compensation: South Dakota Codified Laws 23A-28B-24.

Insurance: Annuity contract proceeds (up to $250 per month): South Dakota Codified Laws 58-12-6 & 58-12-8; Endowment or life insurance policy, proceeds, or cash value (up to $20,000): South Dakota Codified Laws 58-12-4; Fraternal society benefits (unlimited amount): South Dakota Codified Laws 58-37A-18; Health benefits (up to $20,000): South Dakota Codified Laws 58-12-4; Life insurance proceeds (if held by insurance company and if policy prohibits proceeds from being used to pay creditors): South Dakota Codified Laws 58-15-70; Life insurance proceeds (up to $10,000, if beneficiary is spouse or child): South Dakota Codified Laws 43-45-6.

Miscellaneous: None.

Pensions: City employees (unlimited amount): South Dakota Codified Laws 9-16-47; Public employees (unlimited amount): South Dakota Codified Laws 3-12-115; Employee retirement benefit (unlimited amount): South Dakota Codified Laws 48-7A-501 through 48-7A-504.

Personal Property: Bible and books (up to $200), burial plot, church pew, clothing, and food and fuel to last 1 year (unlimited amount for this category unless noted): South Dakota Codified Laws 43-45-2 & 47-29-25; Head of household exemptions: Any personal property (up to $6,000): South Dakota Codified Laws 43-45-4, 5; Non-head of household exemption: Any personal property (up to $4,000): South Dakota Codified Laws 43-45-4.

Real Estate: Real property, including mobile home (unlimited value, up to 1 acre in town or up to 160 acres elsewhere); limited proceeds from sale are exempt for 1 year (up to $30,000; unlimited if over 70, or unmarried widow or widower (husband and wife may not double exemption value): South Dakota Codified Laws 43-31-1, 43-31-2, 43-31-3, 43-31-4, & 45-43-3. (Note: The 2005 Bankruptcy Act limits homestead exemptions to $136,875.00 if you have lived in the state where you are attempting to claim the exemption for less than 40 months (1215 days). This is true even if your state homestead exemption allows for a higher amount.)

Wages: Wages earned up to 60 days prior to filing for bankruptcy (amount needed for support): South Dakota Codified Laws 15-20-12; Wages of prisoners (unlimited amount): South Dakota Codified Laws 24-8-10.

Tennessee

Tennessee residents cannot use the Federal Bankruptcy Exemptions, but may use the Federal Non-Bankruptcy Exemptions listed at the end of this Appendix and the following state exemptions:

Benefits: Aid to aged, blind, disabled, and families with dependent children (unlimited amount): Tennessee Code Annotated 71-2-216, 71-3-121, 71-4-117, & 71-4-1112; Crime victims compensation (up to $5,000 and up to $15,000 total of all personal injury, wrongful death, and crime victims compensation): Tennessee Code Annotated 26-2-111(2)(A) & 29-13-111; Local public assistance (unlimited amount): Tennessee Code Annotated 26-2-111(1)(A); Social Security (unlimited amount): Tennessee Code Annotated 26-2-111(1)(A); Unemployment compensation (unlimited amount): Tennessee Code Annotated 26-2-111(1)(A); Veterans benefits (unlimited amount): Tennessee Code Annotated 26-2-111(1)(B); Workers compensation (unlimited amount): Tennessee Code Annotated 50-6-223; Uniform relocation assistance program (unlimited amount): Tennessee Code Annotated 13-11-115.

Insurance: Accident, health, or disability benefits (unlimited amount): Tennessee Code Annotated 26-2-110; Annuity contract proceeds if payable to dependent (unlimited amount): Tennessee Code Annotated 56-7-203; Disability or illness benefits (unlimited amount): Tennessee Code Annotated 26-2-111(1)(C); Fraternal society benefits (unlimited amount): Tennessee Code Annotated 56-25-1403; Homeowners insurance proceeds (up to $5,000): Tennessee Code Annotated 26-2-304; Life insurance or annuity (unlimited amount): Tennessee Code Annotated 56-7-203.

Miscellaneous: Alimony and child support (if owed for 30 days before filing for bankruptcy): Tennessee Code Annotated 26-2-111(1)(E) & (F).

Pensions: Public employees (unlimited amount): Tennessee Code Annotated 8-36-111; Retirement benefits (unlimited amount): Tennessee Code Annotated 26-2-111 (1)(D); State and local government employees (unlimited amount): Tennessee Code Annotated 26-2-104; Teachers (unlimited amount): Tennessee Code Annotated 49-5-909.

Personal Property: Any personal property, including cash or bank deposits (up to $4,000): Tennessee Code Annotated 26-2-103; Bible, clothing, pictures, portraits, schoolbooks, and storage containers (unlimited amount): Tennessee Code Annotated 26-2-104; Burial plot (unlimited value, up to 1 acre): Tennessee Code Annotated 26-2-305 & 46-2-102; Health aids (unlimited amount): Tennessee Code Annotated 26-2-111(5); Implements, books, and tools of a trade (up to $1,900): Tennessee Code Annotated 26-2-111(4); Lost earnings payments: Tennessee Code Annotated 26-2-111(3); Personal injury recoveries except for pain and suffering (up to $7,500 and up to $15,000 total of all personal injury, wrongful death, and crime victims compensation): Tennessee Code Annotated 26-2-111(2)(B); Wrongful death recoveries (up to $10,000 and up to $15,000 total of all personal injury, wrongful death, and crime victims compensation): Tennessee Code Annotated 26-2-111(2)(C); Scholarship trust fund (unlimited amount): Tennessee Code Annotated 49-4-108; Education system trust fund (unlimited amount): Tennessee Code Annotated 49-7-822 .

Real Estate: Real estate-life estate (please see statute) [unlimited amount]: Tennessee Code Annotated 26-2-302; Real property used as a residence (up to $5,000 and $7,500 for joint owners; if owner is 62 or over and single up to $12,500; if also married, then up to $20,000; if married to spouse who is also 62 or older, then up to $25,000): Tennessee Code Annotated 26-2-301; 2-15 year lease (unlimited amount): Tennessee Code Annotated 26-2-303.

Wages: 75% of earned but unpaid wages, plus $2.50 per week per child (judge may allow more for low-income debtors): Tennessee Code Annotated 26-2-106 & 26-2-107; Wages of debtor deserting family that are in the hands of the family (up to $5,000): Tennessee Code Annotated 26-2-209.

Texas

Texas residents may use either the Federal Bankruptcy Exemptions listed at the end of this Appendix or the state exemptions listed below. If state exemptions are used, then the Federal Non-Bankruptcy Exemptions at the end of this Appendix may also be used.

Benefits: Aid to families with dependent children (unlimited amount): Texas Revised Civil Statutes Annotated, Human Resources 31.040; Medical assistance (unlimited amount): Texas Revised Civil Statutes Annotated, Human Resources 32.036.

Insurance: Fraternal society benefits (unlimited amount): Texas Revised Civil Statutes Annotated, Insurance Code 885.316; Life, health, accident, or annuity benefits, cash value, or proceeds (see limits under "Personal Property"): Texas Revised Civil Statutes Annotated, Insurance Code 1108.051; Life insurance if beneficiary is debtor or debtor's dependent (unlimited amount): Texas Revised Civil Statutes Annotated, Property 42; Texas employee uniform group insurance (unlimited amount): Texas Revised Civil Statutes Annotated, Insurance 1551.011; Texas state college or university employee benefits (unlimited amount): Texas Revised Civil Statutes Annotated, Insurance 1601.001+.

Miscellaneous: Alimony (amount needed for support): Texas Revised Civil Statutes Annotated, Property 42.

Pensions: County and district employees (unlimited): Texas Revised Civil Statutes Annotated, Government 8115; Firefighters: Texas Revised Civil Statutes Annotated 6243e(5) & 6243e.1(104); Judges (unlimited amount): Texas Revised Civil Statutes Annotated, Government 8115; Municipal employees (unlimited amount): Texas Revised Civil Statutes Annotated 6243g, Government 8115; Police officers (unlimited amount): Texas Revised Civil Statutes Annotated 6243d-1(17), 6243j(20), & 6243g-1(23B); Retirement benefits (unlimited amount if tax-deferred): Texas Revised Civil Statutes Annotated, Property 4221; State employees (unlimited amount): Texas Revised Civil Statutes Annotated, Government 8115; Teachers (unlimited amount): Texas Revised Civil Statutes Annotated, Government 8115.

Personal Property: Athletic and sporting equipment, bicycles, boat, books, cattle (12), clothing, equipment, farming or ranching equipment, firearms (2), food, heirlooms, home furnishings, horses or donkeys (2 and saddle, blanket, and bridle for both), jewelry (up to 25% of total exemption), livestock (60), motor vehicle, pets, poultry (120), and tools (NOTE: limits on total of all above personal property, life insurance cash value, and unpaid commissions are up to $30,000 or up to $60,000 for head of family): Texas Revised Civil Statutes Annotated, Property 42; Burial plots (unlimited amount): Texas Revised Civil Statutes Annotated, Property 411; Health aids (unlimited amount): Texas Revised Civil Statutes Annotated, Property 42; Prepaid tuition plans (unlimited amount): Texas Revised Civil Statutes Annotated, Education Code 54.639; Higher education savings plans (unlimited amount): Texas Revised Civil Statutes Annotated, Education Code 54.709.

Real Estate: Real property (unlimited value; up to 1 acre in town, village, city, and 200 acres elsewhere; 100 acres limit if single); must file exemption with county; proceeds of sale are exempt for 6 months: Texas Revised Civil Statutes Annotated, Property 41. (Note: The 2005

Bankruptcy Act limits homestead exemptions to $136,875.00 if you have lived in the state where you are attempting to claim the exemption for less than 40 months (1215 days). This is true even if your state homestead exemption allows for a higher amount.)

Wages: Earned but unpaid wages (unlimited amount): Texas Revised Civil Statutes Annotated, Property 42; Unpaid commissions (up to 75%) [see limits under "Personal Property"]: Texas Revised Civil Statutes Annotated Property 42.

Utah

Utah residents cannot use the Federal Bankruptcy Exemptions, but may use the Federal Non-Bankruptcy Exemptions listed at the end of this Appendix and the following state exemptions:

Benefits: Unemployment compensation (unlimited amount): Utah Code 35A-4-103; Veterans benefits (unlimited amount): Utah Code 78B-5-505; Workers compensation (unlimited amount): Utah Code 34A-2-422; Public assistance benefits (unlimited amount): Utah Code 35A-3-112.

Insurance: Disability, illness, medical, or hospital benefits (unlimited amount): Utah Code 78B-5-505; Fraternal society benefits (unlimited amount): Utah Code 31A-9-603; Life insurance policy [unlimited amount]: Utah Code 78B-5-505; Life insurance proceeds if beneficiary is insured's spouse or dependent (amount needed for support): Utah Code 78B-5-505.

Miscellaneous: Alimony or child support (amount needed for support): Utah Code 78B-5-505; Property of a business partnership (unlimited amount): Utah Code 48-1-22.

Pensions: Any pension (amount needed for support): Utah Code 78B-5-505; Public employees (unlimited amount): Utah Code 49-11-612; Retirement benefits (unlimited amount): Utah Code 78B-5-505.

Personal Property: Animals, books, and musical instruments (up to $500 total): Utah Code 78B-5-506; Appliances and household furnishings: Utah Code 78B-5-505; Artwork depicting, or done by, family member (unlimited amount): Utah Code 78B-5-505; Bed, bedding, carpets, washer, and dryer (unlimited amount): Utah Code 78B-5-505; Burial plot (unlimited amount): Utah Code 78B-5-505; Clothing (unlimited amount, but not furs or jewelry): Utah Code 78B-5-505; Equipment required for military use (unlimited amount): Utah Code 39-1-47; Food and fuel: Utah Code 78B-5-505; Health aids (amount needed): Utah Code 78B-5-505; Heirlooms or sentimental item (up to $500): Utah Code 78B-5-506; Implements, books, and tools of a trade (up to $3,500 total): Utah Code 78B-5-506; Motor vehicle (for business use only and only up to $2,500): Utah Code 78B-5-506; Personal injury recoveries (unlimited amount): Utah Code 78B-5-505; Proceeds for damaged exempt property (up to exemption amount): Utah Code 78B-5-507; Refrigerator, freezer, sewing machine, and stove (unlimited amount): Utah Code 78B-5-505; Wrongful death recoveries (unlimited amount): Utah Code 78B-5-505.

Real Estate: Real property, mobile home used as a residence, or water rights (up to $10,000, if property is jointly owned; each debtor may claim the exemption, but total exemption not to exceed $20,000) (if property is not used as primary residence then up to $5,000 only); must file exemption with county: Utah Code 78B-5-503.

Wages: 75% of earned but unpaid wages (judge may allow more for low-income debtors): Utah Code 70C-7-103.

Vermont

Vermont residents may use either the Federal Bankruptcy Exemptions listed at the end of this Appendix or the state exemptions listed below. If state exemptions are used, then the Federal Non-Bankruptcy Exemptions at the end of this Appendix may also be used.

Benefits: Aid to aged, blind, disabled, families with dependent children, and general assistance (unlimited amount): Vermont Statutes Annotated 33-124; Crime victims compensation (amount needed for support): Vermont Statutes Annotated 12-2740(19)(E); Social Security (amount needed for support): Vermont Statutes Annotated 12-2740(19)(A); Unemployment compensation (unlimited amount): Vermont Statutes Annotated 21-1367; Veterans benefits (amount needed for support): Vermont Statutes Annotated 12-2740(19)(B); Workers compensation (unlimited amount): Vermont Statutes Annotated 21-681.

Insurance: Annuity contract benefits (up to $350 per month): Vermont Statutes Annotated 8-3709; Disability or illness benefits (amount needed for support): Vermont Statutes Annotated 8-3707 & 12-2740(19)(C); Fraternal society benefits (unlimited amount): Vermont Statutes Annotated 8-4478; Group life or health benefits (unlimited amount): Vermont Statutes Annotated 8-3708; Health benefits (up to $200 per month): Vermont Statutes Annotated 8-4086; Life insurance proceeds if beneficiary not the insured (unlimited amount): Vermont Statutes Annotated 8-3706; Life insurance proceeds if policy prohibits proceeds from being used to pay creditors (unlimited amount): Vermont Statutes Annotated 8-3705; Life insurance proceeds (unlimited amount): Vermont Statutes Annotated 8-3708 & 12-2740(19)(H); Supplemental disability benefits (unlimited amount): Vermont Statutes Annotated 8-3707; Unmatured life insurance contract (unlimited amount): Vermont Statutes Annotated 12-2740(18).

Miscellaneous: Alimony or child support (amount needed for support): Vermont Statutes Annotated 12-2740(19)(D); Any property (up to $400): Vermont Statutes Annotated 12-2740(7).

Pensions: Any pensions (unlimited amount): Vermont Statutes Annotated 12-2740 (19)(j); IRAs and Keogh (up to $5,000): Vermont Statutes Annotated 12-2740(16); Municipal employees (unlimited amount): Vermont Statutes Annotated 24-5066; State employees (unlimited amount): Vermont Statutes Annotated 3-476; Teachers (unlimited amount): Vermont Statutes Annotated 16-1946.

Personal Property: Animals, appliances, books, clothing, crops, furnishings, goods, and musical instruments (up to $2,500 total): Vermont Statutes Annotated 12-2740(5); Bank deposits (up to $700): Vermont Statutes Annotated 12-2740(15); Books and tools of a trade (up to $5,000 total): Vermont Statutes Annotated 12-2740(2); Farm crops and animals: bees (3 swarms), crops (up to $5,000), chickens (10), cow, goats (2), horses (2), sheep (10), yoke of oxen or steers, and feed to last through winter: Vermont Statutes Annotated 12-2740 (6), (11)-(13); Farm equipment: chains (2), halters (2), harnesses (2), plow, and yoke: Vermont Statutes Annotated 12-2740(14); Firewood (10 cords), coal (5 tons), heating oil (500 gallons), or bottled gas (500 gallons): Vermont Statutes Annotated 12-2740(9)-(10); Freezer, heating unit, refrigerator, sewing machines, stove, and water heater (unlimited amount): Vermont Statutes Annotated 12-2740(8); Health aids (unlimited amount): Vermont Statutes Annotated 12-2740(17); Jewelry (up to $500, unlimited amount for wedding ring): Vermont Statutes Annotated 12-2740(3), (4); Lost future earnings (unlimited amount): Vermont Statutes Annotated 12-2740 (19)(I); Motor vehicles (up to $2,500): Vermont Statutes Annotated 12-2740(1); Personal injury recoveries (unlimited amount): Vermont Statutes Annotated

12-2740(19)(I); Wrongful death recoveries (unlimited amount): Vermont Statutes Annotated 12-2740(19)(G).

Real Estate: Real property or mobile home (up to $75,000): Vermont Statutes Annotated 27-101.

Wages: 75% of earned but unpaid wages (judge may allow more for low-income debtors, unlimited amount if debtor received welfare within 2 months of filing for bankruptcy): Vermont Statutes Annotated 12-3170.

Virginia

Virginia residents cannot use the Federal Bankruptcy Exemptions, but may use the Federal Non-Bankruptcy Exemptions listed at the end of this Appendix and the following state exemptions:

Benefits: Aid to aged, blind, disabled, families with dependent child, and general relief (unlimited amount): Code of Virginia 63.2-506; Crime victims compensation (unlimited amount, except not for debt for treatment of injury incurred during crime): Code of Virginia 19.2-368.12; Unemployment compensation (unlimited amount): Code of Virginia 60.2-600; Workers compensation (unlimited amount): Code of Virginia 65.2-531.

Insurance: Accident or sickness benefits (unlimited amount): Code of Virginia 38.2-3549; Burial benefits (unlimited amount): Code of Virginia 38.2-4021; Cooperative life insurance benefits (unlimited amount): Code of Virginia 38.2-3811; Fraternal society benefits (unlimited amount): Code of Virginia 38.2-4118; Government group life or accident insurance (unlimited amount): Code of Virginia 51.1-510; Group life insurance policy or proceeds (unlimited amount): Code of Virginia 38.2-3339; Sickness benefits (unlimited amount): Code of Virginia 38.2-3549.

Miscellaneous: Any property for disabled veterans homeowner (up to $2,000): Code of Virginia 34-4.1.

Pensions: City, town, and county employees (unlimited amount): Code of Virginia 51.1-802; Retirement benefits: Code of Virginia 34-34; 75% of earned but unpaid pension payments (judge may allow more for low-income debtors): Code of Virginia 34-29.

Personal Property: [*Note*: Debtor must be a householder to claim any personal property exemption in Virginia.] Bible (unlimited amount): Code of Virginia 34-26(1); Burial plot (unlimited amount): Code of Virginia 34-26(3); Clothing (up to $1,000): Code of Virginia 34-26(4); Crops (unlimited amount): Code of Virginia 8.01-489; Estate sale proceeds (up to amount of unused real estate exemption): Code of Virginia 34-20; Family portraits and heirlooms (up to $5,000 total): Code of Virginia 34-26(2); Farm equipment: fertilizer (up to $1,000), horses (2), mules (2), with gear, pitchfork, plows (2), rake, tractor (up to $3,000), wagon, drag, harvest cradle, and iron wedges (2): Code of Virginia 34-27; Health aids (unlimited amount): Code of Virginia 34-26(6); Household furnishings (up to $5,000): Code of Virginia 34-26(4)(a); Motor vehicle (up to $2,000): Code of Virginia 34-26(8); Personal injury recoveries or causes of action (unlimited amount): Code of Virginia 34-28.1; Pets (unlimited amount): Code of Virginia 34-26(5); Tools, books, and instruments of trade, including motor vehicles (up to $10,000): Code of Virginia 34-26; Uniforms, arms, and equipment required for military use: Code of Virginia 44-96; Wedding and engagement rings (unlimited amount): Code of Virginia 34-26 (1)(a); Prepaid tuition contracts (unlimited amount): Code of Virginia 23-38.81; Unused portion of real estate exemption may be used for personal property: Code of Virginia 34-13.

Real Estate: Real property (up to $5,000 plus $500 per dependent) and homestead for sur-viving spouse or children (up to $15,000); proceeds from the sale of exempt real estate are also exempt; must file homestead declaration before filing for bankruptcy: Code of Virginia 34-4, 34-6, & 64.1-151.3.

Wages: 75% of earned but unpaid wages (judge may allow more for low-income debtors): Code of Virginia 34-29.

Washington

Washington residents may use either the Federal Bankruptcy Exemptions listed at the end of this Appendix or the state exemptions listed below. If state exemptions are used, then the Federal Non-Bankruptcy Exemptions at the end of this Appendix may also be used.

Benefits: Aid to aged and families with dependent children (unlimited amount): Revised Code of Washington Annotated 74.08.210 & 74.13.070; Crime victims compensation (unlimited amount): Revised Code of Washington Annotated 7.68.070; General assistance (unlimited amount): Revised Code of Washington Annotated 74.04.280; Unemployment compensation (unlimited amount): Revised Code of Washington Annotated 50.40.020; Workers compensa-tion (unlimited amount): Revised Code of Washington Annotated 51.32.040.

Insurance: Annuity contract proceeds (up to $2,500 per month): Revised Code of Washington Annotated 48.18.430; Disability proceeds or benefits (unlimited amount): Revised Code of Washington Annotated 48.18.400; Fraternal society benefits (unlimited amount): Revised Code of Washington Annotated 48.36A.180; Group life insurance policy or proceeds (unlim-ited amount): Revised Code of Washington Annotated 48.18.420; Insurance proceeds for destroyed exempt property (up to exemption amount): Revised Code of Washington Anno-tated 6.15.030; Life insurance proceeds if beneficiary is not the insured (unlimited amount): Revised Code of Washington Annotated 48.18.410.

Miscellaneous: Child support payments (unlimited amount): Revised Code of Washington Annotated 6.15.010(3)(d).

Pensions: City employees (unlimited amount): Revised Code of Washington Annotated 41.28.200; IRAs (unlimited amount): Revised Code of Washington Annotated 6.15.020; Public employees (unlimited amount): Revised Code of Washington Annotated 41.40.052; Retirement benefits (unlimited amount): Revised Code of Washington Annotated 6.15.020; State patrol officers (unlimited amount): Revised Code of Washington Annotated 43.43.310; Volunteer firefighters (unlimited amount): Revised Code of Washington Annotated 41.24.240.

Personal Property: Any personal property (up to $2,000; only $200 may be cash, bank de-posits, bonds, stocks, or securities): Revised Code of Washington Annotated 6.15.010(3)(b); Appliances, furniture, home and yard equipment, and household goods (up to $2,700 to-tal; husband and wife may double this amount): Revised Code of Washington Annotated 6.15.010(3)(a); Books (up to $1,500): Revised Code of Washington Annotated 6.15. 010(2); Burial plots (unlimited amount): Revised Code of Washington Annotated 68.24.220; Clothing (unlimited amount, but only up to $1,000 of furs or jewelry): Revised Code of Washington Annotated 6.15.010(1); Farm equipment: equipment, seed, stock, tools, and vehicles (up to $5,000 total): Revised Code of Washington Annotated 6.15.010(4)(a); Food and fuel (amount needed): Revised Code of Washington Annotated 6.15.010(3)(a); Keepsakes and pictures (unlimited amount): Revised Code of Washington Annotated 6.15.010(2); Library, office equip-ment, office furniture, and supplies of attorney, clergy, physician, surgeon, or other professional (up to $5,000 total): Revised Code of Washington Annotated 6.15.010(4)(b); Motor vehicle (up to $2,500; husband and wife may double this amount): Revised Code of Washington Annotated 6.15.010(3)(c); Tools of a trade (up to $5,000): Revised Code of Washington Annotated 6.15.010(4)(c); Professionally prescribed health aids (unlimited amount): Revised Code of Washington Annotated 6.15.010(3)(e); Personal injury awards (up to $16,150): Revised Code of Washington Annotated 6.15.010(3)(f); Building materials for home improvement (unlimited amount): Revised Code of Washington Annotated 60.04.201.

Real Estate: Real property or mobile home (up to $125,000) or unimproved real estate intended to be used for a residence (up to $15,000) Husband and wife may not double real estate exemption amounts; must file exemption with county: Revised Code of Washington Annotated 6.13.010 & 6.13.030 [*Note*: This exemption is for an unlimited value if for property located in Washington and if debtor is seeking to discharge debt for a state income tax assessed on retirement benefits received while a resident of Washington.]

Wages: 75% of earned but unpaid wages (judge may allow more for low-income debtors): Revised Code of Washington Annotated 6.27.150.

West Virginia

West Virginia residents cannot use the Federal Bankruptcy Exemptions, but may use the Federal Non-Bankruptcy Exemptions listed at the end of this Appendix and the following state exemptions:

Benefits: Aid to aged, blind, disabled, families with dependent children, and general assistance (unlimited amount): West Virginia Code 9-5-1; Crime victims compensation (unlimited amount): West Virginia Code 14-2A-24 & 38-10-4(k)(1); Social Security (unlimited amount): West Virginia Code 38-10-4(j)(1); Unemployment compensation (unlimited amount): West Virginia Code 38-10-4(j)(1); Veterans benefits (unlimited amount): West Virginia Code 38-10-4(j)(2); Workers compensation (unlimited amount): West Virginia Code 23-4-18.

Insurance: Fraternal society benefits (unlimited amount): West Virginia Code 33-23-21; Group life insurance policy or proceeds (unlimited amount): West Virginia Code 33-6-28; Health or disability benefits (unlimited amount): West Virginia Code 38-10-4 (j)(3); Life insurance proceeds (unlimited amount): West Virginia Code 38-10-4(k)(3); Unmatured life insurance contract (unlimited amount; accrued dividend, interest, or loan value up to $8,000, if debtor is the insured or 1 debtor is dependent upon): West Virginia Code 38-10-4(g), (h).

Miscellaneous: Alimony and child support (amount needed for support): West Virginia Code 38-10-4(j)(4); Any property (up to $800 plus any unused amount of real estate or burial exemption): West Virginia Code 38-10-4(e); Payments made to prepaid tuition trust fund (unlimited amount): West Virginia Code 38-10-4(k)(6).

Pensions: Public employees (unlimited amount): West Virginia Code 5-10-46; Retirement benefits (amount needed for support): West Virginia Code 38-10-4 (j)(5); Teachers (unlimited amount): West Virginia Code 18-7A-30.

Personal Property: Animals, appliances, books, clothing, crops, furnishings, household goods, and musical instruments (up to $400 per item and $8,000 total): West Virginia Code 38-10-4(c); Burial plot (up to $25,000, if taken instead of real estate exemption): West Virginia Code 38-10-4(a); Health aids (unlimited amount): West Virginia Code 38-10-4(i); Implements, books, and tools of a trade (up to $1,500): West Virginia Code 38-10-4(f); Jewelry (up to $1,000): West Virginia Code 38-10-4(d); Lost future earnings payments (amount needed for support): West Virginia Code 38-10-4(k)(5); Motor vehicle (up to $2,400): West Virginia Code 38-10-4(b); Personal injury recoveries (up to $15,000, but not for pain and suffering): West Virginia Code 38-10-4(k)(4); Wrongful death recoveries (amount needed for support): West Virginia Code 38-10-4(k)(2); Tuition trust fund (unlimited amount): West Virginia Code 38-10-4(k)(6).

Real Estate: Real or personal property used as residence (up to $25,000): West Virginia Code 38-10-4(a).

Wages: 50% of earned but unpaid wages (more possible for low-income debtor): West Virginia Code 38-5A-3.

Wisconsin

Wisconsin residents may use either the Federal Bankruptcy Exemptions listed at the end of this Appendix or the state exemptions listed below. If state exemptions are used, then the Federal Non-Bankruptcy Exemptions at the end of this Appendix may also be used.

Benefits: Aid to families with dependent children and any other social services payments (unlimited amount): Wisconsin Statutes Annotated 49.96; Crime victims compensation (unlimited amount): Wisconsin Statutes Annotated 949.07; Unemployment compensation (unlimited amount): Wisconsin Statutes Annotated 108.13; Veterans benefits (unlimited amount): Wisconsin Statutes Annotated 45.35(8)(b); Workers compensation (unlimited amount): Wisconsin Statutes Annotated 102.27.

Insurance: Federal disability insurance (unlimited amount): Wisconsin Statutes Annotated 815.18(3)(ds); Fraternal society benefits (unlimited amount): Wisconsin Statutes Annotated 614.96; Insurance proceeds for exempt property destroyed within 2 years of filing for bankruptcy (up to amount of exemption): Wisconsin Statutes Annotated 815.18(3)(e); Life insurance proceeds if beneficiary was a dependent of the insured (amount needed for support): Wisconsin Statutes Annotated 815.18(3)(i)(1)(a); Life insurance proceeds if held in trust by insurer and if policy prohibits proceeds from being used to pay creditors: Wisconsin Statutes Annotated 632.42; Unmatured life insurance contract (unlimited amount; accrued dividend, interest, or loan value up to $4,000, if debtor is the insured or 1 debtor is dependent upon): Wisconsin Statutes Annotated 815.18(3)(f).

Miscellaneous: Alimony and child support: Wisconsin Statutes Annotated 815.18(3)(c); Property of a business partnership (unlimited amount): Wisconsin Statutes Annotated 178.21.

Pensions: Firefighters and police officers (unlimited amount): Wisconsin Statutes Annotated 815.18(3)(e) & (f); Military pensions (unlimited amount): Wisconsin Statutes Annotated 815.18 (3)(n); Private or public retirement benefits (amount needed for support): Wisconsin Statutes Annotated 815.18(3)(j); Public employees (unlimited amount): Wisconsin Statutes Annotated 40.08(1).

Personal Property: Animals, appliances, books, clothing, firearms, furnishings, household goods, jewelry, keepsakes, musical instruments, sporting goods, or any other personal property held for personal use (up to $5,000 total): Wisconsin Statutes Annotated 815.18(3)(d); Bank accounts (up to $1,000): Wisconsin Statutes Annotated 815.18(3)(k); Burial plot (unlimited amount): Wisconsin Statutes Annotated 815.18(3)(a); Equipment, inventory, farm products, books, and tools of a trade (up to $7,500 total): Wisconsin Statutes Annotated 815.18(3)(b); Lease or interest in housing co-op (up to real estate exemption amount): Wisconsin Statutes Annotated 1824(6); Lost future earnings recoveries (amount needed for support): Wisconsin Statutes Annotated 815.18(3)(i)(1)(d); Motor vehicles (up to $1,200): Wisconsin Statutes Annotated 815.18(3)(g); Personal injury recoveries (up to $25,000): Wisconsin Statutes Annotated 815.18(3)(i)(1)(c); Wrongful death recoveries (amount needed for support): Wisconsin Statutes Annotated 815.18(3)(i)(1)(b); Fire-fighting equipment belonging to municipality (unlimited amount): Wisconsin Statutes Annotated 815.18(3)(em); State aid to county fairs and agricultural societies (unlimited amount): Wisconsin Statutes Annotated 815.18(3)(df); Tuition trust funds and college savings programs (unlimited amount): Wisconsin Statutes Annotated 14.63 & 14.64.

Real Estate: Real property used, or intended to be used, as a residence, which includes a building, condominium, mobile home, house trailer, or cooperative not less than 1/4 of an acre and not exceeding 40 acres (up to $40,000) husband and wife may not double real estate exemption amount; proceeds from sale of exempt real estate is exempt for 2 years: Wisconsin Statutes Annotated 815.20.

Wages: 75% of earned but unpaid wages (judge may allow more for low-income debtors): Wisconsin Statutes Annotated 815.18(3)(h); Wages used for the purchase of savings bonds (unlimited amount): Wisconsin Statutes Annotated 20.921(1)(e); Wages of inmates under work release programs, in county jails, or in county work camps (unlimited amount): Wisconsin Statutes Annotated 303.065, 303.08, & 303.10.

Wyoming

Wyoming residents cannot use the Federal Bankruptcy Exemptions, but may use the Federal Non-Bankruptcy Exemptions listed at the end of this Appendix and the following state exemptions:

Benefits: Aid to families with dependent children and general assistance (unlimited amount): Wyoming Statutes Annotated 42-2-113; Crime victims compensation (unlimited amount): Wyoming Statutes Annotated 1-40-113; Unemployment compensation (unlimited amount): Wyoming Statutes Annotated 27-3-319; Workers compensation (unlimited amount): Wyoming Statutes Annotated 27-14-702.

Insurance: Annuity contract proceeds (up to $350 per month): Wyoming Statutes Annotated 26-15-132; Disability benefits if policy prohibits proceeds from being used to pay creditors (unlimited amount): Wyoming Statutes Annotated 26-15-130; Fraternal society benefits (unlimited amount): Wyoming Statutes Annotated 26-29-218; Group life or disability policy or proceeds (unlimited amount): Wyoming Statutes Annotated 26-15-131; Life insurance proceeds if held in trust by insurer and if policy prohibits proceeds from being used to pay creditors (unlimited amount): Wyoming Statutes Annotated 26-15-133.

Miscellaneous: Liquor and beer licenses (unlimited amount): Wyoming Statutes Annotated 12-4-604.

Pensions: Criminal investigators and highway patrol (unlimited amount): Wyoming Statutes Annotated 9-3-620; Firefighters and police officers (only payments being received): Wyoming Statutes Annotated 15-5-209; Game and fish wardens (unlimited amount): Wyoming Statutes Annotated 9-3-620; Private or public retirement accounts (unlimited amount): Wyoming Statutes Annotated 1-20-110; Public employees (unlimited amount): Wyoming Statutes Annotated 9-3-426.

Personal Property: Bedding, food, furniture, and household articles (up to $2,000 per person in household if 2 or more people, otherwise $2,000): Wyoming Statutes Annotated 1-20-

106(a)(iii); Bible, schoolbooks, and pictures (unlimited amount): Wyoming Statutes Annotated 1-20-106(a)(i); Burial plot (unlimited amount): Wyoming Statutes Annotated 1-20-106(a)(ii) & 35-8-104; Clothing and wedding rings (up to $1,000): Wyoming Statutes Annotated 1-20-105; Library and equipment of a professional (up to $2,000): Wyoming Statutes Annotated 1-20-106(b); Motor vehicle (up to $2,400): Wyoming Statutes Annotated 1-20-106 (a)(iv); Pre-paid funeral contracts (unlimited amount): Wyoming Statutes Annotated 26-32-102; Tools, motor vehicle, implements, team, and stock-in-trade used in trade or business (up to $2,000): Wyoming Statutes Annotated 1-20-106(b); Medical savings accounts (unlimited amount): Wyoming Statutes Annotated 1-20-111.

Real Estate: Real property or house trailer used as a residence (up to $10,000, $20,000 for joint owners, only up to $6,000 for house trailer; and up to $12,000 for joint owners of house trailer): Wyoming Statutes Annotated 1-20-101, 1-20-102, & 1-20-104.

Wages: 75% of earned but unpaid wages (judge may allow more for low-income debtors): Wyoming Statutes Annotated 1-15-511; Wages of inmates on work release, in community corrections programs, and correctional industry programs (unlimited amount): Wyoming Statutes Annotated 7-16-308, 7-18-114, & 25-13-107; Wages of National Guard members (unlimited amount): Wyoming Statutes Annotated 19-9-501.

Federal Bankruptcy Exemptions

Federal Bankruptcy Exemptions are only available to residents of the following states: Arkansas, Connecticut, District of Columbia (Washington D.C.),Hawaii, Massachusetts, Michigan, Minnesota, New Jersey, New Mexico, Pennsylvania, Rhode Island, South Carolina, Texas, Vermont, Washington, and Wisconsin. If the debtor elects to use the Federal Bankruptcy Exemptions listed here, he or she cannot use either his or her own state exemptions or the Federal Non-Bankruptcy Exemptions listed at the end of this Appendix. Married couples filing jointly may double the exemption amounts listed. Note: Certain tax-exempt pension plan and IRA exemptions are available to all taxpayers.

Benefits: Crime victims compensation (unlimited amount):11 United States Code 522(d)(11)(A); Public assistance (unlimited amount): 11 United States Code 522(d)(10)(A); Unemployment compensation (unlimited amount):11 United States Code 522(d)(10)(A); Social Security (unlimited amount): 11 United States Code 522(d)(10)(A); Veterans benefits (unlimited amount): 11 United States Code 522(d)(10)(B).

Insurance: Disability, illness,or unemployment benefits (unlimited amount): 11 United States Code 522(d)(10)(C);Life insurance proceeds (amount needed for support): 11 United States Code 522(d)(11)(C); Life insurance policy loan value, dividends, or interest (up to $10,775):11 United States Code 522(d)(8); Unmatured life insurance contract (unlimited amount, but not credit insurance policy): 11 United States Code 522(d)(7).

Miscellaneous: Alimony and child support (amount needed for support): 11 United States Code 522(d)(10)(D); Any property (up to $1,075): 11 United States Code 522(d)(5);

Pensions: Retirement benefits (amount needed for support): 11 United States Code 522(d)(10)(E). Note: The following exemptions are available to all taxpayers: Tax exempt retirement accounts (including 401K, 403B, profit-sharing plans, money-purchase plans, SEP IRAs, Simple IRAs, and defined-benefit plans (unlimited amounts): 11 United States Code 522(b)(3)(c); Traditional IRAs and Roth IRAs (up to $1,095,000 per person): 11 United States Code 522(b)(3)(c)(n).

Personal Property: Animals, appliances, books, clothing, crops, furnishings, household goods, and musical instruments (up to $525 per item and up to $10,775 total): 11 United States Code 522(d)(3); One motor vehicle (up to $3,2250): 11 United States Code 522(d)(2); Burial plot ($15,000 in lieu of real estate exemption): 11 United States Code 522(d)(1); Health aids (unlimited amount): 11 United States Code 522(d)(9); Implements,books,and tools of a trade (up to $2,025): 11 United States Code 522(d)(6); Jewelry (up to $1,000): 11 United States Code 522(d)(4); Lost earnings payments (unlimited amount): 11 United States Code 522 (d)(11)(E); Personal injury recoveries (up to $20,200, but not for pain and suffering or pecuniary loss): 11 United States Code 522(d)(11)(D); Wrongful death recoveries (amount needed for support): 11 United States Code 522(d)(11)(B); May use up to $10,125 of any unused homestead (real estate) exemption for any property: 11 United States Code 522(d)(5).

Real Estate: Real property, co-op,or mobile home (up to $20,200): 11 United States Code 522(d)(1); May use up to $10,125 of any unused homestead (real estate) exemption for any property: 11 United States Code 522(d)(5).

Wages: None.

Federal Non-Bankruptcy Exemptions

The following Federal Non-Bankruptcy Exemptions may only be used if the debtor elects to use specific state exemptions.If the debtor elects to use the Federal Bankruptcy Exemptions on the previous page, he or she cannot use the Federal Non-Bankruptcy Exemptions listed here. Note: Certain tax-exempt pension plan and IRA exemptions are available to all taxpayers.

Benefits: Government employee death and disability benefits (unlimited amount): 5 United States Code 8130; Harbor workers death and disability benefits (unlimited amount): 33 United States Code 916; Judges survivor benefits (unlimited amount): 28 United States Code 376; Judicial center directors survivor benefits (unlimited amount): 28 United States Code 376; Lighthouse workers survivor benefits (unlimited amount): 33 United States Code 775; Longshoremen death and disability benefits (unlimited amount): 33 United States Code 916; Military service survivor benefits (unlimited amount): 10 United States Code 1450; Supreme Court Chief Justice administrators survivor benefits (unlimited amount): 28 United States Code 376; U.S.court directors survivor benefits (unlimited amount): 28 United States Code 376; War hazard death or injury compensation (unlimited amount): 42 United States Code 1717.

Insurance: Railroad workers unemployment insurance (unlimited amount): 45 United States Code 352(e).

Miscellaneous: Klamath Indian tribe benefits (unlimited amount): 25 United States Code 543 &545.

Pensions: Civil service employees (unlimited amount): 5 United States Code 8346; Foreign service employees (unlimited amount): 22 United States Code 4060; Military service employees (unlimited amount): 10 United States Code 1440; Social Security (unlimited amount): 42 United States Code 407; Veterans benefits (unlimited amount): 38 United States Code 3101. Note: The following exemptions are available to all taxpayers: Tax exempt retirement accounts (including 401K, 403B, profit-sharing plans, money-purchase plans, SEP IRAs, Simple IRAs, and defined-benefit plans (unlimited amounts): 11 United States Code 522(b)(3)(c); Traditional IRAs and Roth IRAs (up to $1,095,000 per person): 11 United States Code 522(b)(3)(c)(n).

Personal Property: Seamen 's clothing (unlimited amount): 46 United States Code 11110.

Real Estate: None.

Wages: 75%of earned but unpaid wages (judge may allow more for low-income debtors): 15 United States Code 1673; Wages of seamen while on a voyage (unlimited amount): 46 United States Code 11111.

Appendix B

Federal Bankruptcy Courts

Alabama

Middle District

Counties: Autauga, Barbour, Bullock, Butler, Chambers, Chilton, Coffee, Coosa, Convington, Crenshaw, Dale, Elmore, Geneva, Henry, Houston, Lee, Lowndes, Macon, Montgomery, Pike, Randolph, Russell, Tallapoosa (The Court meets in Dothan, Montgomery, Opelika)

U.S. Bankruptcy Court
P.O. Box 1248
Montgomery, AL 36102
(334) 206-6300

Northern District

Counties: Bibb, Blount, Calhoun, Cherokee, Clay, Cleburne, Colbert, Culman, DeKalb, Etowah, Fayette, Franklin, Greene, Jackson, Jefferson, Lamar, Lauderdale, Lawrence, Limestone, Madison, Marion, Marshall, Morgan, Pickens, Saint Claire, Shelby, Sumter, Talladega, Tuscaloosa, Walker, Winston (The Court meets in Anniston, Birmingham, Decatur, Florence, Gadsden, Huntsville, Jasper, Talladega, Tuscaloosa)

U.S. Bankruptcy Court
1800 5th. Ave. North
Birmingham, AL 35203
(205) 714-4000

U.S. Bankruptcy Court
1129 Noble Street, # 117
Anniston, AL 36201
(256) 741-1500

U.S. Bankruptcy Court
1118 Greensboro Avenue
Room 209
Tuscaloosa, AL 35401
(205) 561-1606

U.S. Bankruptcy Court
P.O. Box 2775
Decatur, AL 35602
(256) 340-2717

Southern District

Counties: Baldwin, Choctaw, Clarke, Conecuh, Dallas, Escambia, Hale, Marengo, Mobile, Monroe, Perry, Washington, Wilcox (The Court meets in Mobile and Selma)

U.S. Bankruptcy Court
201 St. Louis St.
Mobile, AL 36602
(334) 441-5391

Alaska

One District

(The Court meets in Anchorage, Fairbanks, Juneau, Ketchikan, Nome)

U.S. Bankruptcy Court
605 West 4th Ave., Ste. 138
Anchorage, AK 99501-2296
(907) 271-2655

Arizona

One District

(The Court meets in Phoenix, Prescott, Yuma)

U.S. Bankruptcy Court
230 N. 1st Ave., Ste. 101
Phoenix, AZ 85003
(602) 682-4000

U.S. Bankruptcy Court
38 South Scott Avenue
Tucson, AZ 85701
(520) 202-7500

U.S. Bankruptcy Court
325 19th. Street, Ste. D
Yuma, AZ 85364
(928) 783-2288

Arkansas

Eastern District

Counties: Arkansas, Chicot, Clay, Cleburne, Cleveland, Conway, Craighead, Crittenden, Cross, Dallas, Desha, Drew, Faulkner, Fulton, Grant, Greene, Independence, Izard, Jackson, Jefferson, Lawrence, Lee, Lincoln, Lonoke, Mississippi, Monroe, Perry, Phillips, Poinsett, Pope, Prairie, Pulaski, Randolph, Saint Francis, Saline, Sharp, Stone, Van Buren, White, Woodruff, Yell (The Court meets in Batesville, Helena, Jonesboro, Little Rock, Pine Bluff)

Western District

Counties: Ashley, Baxter, Benton, Boone, Bradley, Calhoun, Carroll, Columbia, Clark, Crawford, Franklin, Garland, Hempstead, Hot Springs, Howard, Johnson, Lafayette, Little River, Logan, Madison, Marion, Miller, Montgomery, Nevada, Newton, Ouachita, Pike, Polk, Scott, Searcy, Sebastian, Sevier, Union, Washington (The Court meets in El Dorado, Fayetteville, Fort Smith, Harrison, Hot Springs, Little Rock, Texarkana)

U.S. Bankruptcy Court
300 W. 2nd., Ste. 111
Little Rock, AR 72201
(501) 918-5500

California

Central District

Counties: Counties: Los Angeles, Orange, Riverside, San Luis Obispo, Santa Barbara, and Ventura Hills. (The Court meets in Los Angeles, Riverside, San Fernando Valley, Santa Ana, Santa Barbara.)

U.S. Bankruptcy Court
255 East Temple St.
Los Angeles, CA 90012
(213) 894-3118

U.S. Bankruptcy Court
411 W. Fourth St.
Santa Ana, CA 92701
(714) 338-5300
U.S. Bankruptcy Court
3420 Twelfth St.
Riverside, CA 92501
(909) 774-1000

U.S. Bankruptcy Court
1415 State Street
Santa Barbara, CA 93101
(805) 884-4800

U.S. Bankruptcy Court
21041 Burbank Blvd.
Woodland Hills, CA 91367
(818) 587-2900

Eastern District

Counties: Alpine, Amador, Butte, Calaveras, Colusa, El Dorado, Fresno, Glenn, Inyo, Kern, Kings, Lassen, Madera, Mariposa, Merced, Modoc, Mono, Nevada, Placer, Plumas, Sacramento, San Joaquin, Shasta, Sierra, Siskiyou, Solano, Stanislaus, Sutter, Tehama, Trinity, Tulare, Tuolomne, Yolo, Yuba (The Court meets in Bakersfield, Fresno, Modesto, Sacramento)

U.S. Bankruptcy Court
501 I St, Ste. 3-200
Sacramento, CA 95814
(916) 930-4400

U.S. Bankruptcy Court
2656 U.S. Courthouse
2500 Tulare Street,
Ste. 2501
Fresno, CA 93721
(559) 499-5800

U.S. Bankruptcy Court
1130 12th St., Ste. C
Modesto, CA 95354
(209) 521-5160

Northern District

Counties: Alameda, Contra Costa, Del Norte, Humboldt, Lake, Marin, Mendocino, Monterey, Napa, San Benito, Santa Clara, Santa Cruz, San Francisco, San Mateo, Sonoma, Santa Rosa (The Court meets in Eureka, Oakland, Salinas, San Francisco, San Jose, Santa Rosa)

U.S. Bankruptcy Court
235 Pine St., 19th Fl.
P.O. Box 7341
San Francisco, CA 94120-7341
(413) 268-2300

U.S. Bankruptcy Court
280 South First Street,
#3035
San Jose, CA 95113
(408) 535-5118

U.S. Bankruptcy Court
99 South E. St.
Santa Rosa, CA 95404
(707) 525-8539

U.S. Bankruptcy Court
P.O. Box 2070
Oakland, CA 94604
(510) 879-3600

Southern District

Counties: Imperial, San Diego (The Court meets in San Diego)

U.S. Bankruptcy Court
325 West F. St.
San Diego, CA 92101-6991
(619) 557-5620

Colorado

One District

(The Court meets in Denver, Grand Junction, Pueblo)

U.S. Bankruptcy Court
U.S. Custom House
721 19th St.
Denver, CO 80202-2508
(720) 904-7300

Connecticut

One District

(The Court meets in Bridge-port, Hartford, New Haven)

U.S. Bankruptcy Court
450 Main Street
Hartford, CT 06103
(860) 240-3675

U.S. Bankruptcy Court
157 Church St., 18th Fl.
New Haven, CT 06510
(203) 773-2009

U.S. Bankruptcy Court
915 Lafayette Blvd.
Bridgeport, CT 06604
(203) 579-5808

Delaware

One District

(The Court meets in Wilm-ington)

U.S. Bankruptcy Court
824 Market St., 5th Floor
Wilmington, DE 19801
(302) 252-2900

District of Columbia

(The District of Columbia is in its own circuit, the District of Columbia Circuit, and its own district, the District of Columbia District.)
U.S. Bankruptcy Court
4400 U.S. Courthouse Ave.
333 Constitution Ave. NW
Washington, DC 20001
(202) 565-2500

Florida

Middle District

Counties: Baker, Bradford, Brevard, Charlotte, Citrus, Clay, Collier, Columbia, De Soto, Duval, Flagler, Glades, Hamilton, Hardee, Hendry, Hernando, Hillsborough, Lake, Lee, Manatee, Marion, Nassau, Osceola, Orange, Pasco, Pinellas, Polk, Putnam, Sarasota, Seminole, St. John's, Sumter, Suwannee, Union, Volusia (The Court meets in Fort Meyers, Orlando, Jacksonville, Tampa)

U.S. Bankruptcy Court
2110 First Street
Fort Myers, FL. 33901
(813) 301-5065
(Records Kept in Tampa Division)

U.S. Bankruptcy Court
801 N. Florida Ave.
Tampa, FL. 33602
(813) 301-5065

U.S. Bankruptcy Court
300 North Hogan Street
Jacksonville, FL 32202
(904) 301-6500

U.S. Bankruptcy Court
Fairwinds Bldg., #950
135 West Central Blvd.
Orlando, FL 32801
(407) 648-6365

Northern District

Counties: Alachua, Bay, Calhoun, Dixie, Escambia, Franklin, Gadsden, Gilchrist, Gulf, Holmes, Jackson, Jefferson, Lafayette, Leon, Levy, Liberty, Madison, Okaloosa, Santa Rosa, Taylor, Wakulla, Walton, Washington (The Court meets in Gainesville, Panama City, Pensacola, Tallahassee)

U.S. Bankruptcy Court
110 E Park Ave. # 100
Tallahassee, FL 32301
(850) 521-5001

U.S. Bankruptcy Court
U.S. Courthouse
401 SE First Ave., # 243
Gainesville, FL 32601
(352) 380-2400

U.S. Bankruptcy Court
U.S. Courthouse
30 W. Government St.
Panama City, Florida 32401
(850) 769-4556

Southern District

Counties: Broward, Dade, Highlands, Indian River, Martin, Monroe, Okeechobee, Palm Beach County, St. Lucie, Palm Beach County, St. Lucie (The Court meets in Ft. Lauderdale, Miami, West Palm Beach)

U.S. Bankruptcy Court
51 SW First Ave.
Miami, FL 33130
(305) 714-1800

U.S Bankruptcy Court
299 East Broward Blvd.
#310
Fort Lauderdale, FL 33301
(954) 769-5700

U.S. Bankruptcy Court
1515 N. Flagler Drive,
8th Floor,
West Palm Beach, FL 33401
(561) 514-4100

Georgia

Middle District

Counties: Baker, Baldwin, Ben Hill, Berrien, Bibb, Bleckley, Brooks, Butts, Calhoun, Chattahoochee, Clarke, Clay, Clinch, Colquitt, Cook, Crawford, Crisp, Decatur, Dooley, Dougherty, Early, Echols, Elbert, Franklin, Grady, Greene, Hancock, Harris, Hart, Houston, Irwin, Jasper, Jones, Lamar, Lanier, Lee, Lowndes, Macon, Madison, Marion, Miller, Mitchell, Monroe, Morgan, Oconee, Ogelthorpe, Peach, Pulaski, Putnam, Quitman, Randolph, Seminole, Stewart, Sumter, Talbot, Taylor, Terrell, Thomas, Tift, Turner, Twiggs, Upson, Walton, Washington, Webster, Wilcox, Wilkinson, Worth. (The Court meets in Albany, Athens, Columbus, Macon, Thomasville, Valdosta)

U.S. Bankruptcy Court
CB King U.S. Courthouse
Second Floor
201 West Broad Avenue
Albany, GA 31701

U.S. Bankruptcy Court
U.S. Courthouse
115 East Hancock Avenue
Athens, GA 30601

U.S. Bankruptcy Court
U.S. Courthouse
404 North Broad Street
Thomasville, GA 31792

U.S. Bankruptcy Court
U.S. Courthouse
401 North Patterson Street
Valdosta, GA 31601

U.S. Bankruptcy Court
P.O. Box 1957
433 Cherry St.
Macon, GA 31202
(478) 752-3506

U.S. Bankruptcy Court
P.O. Box 2147
Columbus, GA 31902
(706) 649-7837

Northern District

Counties: Banks, Barrow, Bartow, Carroll, Catoosa, Chattooga, Cherokee, Clayton, Cobb, Coweta, Dade, Dawson, Dekalb, Douglas, Fannin, Fayette, Floyd, Forsyth, Fulton, Gilmer, Gordon, Gwinnett, Habersham, Hall, Haralson, Heard, Henry, Jackson, Lumpkin, Meriwether, Murray, Newton, Paulding, Pickens, Pike, Polk, Rabun, Rockdale, Spalding, Stephens, Towns, Troup, Union, Walker, White, Whitfield (The Court meets in Atlanta, Gainesville, Newnan, Rome)

U.S. Bankruptcy Court
75 Spring St. SW, Rm 1340
Atlanta, GA 30303
(404) 215-1000

U.S. Bankruptcy Court
18 Greenville St. 2nd Floor
Newnan, GA 30264
(678) 423-3000

U.S. Bankruptcy Court
600 E. 1st St.
339 Federal Bldg.
Rome, GA 30161
(706) 378-4000

U.S. Bankruptcy Court
121 Spring Street SE, Rm. 120
Gainesville, GA 30501
(678) 450-2700

Southern District
Counties: Appling, Atkinson. Bacon, Brantley, Bryan, Bulloch, Burke, Camden, Candler, Charlton, Chatham, Coffee, Columbia, Dodge, Effingham, Emanuel, Evans, Glascock, Glynn, Jeff Davis, Jefferson, Jenkins, Johnson, Laurens, Liberty, Lincoln, Long, McDuffie, McIntosh, Montgomery, Pierce, Richmond, Screven, Taliaferro, Tatnall, Telfair, Toombs, Treutlen, Ware, Warren, Wayne, Wheeler, Wilkes (The Court meets in Augusta, Brunswick, Dublin, Savannah, Statesboro, Waycoss)
U.S. Bankruptcy Court
P.O. Box 8347
Savannah, GA 31412
912-650-4100

U.S. Bankruptcy Court
P.O. Box 1487
Augusta, GA 30903
(706) 823-6000

U.S. Bankruptcy Court
801 Gloucester St.
Brunswick, GA 31520
(914) 280-1376

Hawaii

One District
(The Court meets in Hilo, Honolulu, Lihue, Wailuku)

U.S. Bankruptcy Court
1132 Bishop St., Ste. 250-L
Honolulu, HI 96813
(808) 522-8100, ext. 116

Idaho

One District
(The Court meets in Boise, Coeur d'Alene, Jerome, Moscow, Pocatello)

U.S. Bankruptcy Court
550 West Fort St.
Boise, ID 83724
(208) 334-1074

Illinois

Central District

Counties: Adams, Brown, Bureau, Cass, Champaign, Christian, Coles, De Witt, Douglas, Edgar, Ford, Fulton, Greene, Hancock, Henderson, Henry, Iroquois, Kankakee, Knox, Livingston, Logan, Macon, Macoupin, Marshall, Mason, Mc-Donough, Mclean, Menard, Mercer, Montgomery, Morgan, Moultrie, Peoria, Piatt, Pike, Putnam, Rock Island, Sangamon, Schuyler, Scott, Shelby, Stark, Tazewell, Vermilion, Warren, Woodford (The Court meets in Bloomington, Danville, Decatur, Galesburg, Kankakee, Paris, Peoria, Quincy, Rock Island, Springfield)

U.S. Bankruptcy Court
226 U.S. Courthouse
600 E. Monroe St.
Springfield, IL 62701
(217) 492-4551

U.S. Bankruptcy Court
130 Federal Bldg.
201 North Vermilion St.
Danville, IL 61832
(217) 431-4820

U.S. Bankruptcy Court
131 Federal Bldg.
100 NE Monroe St.
Peoria, IL 61602
(309) 671-7035

Northern District

Counties: Boone, Carroll, Cook, Dekalb, Du Page, Grundy, Jo Daviess, Kane, Kendall, Lake, La Salle, Lee, McHenry, Ogle, Stephenson, Whiteside, Will, Winnebago (The Court meets in Chicagoe, Joliet, Kane, Rockford, Waukegam, Wheaton)

U.S. Bankruptcy Court
219 South Dearborn St.
Chicago, IL 60604
(312) 435-5694

U.S. Bankruptcy Court
211 South Court St., # 110
Rockford, IL 61101
(815) 987-4350

Southern District

Counties: Alexander, Bond, Calhoun, Clark, Clay, Clinton, Crawford, Cumberland, Edwards, Effingham, Fayette, Franklin, Gallatin, Hamilton, Hardin, Jackson, Jasper, Jefferson, Jersey, Johnson, Lawrence, Madison, Marion, Massac, Monroe, Perry, Pope, Pulaski, Randolph, Richland, St. Claire, Saline, Union, Wabash, Washington, Wayne, White, Williamson (The Court meets in Alton, Benton, East St. Louis, Effingham, Mt. Vernon)

U.S. Bankruptcy Court
750 Missouri Avenue
East St. Louis, IL 62201
(618) 482-9400

U.S. Bankruptcy Court
301 West Main Street
Benton, IL 62812
(618) 435-2200

Indiana

Northern District

Counties: Adams, Allen, Benton, Blackford, Carroll, Cass, De Kalb, Elkhart, Fulton, Grant, Huntington, Jasper, Jay, Kosciusko, La Porte, LaGrange, Lake, Marshall, Miami, Newton, Noble, Porter, Pulaski, Starke, Steuben, St. Joseph, Tippecanoe, Wabash, Warren, Wells, White, Whitley (The Court meets in Fort Wayne, Hammond, Lafayette. South Bend)

U.S. Bankruptcy Court
401 S. Michigan St
South Bend, IN 46634-7003
(574) 968-2100

U.S. Bankruptcy Court
5400 Federal Plaza
Hammond, IN 46320
(219) 852-3575

U.S. Bankruptcy Court
230 North Fourth Street
Lafayette, IN 47901
(765) 420-6300

1188 Federal Bldg
1300 South Harrison St.
Fort Wayne, IN 46802
(219) 420-5100

Southern District

Counties: Bartholomew, Boone, Brown, Clark, Clay, Clinton, Crawford, Davies, Dearborn, Decatur, Delaware, Dubois, Fayette, Floyd, Fountain, Franklin, Greene, Gibson, Hamilton, Hancock, Harrison, Hendricks, Henry, Howard, Jackson, Jefferson, Jennings, Johnson, Knox, Lawrence, Madison, Marion, Martin, Monroe, Montgomery, Morgan, Ohio, Orange, Owen, Parke, Perry, Pike, Posey, Putnam, Randolph, Ripley, Rush, Scott, Shelby, Spencer, Sullivan, Switzerland, Tipton, Union, Vanderburgh, Vermillion, Vigo, Warrick, Washington, Wayne (The Court meets in Evansville, Indianapolis, New Albany, Richmond)

U.S. Bankruptcy Court
110 U.S. Courthouse
121 West Spring Street
New Albany, IN 47150
(812) 542-4540

U.S. Bankruptcy Court
116 U.S Courthouse
46 East Ohio St.
Indianapolis, IN 46204
(317) 229-3800

U.S. Bankruptcy Court
30 N. 7th
Terre Haute, IN 47808
(812) 238-1550

U.S. Bankruptcy Court
101 NW Martin Luther King
352 Federal Bldg.
Evansville, IN 47708
(812) 434-6470

Iowa

Northern District

Counties: Allamakee, Benton, Black Hawk, Bremer, Buchanan, Buena Vista, Butler, Calhoun, Carroll, Cedar, Cerro Gordo, Cherokee, Chickasaw, Clay, Clayton, Crawford, Delaware, Dickinson, Dubuque, Emmet, Fayette, Floyd, Franklin, Grundy, Hamilton, Hancock, Hardin, Howard, Humboldt, Ida, Iowa, Jackson, Jones, Kossuth, Linn, Lyon, Mitchell, Monona, Osceola, O'Brien, Palo Alto, Plymouth, Pocahontas, Sac, Sioux, Tama, Webster, Winnebago, Winneshiek, Woodbury, Worth, Wright (The Court meets in Cedar Rapids. Dubuque, Fort Dodge, Independence, Mason City, Sioux City)

U.S. Bankruptcy Court
P.O. Box 74890
Cedar Rapids, IA 52407
(319) 286-2200
U.S. Bankruptcy Court
P.O. Box 3857
Sioux City, IA 51102
(712) 233-3939

Southern District

Counties: Adair, Adams, Appanoose, Audubon, Boone, Cass, Clarke, Clinton, Dallas, Davis, Decatur, Des Moines, Fremont, Greene, Guthrie, Harrison, Henry, Jasper, Jefferson, Johnson, Keokuk, Lee, Louisa, Lucas, Madison, Mahaska, Marion, Marshall, Mills, Monroe, Montgomery, Muscatine, Page, Polk Pottawattanie, Poweshiek, Ringgold, Scott, Shelby, Story, Taylor, Union, Van Buren, Wapello, Warren, Washington, Wayne (The Court meets in Council Bluffs, Davenport, Des Moines)

U.S. Courthouse Annex
110 E. Court Ave.
Des Moines, IA 50309-2050
(515) 284-6230

Kansas

One District

(The Court meets in Kansas City, Topeka, Wichita)

U.S. Bankruptcy Court
401 North Market St.
Wichita, KS 67202
(316) 269-6486

U.S. Bankruptcy Court
500 State Ave. Room 161
Kansas City, KS 66101
(913) 551-6732

U.S. Bankruptcy Court
444 SE Quincy St.
Room 240
Topeka, KS 66683
(785) 295-2750

Kentucky

Eastern District

Counties: Anderson, Bath, Bell, Boone, Bourbon, Boyd, Boyle, Bracken, Breathitt, Campbell, Carroll, Carter, Clark, Clay, Elliot, Estill, Fayette, Fleming, Floyd, Franklin, Gallatin, Garrard, Grant, Greenup, Harlan, Harrison, Henry, Jackson, Jessamine, Johnson, Kenton, Knott, Knox, Laurel, Lawrence, Lee, Leslie, Letcher, Lewis, Lincoln, McCreary, Madison, Magoffin, Martin, Mason, Menifee, Mercer, Montgomery, Morgan, Nicholas, Owen, Owsley, Pendleton, Perry, Pike, Powell, Pulaski, Robertson, Rockcastle, Rowan, Scott, Shelby, Trimble, Wayne, Whitley, Wolfe, Woodford (The Court meets in Ashland, Covington, Frankfurt, Lexington, London, Pikeville)

U.S. Bankruptcy Court
P.O. Box 1111
Lexington, KY 40588
(859) 233-2608

Western District

Counties: Adair, Allen, Ballard, Barren, Breckinridge, Bullit, Butler, Caldwell, Calloway, Carlisle, Casey, Christian, Clinton, Crittenden, Cumberland, Daviess, Edmonson, Fulton, Graves, Grayson, Green, Hancock, Hardin, Hart, Henderson, Hickman, Hopkins, Jefferson, Larue, Livingston, Logan, Lyon, McCracken, McClean, Marion, Marshall, Meade, Metcalf, Monroe, Muhlenberg, Nelson, Ohio, Oldham, Russell, Simpson, Spencer, Taylor, Todd, Trigg, Union, Warren, Washington, Webster (The Court meets in Bowling Green, Louisville, Owensboro, Paducah)

U.S. Bankruptcy Court
601 West Broadway
Louisville, KY 40202
(502) 627-5700

U.S. Courthouse
423 Fredrica St.
Owensboro, KY 42301
(502) 627-5700

U.S. Bankruptcy Court
241 E. Main St.
Bowling Green, KY 42101
(502) 627-5700

U.S. Courthouse
501 Broadway
Paducah, KY 42001
(502) 627-5700

Louisiana

Eastern District

Parishes: Assumption, Jefferson, Lafourche, Orleans, Plaquemines, Saint Bernard, Saint Charles, Saint James, Saint John the Baptist, Saint Tammany, Tangipahoa, Terrebonne, Washington (The Court meets in New Orleans)

U.S. Bankruptcy Court
601 Hale Boggs Federal Bldg. 500 Poydras St.
New Orleans, LA 70130-3386 (504) 589-7878

Middle District

Parishes: Ascension, East Baton Rouge, East Feliciana, Iberville, Livingston, Pointe Coupee, Saint Helena, West Baton Rouge, West Feliciana (The Court meets in Baton Rouge)

U.S. Bankruptcy Court
707 Florida St., Ste 119
Baton Rouge, LA 70801
(225) 389-0211

Western District

Parishes: Acadia, Allen, Avoyelles, Beauregard, Bienvile, Bossier, Caddo, Calcasieu, Caldwell, Cameron, Catahoula, Claiborne, Concordia, De Sota, East Carroll, Evangeline, Franklin, Grant, Iberia, Jackson, Jefferson Davis, La Salle, Lafayette, Lincoln, Madison, Morehouse, Natchitoches, Ouachita, Rapides, Red River, Richland, Sabine, Saint Landry, Saint Martin, Saint Mary, Tensas, Union, Vermilion, Vernon, Webster, West Carroll, Winn (The Court meets in Alexandria, Lake Charles, Monroe, Lafayette-Opelousas, Shreveport)

U.S. Bankruptcy Court
300 Fannin St.
Shreveport, LA 71101
(318) 676-4267

U.S. Bankruptcy Court
300 Jackson St. Ste. 116
Alexandria, LA 71301
(318) 445-1890

U.S. Bankruptcy Court
214 Jefferson Street
Lafayette, LA 70501
(337) 262-6800

Maine

One District

(The Court meets in Augusta, Bangor, Portland)

U.S. Bankruptcy Court
537 Congress St.
Portland, ME 04101
(207) 780-3482

U.S. Bankruptcy Court
202 Harlow St.
Bangor, ME 04401
(207) 945-0348

Maryland

One District

(The Court meets in Baltimore, Greenbelt, Salisbury)

U.S. Bankruptcy Court
101 West Lombard St.
Baltimore, MD 21201
(410) 962-2688

U.S. Bankruptcy Court
6500 Cherry Wood Ln.
Greenbelt, MD 20770
(301) 344-8018

U.S. Bankruptcy Court
129 East Main Street, # 104
Salisbury, MD 21801
(410) 962-2688

Massachusetts

One District
(The Court meets in Boston, Hyannis, Springfield, Worcester)

U.S. Bankruptcy Court
Thomas O'Neil Federal Bldg.
10 Causeway St.
Boston, MA 02222-1074
(617) 565-8950

U.S. Bankruptcy Court
Donohue Federal Building
595 Main St., Rm. 211
Worcester, MA 01608-2076
(508) 770-8900

Michigan

Eastern District
Counties: Alcona, Alpena, Arenac, Bay, Cheboygan, Clare, Crawford, Genesee Gladwin, Gratiot, Huron, Iosco, Isabella, Jackson, Lapeer, Lenawee, Livingston, Macomb, Midland, Monroe, Montgomery, Oakland, Ogemaw, Oscoda, Otsego, Presque Isle, Roscommon, Saginaw, Saint Clair, Sanilac, Shiawassee, Tuscola, Washtenaw, Wayne (The Court meets in Bay City, Detroit, Flint)

U.S. Bankruptcy Court
211 W. Fort St., 21 st. Floor
Detroit, MI 48226
(313) 234-0068

U.S. Bankruptcy Court
111 1st. St.
Bay City, MI 48707
(989) 894-8840

U.S. Bankruptcy Clerk
226 West 2nd. St.
Flint, MI 48502
(810) 235-4126

Western District
Counties: Alger, Allegan, Antrim, Baraga, Barry, Benzie, Berrien, Branch, Calhoun, Cass, Charlevoix, Chippewa, Clinton, Delta, Dickinson, Eaton, Emmet, Gogebic, Grand Traverse, Hillsdale, Houghton, Ingham, Ionia, Iron, Kalamazoo, Kalkaska, Kent, Keweenaw, Lake, Leelanau, Luce, Mackinac, Manistee, Marquette, Mason, Mecosta, Menominee, Missaukee, Montcalm, Muskegon, Newaygo, Oceana, Ontonagon, Osceola, Ottawa, Saint Joseph, Schoolcraft, Van Buren, Wexford (The Court meets in Grand Rapids, Kalamazoo, Lansing, Marquette, Traverse City)

U.S. Bankruptcy Court
One Division Avenue, N.,
200
Grand Rapids, MI 49503
(616) 456-2693

U.S. Bankruptcy Court
202 W. Washington St.
Marquette, MI 49855
(906) 226-2117

Minnesota

One District

(The Court meets in Duluth, Fergus Falls, Minneapolis, St. Paul)

U.S. Bankruptcy Court
301 U.S. Courthouse
300 South Fourth St.
Minneapolis, MN 55415
(612) 664-5200

U.S. Bankruptcy Court
416 U.S. Courthouse
515 W. 1st. St.
Duluth, MN 55802
(218) 529-3600

U.S. Bankruptcy Court
204 U.S. Courthouse
118 South Mill St.
Fergus Falls, MN 56537
(218) 739-4671

Mississippi

Northern District

Counties: Alcorn, Attala, Benton, Bolivar, Calhoun, Carroll, Chickasaw, Choctaw, Clay, Coahoma, De Soto, Grenada, Humphreys, Itawamba, Lafayette, Lee, Leflore, Lowndes, Marshall, Monroe, Montgomery, Oktibbeha, Panola, Pontotoc, Prentiss, Quitman, Sunflower, Tallahtchie, Tate, Tippah, Tishomingo, Tunica, Union, Washington, Webster, Winston, Yalobusha (The Court meets in Aberdeen, Greenville, Oxford)

U.S. Bankruptcy Court
703 Hwy. 145 North
Aberdeen MS 39730
(662) 369-2596

Southern District

Counties: Adams, Amite, Clairborne, Clarke, Copiah, Covington, Forrest, Franklin, George, Greene, Hancock, Harrison, Hinds, Holmes, Issaquena, Jackson, Jasper, Jefferson, Jefferson Davis, Jones, Kemper, Lamar, Lauderdale, Lawrence, Leake, Lincoln, Madison, Marion, Neshoba, Newton, Noxubee, Pearl River, Perry, Pike, Rankin, Scott, Sharkey, Simpson, Smith, Stone, Walthall, Warren, Wilkinson, Yazoo) (The Court meets in Biloxi, Gulfport, Hattiesburg, Jackson, Meriden, Natchez, Vicksburg)

U.S. Bankruptcy Court
P.O. Box 2448
Jackson, MS 39225
(601) 965-5301

U.S. Bankruptcy Court
2012 15th Street
Gulfport, MS 39501
(228) 563-1790

Missouri

Eastern District

Counties: Adair, Audrain, Bollinger, Butler, Cape Girardeau, Carter, Chariton, City of St. Louis, Clark, Crawford, Dent, Dunklin, Franklin, Gasconade, Iron, Jefferson, Knox, Lewis, Lincoln, Linn, Macon, Madison, Maries, Marion, Mississippi, Monroe, Montgomery, New Madrid, Pemiscot, Perry, Phelps, Pike, Ralls, Randolph, Reynolds, Ripley, Saint Charles, Saint Francois, Saint Genevieve, Schuyler, Scotland, Scott, Shannon, Shelby, Stoddard, St. Louis, Warren, Washington, Wayne (The Court meets in Cape Girardeau, Hannibal, St. Louis)

U.S. Bankruptcy Court
111 South Tenth St, 4th Fl.
St. Louis, MO. 63102
(314) 244-4500

Western District

Counties: Andrew, Atchison, Barry, Barton, Bates, Benton, Boone, Buchanan, Caldwell, Callaway, Camden, Carroll, Cass, Cedar, Christian, Clay, Clinton, Cole, Cooper, Dade, Dallas, Daviess, DeKalb, Douglas, Gentry, Greene, Grundy, Harrison, Henry, Hickory, Holt, Howard, Howell, Jackson, Jasper, Johnson, Laclede, Lafayette, Lawrence, Livingston, McDonald, Mercer, Miller, Moniteau, Morgan, Newton, Nodaway, Oregon, Osage, Ozark, Pettis, Platte, Polk, Pulaski, Putnam, Ray, Saint Clair, Saline, Stone, Sullivan, Taney, Texas, Vernon, Webster, Worth, Wright (The Court meets in Jefferson City, Joplin, Kansas City, Springfield, St. Joseph)

U.S. Courthouse
400 E. 9th St.
Kansas City, MO 64106
(816) 512-1800

Montana

One District

(The Court meets in Billings, Butte, Great Falls, Missoula)

U.S. Bankruptcy Court
273 Federal Bldg.
400 North Main St.
Butte, MT 50701
(406) 782-1043

Nebraska

One District

(The Court meets in Lincoln, North Platte, Omaha)

U.S. Bankruptcy Court
111 S. 18th Plaza #1125
Omaha, NE 68101
(402) 661-7484

U.S. Bankruptcy Court
100 Centennial Mall North.
#463
Lincoln, NE 68508
(402) 437-5442

Nevada

One District

(The Court meets in Elko, Ely, Las Vegas, Reno)

U.S. Bankruptcy Court
300 Las Vegas Blvd. South
Las Vegas, NV 89101
(702) 388-6257

U.S. Bankruptcy Court
300 Booth St. Rm. 1109
Reno, NV 89509
(775) 784-5599

New Hampshire

One District

(The Court meets in Manchester)

U.S. Bankruptcy Court
1000 Elm Street, # 1001
Manchester, NH 03101
(603) 222-2600

New Jersey

One District

(The Court meets in Camden, Newark, Trenton)

U.S. Bankruptcy Court
50 Walnut St., 3rd Floor
Newark, NJ 07102
(973) 645-2322

U.S. Bankruptcy Court
400 Cooper Street
Camden, NJ 08101
(856) 757-5485

U.S. Bankruptcy Court
U.S. Courthouse
402 East State St.
Trenton, NJ 08608
(609) 989-2200

New Mexico

One District

(The Court meets in Albuquerque, Las Cruces, Roswell)

U.S. Bankruptcy Court
P.O. Box 546
Albuquerque, NM 87103
(505) 348-2500

New York

Eastern District

Counties: Counties: Kings, Nassau, Queens, Richmond, Suffolk. Waters within the counties of Bronx and New York are shared with the Southern District (The Court meets in Brooklyn, Hauppauge, Westbury)

U.S. Bankruptcy Court
271 Cadman Plaza East
Brooklyn, NY 11201
(347) 394-1700

U.S. Bankruptcy Court
Long Island Federal Courthouse
290 Federal Plaza
Central Islip, NY 11722
(631) 712-6200

Northern District

Counties: Albany, Broome, Cayuga, Chenango, Clinton, Columbia, Cortland, Delaware, Essex, Franklin, Fulton, Greene, Hamilton, Herkimer, Jefferson, Lewis, Madison, Montgomery, Oneida, Onondaga, Oswego, Otsego, Rensselaer, Saint Lawrence, Saratoga, Schenctedy, Schoharie, Tioga, Tompkins, Ulster, Warren, Washington (The Court meets in Albany, Syracuse, Utica)

U.S. Bankruptcy Court
445 Broadway Street
Albany, NY 12207
(518) 257-1661

U.S. Bankruptcy Court
Alexander Pernie Courthouse
10 Broad St., Rm. 230
Utica, NY, 13501
(315) 793-8101

U.S. Bankruptcy Court
100 South Salina Street
Syracuse, NY 13202
(315) 295-1600

Southern District

Counties: Bronx, Dutchess, New York, Orange, Putnam, Rockland, Sullivan, Westchester, Waters within the counties of Kings, Nassau, Queens, Richmond and Suffolk (The Court meets in New York, Poughkeepsie, White Plains)

U.S. Bankruptcy Court
One Bowling Green, 6th Fl.
New York, NY 10004-11408
(212) 668-2870

U.S Bankruptcy Court
355 Main Street
Poughkeepsie, NY 12601
(845) 452-4200

U.S. Bankruptcy Court
300 Quarropas, St.
White Plains, NY 10601
(914) 390-4060

Western District

Counties: Allegheny, Cattaraugus, Chautauqua, Chemug, Erie, Genesee, Livingston, Monroe, Niagara, Ontario, Orleans, Schuyler, Seneca, Steuben, Wayne, Wyoming, Yates (The Court meets in Batavia, Buffalo, Mayville, Niagara Falls, Olean, Rochester, Watkins Glenn)

U.S. Bankruptcy Court
250 U.S. Courthouse
300 Perl St., Ste. 250
Buffalo, NY 14202
(716) 551-4130

U.S. Bankruptcy Court
234 U.S. Courthouse
100 State St.
Rochester, NY 14614
(716) 263-3148

North Carolina

Eastern District

Counties: Beaufort, Bertie, Bladen, Brunswick, Camden, Carteret, Chowan, Columbus, Craven, Cumberland, Currituck, Dare, Duplin, Edgecombe, Franklin, Gates, Granville, Greene, Halifax, Harnett, Hertford, Hyde, Johnston, Jones, Lenoir, Martin, Nash, New Hanover, Northhampton, Onslow, Pamlico, Pasquotank, Pender, Perquimans, Pitt, Robeson, Sampson, Tyrrell, Vance, Wake, Warren, Washington, Wayne, Wilson (The Court meets in Elizabeth City, Fayetteville, New Bern, Raleigh, Wilmington, Wilson)

U.S. Bankruptcy Court
P.O. Drawer 2807
Wilson, NC 27894-2807
(252) 237-0248 x143
(919) 846-4752 (Raleigh)

Middle District

Counties: Alamance, Cabburus, Caswell, Chatham, Davidson, Davie, Durham, Forsyth, Guilford, Hoke, Lee, Montgomery, Moore, Orange, Person, Randolph, Richmond, Rockingham, Rowan, Scotland, Stanley, Stokes, Surry, Yadkin (The Court meets in Durham, Greensboro, Winston-Salem)

U.S. Bankruptcy Court
P.O. Box 26100
Greensboro, NC 27402
(336) 358-4000

U.S. Bankruptcy Court
226 S. Liberty Street
Winston-Salem, NC 27100
(336) 397-7785

Western District

Counties: Alexander, Allegheny, Anson, Ashe, Avery, Burncombe, Burke, Caldwell, Catawba, Cherokee, Clay, Gaston, Graham, Haywood, Henderson, Iredell, Jackson, Lincoln, Macon, Madison, McDowell, Mecklenburg, Mithchell, Polk, Rutherford, Swain, Transylvania, Union, Watauga, Wilkes, Yancey (The Court meets in Ashville, Bryson, Charlotte, Shelby, Wilkesboro)

U.S. Bankruptcy Court
Federal Bldg.
401 West Trade St.
Charlotte, NC 28202
(704) 350-7500

North Dakota

One District

(The Court meets in Bismark, Fargo, Grand Forks, Minot)

U.S. Bankruptcy Court
655 First Ave. North, # 210
Fargo, ND 58102
(701) 297-7111

Ohio

Northern District

Counties: Allen, Ashland, Ashtabula, Auglaize, Carroll, Columbiana, Crawford, Cuyahoga, Defiance, Erie, Fulton, Geauga, Hanckock, Hardin, Henry, Holmes, Huron, Lake, Lorain, Lucas, Mahoning, Marion, Medina, Mercer, Ottawa, Paulding, Portage, Putnam, Richland, Sandusky, Seneca, Stark, Summit, Trumbull, Tuscarawas, Van Wert, Wayne, Williams, Woods, Wyandot (The Court meets in Akron, Canton, Cleveland, Jefferson, Masnfield, Toledo, Youngstown)

U.S. Bankruptcy Court
U.S. Courthouse
201 Superior Avenue
Cleveland, OH 44114
(216) 615-4300

U.S. Bankruptcy Court
455 U.S. Courthouse
2 South Main St.
Akron, OH 44308
(330) 252-6100

U.S. Bankruptcy Court
201 Cleveland Ave. SW
Canton, OH 44702
(330) 458-2120

411 U.S. Bankruptcy Court

1716 Spielbusch Ave.
Toledo, OH 43604
(419) 213-5600

U.S. Bankruptcy Court
10 East Commerce Street
Youngstown, OH 44503
(330) 742-0900

Southern District

Counties: Adams, Athens, Belmont, Brown, Butler, Champaign, Clark, Clermont, Clinton, Coshocton, Darke, Delaware, Fairfield, Fayette, Franklin, Gallia, Greene, Guernsy, Hamilton, Harrison, Highland, Hocking, Jackson, Jefferson, Knox, Lawrence, Licking, Logan, Madison, Meigs, Miami, Monroe, Montgomery, Morgan, Morrow, Muskingum, Noble, Perry, Pickaway, Pike, Preble, Ross, Scioto, Shelby, Union, Vinton, Warren, Washington (The Court meets in meets in Cincinnati, Columbus, Dayton, Portsmouth, Steubenville, Zanesville)

U.S. Bankruptcy Court
170 North High Street
Columbus, OH 43215
(614) 469-6638

U.S. Bankruptcy Court
120 W. 3rd. St.
Dayton, OH 45402
(937) 225-2516

Oklahoma

Eastern District

Counties: Counties: Adair, Atoka, Bryan, Carter, Cherokee, Choctaw, Coal, Haskell, Hughes, Johnston, Latimer, Le Flore, Love, McCurtin, McIntosh, Marshall, Murray, Muskogee, Ofkuskee, Okmulgee, Pittsbug, Pontotoc, Seminole, Sequoyah, Wagoneer (The Court meets in Okmulgee)

U.S. Bankruptcy Court
P.O. Box 1347
Okmulgee, OK 74447
(918) 758-0126

Northern District

Counties: Craig, Creek, Delaware, Mayes, Nowata, Osage, Ottawa, Pawnee, Rogers, Tulsa, Washington (The Court meets in meets in Tulsa)

U.S. Bankruptcy Court
224 South Boulder St. Ste. 105
Tulsa, OK 74103
(918) 581-7181

Western District

Counties: Alfalfa, Beaver, Beckham, Blaine, Caddo, Canadian, Cimarron, Cleveland, Comanche, Cotton, Custer, Dewey, Ellis, Garfield, Garvin, Grady, Grant, Greer, Harmon, Harper, Jackson, Jefferson, Kay, Kingfisher, Kiowa, Lincoln, Logan, Major, McClain, Noble, Oklahoma, Payne, Pottawatomie, Roger Mills, Stephens, Texas, Tillman, Washita, Woods, Woodward (The Court meets in Lawton, Oklahoma City)

U.S. Bakruptcy Court
215 Dean A. McGee Ave,
Oklahoma City, OK 73102
(405) 609-5700

Oregon

One District

(The Court meets in Bend, Coos Bay, The Dalles, Eugene, Klamath Falls, Medford, Pendleton, Portland, Roseburg, Seaside)

U.S. Bankruptcy Court
1001 SW Fifth Ave. #700
Portland, OR 97204
(503) 326-1500

U.S. Bankruptcy Court
405 E. 8th Ave. # 2600
Eugene, OR 97401
(541) 431-4000

Pennsylvania

Eastern District

Counties: Berks, Bucks, Chester, Delaware, Lancaster, Lehigh, Montgomery, Northampton, Philadelphia, (The Court meets in Allentown, Doylestown, Lancaster, Philadelphia, Reading)

U.S. Bankruptcy Court
900 Market St., Rm. 400
Philadelphia, PA 19107
(215) 408-2800

U.S. Bankruptcy Court
400 Washington, St., Rm. 300
Reading, PA 19601
(610) 320-5255

Middle District

Counties: Adams, Bradford, Cameron, Carbon, Centre, Clinton, Columbia, Cumberland, Dauphin, Franklin, Fulton, Huntington, Juniata, Lacawanna, Lebanon, Luzerne, Lycoming, Mifflin, Monroe, Montour, Northumberland, Perry, Pike, Potter, Schuylkill, Snyder, Sullivan, Susquehanna, Tioga, Union, Wayne, Wyoming, York (The Court meets in Harrisburg, Scranton, Wilke-Barre, Williamsport)

U.S. Bankruptcy Court
197 South Main St.
Wilkes-Barre, PA 18701
(717) 826-6450

U.S. Bankruptcy Court
228 Walnut Street, Rm. 320
Harrisburg, PA 17101
(717) 901-2800

Western District

Counties: Allegheny, Armstrong, Beaver, Bedford, Blair, Butler, Cambria, Clarion, Clearfield, Crawford, Elk, Fayette, Forest, Greene, Indiana, Jefferson, Lawrence, McKean, Mercer, Somerset, Venango, Warren, Washington, Westmoreland (The Court meets in Erie, Johnston, Meadville, Mercer, Pittsburgh, Warren)

U.S. Bankruptcy Court
5414 U.S. Steel Tower
600 Grant St.
Pittsburgh, PA 15219
(412) 644-2700

U.S. Bankruptcy Court
17 South Park Row
Erie, PA 16501
(814) 464-9740

Rhode Island

One District

(The Court meets in Providence)

U.S. Bankruptcy Court
380 Westminster Mall
Providence, RI 02903
(401) 626-3100

South Carolina

One District

(The Court meets in Charleston, Columbia, Spartanburg)

U.S. Bankruptcy Court
1100 Laurel Street
Columbia, SC 29201
(803) 765-5209

South Dakota

One District (The Court meets in Aberdeen, Pierre, Rapid City, Sioux Falls)

U.S. Bankruptcy Court
104 Federal Bldg.
400 South Phillips Ave.
Sioux Falls, SD 57104
(605) 357-2400

U.S. Bankruptcy Court
203 Federal Bldg.
225 South Pierre St.
Pierre, SD 57501
(605) 945-4460

Tennessee

Eastern District

Counties: Anderson, Bedford, Bledsoe, Blount, Bradley, Campbell, Carter, Claiborne, Cocke, Coffee, Franklin, Grainger, Greene, Grundy, Hamblen, Hamilton, Hancock, Hawkins, Jefferson, Johnson, Knox, Lincoln, Loudon, Marion, McMinn, Meigs, Monroe, Moore, Morgan, Polk, Rhea, Roane, Scott, Sequatchie, Sevier, Sullivan, Unicoi, Union, Van Buren, Warren, Washington. (The Court meets in Chattanooga, Knoxville, Greeneville, Winchester)

U.S. Bankruptcy Court
31 E. 11th St.
Chattanooga, TN 37402
(423) 752-5163

U.S. Bankruptcy Court
800 Market Street
Knoxville, TN 37902
(865) 545-4279

Middle District

Counties: Cannon, Cheatham, Clay, Cumberland, Davidson, DeKalb, Dickson, Fentress, Giles, Hickman, Houston, Humphreys, Jackson, Lawrence, Lewis, Macon, Marshall, Maury, Montgomery, Overton, Pickett, Putnam, Robertson, Rutherford, Smith, Stewart, Sumner, Trousdale, Wayne, White, Williamson, Wilson (The Court meets in Columbia, Cookeville, Nashville)

U.S. Bankruptcy Court
U.S. Customs House
701 Broadway
Nashville, TN 37203
(615) 736-5584

Western District

Counties: Benton, Carroll, Chester, Crockett, Decatur, Dyer. Fayette, Gibson, Hardeman, Hardin, Haywood, Henderson, Henry, Lake, Lauderdale, McNairy, Madison, Obion, Perry, Shelby, Tipton, Weakley (The Court meets in Jackson, Memphis)
U.S. Bankruptcy Court
200 Jefferson Ave.
Memphis, TN 38103
(901) 328-3500

Texas

Eastern District

Counties: Anderson, Angelina, Bowie, Camp, Cass, Cherokee, Collin, Cooke, Delta, Denton, Fannin, Franklin, Grayson, Gregg, Hardin, Harrison, Henderson, Hopkins, Houston, Jasper, Jefferson, Lamar, Liberty, Marion, Morris, Nacogdoches, Newton, Orange, Panola, Polk, Rains, Red River, Rusk, Sabine, San Augustine, Shelby, Smith, Titus Trinity, Tyler, Upshur, Van Zandt, Wood (The Court meets in Beaumont, Plano, Tyler)

U.S. Bankruptcy Court
110 North College Ave
Tyler, TX 75702
(903) 590-3200

U.S. Bankruptcy Court
660 North Central Expressway
#300B
Plano, Texas 75074
(972) 509-1240

Northern District

Counties: Archer, Armstrong, Bailey, Baylor, Borden, Brisco, Brown, Callahan, Carson, Castro, Childres, Clay, Cochran, Coke, Coleman, Collingsworth, Comanche, Concho, Cottle, Crockett, Crosby, Dallam, Dallas, Dawson, Deaf Smith, Dickens, Donley, Eastland, Ellis, Erath, Fisher, Floyd, Foard, Gaines, Garza, Glasscock, Gray, Hale, Hall, Hansford, Hardeman, Hartley, Haskell, Hemphill, Hockley, Hood, Howard, Hunt, Hutchinson, Irion, Jack, Johnson, Jones, Kaufman, Kent, King, Knox, Lamb, Lipscomb, Lubbock, Lynn, Menard, Mills, Mitchell, Montague, Moore, Motley, Navarro, Nolan, Ochiltree, Oldham, Palo, Parker, Parmer, Pinto, Potter, Randall, Reagan, Roberts, Rockwall, Runnels, Schleicher, Scurry, Shackleford, Sherman, Stephens, Sterling, Stonewall, Sutton, Swisher, Tarrant, Taylor, Terry, Throckmorton, Tom Green, Wheeler, Wichita, Wilbarger, Wise, Yoakum, Young (The Court meets in Albilene, Amarillo, Dallas, Fort Worth, Lubbock, San Angelo, Wichita Falls)

U.S. Bankruptcy Court
1100 Commerce St.
Dallas, TX 75242
(214) 753-2000

U.S. Bankruptcy Court
U.S. Courthouse
501 W. 10th St.
Fort Worth, TX 76102
(817) 333-6000

U.S. Bankruptcy Court
306 Federal Building
1205 Texas Ave.
Lubbock, TX 79401
(806) 472-5000

Southern District

Counties: Aransas, Austin, Bee, Brazoria, Brazos, Brooks, Calhoun, Cameron, Chambers, Colorado, De Witt, Duval, Fayette, Fort Bend, Galveston, Goliad, Grimes, Harris, Hidalgo, Jackson, Jim Wells, Jim Hogg, Kenedy, Kleberg, La Salle, Lavaca, Live Oak, Madison, Matagorda, McMullen, Montgomery, Nueces, Refugio, San Jacinto, San Patricio, Starr, Victoria, Walker, Waller, Webb, Wharton, Willacy, Zapata (The Court meets in Brownsville, Corpus Christi, Galveston, Houston, McAllen, Laredo, Victoria)

U.S. Bankruptcy Court
P.O. Box 61010
Houston, TX 77008
(713) 250-5500

U.S Bankruptcy Court
1133 N. Shoreline Blvd.
Corpus Christi, TX 78401
(361) 888-3484

Western District

Counties: Andrews, Atascosa, Bandera, Bastrop, Bell, Bexar, Blanco, Bosque, Brewster, Burleson, Burnet, Caldwell, Comal, Coryell, Crane, Culberson, Dimmit, Ector, Edwards, El Paso, Falls, Freestone, Frio, Gillespie, Gonzales, Guadaloupe, Hamilton, Hays, Hill, Hudspeth, Jeff Davis, Karnes, Kendall, Kerr, Kimble, Kenney, Lampasas, Lee, Leon, Limestone, Llano, Loving, Martin, Mason, Maverick, McCulloch, McLennan, Medina, Midland, Milam, Pecos, Presidio, Real, Reeves, Robertson, San Saba, Somervell, Terrell, Travis, Upton, Uvalde, Val Verde, Ward, Washington, Williamson, Wilson, Winkler, Zavala (The Court meets in Austin, El Paso, Midland, San Antonio, Waco)

U.S. Courthouse
615 East Houston Street
San Antonio, Texas 78295-1439
(210) 472-6720

U.S. Bankruptcy Court
903 San Jacinto Blvd. #322
Austin, TX 78701
(512) 916-5237

U.S. Bankruptcy Court
100 E. Wall St., Rm. P163
Midland, TX 79701
(432) 683-1650

U.S. Bankruptcy Court
8515 Lockheed
El Paso, Texas 79925
(915) 779-7362

U.S. Bankruptcy Court
800 Franklin Avenue #140
Waco, Texas 76701
(254) 750-1528

Utah

One District
(The Court meets in Ogden, Salt Lake City)

U.S. Bankruptcy Court
301 U.S. Courthouse
350 South Main St.
Salt Lake City, UT 84101
(801) 524-6687

Vermont

One District
(The Court meets in Montpelier, Rutland)

U.S. Bankruptcy Court
67 Merchant's Row
Rutland, VT 05702
(802) 776-2032

Virginia

Eastern District

Counties: Accomack, Amelia, Arlington, Brunswick, Caroline, Charles City, Chesterfield, Dinwiddie, Essex, Fairfax, Fauquier, Gloucester, Goochland, Greensville, Hanover, Henrico, Isle of Wight, James City, King and Queen, King George, King, William, Lancaster, Loudoun, Louisa, Lunenberg, Mathews, Mecklenberg, Middlesex, New Kent, Northampton, Northumberland, Nottoway, Powhatan, Prince Edward, Prince George, Prince William, Richmond, Southampton, Spotsylvania, Stafford, Surry, Sussex, Westmoreland, York (The meets in Alexandria, Newport News, Norfolk, Richmond)

U.S. Bankruptcy Court
1100 E. Main St. Ste. 301
Richmond, VA 23219
(804) 916-2400

U.S. Bankruptcy Court
200 S. Washington Street
Alexandria, VA 22314
(703) 258-1200

U.S. Bankruptcy Court
600 Granby, Rm.400
Norfolk, VA 23510
(757) 222-7500

U.S. Bankruptcy Court
2400 West Avenue
Newport News, VA 23607
(757) 222-7500

Western District

Counties: Albermarle, Allegheny, Amherst, Appomattox, Augusta, Bath, Bedford, Bland, Botetourt, Buchanan, Buckingham, Campbell, Carroll, Charlotte, Clarke, Craig, Culpeper, Cumberland, Dickenson, Floyd, Fluvanna, Franklin, Frederick, Giles, Grayson, Greene, Halifax, Henry, Highland, Lee, Madison, Montgomery, Nelson, Page, Patrick, Pittsylvania, Pulaski, Rappahannock, Roanoke, Rockbridge, Rockingham, Russell, Scott, Shenandoah, Smyth, Tazewell, Warren, Washingon, Wise, Wythe (The Court meets in Abington, Big Stone Gap, Charlottesville, Danville, Harrisonburg, Lynchburg, Roanoke, Staunton)

U.S. Bankruptcy Court
210 Church Ave.
Roanoke, VA 24011
(540) 857-2391

U.S. Bankruptcy Court
1101 Court St., #166
Lynchburg, VA 24504
(434) 845-0317

U.S. Bankruptcy Court
116 N. Main St., #223
Harrisonburg, VA 22802
(540) 434-8327

Washington

Eastern District

Counties: Adams, Asotin, Benton, Chelan, Columbia, Douglas, Ferry, Franklin, Garfield, Grant, Kittitas, Klickitat, Lincoln, Okanogan, Pend Oreille, Spokane, Stevens, Walla Walla, Whitman, Yakima (The meets in Ephrata, Richland, Spokane, Yakima)

U.S. Bankruptcy Court
P.O. Box 2164
Spokane, WA 99201
(509) 353-2404

U.S. Bankruptcy Court
402 East Yakima Ave,
Ste. 200
Yakima, WA 98901
(509) 454-5660

Western District

Counties: Clallam, Clark, Cowlitz, Grays Harbor, Island, Jefferson, King, Kitsap, Lewis, Mason, Pacific, Pierce, San Juan, Skagit, Skamania, Snohomish, Thurston, Whakiakum, Whatcom (The Court meets in Bremerton, Everett, Kelso, Seattle, Tacoma, Vancouver)

U.S. Bankruptcy Court
700 Stewart St., #6301
Seattle, WA 98101
(206) 370-5200
U.S. Bankruptcy Court
1717 Pacific Ave.
Tacoma, WA 98402
(253) 882-3900

West Virginia

Northern District

Counties: Barbour, Berkeley, Braxton, Brooke, Calhoun, Doddridge, Gilmer, Grant, Hampshire, Hancock, Hardy, Harrison, Jefferson, Lewis, Marion, Marshall, Mineral, Monongalia, Morgan, Ohio, Pendleton, Pleasants, Pocahontas, Preston, Randolph, Ritchie, Taylor, Tucker, Tyler, Upshur, Webster, and Wetzel (The Court meets in Wheeling, Clarksburg, Martinsburg, Elkins)

U.S. Bankruptcy Court
P.O. Box 70
Wheeling, WV 26003
(304) 233-1655

U.S. Bankruptcy Court
324 Main Street
P.O. Box 2506
Clarksburg, WV 26302
(304) 623-7866

Southern District

Counties: Boone, Cabell, Clay, Fayette, Greenbrier, Jackson, Kanawha, Lincoln, Logan, Mason, McDowell, Mercer, Mingo, Monroe, Nicholas, Putnam, Raleigh, Roane, Summers, Wayne, Wirt, Wood, Wyoming (The Court meets in Beckley, Bluefield, Charleston, Huntington, Parkersburg)

U.S. Bankruptcy Court
300 Virginia St. E.
Charleston, WV 25301
(304) 347-3003

U.S. Bankruptcy Court
110 North Herber St.
Beckley, WV 25801
(304) 253-7402

Wisconsin

Eastern District

Counties: Brown, Calumet, Dodge, Door, Florence, Fond du Lac, Forest, Green Lake, Kenosha, Kewaunee, Langlade, Manitowoc, Marinette, Marquette, Menominee, Milwaukee, Oconto, Outagamie, Ozaukee, Racine, Shawano, Sheboygan, Walworth, Washington, Waukesha, Waupaca, Waushara, Winnebago (The Court meets in Green Bay, Kenosha, Manitowoc, Milwaukee, Oshkosh, Racine)

U.S. Bankruptcy Court
126 U.S. Courthouse
517 East Wisconsin Ave.
Milwaukee, WI 53202
(414) 297-3291

Western District

Counties: Adams, Ashland, Barron, Bayfield, Buffalo, Burnett, Chippewa, Clark, Columbia, Crawford, Dane, Douglas, Dunn, Eau Claire, Grant, Green, Iowa, Iron, Jackson, Jefferson, Juneau, La Crosse, Lafayette, Lincoln, Marathon, Monroe, Oneida, Pepin, Pierce, Polk, Portage, Price, Richland, Rock, Rusk, Saint Croix, Sauk, Sawyer, Taylor, Trempealeau, Vernon, Vilas, Washburn, Wood (The Court meets in Eau Claire, La Crosse, Madison, Wausau)

U.S. Bankruptcy Court
P.O. Box 548
Madison, WI 53701-0548
(608) 264-5178

U.S. Bankruptcy Court
P.O. Box 5009
500 South Barstow St.
Eau Claire, WI 54702
(715) 839-2980

Wyoming

One District

(The Court meets in Casper, Cheyenne)

U.S. Bankruptcy Court
2120 Capitol Ave.
Cheyenne WY 82001
(307) 433-2200

U.S. Bankruptcy Court
111 S. Wolcott St.
Casper, WY 82601
(307) 232-2650

Appendix C

Approved Credit Counseling Agencies

Note: After each listing, it is noted whether the agency provides counseling services in person, via telephone, or on the internet. You should also check the U.S. Bankruptcy Trustee Service website for periodic updates to this list: **www.usdoj.gov/ust/eo/bapcpa/ccde/cc_approved.htm#AL**

For All States

Consumer Credit Counseling Service of Greater Atlanta Inc.
100 Edgewood Avenue #1800
Atlanta, GA 30303
866-672-2227
www.cccsinc.org
In Person (not available in all judicial districts), Telephone and Internet

Consumer Credit Counseling Services of San Francisco
595 Market Street, #1500
San Francisco, CA 94105
800-777-7526
www.cccssf.org
In Person (not available in all judicial districts), Telephone and Internet

Consumer Credit Management, Inc.
28124 Orchard Lake Rd.
Suite 102
Farmington Hills, MI 48334
888-821-4357
www.ccmcanhelp.com
In Person, Telephone, Internet

Credit Advisors Foundation
1818 South 72nd Street
Omaha, NE 68124
800-942-9027
www.yourbankruptcypartner.com
In Person (not available in all judicial districts), Telephone and Internet

Credit Counseling Centers of America
9330 LBJ Freeway # 900
Dallas, TX
75379-8039

800-493-2222
www.cccamerica.org
In Person (not available in all judicial districts), Telephone and Internet

Hummingbird Credit Counseling and Education, Inc.
3737 Glenwood Ave.
Suite 100
Raleigh, NC 27612
800-645-4959
www.hbcce.org
Telephone and Internet

Garden State Consumer Credit Counseling, Inc.
225 Willowbrook Road
Freehold, NJ 07728
732-409-6281
www.novadebt.org
In Person (may not be available in all Judicial districts), Telephone and Internet

GreenPath, Inc.
38505 Country Club Drive,
Suite 210
Farmington Hills, MI
48331-3429
800-630-6718
www.greenpathbk.com
In Person (not available in
all judicial districts), and
Telephone

Institute for Financial
Literacy, Inc.
449 Forest Avenue #12
Portland, ME 04101
207-879-0389
www.financiallit.org
Telephone and Internet

Money Management
International Inc.
9009 West Loop South 7th
Fl
Houston, TX 77096-1719
888-845-5669
moneymanagement.org
In Person (not available
in all judicial districts),
Telephone and Internet

Springboard Nonprofit
Consumer Credit
Management Inc.
4351 Latham Street
Riverside, CA 92501
800-947-3752
www.bkhelp.org
In Person (not available
in all judicial districts),
Telephone and Internet

Alabama

Bankruptcy cases in
Alabama are not under the
jurisdiction of the United
States Trustee Program.
Questions regarding
bankruptcy cases filed in

Alabama should be directed
to the Administrative Office
of the U.S. Courts:

Administrative Office of the
U.S. Courts
Bankruptcy Judges
Division
1 Columbus Circle NE,
#4-250
Washington, D.C. 20544
Phone: 202-502-1900

Alaska

Consumer Credit
Counseling Service of
Alaska
208 E. 4th Avenue
Anchorage, AK 99501
907-279-6501
www.cccsofak.com
In Person and Telephone

Arizona

See Agency listing "**For
All States**" at beginning of
listings.

Arkansas

Eastern District of
Arkansas

ClearPoint Financial
Solutions, Inc.
8000 Franklin Farms Dr.
Richmond, VA 23229
877-422-9046
In Person and Telephone

Consumer Credit
Counseling of Springfield
Missouri Inc.
1515 S. Glenstone

Springfield, Missouri 65804
800-882-0808
www.cccsoftheozarks.org
In Person, Telephone,
Internet

Credit Counseling of
Arkansas, Inc.
1111 Zion Road
Fayetteville, AR 72703
800-889-4916
www.ccoacares.com
In Person, Telephone,
Internet

Western District of
Arkansas

ClearPoint Financial
Solutions, Inc.
8000 Franklin Farms Drive
Richmond, VA 23229
877-422-9044
www.clearpointfinancialsolu
tions.org
In Person and Telephone

Consumer Credit
Counseling of Springfield
Missouri Inc.
1515 S. Glenstone
Springfield, Missouri 65804
800-882-0808
www.cccsoftheozarks.org
In Person, Telephone,
Internet

Consumer Credit
Counseling Services of
North Central Texas
901 North McDonald # 600
McKinney, TX 75069
800-856-0257
www.cccsnct.org
In Person, Telephone,
Internet

Credit Counseling of
Arkansas, Inc.
1111 Zion Road
Fayetteville, AR 72703
800-889-4916
www.ccoacares.com
In Person, Telephone,
Internet

California

Central District of California

Consumer Credit
Counseling Service of
Ventura County, Inc.
80 N. Wood Road Suite 200
Camarillo, CA 93010
800-540-2227
www.gotdebt.org
In Person, Telephone,
Internet

Consumer Credit
Counselors of Kern County
5300 Lennox Avenue # 200
Bakersfield, CA 93309
800-272-2482
www.californiacccs.org
In Person, Telephone,
Internet

Consumer Credit
Counselors of Orange
County
1920 Old Tustin Avenue
Santa Ana, CA 92832
888-289-8230
www.cccsoc.org
In Person and Telephone

Eastern District of California

Consumer Credit
Counseling Service of

Southern Oregon Inc.
820 Crater Lake Ave, # 202
Medford, OR 97504
541-779-2273
www.cccsso.org
In Person and Telephone

Consumer Credit
Counselors of Kern County
5300 Lennox Avenue # 200
Bakersfield, CA 93309
800-272-2482
www.californiacccs.org
In Person, Telephone,
Internet

Consumer Credit
Counselors of Orange
County
1920 Old Tustin Avenue
Santa Ana, CA 92832
888-289-8230
www.cccsoc.org
In Person and Telephone

Consumer Credit
Counselors of the Twin
Cities
718-B Bridge Street
Yuba City, CA 95991
800-388-2227
In Person and Telephone

Northern District of California

Consumer Credit
Counseling Service of the
North Coast
1309 11th Street
Suite 104
Arcata, CA 95521
800-762-1811
www.cccsnojuggle.org
In Person and Telephone

Consumer Credit
Counseling Service of
Ventura County, Inc.

80 N. Wood Road # 200
Camarillo, CA 93010
800-540-2227
www.gotdebt.org
In Person, Telephone,
Internet

Consumer Credit
Counselors of Kern County
5300 Lennox Avenue # 200
Bakersfield, CA 93309
800-272-2482
www.californiacccs.org
In Person, Telephone,
Internet

Consumer Credit
Counselors of Orange
County
1920 Old Tustin Avenue
Santa Ana, CA 92832
888-289-8230
www.cccsoc.org
In Person and Telephone

Southern District of California

Consumer Credit
Counselors of Kern County
5300 Lennox Avenue # 200
Bakersfield, CA 93309
800-272-2482
www.californiacccs.org
In Person, Telephone,
Internet

Consumer Credit
Counselors of Orange
County
1920 Old Tustin Avenue
Santa Ana, CA 92832
888-289-8230
www.cccsoc.org
In Person and Telephone

Colorado

Community Credit
Counseling Service
2009 Wadsworth Blvd., #200
Lakewood, CO 80215
303-233-2773
www.bkcounselor.org
In Person and Telephone

Consumer Credit
Counseling Service of
Northern Colorado and
Southeast Wyoming
1247 Riverside Avenue
Fort Collins, CO 80524
800-424-2227
www.cccsnc.org
In Person and Telephone

Connecticut

See Agency listing **"For
All States"** at beginning of
listings.

Delaware

Consumer Credit
Counseling Service of
Maryland and Delaware Inc.
757 Frederick Road 2nd Fl.
Baltimore, Maryland 21228
800-642-2227
www.cccs-inc.org
In Person and Telephone

District of Columbia

ClearPoint Financial
Solutions, Inc.
8000 Franklin Farms Dr.
Richmond, VA 23229
877-422-9045
www.clearpointfinancialsolu

tions.org
In Person and Telephone

Consumer Credit
Counseling Service of
Maryland and Delaware Inc.
757 Frederick Road 2nd Fl.
Baltimore. Maryland 21228
800-642-2227
www.cccs-inc.org
In Person and Telephone

Florida

Middle District of Florida

Consumer Credit
Counseling Service of
Central Florida and the
Florida Gulf Coast, Inc.
3670 Maguire Blvd. #103
Orlando, Fl 32803
800-741-7040
www.cccsfl.org
In Person, Telephone,
Internet

Family Counseling Center
of Brevard, Inc.
220 Coral Sands Drive
Rockledge, FL 32955
321-259-1070
www.cccsbrevard.org
In Person and Telephone

Family Foundations of
Northeast Florida, Inc.
1639 Atlantic Boulevard
Jacksonville, FL 32207
904-396-4846
www.familyfoundationsjax
.org
In Person, Telephone,
Internet

Northern District of Florida

Consumer Credit
Counseling Service of
Central Florida and the
Florida Gulf Coast, Inc.
3670 Maguire Blvd., #103
Orlando, Fl 32803
800-741-7040
www.cccsfl.org
In Person, Telephone,
Internet

Consumer Credit
Counseling Service of
Mid-Florida, Inc.
1539 NE 22nd Avenue
Ocala, FL 34470
800-245-1865
In Person and Telephone

Family Counseling Service,
Inc.
1639 Atlantic Boulevard
Jacksonville, FL 32207
904-396-4846
www.fcsjax.org
In Person, Telephone,
Internet

Southern District of Florida

Family Foundations of
Northeast Florida, Inc.
1639 Atlantic Boulevard
Jacksonville, FL 32207
904-396-4846
www.familyfoundationsjax
.org
In Person, Telephone,
Internet

283

Georgia

Middle District of Georgia

Consumer Credit Counseling Service of Middle Georgia Inc.
277 Martin Luther King Jr. Blvd., Suite 202
Macon, GA 31201
800-446-7123
www.cccsmacon.org
In Person and Telephone

Consumer Credit Counseling Service of Southwest Georgia
409 North Jackson Street
Albany, GA 31701
800-309-3358
www.cccsalbany.org
In Person, Telephone, Internet

The Family Center of Columbus, Inc.
1350 15th Avenue
Columbus, GA 31902
800-757-2227
www.cccs-wga.com
In Person, Telephone, Internet

Northern District of Georgia

Consumer Credit Counseling Service of Middle Georgia Inc.
277 Martin Luther King Jr. Blvd., Suite 202
Macon, GA 31201
800-446-7123
www.cccsmacon.org
In Person and Telephone

The Family Center of Columbus, Inc.
1350 15th Avenue
Columbus, GA 31902
800-757-2227
www.cccs-wga.com
In Person, Telephone, Internet

Partnership for Families, Children and Adults
2245 Olan Mills Drive
Chattanooga, TN 37421
423-490-5620
www.partnershipfca.com
In Person, Telephone, Internet

Southern District of Georgia

Consumer Credit Counseling Service of Middle Georgia Inc.
277 Martin Luther King Jr. Blvd., Suite 202
Macon, GA 31201
800-446-7123
www.cccsmacon.org
In Person and Telephone

Consumer Credit Counseling Service of the Savannah Area Inc.
7505 Waters Ave. # C-11
Savannah, GA 31406
912-691-2227
www.cccssavannah.org
In Person, Telephone, Internet

Consumer Credit Counseling Service of Southwest Georgia
409 North Jackson Street
Albany, GA 31701
800-309-3358
www.cccsalbany.org
In Person, Telephone, Internet

Family Counseling Service, Inc.
1639 Atlantic Boulevard
Jacksonville, FL 32207
904-396-4846
www.familyfoundationsjax.org
In Person, Telephone, Internet

JcVision and Associates Inc.
135-G East M.L. King Jr. Dr.
Hinesville, GA 31313
1-866-396-4243
www.jcvision.com
In Person and Telephone

Hawaii

See Agency listing **"For All States"** at beginning of listings.

Idaho

Consumer Credit Counseling Service of Northern Idaho, Inc.
1113 Main Street
Lewiston, ID 83501
800-556-0127
www.cccsnid.org
In Person and Telephone

Illinois

Central District of Illinois

Central Illinois Debt Management and Credit Education, Inc.
719 Main street
Peoria, IL 61602
888-671-2227
www.cidmce.org
In Person

Chestnut Health System, Inc.
1003 Martin Luther King Dr.
Bloomington, IL 61701
800-615-3022
www.chestnut.org/credit
In Person and Telephone

Northern District of Illinois

Chestnut Health System, Inc.
1003 Martin Luther King Dr.
Bloomington, IL 61701
800-615-3022
www.chestnut.org
In Person and Telephone
Consumer Credit
Counseling Service of
McHenry County, Inc.
400 Russel Court
Woodstock, IL 60098
800-815-2227
www.illinoiscccs.org
In Person and Telephone

Indiana

Northern District of Indiana

Consumer Credit
Counseling Inc. of
Northeastern Indiana
4105 W. Jefferson Blvd.
Ft. Wayne, IN 46804
800-432-0420
www.financialhope.org
In Person and Telephone

Comprehensive Credit
Counseling of Rural
Services of Indiana, Inc.
60918 US 31 South
South Bend, IN 46614
800-288-6581
www.comprehensivecreditc
ounseling.com
In Person and Telephone

Southern District of Indiana

Consumer Credit
Counseling Inc. of
Northeastern Indiana
4105 W. Jefferson Blvd.
Ft. Wayne, IN 46804
800-432-0420
www.financialhope.org
In Person and Telephone

Iowa

Northern District of Iowa

Consumer Credit
Counseling Service of
Nebraska, Inc.
8805 Indian Hills Drive #105
Omaha, NE 68114
877-494-2227
www.cccsn.org
In Person and Telephone

Consumer Credit
Counseling Service of
Northeastern Iowa, Inc.
1003 West 4th Street
Waterloo, IA 50702
800-714-4388
www.cccsia.org
In Person, Telephone,
Internet

Southern District of Iowa

Consumer Credit
Counseling Service of
Nebraska, Inc.
8805 Indian Hills Drive # 105
Omaha, NE 68114
877-494-2227
www.cccsn.org
In Person and Telephone

Kansas

Consumer Credit
Counseling of Springfield
Missouri Inc.
1515 S. Glenstone
Springfield, Missouri 65804
800-882-0808
www.cccsoftheozarks.org
In Person, Telephone,
Internet

Consumer Credit
Counseling Service, Inc.
1201 W. Walnut
Salina, KS 67401
888-257-6899
www.kscccs.org
In Person and Telephone

Housing and Credit
Counseling, Inc.
1195 SW Buchanan # 101
Topeka, KS 66604
800-383-0217
www.hcci-ks.org
In Person, Telephone,
Internet

Kentucky

Consumer Credit
Counseling Service of
Huntington, Inc.
1102 Memorial Blvd.
Huntington, WV 25701
888-534-4387
www.goodwillhunting.org
In Person, Telephone,
Internet

285

Louisiana

Eastern District of Louisiana

The requirement to obtain pre-bankruptcy credit counseling in this judicial district is currently waived until further notice (December 2008).

Middle District of Louisiana

Consumer Credit Counseling Service of Greater New Orleans, Inc.
1215 Prytania Street, #424
New Orleans, LA 70130
800-880-2221
www.cccsno.org
Telephone

Western District of Louisiana

Consumer Credit Counseling Service of Greater New Orleans, Inc.
1215 Prytania Street, #424
New Orleans, LA 70130
800-880-2221
www.cccsno.org
Telephone

Maine

See Agency listing "**For All States**" at beginning of listings.

Maryland

ClearPoint Financial Solutions, Inc.
8000 Franklin Farms Dr.
Richmond, VA 23229
877-422-9044
www.clearpointfinancialsolutions.org
In Person and Telephone

Consumer Credit Counseling Service of Maryland and Delaware Inc.
757 Frederick Rd, 2nd Floor
Baltimore, MD 21228
800-642-2227
www.cccs-inc.org
In Person and Telephone

Massachusetts

Money Management International, Inc.
9009 West Loop S, 7th FL.
Houston, TX 77096
888-845-5669
www.moneymanagment.org
In Person, Telephone, Internet

Michigan

See Agency listing "**For All States**" at beginning of listings.

Minnesota

FamilyMeans
1875 Northwestern Ave.
Stillwater, MN 55082
800-780-2890
www.familymeans.org
In Person, Telephone, Internet

Family Service Association of Sheboygan, Inc.
1930 North 8th Street
Sheboygan, WI 53081
800-350-2227
www.cccsonline.org
Telephone, Internet

Lutheran Social Services of Minnesota
424 West Superior St., #600
Duluth, MN 55802
888-577-2227
www.lssmn.org/debt
In Person, Telephone, Internet

Mississippi

Southern District of Mississippi

See Agency listing "**For All States**" at beginning of listings.

Northern District of Mississippi

See Agency listing "**For All States**" at beginning of listings.

Missouri

ClearPoint Financial Solutions, Inc.
8000 Franklin Farms Dr.
Richmond, VA 23229
877-422-9044
www.clearpointfinancialsolutions.org
In Person and Telephone

Consumer Credit
Counseling of Springfield
Missouri Inc.
1515 S. Glenstone
Springfield, MO 65804
800-882-0808
www.cccsoftheozarks.org
In Person, Telephone,
Internet

Montana

Consumer Credit
Counseling Service of
Montana, Inc.
2022 Central Avenue
Great Falls, MT 59401
877-275-2227
www.cccsmt.org
In Person, Telephone,
Internet

Nebraska

Consumer Credit
Counseling Service of
Nebraska, Inc.
8805 Indian Hills Drive #105
Omaha, NE 68114
877-494-2227
www.cccsn.org
In Person and Telephone

Nevada

Consumer Credit
Counseling Service of
Southern Nevada
2650 South Jones
Las Vegas, NV 89146
800-451-4505
www.cccsnevada.org
In Person and Telephone

Family Counseling Service
of Northern Nevada
575 E. Plumb Lane #101
Reno, NV 89502
775-322-6557
www.fcsnv.org
In Person, Telephone,
Internet

New Hampshire

Consumer Credit
Counseling Service of NH &
VT, Inc.
105 Loudon Road
Bldg #1
Concord, NH 03301
603-224-6593
www.cccsnh-vt.org
In Person, Telephone

New Jersey

Consumer Credit and
Budget Counseling, Inc.
299 South Shore Road,
US Route 9 South
Marmora, NJ 08223
888-738-8233
www.cc-bc.com
In Person, Telephone,
Internet

Consumer Credit
Counseling Service of
Delaware Valley, Inc.
1515 Market Street # 1325
Philadelphia, PA 19102
800-989-2227
In Person and Telephone

Family Guidance Center,
1931 Nottingham Way
Hamilton, NJ 08619
609-586-2574
www.fgccorp.org
In Person and Telephone

New Mexico

Young Women's Christian
Association of El Paso
Texas
1600 Brown
El Paso, Texas 79902
888-533-7502
In Person and Telephone

New Mexico Project for
Financial Literacy, Inc.
60 Castle Rock Road SE
Rio Rancho, NM 87124
505-994-4686
In Person, Telephone

New York

Eastern District of New York

Consumer Credit
Counseling Service of
Buffalo, Inc.
40 Gardenville Parkway
West Seneca, NY 14224
716-712-2060
www.cccsbuff.org
In Person, Telephone,
Internet

Consumer Credit
Counseling Service of
Rochester Inc.
50 Chestnut Plaza
Rochester, NY 14604
888-724-2227
www.cccsroch.org
In Person (not available in
all judicial districts), and
Telephone

Northern District of New York

Consumer Credit
Counseling Service of
Buffalo, Inc.
40 Gardenville Parkway
West Seneca, NY 14224
716-712-2060
www.cccsbuff.org
In Person, Telephone,
Internet

Consumer Credit
Counseling Service of
Central New York Inc.
500 South Salina St. # 600
Syracuse, New York 13202
800-479-6026
www.credithelpny.org
In Person, Telephone,
Internet

Consumer Credit
Counseling Service of
Rochester Inc.
50 Chestnut Plaza
Rochester, NY 14604
888-724-2227
www.cccsroch.org
In Person (not available in
all judicial districts), and
Telephone

Southern District of New York

Consumer Credit
Counseling Service of
Rochester Inc.
50 Chestnut Plaza
Rochester, NY 14604
888-724-2227
www.cccsroch.org
In Person (not available in
all judicial districts), and
Telephone

Western District of New York

Consumer Credit
Counseling Service of
Buffalo, Inc.
40 Gardenville Parkway
West Seneca, NY 14224
716-712-2060
www.cccsbuff.org
In Person, Telephone,
Internet

Consumer Credit
Counseling Service of
Central New York Inc.
500 South Salina St. #600
Syracuse, New York 13202
800-479-6026
www.credithelpny.org
In Person, Telephone,
Internet

Consumer Credit
Counseling Service of
Rochester Inc.
50 Chestnut Plaza
Rochester, NY 14604
888-724-2227
www.cccsroch.org
In Person (not available in
all judicial districts), and
Telephone

North Carolina

Bankruptcy cases in
North Carolina are not
under the jurisdiction of
the United States Trustee
Program. Questions
regarding bankruptcy cases
filed in North Carolina
should be directed to the
Administrative Office of the
U.S. Courts:

Administrative Office of the
U.S. Courts
Bankruptcy Judges Division
1 Columbus Circle NE 4-250
Washington, D.C. 20544
Phone: 202-502-1900

North Dakota

Village Family Service Center
1201 25th Street South
Fargo, ND 58106
800-450-4019
www.helpwithmoney.org
In Person, Telephone,
Internet

Ohio

Northern District of Ohio

Family and Community
Services, Inc.
143 Gougler Avenue
Kent, OH 44240
330-677-4124
www.portagefamilies.org
In Person and Telephone

Family Service Agency
535 Marmion Avenue
Youngstown, OH 44502
330-782-5664
www.familyserviceagency.com
In Person

Northwest Family Services
799 S. Main Street
Lima, OH 45804
877-287-2227
www.consumercreditcounse
lingohio.org
In Person and Telephone

Southern District of Ohio

Consumer Credit
Counseling Service of
Huntington, Inc.
1102 Memorial Blvd.
Huntington, WV 25701
888-534-4387
www.goodwillhunting.org
In Person, Telephone,
Internet

LifeSpan Inc.
1900 Fairgrove Avenue
Hamilton, OH 45011
513-868-3210
www.lifespanohio.org
In Person, Telephone,
Internet

Graceworks Lutheran
Services
3131 S. Dixie, Suite 300
Dayton, OH 45439
937-643-2227
www.graceworks.org
In Person, Telephone,
Internet

Northwest Family Services
530 S. Main Street
Lima, OH 45804
877-287-2227
www.consumercreditcounse
lingohio.org
In Person and Telephone

Oklahoma

Eastern District of Oklahoma

Consumer Credit
Counseling Service of
Central Oklahoma
3230 N. Rockwell
Bethany, OK 73008
800-916-4522
www.cccsok.org
In Person, Telephone,
Internet

Consumer Credit
Counseling of Springfield
Missouri Inc.
1515 S. Glenstone
Springfield, Missouri 65804
800-882-0808
www.cccsoftheozarks.org
In Person, Telephone,
Internet

Consumer Credit
Counseling Services of
North Central Texas
901 North McDonald, # 600
McKinney, TX 75069
800-856-0257
www.cccsnct.org
In Person, Telephone,
Internet

Credit Counseling of
Arkansas, Inc.
1111 Zion Road
Fayetteville, AR 72703
800-889-4916
www.ccoacares.com
In Person, Telephone,
Internet

Northern District of Oklahoma

Consumer Credit
Counseling of Springfield
Missouri Inc.
1515 S. Glenstone
Springfield, Missouri 65804
800-882-0808
www.cccsoftheozarks.org
In Person, Telephone,
Internet

Credit Counseling Centers
of Oklahoma Inc.
4646 South Harvard
Tulsa, OK 74135
800-324-5611
In Person, Telephone,
Internet

Western District of Oklahoma

Consumer Credit
Counseling Service of
Central Oklahoma
3230 N. Rockwell
Bethany, OK 73008
800-916-4522
www.cccsok.org
In Person, Telephone,
Internet

Oregon

ClearPoint Financial
Solutions, Inc.
8000 Franklin Farms Dr.
Richmond, VA 23229
877-422-9044
www.clearpointfinancialsolu
tions.org
In Person, Telephone,
Internet

Consumer Credit
Counseling Service of
Linn-Benton Inc.
214 NW Hickory
Albany, OR 97321
541-926-5843
In Person

Consumer Credit
Counseling Service of
Southern Oregon Inc.
820 Crater Lake Ave, # 202
Medford, OR 97504
541-779-2273
www.cccsso.org
In Person, Telephone,
Internet
Consumer Credit
Counseling Service of the
Tri-Cities, Inc.
401 N. Morain
Kennewick, WA 99336
800-201-2181
www.cccswaor.org
In Person and Telephone

Douglas Consumer Credit
Counseling
849 SE Mosher
Roseburg, OR 97470
541-673-3104
In Person and Telephone

Pennsylvania

Eastern District of Pennsylvania

Advantage Credit
Counseling Service Inc.
River Park Commons
2403 Sidney Street #400
Pittsburgh, PA 15203
888-511-2227
www.advantageccs.org
In Person, Telephone

Consumer Credit
Counseling Service of
Delaware Valley, Inc.
1515 Market Street #1325
Philadelphia, PA 19102
800-989-2227
www.cccsdv.org
In Person and Telephone

Middle District of Pennsylvania

Advantage Credit
Counseling Service Inc.
River Park Commons
2403 Sidney Street, # 400
Pittsburgh, PA 15203
888-511-2227
www.advantageccs.org
In Person, Telephone

Consumer Credit
Counseling Service of
Northeastern PA, Inc.
401 Laurel Street
Pittston, PA 18640
800-922-9537
www.cccsnepa.org
In Person, Telephone,
Internet

Western District of Pennsylvania

Advantage Credit
Counseling Service Inc.
River Park Commons
2403 Sidney Street
Suite 400
Pittsburgh, PA 15203
888-511-2227
In Person, Telephone

Consumer Credit
Counseling Service of
Northeastern PA, Inc.
401 Laurel Street
Pittston, PA 18640
800-922-9537
www.cccsnepa.org
In Person, Telephone,
Internet

Rhode Island

See Agency listing **"For All States"** at beginning of listings.

South Carolina

Compass of Carolina
1100 Rutherford Road
Greenville, SC 29609
800-203-9692
www.compassofcarolina.org
In Person

Consumer Credit
Counseling Service of the
Savannah Area Inc.
7505 Waters Ave., # C-11
Savannah, GA 31406
912-691-2227
www.cccssavannah.org
In Person, Telephone,
Internet

Family Service Center of
South Carolina
2712 Middleburg Drive
Suite 207-A
Columbia, SC 29204
800-223-9213
www.fsconline.org
In Person, Telephone,
Internet

Family Service Inc.
4925 Lacross Road,#215
North Charleston, SC
29406
800 232 6489
www.familyserviceschassc
.com
In Person, Telephone,
Internet

South Dakota

Lutheran Social Services of
South Dakota
705 E. 41 St., Suite 100
Sioux Falls, SD 57105
888-258-2227
www.lsssd.org
In Person, Telephone,
Internet

Tennessee

Eastern District of Tennessee

Partnership for Families,
Children and Adults, Inc.
2245 Olan Mills Drive
Chattanooga, TN 37421
423-490-5620
www.partnershipfca.com
In Person, Telephone,
Internet

Middle District of Tennessee

Partnership for Families,
Children and Adults, Inc.
2245 Olan Mills Drive
Chattanooga, TN 37421
423-490-5620
www.partnershipfca.com
In Person, Telephone,
Internet

Western District of Tennessee

2nd Chance Budget and
Debt Family Counseling
Services Inc.
2600 Poplar Avenue, # 519
Memphis, TN 38112
901-323-0609
In Person

Partnership for Families,
Children and Adults, Inc.
2245 Olan Mills Drive
Chattanooga, TN 37421
423-490-5620
www.partnershipfca.com
In Person, Telephone,
Internet

Texas

Eastern District of Texas

Consumer Credit
Counseling Services of
North Central Texas
901 North McDonald, Ste.
600
McKinney, TX 75069
800-856-0257
www.cccsnct.org
In Person, Telephone,
Internet

Northern District of Texas

Consumer Credit
Counseling Services of
North Central Texas
901 North McDonald, Ste.
600
McKinney, TX 75069
800-856-0257
www.cccsnct.org
In Person, Telephone,
Internet

Southern District of Texas

Consumer Credit
Counseling Service of
Greater San Antonio
6851 Citizens Parkway #
100
San Antonio, TX 78229
210-979-4300
www.cccssa.org
In Person, Telephone,
Internet

Consumer Credit
Counseling Service of
South Texas
1706 South Padre Island Dr.
Corpus Christi, TX 78416
800-333-4357
www.cccsstx.org
In Person, Telephone,
Internet

Western District of Texas

Consumer Credit
Counseling Service of
Greater San Antonio
6851 Citizens Parkway,
Suite 100
San Antonio, TX 78229
210-979-4300
www.cccssa.org
In Person, Telephone,
Internet

Young Women's Christian
Association of El Paso
Texas
1600 Brown
El Paso, Texas 79902
888-533-7502
In Person and Telephone

Utah

Consumer Credit
Counseling Service of
Southern Nevada
2650 South Jones
Las Vegas, NV 89146
800-451-4505
www.cccsnevada.org
In Person, Telephone,
Internet

Vermont

See Agency listing "**For All States**" at beginning of listings.

Virginia

Eastern District of Virginia

Center for Child a Family
Service Inc.
2021 Cunningham Dr.,
Ste. 4001
Hampton, VA 23666
757-826-2227
In Person

ClearPoint Financial
Solutions, Inc.
8000 Franklin Farms Dr.
Richmond, VA 23229
877-422-9044
www.clearpointfinancialsolu
tions.org
In Person, Telephone,
Internet

Western District of Virginia

ClearPoint Financial
Solutions, Inc.
8000 Franklin Farms Dr.
Richmond, VA 23229
877-422-9044
www.clearpointfinancialsolu
tions.org
In Person, Telephone,
Internet

Washington

Eastern District of Washington

ClearPoint Financial
Solutions, Inc.
8000 Franklin Farms Dr.
Richmond, VA 23229
877-422-9044
www.clearpointfinancialsolu
tions.org
In Person, Telephone,
Internet

Consumer Credit
Counseling Service of
Northern Idaho, Inc.
1113 Main Street
Lewiston, ID 83501
800-556-0127
www.cccsnid.org
In Person and Telephone

Consumer Credit
Counseling Service of the
Tri Cities, Inc.
401 N. Morain
Kennewick, WA 99336
800-201-2181
www.cccswaor.org
In Person and Telephone

Consumer Credit
Counseling Service of
Yakima Valley
1115 W Lincoln Ave, #119
Yakima, WA 98902
800-273-6897
www.cccsyakima.org
In Person and Telephone

Western District of Washington

ClearPoint Financial
Solutions, Inc.
8000 Franklin Farms Dr.
Richmond, VA 23229
877-422-9044
www.clearpointfinancialsolu
tions.org
In Person, Telephone,
Internet

Consumer Credit
Counseling Service of the
Tri Cities, Inc.
401 N. Morain
Kennewick, WA 99336
800-201-2181
www.cccswaor.org
In Person and Telephone

West Virginia

Northern District of West Virginia

Consumer Credit
Counseling Service of
Southern West Virginia
1219 Ohio Avenue
Dunbar, WV 25064
800-281-5969
www.cccswv.com
Telephone and Internet

Consumer Credit
Counseling Service of the
Mid-Ohio Valley, Inc.
2715 Murdoch Avenue B-4
Parkersburg, WV 26101
866-481-4752
www.wvcccs.org
Telephone and Internet
Criss-Cross, Inc.
209 W. Pike Street, #B

Clarksburg, WV 26301
304-623-0921
www.criss-crosswv.org
In Person

Southern District of West Virginia

Consumer Credit
Counseling Service of
Huntington
1102 Memorial Blvd.
Huntington, WV 25701
888-534-4387
www.goodwillhunting.org
In Person, Telephone,
Internet
Consumer Credit
Counseling Service of
Southern West Virginia
1219 Ohio Ave
Dunbar, WV 25064
800-281-5969
www.cccswv.com
In Person, Telephone,
Internet

Consumer Credit
Counseling Service of the
Mid-Ohio Valley, Inc.
2715 Murdoch Avenue B-4
Parkersburg, WV 26101
866-481-4752
www.wvcccs.org
Telephone and Internet

Wisconsin

Eastern District of Wisconsin

Aurora Family Service
4915 South Howell Ave.,
Ste. 102
Milwaukee, WI 53207
888-799-2227
www.creditcounselingwi.org
In Person, Telephone,
Internet

FamilyMeans
1875 Northwestern Ave
Stillwater, MN 55082
800-780-2890
www.familymeans.org
In Person, Telephone,
Internet
Family Service Association
of Sheboygan, Inc.
1930 North 8th Street
Sheboygan, WI 53081
800-350-2227
www.cccsonline.org
In Person, Telephone,
Internet

Family Services of
Southern Wisconsin and
Northern Illinois Inc.
423 Bluff Street
Beloit, WI 53511
608-365-1244
www.cccsbeloit.org
In Person, Telephone,
Internet

Western District of Wisconsin

Catholic Charities of the
Diocese of La Crosse, Inc.
3710 East Ave.
La Crosse, WI 54601
888-654-5294
www.cclse.org
In Person

FamilyMeans
1875 Northwestern Ave
South
Stillwater, MN 55082
800-780-2890
www.familymeans.org
In Person, Telephone,
Internet

Family Service Association
of Sheboygan, Inc.
1930 North 8th Street
Sheboygan, WI 53081
800-350-2227
www.cccsonline.org
In Person, Telephone,
Internet

Family Services of
Southern Wisconsin and
Northern Illinois Inc.
423 Bluff Street
Beloit, WI 53511
608-365-1244
www.cccsbeloit.org
In Person, Telephone,
Internet

Wyoming

Consumer Credit
Counseling Service of
Montana, Inc.
2022 Central Avenue
Great Falls, MT 59401
877-275-2227
www.cccsmt.org
In Person, Telephone,
Internet

Consumer Credit
Counseling Service of
Northern Colorado and
Southeast Wyoming
1247 Riverside Avenue
Fort Collins, CO 80524
800-424-2227
www.cccsnc.org
In Person and Telephone

Appendix D

Approved Debtor Education

Note: After each listing, it is noted whether the agency provides counseling services in person, via telephone, or on the internet. You should also check the U.S. Bankruptcy Trustee Service website for periodic updates to this list:
www.usdoj.gov/ust/eo/bapcpa/ccde/de_approved.htm#AL

Alabama

Bankruptcy cases in Alabama are not under the jurisdiction of the United States Trustee Program. Questions regarding bankruptcy cases filed in Alabama should be directed to the Administrative Office of the U.S. Courts:

Administrative Office of the U.S. Courts
Bankruptcy Judges Division
1 Columbus Circle, N.E., # 4-250
Washington, D.C. 20544
Phone: 202-502-1900

Alaska

See Agency listing "**For All States**" at beginning of listings.

Arizona

Academy of Financial Literacy
2105 E. Oakland Street
Chandler, AZ 85225
877-833-2867
www.academyoffinancialliteracy.com
Telephone and Internet

AAA Personal Finance Education
252 N. Los Altos Ave., #433
Tuscon, AZ 85705
877-AAA-4547
www.aaapersonalfinance.com
Internet

Arkansas

Eastern District of Arkansas

Consumer Credit Counseling of Springfield, Missouri, Inc.
1515 S. Glenstone
Springfield, Missouri 65804
800-882-0808
www.cccsoftheozarks.org
Telephone and Internet

Economic Opportunity Agency of Washington County, Inc.
614 E Emma Ave, # M401
Springdale, AR 72764
479-872-7479
www.tabde.org
Internet

Family Service Agency, Inc.
628 West Broadway, # 203
North Little Rock, AR 72114
501-753-0202
www.helpingfamilies.org
In Person and Internet

Western District of Arkansas

Consumer Credit
Counseling of Springfield,
Missouri, Inc.
1515 S. Glenstone
Springfield, Missouri 65804
800-882-0808
ww.cccsoftheozarks.org
In Person, Telephone,
Internet

Consumer Credit
Counseling Service of North
Central Texas
901 N. McDonald St, #600
McKinney, TX 75069
800-856-0257
www.cccsnct.org
Internet

Economic Opportunity
Agency of Washington
County, Inc.
614 E Emma Ave, #M401
Springdale, AR 72764
479-872-7479
www.tabde.org
In Person and Internet

Family Service Agency, Inc.
628 West Broadway, # 203
North Little Rock, AR 72114
501-753-0202
www.helpingfamilies.org
In Person and Internet

California

Central District of California

Amrane Cohen
Chapter 13 Trustee
770 The City Dr. S, #3300
Orange, CA 92868
714-621-0200
www.ch13ac.com
In Person - Only approved
in cases where the provider
is appointed as the trustee.

Rod Danielson
Chapter 13 Trustee
3435 14th Street, #100
Riverside, CA 92501
951-826-8000
www.rodan13.com
In Person - Only approved
in cases where the provider
is appointed as the trustee.

Eastern District of California

Consumer Credit
Counseling Service of
Southern Oregon, Inc.
820 Crater Lake Ave,# 202
Medford, Oregon 97504
541-779-2273
www.cccsso.org
In Person and Internet

Lawrence Loheit
Chapter 13 Trustee
10265 Rockingham Dr,#180
Sacramento, CA 95827
916-856-8000
www.loheit13.com
In Person - Only approved
in cases where the provider
is appointed as the trustee.

Jan P. Johnson
Chapter 13 Trustee
2535 Capitol Oaks Dr, #100
Sacramento, CA 95833
916-239-6613
www.jpj13trustee.com
In Person - Only approved
in cases where the provider
is appointed as the trustee.

Northern District of California

Martha G. Bronitsky
Chapter 13 Trustee
24301 Southland Dr. # 200
Hayward, CA 94545
510-266-5580
oak13.com
In Person - Only approved
in cases where the provider
is appointed as the trustee.

Consumer Credit
Counseling Service of the
North Coast
1309 11th Street, # 104
Arcata, CA 95521
707-822-8536
www.cccsnojuggle.org
Internet

Southern District of California

A Better Financial
Education, Inc.
One Capitol Mall, # 200
Sacramento, CA 95814
877-930-9600www.SmartM
oneySense.com
Internet

Colorado

Consumer Credit
Counseling Service of
Greater Dallas, Inc.
8737 King George Dr. #200
Dallas, TX 75235
800-249-2227
www.cccs.net
In Person, Telephone,
Internet

Consumer Credit
Counseling Service of N.
Colorado and SE Wyoming
1247 Riverside Avenue
Fort Collins, CO 80524
800-424-2227
In Person

Connecticut

Money Management
International, Inc.
9009 West Loop South, 7th
Floor
Houston, TX 77096
888-845-5669www.moneym
anagement.org
In Person, Telephone,
Internet

Delaware

See Agency listing "**For
All States**" at beginning of
listings.

District of
Columbia

See Agency listing "**For
All States**" at beginning of
listings.

Florida

Middle District of
Florida

Consumer Credit
Counseling Service of the
Midwest, Inc.
4500 East Broad Street
Columbus, OH 43213
800-355-2227
www.cccservices.com
In Person and Internet

Douglas W. Neway
Chapter 13 Trustee
200 West Forsyth St.,#1520
Jacksonville, Florida 32202
904-358-6465
ch13jaxfl.com
In Person - Only approved
in cases where the provider
is appointed as the trustee.

Laurie K. Weatherford
Chapter 13 Trustee
150 N. Orange Ave, # 450
Orlando, Fl 32801
407-648-8841
www.c13orl.com
In Person

Northern District of
Florida

Consumer Credit
Counseling Service of the
Midwest, Inc.
4500 East Broad Street
Columbus, OH 43213
800-355-2227
www.cccservices.com
In Person and Internet

Southern District of
Florida

Consumer Credit
Counseling Service of the
Midwest, Inc.
4500 East Broad Street
Columbus, OH 43213
800-355-2227
www.cccservices.com
In Person and Internet

Georgia

Middle District of
Georgia

Consumer Credit
Counseling Service of
Middle Georgia, Inc.
277 Martin Luther King, Jr.
Blvd., # 202
Macon, GA 31201
800-446-7123
www.cccsmacon.org
In Person and Internet
Consumer Credit
Counseling Service of
Southwest Georgia
409 North Jackson Street
Albany, GA 31701
229-883-0909
www.cccsalbany.org
In Person and Telephone

Lamar Purvis, Jr., P.C., CPA
411 South Grant Street
Fitzgerald, GA 31750
229-423-6581
www.llpcpa.com
In Person

Northern District of Georgia

Consumer Credit
Counseling Service of
Middle Georgia, Inc.
277 Martin Luther King, Jr.
Blvd., # 202
Macon, GA 31201
800-446-7123
www.cccsmacon.org
Internet

Partnership for Families,
Children, & Adults
2245 Olan Mills Drive
2300
Chattanooga, TN 37421
423-490-5620
www.partnershipfca.com
In Person

Southern District of Georgia

Consumer Credit
Counseling Service of
Middle Georgia, Inc.
277 Martin Luther King, Jr.
Blvd., # 202
Macon, GA 31201
800-446-7123
www.cccsmacon.org
Internet

Consumer Credit
Counseling Service of
Southwest Georgia
409 North Jackson Street
Albany, GA 31701
229-883-0909
www.cccsalbany.org
Telephone

Fleet and Family Support
Center
Naval Submarine Base
Kings Bay, GA 31547
912-573-4512

www.subasekb.navy.mil/
FFSC/FFSC.htm
In Person

Hawaii

Howard M. S. Hu, Chapter
13 Trustee
1132 Bishop Street,# 301
Honolulu, HI 96813
808-526-3083
In Person

Idaho

Consumer Financial
Solutions
1090 N Cole Road
Boise, ID 83704
208-375-8140
www.cfsidaho
In Person, Internet

Illinois

Central District of Illinois

Eastern Iowa Community
College District
306 West River Drive
Davenport, IA 52801
888-336-3907
www.eicc.edu
In Person

Northern District of Illinois

Eastern Iowa Community
College District
306 West River Drive
Davenport, IA 52801
888-336-3907
www.eicc.edu
In Person

Glenn Stearns
Chapter 13 Trustee
4343 Commerce Ct, #120
Lisle, IL 60532
630-577-1313
www.lisle13.com
In Person - Only approved
in cases where the provider
is appointed as the trustee.

Southern District of Illinois

Accountax School of
Business, Incorporated
5636 Crestwood Rd.
Matteson, IL 60443
866-720-4547
www.accountax.us
Internet

Indiana

Northern District of Indiana

Debra L. Miller
Chapter 13 Trustee
100 East Wayne Steert, #
210
South Bend, IN 46634
574-251-1493
www.trustee13.com
In Person - Only approved
in cases where the provider
is appointed as the trustee.

David A. Rosenthal
Chapter 13 Trustee
408 Main Street
Lafayette, IN 47902
765-742-8248
In Person - Only approved
in cases where the provider
is appointed as the trustee.

Southern District of Indiana

Consumer Credit
Counseling Service of the
Midwest, Inc.
4500 East Broad Street
Columbus, OH 43213
800-355-2227
www.cccservices.com
In Person and Internet

Iowa

Northern District of Iowa

Consumer Credit Counseling
Service of Northeastern Iowa,
Inc.
1003 West 4th Street
Waterloo, IA 50702
800-714-4388
www.cccsia.org
In Person, Telephone,
Internet

Eastern Iowa Community
College District
306 West River Drive
Davenport, IA 52801
888-336-3907
www.eicc.edu
In Person

Horizon Consumer Credit
Counseling Service
819 5th Street, SE
Cedar Rapids, IA 52401
319-398-3576
www.horizonsfamily.org
In Person, Internet

Southern District of Iowa

Consumer Credit Counseling
Service of Northeastern Iowa,
Inc.
1003 West 4th Street
Waterloo, IA 50702
800-714-4388
www.cccsia.org
In Person, Telephone,
Internet

Eastern Iowa Community
College District
306 West River Drive
Davenport, IA 52801
888-336-3907
www.eicc.edu
In Person

Horizon Consumer Credit
Counseling Service
819 5th Street, SE
Cedar Rapids, IA 52401
319-398-3576
www.horizonsfamily.org
In Person, Internet

Kansas

Consumer Credit
Counseling of Springfield,
Missouri, Inc.
1515 S. Glenstone
Springfield, MO 65804
800-882-0808
www.cccsoftheozarks.org
Telephone, Internet

Consumer Credit
Counseling Service of the
Midwest, Inc.
4500 East Broad Street
Columbus, OH 43213
800-355-2227
www.cccservices.com
In Person and Internet

Housing and Credit
Counseling, Inc.
1195 SW Buchanan
101
Topeka, Kansas 66604
785-234-0217
www.hcci-ks.org
In Person

K-State Research and
Extension - Sedgwick
County
Sedgwick County Extension
Education Center
7001 W. 21st Street N.
Wichita, KS 67205-1759
316-722-7721
http://ww.sedgwick.ksu.edu/
DesktopDefault.aspx
In Person

Kentucky

Eastern District of Kentucky

Consumer Credit
Counseling Service of the
Midwest, Inc.
4500 East Broad Street
Columbus, OH 43213
800-355-2227
www.cccservices.com
In Person and Internet

Western District of Kentucky

Consumer Credit
Counseling Service of the
Midwest, Inc.
4500 East Broad Street
Columbus, OH 43213
800-355-2227
www.cccservices.com
In Person and Internet

Louisiana

Eastern District of Louisiana

The requirement to obtain debtor education in this judicial district is currently waived until further notice (December 2008)

Foster Human Resources Solutions, LLC
1501-A Wimbledon Drive
Alexandria, LA 71301
318-448-8693
In Person

Middle District of Louisiana

Consumer Credit Counseling Service of Greater New Orleans, Inc.
1215 Prytania Street, # 424
New Orleans, LA 70130
504-529-2396
www.cccsno.org
Telephone and Internet

Western District of Louisiana

Willie Banks, Jr.
Chapter 13 Trustee
2009 Pecan Park Ave, # C
Alexandria, LA 71303
318-448-1306
In Person - Only approved in cases where the provider is appointed as the trustee.

Consumer Credit Counseling Service of North Central Texas

901 N. McDonald St, # 600
McKinney, TX 75069
800-856-0257
www.cccsnct.org
In Person

Keith Rodriguez
Chapter 13 Trustee
700 St. John Street, # 201
Lafayette, LA 70502
337-233-4413
In Person - Only approved in cases where the provider is appointed as the trustee.

Maine

Institute for Financial Literacy, Inc.
449 Forest Avenue, # 12
Portland, ME 04101
207-879-0389
www.financiallit.org
In Person, Telephone, Internet

Maryland

Consumer Credit Counseling Service of Maryland & Delaware, Inc.
757 Frederick Road, 2nd Floor
Baltimore, MD 21228
410-747-2050
www.cccs-inc.org
In Person, Internet

Massachusetts

See Agency listing **"For All States"** at beginning of listings.

Michigan

Eastern District of Michigan

Carl L. Bekofske
Chapter 13 Trustee
510 W. Court Street
Flint, MI 48503
810-238-4675
flint13.com
In Person - Only approved in cases where the provider is appointed as the trustee.

Northwest Family Services
799 S. Main Street
Lima, OH 45804
877-287-2227
www.consumercreditcounselingohio.org
In Person and Telephone

Western District of Michigan

Brett N. Rodgers, Chapter 13 Trustee
50 Louis Street NW, # 700
Grand Rapids, MI 49503
616-454-9782
www.rodgersch13.com
In Person

Minnesota

Village Family Service Center
1201 25th Street, South
Fargo, ND 58106
800-450-4019
www.helpwithmoney.org
In Person, Telephone, Internet

Mississippi

Northern District of Mississippi

Family Service Agency, Inc.
628 West Broadway, # 203
North Little Rock, AR 72114
501-753-0202
www.helpingfamilies.org
In Person and Internet

Southern District of Mississippi

Mississippi State University Extension, School of Human Sciences
128 Lloyd Ricks Building
Mississippi State, MS 39762
662-325-3080
www.msstate.edu
In Person

Missouri

Eastern District of Missouri

Consumer Credit Counseling of Springfield, Missouri, Inc.
1515 S. Glenstone
Springfield, MO 65804
800-882-0808
www.cccsoftheozarks.org
In Person, Telephone, Internet

Consumer Credit Counseling Service of the Midwest, Inc.
4500 East Broad Street
Columbus, OH 43213
800-355-2227
www.cccservices.com
In Person and Internet

Economic Opportunity Agency of Washington County, Inc.
614 E Emma Ave, # M401
Springdale, AR 72764
479-872-7479
www.tabde.org
In Person, Internet

Western District of Missouri

Consumer Credit Counseling of Springfield, Missouri, Inc.
1515 S. Glenstone
Springfield, Missouri 65804
800-882-0808
www.cccsoftheozarks.org
In Person, Telephone, Internet

Consumer Credit Counseling Service of the Midwest, Inc.
4500 East Broad Street
Columbus, OH 43213
800-355-2227
www.cccservices.com
In Person and Internet

Economic Opportunity Agency of Washington County, Inc.
614 East Emma Ave, #M401
Springdale, AR 72764
479-872-7479
www.tabde.org
In Person and Internet

Montana

Consumer Credit Counseling Service of MT
2022 Central Avenue
Great Falls, MT 59401
877-275-2227
In Person, Telephone, Internet

Nebraska

Arbor Investments
1850 South 72nd Street
Omaha, NC 68124
800-625-7725
www.arbored.com
In Person, Telephone, Internet

Nevada

Consumer Credit Counseling Service of Southern Nevada and Utah
2650 South Jones
Las Vegas, NV 89146
800-451-4505
www.cccsnevada.org
In Person, Internet

New Hampshire

Consumer Credit Counseling Service of NH & VT
105 Loudon Road, Building #1
Concord, NH 03302
800-327-6778
www.cccsnh-vt.org
In Person

New Jersey

Isabel C. Balboa
Chapter 13 Trustee
535 Route 38, # 580
Cherry Hill, NJ 08002
856-663-5002
In Person - Only approved in cases where the provider is appointed as the trustee.

Consumer Credit Counseling Service of Delaware Valley, Inc.
1515 Market Street
1325
Philadelphia, PA 19102
800-989-2227
www.cccsdv.org
In Person

New Mexico

Consumer Credit Counseling Service of Greater Dallas, Inc.
8737 King George Dr. #200
Dallas, TX 75235
800-249-2227
www.cccs.net
In Person, Telephone, Internet

New York

Eastern District of New York

All States Connections, LLC
126 Canterbury Square
Buffalo, NY 14221
800-948-9052
newyorklearningconnectio
ns.com
Telephone

Northern District of New York

Consumer Credit Counseling Service of Central New York, Inc.
500 South Salina St., # 600
Syracuse, NY 13202
800-479-6026
www.credithelpny.org
In Person, Internet

Credit Education Bureau
19 Prince Street
Rochester, NY 14607
585-256-6080
www.crediteducationbureau
.com
In Person

Judith Linder
235 Pangborn Road
Hastings, NY 13076
315-420-4567
In Person

Southern District of New York

Credit Education Bureau
19 Prince Street
Rochester, NY 14607
585-256-6080
www.crediteducationburea
u.com
In Person

Western District of New York

Consumer Credit Counseling Service of Central New York, Inc.
500 South Salina St., # 600
Syracuse, NY 13202
800-479-6026
www.credithelpny.org
In Person, Internet
Credit Education Bureau
19 Prince Street
Rochester, NY 14607
585-256-6080
www.crediteducationbureau
.com
In Person

North Carolina

Bankruptcy cases in North Carolina are not under the jurisdiction of the United States Trustee Program. Questions regarding bankruptcy cases filed in North Carolina should be directed to the Administrative Office of the U.S. Courts:

Administrative Office of the U.S. Courts
Bankruptcy Judges Division
1 Columbus Circle NE
#4-250
Washington, D.C. 20544
Phone: 202-502-1900

North Dakota

The Village Family Service Center
1201 25th Street, South
Fargo, ND 58106
800-450-4019
www.helpwithmoney.org
In Person, Telephone, Internet

Ohio

Northern District of Ohio

Catholic Social Services of Summit County, Inc.
640 North Main Street
Akron, OH 44310
330-762-7481
www.csssc.org
In Person

Consumer Credit
Counseling Service of the
Midwest, Inc.
4500 East Broad Street
Columbus, OH 43213
800-355-2227
www.cccservices.com
In Person and Internet

Family Service Agency
535 Marmion Avenue
Youngstown, OH 44502
330-782-5664
www.familyserviceagency
.com
In Person

Northwest Family Services
799 S. Main Street
Lima, OH 45804
877-287-2227
www.consumercreditcounse
lingohio.org
In Person and Telephone

Southern District of Ohio

Consumer Credit Counseling
Service of the Mid Ohio
Valley, Inc.
2715 Murdoch Avenue B-4
Parkersburg, WV 26101
866-481-4752
www.wvcccs.org
In Person

Consumer Credit
Counseling Service of the
Midwest, Inc.
4500 East Broad Street
Columbus, OH 43213
800-355-2227
www.cccservices.com
In Person and Internet

Graceworks Lutheran
Services
3131 S. Dixie, # 300
Dayton, OH 45439
937-643-2227
www.graceworks.org
In Person

Northwest Family Services
799 S. Main Street
Lima, OH 45804
877-287-2227
www.consumercreditcounse
lingohio.org
In Person and Telephone

Frank M. Pees
Chapter 13 Trustee
130 E. Wilson Bridge Road,
200
Worthington, OH 43085
614-436-6700
www.13network.com
In Person - Only approved
in cases where the provider
is appointed as the trustee.

Oklahoma

Eastern District of Oklahoma

Consumer Credit
Counseling Service of
Greater Dallas, Inc.
8737 King George Dr. #200
Dallas, TX 75235
800-249-2227
www.cccs.net
In Person, Telephone,
Internet

Consumer Credit
Counseling Service of North
Central Texas
901 N. McDonald St., # 600
McKinney, TX 75069
800-856-0257
www.cccsnct.org
In Person and Internet

Consumer Credit
Counseling of Springfield,
Missouri, Inc.
1515 S. Glenstone
Springfield, MO 65804
800-882-0808
www.cccsoftheozarks.org
Telephone, Internet

Credit Counseling Centers
of Oklahoma, Inc.
4646 South Harvard
Tulsa, OK 74135
800-324-5611
www.cccsofok.org
In Person and Internet

Western District of Oklahoma

Economic Opportunity
Agency of Washington
County, Inc.
614 East Emma Ave, #
M401
Springdale, AR 72764
479-872-7479
www.tabde.org
In Person and Internet

John Hardeman
Chapter 13 Trustee
321 Dean A. McGee
Avenue
Oklahoma City, OK 73101
405-236-4843
In Person - Only approved
in cases where the provider
is appointed as the trustee.

Oregon

Consumer Credit
Counseling Service of
Coos-Curry, Inc.
375 South 4th Street, # 100
Coos Bay, OR 97420
541-267-7040
www.cccscoos.org
In Person

Consumer Credit
Counseling Service of
Josephine County
1314 NE Foster Way
Grants Pass, OR 97526
541-479-6002
www.cccsgrantspass.com
In Person

Consumer Credit
Counseling Service of
Linn-Benton, Inc.
214 NW Hickory
Albany, OR 97321
541-926-5843
www.cccs-lb.org
In Person

Consumer Credit Counseling
Service of Southern Oregon,
Inc.
820 Crater Lake Ave, # 202
Medford, Oregon 97504
541-779-2273
www.cccsso.org
In Person

Consumer Credit
Counseling Service of the
Tri-Cities, Inc.
401 N. Morain
Kennewick, WA 99336
509-737-1973
www.cccswaor.org
In Person

Douglas Consumer Credit
Counseling Service
849 SE Mosher
Roseburg, OR 97470
541-673-3104
www.cccsdouglas.org
In Person

Pennsylvania

Eastern District of Pennsylvania

Advantage Credit
Counseling Service, Inc.
River Park Commons
2403 Sidney Street, # 400
Pittsburgh, PA 15203
888-511-2227
www.advantageccs.org
In Person and Internet

Consumer Credit
Counseling Service of
Delaware Valley, Inc.
1515 Market Street, # 1325
Philadelphia, PA 19102
800-989-2227
www.cccsdv.org
In Person

Middle District of Pennsylvania

Advantage Credit
Counseling Service, Inc.
River Park Commons
2403 Sidney Street, # 400
Pittsburgh, PA 15203
888-511-2227
www.advantageccs.org
In Person and Internet

Western District of Pennsylvania

Advantage Credit
Counseling Service, Inc.
River Park Commons
2403 Sidney Street, # 400
Pittsburgh, PA 15203
888-511-2227
www.advantageccs.org
In Person and Internet
Consumer Credit
Counseling Service of the
Midwest, Inc.
4500 East Broad Street
Columbus, OH 43213
800-355-2227
www.cccservices.com
In Person and Internet

Rhode Island

ABC Community Education
Services, LLC
97 Sheffield Avenue
Pawtucket, RI 02860
800-987-1924
www.edebtclass.com
Internet

South Carolina

Family Services, Inc.
4925 Lacross Road, # 215
N. Charleston, SC 29406
800-232-6489
In Person

South Dakota

The Village Family Service Center
1201 25th Street, South
Fargo, ND 58106
800-450-4019
www.helpwithmoney.org
In Person, Telephone, Internet

Tennessee

Eastern District of Tennessee

Consumer Credit
Counseling Service of the
Midwest, Inc.
4500 East Broad Street
Columbus, OH 43213
800-355-2227
www.cccservices.com
In Person and Internet

Partnership for Families, Children, & Adults
2245 Olan Mills Dr., # 2300
Chattanooga, TN 37421
423-490-5620
www.partnershipfca.com
In Person

The University of
Tennessee Extension
218 Morgan Hall
Knoxville, TN 37996-4512
865-974-8198
www.fcs.tennessee.edu
In Person

Middle District of Tennessee

Consumer Credit
Counseling Service of the
Midwest, Inc.
4500 East Broad Street
Columbus, OH 43213
800-355-2227
www.cccservices.com
In Person and Internet

Henry E. Hildebrand, III
Chapter 13 Trustee
500 Church Street, 3rd Fl.
Nashville, TN 37219
615-244-1101
In Person - Only approved
when the provider is appointed
as the trustee.

The University of
Tennessee Extension
218 Morgan Hall
Knoxville, TN 37996-4512
865-974-8198
www.fcs.tennessee.edu
In Person

Family Service Agency, Inc.
628 West Broadway, # 203
North Little Rock, AR 72114
501-753-0202
www.helpingfamilies.org
In Person and Internet

The Memphis Housing
Resource Center
2400 Poplar, # 220
Memphis, TN 38112
901-529-1151
www.mhrc.info
In Person

The University of
Tennessee Extension
218 Morgan Hall
Knoxville, TN 37996-4512
865-974-8198
www.fcs.tennessee.edu
In Person

Texas

Eastern District of Texas

Consumer Credit
Counseling Service of
Greater Dallas, Inc.
8737 King George Dr., #200
Dallas, TX 75235
800-249-2227
www.cccs.net
In Person, Telephone, Internet
Consumer Credit
Counseling Service of North
Central Texas
901 N. McDonald St., #600
McKinney, TX 75069
800-856-0257
www.cccsnct.org
In Person and Internet

Janna L. Countryman
Chapter 13 Trustee
500 N. Central Expway, # 350
Plano, TX 75074
972-943-2580
In Person - Only approved
when the provider is
appointed as the trustee.

Jane Jolley
713 Preston Place
Grapevine, TX 76051
888-533-3423
jjandpartners.com
In Person, Telephone, Internet

Ronald E. Stadtmueller
Chapter 13 Trustee
110 North College Ave, #1200
Tyler, TX 75702
903-593-7777
In Person - Only approved
when the provider is
appointed as the trustee.

Northern District of Texas

Consumer Credit
Counseling Service of
Greater Dallas, Inc.
8737 King George Dr. #200
Dallas, TX 75235
800-249-2227
www.cccs.net
In Person, Telephone,
Internet
Consumer Credit
Counseling Service of North
Central Texas
901 N. McDonald St., # 600
McKinney, TX 75069
800-856-0257
www.cccsnct.org
In Person and Internet

Jane Jolley
713 Preston Place
Grapevine, TX 76051
888-533-3423
jjandpartners.com
In Person and Telephone

Walter O'Cheskey
Chapter 13 Trustee
6308 Iola Avenue
Lubbock, TX 79424
806-748-1980
In Person - Only approved
when the provider is
appointed as the trustee.

Tom Powers
Chapter 13 Trustee
125 E. John Carpenter
Freeway, # 1100
Irving, TX 75062
214-855-9200
In Person - Only approved
when the provider is
appointed as the trustee.

Tim Truman
Chapter 13 Trustee
6851 NE Loop 820, # 300
Fort Worth, TX 76180
817-770-8500
In Person - Only approved
when the provider is
appointed as the trustee.

Robert B. Wilson
Chapter 13 Trustee
1500 Broadway, # 300
Lubbock, TX 79401
806-740-0114
In Person - Only approved
when the provider is
appointed as the trustee.

Southern District of Texas

Cindy Boudloche
Chapter 13 Trustee
555 N. Carancahua, # 600
Corpus Christi, TX 78478
361-883-5786
www.ch13boudloche.com
In Person - Only approved
when the provider is
appointed as the trustee.

Consumer Credit
Counseling Service of
Greater Dallas, Inc.
8737 King George Dr. #200
Dallas, TX 75235
800-249-2227
www.cccs.net
In Person, Telephone,
Internet

Western District of Texas

Consumer Credit
Counseling Service of
Greater Dallas, Inc.
8737 King George Dr. #200
Dallas, TX 75235
800-249-2227
www.cccs.net
In Person, Telephone,
Internet

Stuart Cox
Chapter 13 Trustee
1760 N. Lee Trevino
El Paso, Texas 79936
915-598-6769
In Person - Only approved
when the provider is
appointed as the trustee.

Ray Hendren
Chapter 13 Trustee
8310 Capital of Texas
Highway N, # 475
Austin, TX 78731
512-474-6309
www.13network.com
In Person - Only approved
when the provider is
appointed as the trustee.

Deborah B. Langehennig
Chapter 13 Trustee
3801 South Capital of
Texas Highway, # 320
Austin, TX 78704
www.ch13austin.com
In Person - Only approved
when the provider is
appointed as the trustee.

Marion A. Olson, Jr.
Chapter 13 Trustee
1020 N.E. Loop 410, #800
San Antonio, TX 78209
210-824-1460
In Person - Only approved
when the provider is
appointed as the trustee.

Utah

Utah State University
Cooperative Extension
Service
4900 Old Main Hill
Logan, UT 84322
801-468-2846
www.extension.usu.edu
In Person

Vermont

Consumer Credit
Counseling Service of NH
& VT
105 Loudon Rd, Building #1
Concord, NH 03301
800-327-6778
www.cccsnh-vt.org
In Person

Virginia

Eastern District of Virginia

Center for Child and Family
Services, Inc.
2021 Cunningham Dri.
#400
Hampton, VA 23666
757-826-2227
In Person

Gerald M. O'Donnell
Chapter 13 Trustee
211 North Union St. #240
Alexandria, VA 22314
703-836-2226
In Person - Only approved
in cases where the provider
is appointed as the trustee.

Virginia Cooperative
Extension
101 Wallace Hall (0410)
Blacksburg, VA 24061
540-231-3497
www.ext.vt.edu/
personalfinance
In Person and Internet

Western District of Virginia

Herbert L. Beskin
Chapter 13 Trustee
401 East Market St. #202
Charlottesville, VA 22902
434-817-9915
In Person - Only approved
in cases where the provider
is appointed as the trustee.

Virginia Cooperative
Extension
101 Wallace Hall (0410)
Blacksburg, VA 24061
540-231-3497
www.ext.vt.edu/
personalfinance
In Person and Internet

Washington

Eastern District of Washington

Consumer Credit
Counseling Service of the
Tri-Cities, Inc.
401 N. Morain
Kennewick, WA 99336
509-737-1973
www.cccswaor.org
In Person

Consumer Credit
Counseling Service of
Yakima Valley
1115 West Lincoln Ave.
#119
Yakima, WA 98902
800-273-6897
www.cccsyakima.org
In Person

Western District of Washington

Consumer Credit
Counseling Service of the
Tri-Cities, Inc.
401 N. Morain
Kennewick, WA 99336
509-737-1973
www.cccswaor.org
In Person

Consumer Credit
Counseling Service of
Yakima Valley
1115 West Lincoln Ave,
#119
Yakima, WA 98902
800-273-6897
www.cccsyakima.org
In Person

Consumer Education and
Training Services
1200 Fifth Avenue, # 600
Seattle, WA 98101
206-267-7017
www.centsprogram.com
In Person and Internet

West Virginia

Northern District of West Virginia

Consumer Credit Counseling
Service of the Mid Ohio
Valley, Inc.
2715 Murdoch Avenue B-4
Parkersburg, WV 26101
866-481-4752
www.wvcccs.org
In Person

CRISS-CROSS, Inc.
209 W. Pike Street
Clarksburg, WV 26301
304-623-0921
www.criss-crosswv.org
In Person

Southern District of West Virginia

Consumer Credit Counseling
Service of the Mid Ohio
Valley, Inc.
2715 Murdoch Avenue B-4
Parkersburg, WV 26101
866-481-4752
www.wvcccs.org
In Person

Wisconsin

Eastern District of Wisconsin

Aurora Family Service
4915 S. Howell Ave. #102
Milwaukee, WI 53207
888-799-2227
www.creditcounselingwi.org
In Person

Catholic Charities of the
Diocese of Green Bay, Inc.
1825 Riverside Drive
Green Bay, WI 54301
920-437-7531
www.gbdioc.org
In Person

Family Services of Southern
Wisconsin and Northern
Illinois, Inc.
423 Bluff Street
Beloit, WI 53511
608-365-1244
www.cccsbeloit.com
In Person

Financial Information &
Service Center
921 Midway Road
Menasha, WI 54952
920-886-1000
www.fisc-cccs.org
In Person

Western District of Wisconsin

Family Services of Southern
Wisconsin and Northern
Illinois, Inc.
423 Bluff Street
Beloit, WI 53511
608-365-1244
www.cccsbeloit.com
In Person and Internet

Financial Information &
Service Center
921 Midway Road
Menasha, WI 54952
920-886-1000
www.fisc-cccs.org
In Person

Wyoming

Consumer Credit
Counseling Service of MT,
Inc.
2022 Central Avenue
Great Falls, MT 59401
877-275-2227
www.cccsmt.org
In Person, Telephone,
Internet

Consumer Credit
Counseling Service of N.
Colorado and SE Wyoming
1247 Riverside Avenue
Fort Collins, CO 80524
800-424-2227
www.cccsnc.org
In Person

Glossary

Bankruptcy Legal Terms

Annuity: An insurance contract that pays the insured person during his or her life, rather than paying a beneficiary after the insured person's death. An annuity is a type of retirement plan.

Asset: Anything of value. May be real estate or personal property. Personal property can be tangible or intangible property.

Attachment: The seizure or repossession of property by a governmental agent. Generally, attachment is carried out by a county sheriff or the Internal Revenue Service.

Automatic stay: An court order from the bankruptcy court that goes into effect automatically upon filing for bankruptcy. It orders creditors to stop taking any further action to collect on any debts owed by the debtor filing for bankruptcy including lawsuits, garnishments, foreclosures, and collections.

Bankruptcy Code: The U.S. Bankruptcy Code is the set of United States laws relating to bankruptcy. The laws are contained in Title 11, Sections 101-1330 of the United States Code.

Bankruptcy Court Rules: In addition to the Bankruptcy Code, there are three further sets of rules that govern the procedures in bankruptcy courts: the Federal Rules of Bankruptcy Procedure, the Federal Rules of Civil Procedure, and Local Bankruptcy Court Rules. Local bankruptcy court rules may not conflict with any of the federal rules.

Bankruptcy Courts: The United States is divided into various bankruptcy court districts. All bankruptcy court districts are referenced by the name of the state (for example, Federal Bankruptcy Court, Idaho District). Many districts are also referenced geographically, if there is more than one district within the state (i.e., Southern District of Illinois).

Bankruptcy estate: All property, whether real estate or personal property, that is owned by a debtor who files for bankruptcy. Control over the bankruptcy estate is given to the court by filing for bankruptcy.

Bankruptcy petition: A formal request of the court for the protection of the federal bankruptcy laws.

Bankruptcy petition preparer: A private non-lawyer paralegal who can assist persons in preparing the legal papers necessary for bankruptcy. He or she cannot, however, provide any legal advice. Preparers are now authorized and regulated by the Bankruptcy Code.

Bankruptcy trustee: A person who is appointed by the bankruptcy court to handle the bankruptcy estate of a debtor. The trustee will examine the papers, handle the creditors' meeting, collect and sell any non-exempt property, and pay off the creditors.

Chapter 7: The chapter of the Bankruptcy Code that provides for "liquidation" (the sale of the debtor's non-exempt property and distribution of the proceeds to the creditors).

Chapter 11: The chapter of the Bankruptcy Code that provides for reorganization (usually of a corporation or partnership).

Chapter 12: The chapter of the Bankruptcy Code that provides for an adjustment of the debts of a family farmer.

Chapter 13: The chapter of the Bankruptcy Code that provides for an adjustment of the debts of an individual with a regular income.

Claim: A creditor's assertion of a right to payment from a debtor.

Codebtor: A person who is jointly liable on a particular debt, either because of cosigning on the debt, acting as a guarantor on the debt, or by virtue of being a spouse or partner of the debtor.

Collateral: Property used to guarantee payment for a secured debt.

Cosignor: A person who has also signed a loan or contract with another and who is jointly liable on the loan or contract.

Common-law property: Property in those states that follow common-law property rules. In general, the ownership of common-law property is determined by the name on the title document for the property. This is true for married couples also, with the exception of gifts or inheritances that are received jointly and thus held jointly. See also *community property*.

Community debts: Those debts incurred during marriage in those states that follow community-property rules. See also *community property*.

Community property: Property held by a husband and wife in those states that follow community-property law rules (Alaska, Arizona, California, Idaho, Louisiana, Nevada, New Mexico, Texas, Washington, and Wisconsin). Generally, all property that either spouse receives during their marriage is owned jointly by both spouses and is referred to as community property. See also *common-law property*.

Contingent debt: A known debt with an uncertain value that has yet to be resolved by a court.

Creditor: A creditor is a person or entity (corporation, partnership, etc.) who is owed a debt of some type. Creditors may be secured creditors who hold the title or a lien or some form of collateral for the debt. Creditors may also be unsecured creditors who have no security for the debt.

Creditors' meeting: This meeting is held in all Chapter 7 bankruptcies approximately one month after filing. It is attended by the bankruptcy trustee and the debtor(s). It may also be attended by any of the creditors. At this meeting, the bankruptcy papers will be examined, priority claims determined, and the property that is exempt will be resolved.

Debtor: A debtor is a person (or entity) who owes a debt of some kind. The persons or entities who file for bankruptcy are referred to as "debtors" in the court papers.

Debts: A debt is an obligation of some type that is owed to another person or entity. A debt may be secured if collateral of some type has been pledged or if a lien exists against some type of property. A debt may also be unsecured if there is no collateral securing the debt. Debts may also be further classified as "contingent", "liquidated," "unliquidated." See also *contingent debt*, *liquidated debt*, or *unliquidated debt*.

Disability benefits: Payments made to a person under a disability insurance plan because of injury, disability, or sickness.

Discharge: The total elimination of all dischargeable debts. This is the final result of a Chapter 7 bankruptcy. A discharge also prohibits creditors from communicating in any way with the debtor regarding the discharged debts.

Dischargeable debts: Those debts that may, by bankruptcy law, be discharged (eliminated) by a bankruptcy action. See also *non-dischargeable debts.*

Disputed debts: Those debts that a debtor claims are in error, either in part or in whole.

Equity: The value of a debtor's interest in property that remains after all liens or creditor's interests (such as a mortgage) are deducted.

ERISA benefits: Payments made to a person under a pension or retirement plan that qualifies under the Federal Employees Retirement Income Security Act. IRAs, KEOGHs, and many other pensions are ERISA plans. Ask your retirement plan administrator.

Execution: The process of seizing and selling property under a court order or judgment for a money judgment against a person or entity.

Executory contract: A contract that is not fully completed, which has some obligation or action yet to be fulfilled.

Exempt property: Property that may not be seized, repossessed by a private creditor, or executed against by a government agent because of debts that the owner has incurred. Property may be exempt based on either state or federal law.

Expenditure: Money that is, or will be, spent by a debtor.

Family farm bankruptcy: A Chapter 12 bankruptcy. Similar to a Chapter 13 bankruptcy, but which is available only to those debtors who fit the description of a "family farmer."

Fee simple: Referst to full ownership.

Fraternal society benefits: Group life or other insurance benefits that are maintained and paid to members by fraternal societies, such as the Elks, Masons, Moose, etc.

Fraudulent transfer: A transfer of property by a debtor with the intent to defraud creditors.

Group Insurance: A single insurance policy under which a group of persons is covered. Often, employee insurance plans are based on group insurance policies.

Guarantor: A person who has agreed to guarantee payment on a debt should the original debtor fail to keep up on the required payments.

Health aids: Items or material that a person uses to maintain his or her own health, such as a wheelchair.

Health benefits: Payments made to a person under a health insurance policy.

Homestead declaration: A document that is placed on county property records that asserts your homestead exemption. Filing such a declaration is a requirement in certain states in order to take advantage of your homestead exemption. Check your state's listing in Appendix B.

Homestead exemption: A state or federal exemption that protects a personal residence from being seized to pay for the owner's debts. Is often limited to only a certain dollar value.

Household goods: Non-disposable items that are used to maintain a household, such as dishes, utensils, pots and pans, lamps, radios, etc.

Income: Money that is, or will be, earned by a debtor.

Insider: Any relative of an individual debtor.

Insurance benefits: Payments made to a person under an insurance policy.

Intangible property: Property that has no actual existence, such as stocks, bonds, copyrights, trademarks, etc. These items may be represented by some type of document, but the property itself has no physical existence. See also *tangible property*.

Involuntary bankruptcy: A bankruptcy action that is instituted by creditors against a debtor who has defaulted on debt obligations.

Joint petition: A single bankruptcy petition filed by a husband and wife together.

Joint tenancy: Joint ownership of property in which the owners of the property hold equal undivided ownership interest in the property and in which each owner has the right of survivorship (the survivor will automatically inherit the other's interest on death).

Judgment: The final determination by a court of the matter before that court.

Judgment lien: A real estate lien that has been established by a court order or judgment. The lien is recorded on official records and generally must be satisfied before the property is sold.

Lessee: A tenant.

Lessor: A landlord.

Liability: A legal obligation or debt.

Lien: A legal claim against property for the payment of a debt.

Life insurance: A contract under which an insurance company agrees to pay a specified sum to a beneficiary upon the death of the insured person.

Liquidate: To sell a debtor's property and pay off any debts. To finally settle all debts.

Liquidated debt: A debt for which a court judgment has been issued.

Liquidation bankruptcy: A Chapter 7 bankruptcy. A bankruptcy in which all non-exempt property is sold to pay off all debts.

Lost future earnings: The amount of money awarded in a personal injury lawsuit to cover the amount of future income that the plaintiff is determined to have lost because of the injury.

Mailing list: A particular column and row arrangement of mailing addresses. It is required by many bankruptcy courts in order to make duplicate mailing labels for notification of creditors and other parties to a bankruptcy.

Matured life Insurance benefits: Life insurance benefits that are currently payable to a beneficiary (because the insured person has already died).

Motor vehicle: Any vehicle that is powered by a mechanical engine.

Nature of lien: The type of lien: either a tax, judgment, child support, or mechanic's lien.

Necessities: Items that are necessary to sustain life. Generally, food, clothing, and medical care are considered necessities.

Non-dischargeable debts: Those debts that cannot be eliminated in a bankruptcy proceeding. Certain taxes, student loans, alimony, child support, and other debts are non-dischargeable. See also *dischargeable debts*.

Non-purchase money debt: A debt that is incurred other than to purchase the collateral for the debt, such as a home equity loan.

Pain and suffering payments: The amount of money awarded in a personal injury lawsuit to cover the amount of pain and suffering that the plaintiff is determined to have suffered because of the injury.

Pension benefits: Benefits that a person receives or will receive upon retirement. Generally received from some type of pension fund.

Personal injury causes of action: The right to file a suit and claim a right to compensation for personal injuries that may have occurred.

Personal Property: All property, either intangible or tangible, that is not real estate. See also *real estate*.

Possessory lien: A right to seize and sell property that attaches to the property by law, such as a moving company's right to sell property that it has moved and which has not been paid for.

Possessory non-purchase money debt: A debt that is incurred other than to purchase the collateral for the debt, and for which the creditor obtains possession of the collateral, such as a loan by a pawnshop for a pawned item.

Priority claims: Those claims for unsecured debts that, by law, are to be paid off in a bankruptcy before any other unsecured debts are paid. The most common priority claim is for the payment of taxes.

Proof of Claim by Mail: A written statement describing why a debtor owes a creditor money. There is an official form for this.

Proof of Service: An official statement under oath that a person has delivered to (served) another a specific legal document.

Purchase money debt: A debt that is incurred to purchase the property which is the collateral for the debt.

Reaffirmation of a debt: An agreement by a debtor to pay off a debt, regardless of bankruptcy. Must be approved by both the creditor and the bankruptcy court. A reaffirmed debt is not eliminated by bankruptcy, even if the debt was dischargeable. Generally done for the purpose of keeping collateral or mortgaged property that would otherwise be subject to repossession.

Real estate: All land and any items that are permanently attached to the land, such as buildings.

Redemption of property: In bankruptcy, a debtor may purchase personal property that is subject to a creditor's lien by payment of the market value of the property.

Reorganization bankruptcy: A Chapter 11 bankruptcy under which a business attempts to reorganize its affairs in order to satisfy its debt obligations.

Repossession: The taking, by a creditor of a defaulted-upon loan, of the collateral for the loan.

Retirement benefits: Those benefits that are paid to persons by reason of their retirement from a job or by virtue of their employment for a certain number of years.

Secured claim: Any mortgage, deed of trust, loan, lien, or other claim against a property, that is in writing and for which the property acts as collateral.

Secured debts: Debts for which the creditors have some form of security for their repayment, such as collateral or a lien.

Security interest: A creditor's right to possess property held as collateral, upon a debtor's default on a loan.

Setoff: The application by a creditor of other assets of a debtor to lessen the amount of debt, such as the application of a debtor's bank account balance to a pay off a defaulted loan.

Tangible property: Property that has existence, that may be touched. See also *intangible property*.

Tenancy by the entireties: A form of joint ownership of property by wives and husbands only (only in certain states). Similar to joint tenancy with a right of survivorship, but for married couples only.

Tools: Those items that are necessary to perform a certain type of work. For bankruptcy, any items that are used in a trade or business may generally qualify as a tool, including computers, motor vehicles, etc.

Trustee: The bankruptcy trustee is a person who is appointed by the Bankruptcy Court to act as watchdog over the bankruptcy process by monitoring the conduct of bankruptcy parties and private estate trustees, overseeing related administrative functions, and acting to ensure compliance with applicable laws and procedures. He or she also identifies and helps investigate bankruptcy fraud and abuse

Unexpired lease: A lease that is still in force.

Unliquidated debt: A known, undisputed debt that has not been the subject of a court action.

Unsecured nonpriority debts: Those debts that have no collateral pledged and which are not priority debts by law.

Unsecured priority debts: See *priority claims*.

Voluntary bankruptcy: A bankruptcy that is voluntarily filed by the debtor in an effort to obtain relief from debts.

Wages: The amount of money paid on a regular basis for work.

Wrongful death benefits: The amount of money awarded in a wrongful death lawsuit to compensate the plaintiff for having to live without the deceased person.

Index

Nova Publishing Company
Small Business and Consumer Legal Books and Software

Legal Toolkit Series

Estate Planning Toolkit	ISBN 13: 9781892949448	Book w/CD	$39.95
Business Start-Up Toolkit	ISBN 13: 9781892949431	Book w/CD	$39.95
No-Fault Divorce Toolkit (available March 2009)	ISBN 13: 9781892949356	Book w/CD	$39.95
Legal Forms Toolkit (available July 2009)	ISBN 13: 9781892949486	Book w/CD	$39.95
Personal Bankruptcy Toolkit	ISBN 13: 9781892949424	Book w/CD	$29.95

Law Made Simple Series

Advance Health Care Directives Simplified	ISBN 13: 9781892949233	Book w/CD	$24.95
Living Trusts Simplified	ISBN 0935755519	Book w/CD	$28.95
Personal Legal Forms Simplified (3rd Edition)	ISBN 0935755977	Book w/CD	$28.95
Powers of Attorney Simplified	ISBN 13: 9781892949400	Book w/CD	$24.95

Small Business Made Simple Series

Corporation: Small Business Start-up Kit (2nd Edition)	ISBN 1892949067	Book w/CD	$29.95
Employer Legal Forms Simplified	ISBN 13: 9781892949264	Book w/CD	$24.95
Landlord Legal Forms Simplified	ISBN 13: 9781892949240	Book w/CD	$24.95
Limited Liability Company: Start-up Kit (3rd Edition)	ISBN 13: 9781892949370	Book w/CD	$29.95
Partnership: Start-up Kit (2nd Edition)	ISBN 1892949075	Book w/CD	$29.95
Real Estate Forms Simplified	ISBN 0935755091	Book w/CD	$29.95
S-Corporation: Small Business Start-up Kit (3rd Edition)	ISBN 13: 9781892949363	Book w/CD	$29.95
Small Business Accounting Simplified (4th Edition)	ISBN 1892949172	Book only	$24.95
Small Business Bookkeeping System Simplified	ISBN 0935755748	Book only	$14.95
Small Business Legal Forms Simplified (4th Edition)	ISBN 0935755985	Book w/CD	$29.95
Small Business Payroll System Simplified	ISBN 0935755551	Book only	$14.95
Sole Proprietorship: Start-up Kit (2nd Edition)	ISBN 1892949083	Book w/CD	$29.95

Legal Self-Help Series

Divorce Yourself: The National Divorce Kit (6th Edition)	ISBN 1892949121	Book w/CD	$39.95
Prepare Your Own Will: The National Will Kit (6th Edition)	ISBN 1892949156	Book w/CD	$29.95

National Legal Kits

Simplified Divorce Kit (3rd Edition)	ISBN 13: 9781892949394	Book only	$24.95
Simplified Family Legal Forms Kit (2nd Edition)	ISBN 13: 9781892949417	Bookw/CD	$19.95
Simplified Incorporation Kit	ISBN 1892949334	Book w/CD	$19.95
Simplified Limited Liability Company Kit	ISBN 1892949326	Book w/CD	$19.95
Simplified Living Will Kit (2nd Edition)	ISBN 13: 9781892949445	Book only	$19.95
Simplified S-Corporation Kit	ISBN 1892949318	Book w/CD	$19.95
Simplified Will Kit (3rd Edition)	ISBN 1892949385	Book w/CD	$19.95

Ordering Information

Distributed by:
National Book Network
4501 Forbes Blvd. Suite 200
Lanham, MD 20706

Shipping: $4.50 for first & $.75 for additional
Phone orders with Visa/MC: (800) 462-6420
Fax orders with Visa/MC: (800) 338-4550
Internet: www.novapublishing.com
Free shipping on all internet orders (within in the U.S.)